# 'NOW IS THE PSYCHOLOGICAL MOMENT'

## EARLE PAGE AND THE IMAGINING OF AUSTRALIA

# 'NOW IS THE PSYCHOLOGICAL MOMENT'

## EARLE PAGE AND THE IMAGINING OF AUSTRALIA

**STEPHEN WILKS**

*Ah, but a man's reach should exceed his grasp,*
*Or what's a heaven for?*
Robert Browning, 'Andrea del Sarto'

*The man who makes no mistakes does not usually make anything.*
Edward John Phelps

**Earle Page as seen by L.F. Reynolds in** *Table Talk***, 21 October 1926.**

Published by ANU Press
The Australian National University
Acton ACT 2601, Australia
Email: anupress@anu.edu.au

Available to download for free at press.anu.edu.au

ISBN (print): 9781760463670
ISBN (online): 9781760463687

WorldCat (print): 1198529303
WorldCat (online): 1198529152

DOI: 10.22459/NPM.2020

This title is published under a Creative Commons Attribution-NonCommercial-NoDerivatives 4.0 International (CC BY-NC-ND 4.0).

The full licence terms are available at
creativecommons.org/licenses/by-nc-nd/4.0/legalcode

This publication was awarded a College of Arts and Social Sciences PhD Publication Prize in 2018. The prize contributes to the cost of professional copyediting.

Cover design and layout by ANU Press. Cover photograph: Earle Page strikes a pose in early Canberra. Mildenhall Collection, NAA, A3560, 6053, undated.

This edition © 2020 ANU Press

# CONTENTS

Illustrations . . . . . . . . . . . . . . . . . . . . . . . . . . . . . . . . . . . . . . . . . ix
Acknowledgements . . . . . . . . . . . . . . . . . . . . . . . . . . . . . . . . . . xi
Abbreviations . . . . . . . . . . . . . . . . . . . . . . . . . . . . . . . . . . . . . .xiii
Prologue: 'How Many Germans Did You Kill, Doc?' . . . . . . . . . . . . . xv
Introduction: 'A Dreamer of Dreams'. . . . . . . . . . . . . . . . . . . . . . . .1
1. Family, Community and Methodism: The Forging of Page's
   World View. . . . . . . . . . . . . . . . . . . . . . . . . . . . . . . . . . . . . . . .17
2. 'We Were Determined to Use Our Opportunities to the Full':
   Page's Rise to National Prominence . . . . . . . . . . . . . . . . . . . . .59
3. The Use of Power: Treasurer Page Pursues His
   National Vision . . . . . . . . . . . . . . . . . . . . . . . . . . . . . . . . . . . .109
4. Government and Party: The Basis of Page's Power . . . . . . . . .135
5. Page and the Final Throes of the Bruce–Page Government:
   Challenging the Nation through Planning and Federalism . . . . .151
6. Page Audacious: The 1930s. . . . . . . . . . . . . . . . . . . . . . . . . .179
7. Post-War Page: Hopes amidst Frustrations . . . . . . . . . . . . . . .241
8. Page Indefatigable: His Last Years in Public Life . . . . . . . . . . .287
Conclusions: 'A Man's Reach Should Exceed His Grasp' . . . . . . . .325
Bibliography . . . . . . . . . . . . . . . . . . . . . . . . . . . . . . . . . . . . . . . .335
Index . . . . . . . . . . . . . . . . . . . . . . . . . . . . . . . . . . . . . . . . . . . .379

# ILLUSTRATIONS

Figure 1: Earle Page strikes a pose in early Canberra. Mildenhall Collection, NAA, A3560, 6053, undated. . . . . . . . . . . . . . . . . . . . 3

Figure 2: 'He went about doing good': Earle Page panel, Page Memorial Window, Wesley and St Aidan's Uniting Church, Canberra . . . . . . . . . . . . . . . . . . . . . . . . . . . . . . . . . . . 24

Figure 3: Charles and Annie Page with their family, c. 1890. . . . . . . . 28

Figure 4: Page's beloved Clarence Valley region. . . . . . . . . . . . . . . . . . 29

Figure 5: Ulrich Ellis . . . . . . . . . . . . . . . . . . . . . . . . . . . . . . . . . . . . . . . 55

Figure 6: Sydney and the North, *New State Magazine*, June 1923. . . . 83

Figure 7: The new Bruce–Page Ministry at its swearing-in ceremony, 1923 . . . . . . . . . . . . . . . . . . . . . . . . . . . . . . . . . . . . . . . 96

Figure 8: Charles Hardy, c. 1931: Regional demagogue pictured in respectable mode . . . . . . . . . . . . . . . . . . . . . . . . . . . . . . . . . . 189

Figure 9: Earle Page with Ethel Page on his return to Australia, August 1942 . . . . . . . . . . . . . . . . . . . . . . . . . . . . . . . . . . . . . . . . 253

Figure 10: Post-war Australia divided into 97 Regional Development Committees, as seen by the Chifley Government . . . . . . . . . . . 267

Figure 11: Cover of Page's 1944 booklet, *Clarence River Hydro-Electric Gorge Scheme* . . . . . . . . . . . . . . . . . . . . . . . . . . . . 279

Figure 12: The new Menzies Ministry 1949 . . . . . . . . . . . . . . . . . . . . 294

# ACKNOWLEDGEMENTS

This is a study of the ideas held by an intelligent, dedicated, somewhat eccentric visionary, and of his attempts to shape the young Australian nation.

It challenges, I hope convincingly, misconceptions about Earle Page. It sets him in wide context, both in terms of what was happening around him and of trying to interpret the implications his career has for Australia's history. It contributes to filling a gap in perceptions of the Australian past and may also have relevance for today's political environment surrounding national development policy.

Thanks foremost and immensely to Professor Nicholas Brown of The Australian National University School of History, my supervisor for the thesis that formed the basis for this book. Thanks also to Frank Bongiorno, Peter Stanley, Linda Botterill, James Walter, A.J. Brown and Brian Costar; staff and students of the School of History, ANU, including those in the National Centre of Biography; and Kent Fedorowich of the University of the West of England.

Also staff of the National Library of Australia; the University of New England and Regional Archives; the University of Melbourne Archives; the National Archives of Australia; Wesley and St Aidan's Uniting Church; ANU Archives; the University of Sydney Archives; Hardie Grant Travel; and of the Museum of Australian Democracy, notably David Jolliffe. Louise Graul searched for traces of Page in the archives of Sydney Boys High School. Paul Davey, historian of the Country Party and its later incarnations, also provided assistance. Patrick Robertson volunteered to recatalogue the Page papers in the National Library of Australia, undertaken well after I had conducted most of my research but still a signal development that will ease the path for future researchers of Page's rich life. I am also very grateful to friend and neighbour Peter

Stevens for his personal generosity in volunteering his time to comment on early drafts. Geoff Hunt was not only a highly skilled copyeditor, but also a valued source of wider advice.

I met several people who encountered Page in person, including the late Ann Moyal who undertook the formidable task of editing the draft of his *Truant Surgeon*. In doing so, she turned this memoir into Australia's foremost prime ministerial autobiography. Helen Snyders and Geoff Page, members of the inestimable Page clan, were both immensely helpful with documents and personal recollections. Thanks too to Jim and Philippa Page and all the residents of Heifer Station: Earle Page's attachment to his home base and the gloriously fertile Clarence River region is eminently understandable. And to Max Ellis, son of the highly observant pioneering chronicler of the Country Party and the new state cause. I alone am responsible for opinions and errors.

Lastly and most importantly, my very special thanks to Jenni for her tolerance over years of my incessant tapping and self-imposed seclusion. No one could have been more loving and supportive. And of course Jim, inevitably.

This research was supported by an Australian Government Research Training Program (RTP) Scholarship.

Some of the capitalisation and spelling of common terms appearing in quotes has been made consistent with usage in the rest of this volume. Units of electricity replicate the original usage employed in each quote and source.

Stephen Wilks,
The Australian National University,
Canberra

# ABBREVIATIONS

| | |
|---|---|
| AAC | Australian Agricultural Council |
| ACPA | Australian Country Party Association |
| AFFO | Australian Farmers' Federal Organisation |
| AIF | Australian Imperial Force |
| AIPS | Australian Institute of Political Science |
| ALP | Australian Labor Party |
| ANU | The Australian National University |
| BMA | British Medical Association (Australia) |
| CRCC | Clarence River County Council |
| CSIR | Council for Scientific and Industrial Research |
| CSIRO | Commonwealth Scientific and Industrial Research Organisation |
| DMC | Development and Migration Commission |
| EPP | Earle Page Papers, National Library of Australia |
| FRM | Federal Reconstruction Movement |
| FSA | Farmers and Settlers' Association |
| MHR | Member of the House of Representatives |
| MLA | Member of the Legislative Assembly |
| MLC | Member of the Legislative Council |
| MP | Member of Parliament |
| NAA | National Archives of Australia |
| NHMRC | National Health and Medical Research Council |
| NLA | National Library of Australia |
| RRC | Rural Reconstruction Commission |

| | |
|---|---|
| SEC | State Electricity Commission of Victoria |
| TVA | Tennessee Valley Authority |
| UAP | United Australia Party |
| UCM | United Country Movement |
| UCP | United Country Party of New South Wales |
| UNE | University of New England |
| USSR | Union of Soviet Socialist Republics |
| VFU | Victorian Farmers' Union |
| WEA | Workers' Educational Association |

# PROLOGUE
## 'How Many Germans Did You Kill, Doc?'

Late on the morning of 20 April 1939, Earle Page – surgeon, grazier, newspaper proprietor, treasurer and prime minister – delivered the most notorious speech ever heard in the parliament of Australia. His carefully worded but scandalously bitter attack on the personal fitness of Robert Menzies to serve as prime minister not only earned Page outraged condemnation at the time, but also has grossly distorted perceptions of him ever since.

This is despite Page having been the most remarkable visionary to hold political power in Australia. His determined efforts to realise the nation's economic potential by recasting it as a decentralised, regionalised and rationally planned society have never been laid out with proper justice to the richness of this vision. He was effervescent, intelligent and persistent. The main constraint on the man was his own tendency to overestimate how eminently practical his plans surely were.

Page was himself prime minister when he launched his attack on Menzies. He had been sworn in 13 days before on a caretaker basis following the death in office of Joseph Lyons from heart failure. The much-loved Lyons had led the United Australia Party (UAP), the senior partner in a governing coalition with the Country Party of which Page had himself been federal parliamentary leader since 1921. The choice of Page to step into the prime ministership was aided by the UAP's lack of a deputy leader when Lyons died. This was as Menzies – comparatively young, determined and prone to an arrogance that extended to indiscreetly imitating Page's mannerisms – had recently resigned as Lyons's deputy over the government's about-face on implementing a national insurance scheme. As war seemed an imminent possibility, Page was sworn in with the full powers of the prime ministership. He accepted his commission from the governor-general with the intention of resigning once the UAP had elected a new leader, and of not serving as a member of a coalition government should Menzies be chosen. Eleven days later, the UAP party room did just that.

Since 1934 Page had sat in the Cabinet alongside Menzies, and even accompanied him on trade delegations to Britain in 1936 and 1938. Page's parliamentary attack on his erstwhile ministerial colleague was made all the more dramatic by the lack of public warning. It had just become known that the Country Party would not serve under Menzies, due foremost to his insistence on choosing all members of a coalition ministry including those from the Country Party. And it was widely appreciated that his personal relations with Page were decidedly poor. But to publicly condemn Menzies on the grounds that he had not volunteered for the Australian Imperial Force (AIF) during the Great War – to effectively brand him an abject coward – went far beyond anything previously heard in the parliament.

That Page was clearly not just speaking intemperately in a sudden flare of anger added to the sense of outrage. His very precise and ordered speech had obviously been carefully crafted. Page's future daughter-in-law later recalled repeatedly typing drafts of the speech with and then without the offending passage as he uncharacteristically vacillated. Only his wife and a select few parliamentary colleagues were taken into his confidence. Page's current and former deputies Harold Thorby and Tom Paterson both tried in vain to dissuade him. His political secretary, Massey Stanley, took it upon himself to neuter his boss's intended text: Page tore the result into shreds with a chuckle.

Accounts vary as to whether the acerbic Archie Cameron, later to succeed Page as Country Party leader, also counselled caution or instead provided the fatal encouragement to go ahead: the latter would have been much more in character. The day before the attack, Page drove into the Brindabella Range outside Canberra with Cameron and Ulrich Ruegg Ellis. Ellis was an acute observer of federal politics who had known Page since 1921 and served as his political secretary 1928–36. Page did not embark on this trip so as to let himself be dissuaded. On the contrary, he was seeking to calm his nerves for what he was about to do. He felt confident that he could end Menzies's political career, if not at once at least eventually. Page had convinced himself that he could match his effort of 1923 when he had made the replacement of Prime Minister William Morris 'Billy' Hughes by Stanley Bruce a condition of the Country Party's preparedness to join a coalition with the urban-based conservatives.

Page began the parliamentary day of 20 April conventionally enough. A distant predecessor of his as member for the north-eastern New South Wales seat of Cowper, one Francis Clarke, had just died. This aroused little interest other than a noting of Clarke's having surrendered a seat he earlier held in the New South Wales Parliament so that Edmund Barton could resume his status as an MP and thus his formal role in the Federation movement. Opposition leader John Curtin and then Menzies briefly added to Page's words of condolence. Following a few further formalities, Page began to deliver his prepared statement.

Page did not launch into the attack at once. His very deliberate choice of words slowly built a sense of tension as it became increasingly clear that he was working towards something momentous. Page spoke of Menzies having personally advised him that he had just become UAP leader, to which Page's very proper response had been an assurance that he would vacate the prime ministership whenever this suited. But Page still felt 'compelled to take up the question as to who was to be the new leader of the UAP', especially as there was a need for someone with the right public record to 'lead a united national effort' and 'inspire the people of Australia'.[1]

Page's penchant for demonstrative cleverness was reflected in how he structured the progression of his speech. Twenty-four days ago, said Page, Menzies had resigned from Lyons's Cabinet over the national insurance scheme issue. Twenty-four weeks ago, he had made a speech on leadership to the Constitutional Club in Sydney, widely interpreted as a veiled attack on Prime Minister Lyons. And then, the climax. In Page's words:

> When, 24 years ago, Australia was in the midst of the Gallipoli campaign, Mr Menzies was a member of the Australian Military Forces, and held the King's Commission. In 1915, after being in the service for some years, he resigned his commission and did not go overseas. I am not questioning the reasons why anyone did not go to the war. All I say is that if the right honourable gentleman cannot satisfactorily and publicly explain to a very

---

1   *Sydney Morning Herald*, 21 April 1939, p. 12.

great body of people in Australia who did participate in the war his failure to do so, he will not be able to get that maximum effort out of the people in the event of war.[2]

In other words, Menzies was of such poor character he was not fit to succeed to the prime ministership. Page had raised the great unmentionable of who had and had not volunteered for active service. Whispers about this had long dogged Menzies. It was why he had not been invited to join the Melbourne Club: when the offer was finally made after he became prime minister, he appears to have elected to quietly decline. Page spoke also of his attempt to entice Stanley Bruce back from the Australian High Commission in London to again become prime minister. Given the seeming likelihood of war, Page was convinced that Bruce should head a national government of all parties and contrasted this with the one-party government that Menzies seemed set to lead.

Page's accusation had an immediate impact, but hardly of the sort he had hoped for. There were at once 'wild scenes' in the House, with 'uproar and cries of "shame"' reported the *Sydney Morning Herald*.[3] The MP for Hunter, Rowley James, was one of the few to make himself clear to the Hansard reporters with his cry of 'That is dirt!'[4] (Verbatim newspaper reports captured a fuller record than did Hansard, including slightly blunter choices of words by both Page and Menzies.) Other members loudly affirmed that they had not gone to the war either, providing history with the unique sight of Labor members shouting in defence of Robert Menzies. Yet Page was deterred neither by the tumult nor by snide references to his own brief war service as an army doctor. The Opposition's Joe Gander pointedly inquired 'How many Germans did you kill, Doc?'[5]

Menzies himself tried to interject but was drowned out. His wife Pattie, sitting in the public gallery, left at once and henceforth never spoke to Page again. Immediately after Page concluded, Menzies rose to deliver his rejoinder. That his right arm was in a dark sling unintentionally added to his innately considerable gravitas – even if, far from being a war wound, it was the result of a fall on a Canberra footpath on the very morning of the UAP party room vote two days earlier.

---

2  Ibid., p. 12.
3  Ibid., p. 12.
4  *Commonwealth Parliamentary Debates*, 20 April 1939, p. 16.
5  *Sydney Morning Herald*, 21 April 1939, p. 12.

Speaking off the cuff, Menzies said ambiguously that he had 'received whispers' about why the Country Party would not join with him in government. He then proceeded to answer Page's case against him point by point. His resignation from Cabinet over national insurance was in keeping with a pledge to his electors and so was in fact 'one of the more respectable actions of my life'. The speech to the Constitutional Club had merely been an affirmation that 'the success of democracy would depend upon leadership and loyalty to leadership'.[6]

As for the attack on his personal integrity, this was 'not novel'. It was part of the 'stream of mud through which I have waded at every election campaign'. Menzies had not resigned anything, but had served out his period of compulsory training like any other universal trainee, which extended – though he did not make this clear in the speech – right through the war and up to 1921. His not joining the AIF arose from 'a man's intimate and personal family affairs'. Mention of two of his brothers having enlisted made it implicitly clear that he had been constrained by a binding family decision that he was the one to stay at home. Specifying that they had served in the infantry may have been a jab at Page not having been a frontline soldier himself. Menzies concluded, according to the press accounts, that as prime minister he would 'exhibit none of those miserable paltry traits' shown by Page 'in the most remarkable attack I have heard in my public career'.[7]

It was immediately obvious that Page had made a massive miscalculation. The next day the *Sydney Morning Herald* denounced his 'despicable attack' as 'a violation of the decencies of debate without parallel in the annals of the Federal Parliament'.[8] The Melbourne *Argus* thought that Page 'emerges with a stain on his record which would seem to be permanent'.[9] Page's political standing was severely damaged: five months later he finally resigned as leader of the Country Party. Despite a rather nominal reconciliation with Menzies in October of the following year, Page never directly apologised or disowned his infamous speech. Nor was it quite the last parliamentary airing of Menzies's lack of a war record. Sixteen years later, amidst a debate on the Petrov Royal Commission, the Labor member Dan Curtin demanded of Menzies 'what about your

---

6   Ibid., p. 12.
7   Ibid., p. 12.
8   Ibid., p. 10.
9   Melbourne *Argus*, 21 April 1939, p. 10.

military record?' Menzies retorted with a tart suggestion to instead 'ask Bert and Eddie', a reference to the Labor leader Herbert Vere Evatt and his colleague Eddie Ward having also spent the war at home.[10]

Page was not normally vindictive. So why this extraordinary transgression of an unspoken parliamentary taboo? The immediate trigger was his angry conviction that Menzies's attacks on Lyons – if such they were – had imposed stress that hastened Lyons's death. But Page's outrage also had a more substantive policy base in the recent failure of his attempt to create a powerful national economic planning agency. Menzies had made clear to Page his disdain for this audacious venture. Like almost everything that Page did, his actions of 20 April 1939 drew on his determination to engineer a very different Australia.

---

10   *Commonwealth Parliamentary Debates*, 25 October 1955, p. 2.

# INTRODUCTION
## 'A Dreamer of Dreams'

The idealism and tireless activism of Earle Page sparked radically differing reactions. H.P. Moss, Commonwealth electricity supply controller, saw him as 'a dreamer of dreams with a firm hold on mother earth'.[1] Former prime minister Stanley Bruce recalled that Page as his treasurer was so 'bursting with energy' that he routinely had to be advised 'my dear Page, for God's sake go away and have your head read'. But Bruce added that 'if you had the patience to listen to Page, he'd come up with a helluva good idea now and then'.[2] Page's Country Party colleague Arthur Fadden was once heard to shout amid an evening group drinking session when Page briefly absented himself 'he's a dribbling, doddering old halfwit!'[3] Much later, political scientist Don Aitkin judged Page to be 'almost without question the most inventive federal politician of the twentieth century', yet also 'the most under-regarded politician of the federal arena'.[4]

Earle Page was not merely one of Australia's longest serving senior politicians. His entire career was dedicated to remarkably consistent but pragmatically opportunistic efforts to shape the still formative Australian nation according to his very personal vision of its economic and social future. He influenced conventional policy, both directly through his membership of governments and indirectly through his impact on what ideas were foremost in public debate.

---

1    Quoted in foreword to Earle Page, *Clarence River Hydro-Electric Gorge Scheme*, *The Bulletin Newspaper*, Sydney, August 1944.
2    Quoted in Cecil Edwards, *Bruce of Melbourne: Man of Two Worlds*, William Heinemann, London, 1965, p. 82.
3    Recalled by publisher Peter Ryan in *It Strikes Me: Collected Essays 1994–2010*, Quadrant Books, Sydney, 2011, p. 266.
4    Don Aitkin, 'Page, Earle Christmas Grafton', in Graeme Davison, John Hirst and Stuart Macintyre (eds), *The Oxford Companion to Australian History*, Oxford University Press, Melbourne, 1998, pp. 488–9.

This book is a biographically based examination of how Australian politics interacted with applied ideas about shaping the entire nation, from the early post-Federation years when the fundamentals of the new Commonwealth were an open issue, up to mid-century when Australian politics and policy seemed more settled. Page's determination to make Australia a decentralised, regionalised and rationally planned nation tapped into wider debate about the disposition of population and industry, economic development and the structures of government. For all his idiosyncrasies, assessing his most distinctive ideas and initiatives concerning national development helps chart what specific issues were important and the extent of their wider support during his many years in politics. This points to broader conclusions on the place in Australian history of great ambitions to invigorate the nation's economy and society – often described as nation-building, but to which I apply the term *developmentalism*.

Page was one of many important Australian leaders – figures as diverse as Prime Minister Ben Chifley, South Australian Premier Thomas Playford and Country Party leader John 'Black Jack' McEwen – who assumed that such a vast and formative nation was surely open to the aggressive exploitation of natural resources and the fostering of new industries. Although Page drew on ideas promoted by other public figures, he uniquely moulded them into a coherent vision that was very much his own. Yet Page has received little serious attention from historians. Aside from a focus on the drama of his 1939 assault on Menzies, he is often cast as merely reflective of the mainstream of the Country Party and hence solely intent on securing resources for rural interests. This is to greatly underestimate the originality and significance of his imagining of Australia.

Over decades, Page used the striking phrase 'now is the psychological moment'. This had fairly wide currency before him: prominent early users include Joseph Conrad, Mark Twain and Alexander Wheelock Thayer in his famed biography of Beethoven. These words, or slight variations, appeared in Page's public statements, private correspondence, official documents and memoirs to mark whenever he thought that the stars had at last aligned to provide the public and political support needed to achieve one of his treasured policy goals. He used this phrase in connection with issues as diverse as new states, hydroelectricity, economic planning and national insurance.

**Figure 1: Earle Page strikes a pose in early Canberra. Mildenhall Collection, NAA, A3560, 6053, undated.**
Source: Courtesy of National Archives of Australia.

This favoured phrase was much more than just a rhetorical device. It encapsulated Page's realisation that his vision of the nation was usually far ahead of what views were held by nearly all of his political peers and the wider public. It also suggested a sense that his ideas still had potential to appeal to the Australian public at a time when the future of their nation remained an open issue. The result was that Page pursued different issues at particular times according to what appeared politically feasible – his seizing of the psychological moment. He pursued regionalism, for example, in the mid-1920s when the new state movement peaked. In the late 1930s, he demanded economic planning as preparations for war and the illness of Lyons presented him with a rare opportunity. In the latter 1940s, he was determined to dam the Clarence River for hydroelectricity as a post-war reconstruction initiative.

'NOW IS THE PSYCHOLOGICAL MOMENT'

# Who was Earle Page – and why does he matter?

Earle Christmas Grafton Page was born on 8 August 1880 in Grafton in north-eastern New South Wales, about 630 kilometres north of Sydney. He was a rural surgeon who helped found the federal Country Party – today's National Party – and was its longest serving leader, from April 1921 until September 1939. His membership of the House of Representatives from 1919 until his death on 20 December 1961 makes Page Australia's third longest serving federal parliamentarian, after Billy Hughes and Philip Ruddock, but Page outstrips both by having held the same seat for the longest continuous period. He was a Cabinet minister for a total of 20 years, and de facto deputy prime minister under Stanley Bruce (1923–29) and Joseph Lyons (1934–39). (The deputy prime ministership was not a formal title at these times.) He held the portfolios of Treasury (1923–29), Commerce (1934–39, 1940–41) and Health (1937–38), but spent most of the 1940s on the political outer before resuming the Health portfolio (1949–56). In 1941–42 he was Australian minister resident in London, serving in Churchill's War Cabinet at the height of the crisis in Anglo-Australian relations in the wake of Japan's entry into the war.

Page's service as caretaker prime minister lasted for a mere 19 days from 7 to 26 April 1939. It nonetheless accords him recognition he would not otherwise have – such standard prime ministerial markers as the naming of a suburb in Canberra, his visage on a 1975 postage stamp and a display in the Museum of Australian Democracy. Only Frank Forde had a shorter prime ministerial career, one week during July 1945. Page is well known for his crucial roles in creating the urban–rural conservative coalition that has been a fundamental feature of Australian national politics since 1923, in resetting the financial relationship between the Commonwealth and states via the 1927 Financial Agreement, and in pioneering a program of publicly subsidised health insurance during the 1950s. Potted biographies usually also raise his less successful efforts to create a new state in northern New South Wales.

Impressive as these achievements are, they are just shards of Page's wider vision for the transformation of the nation, his ultimate aim throughout five decades in public life. Page's own listing of his specific policy ideals varied from time to time, but there were several that he held with near-total consistency. Population and industry were to be decentralised to the countryside. The governance of the nation was to be radically recast into semi-autonomous regional authorities, thereby encouraging local engagement with social and economic development but still in accordance with policies set by a strong central government. National economic planning was needed to guide the location of infrastructure and new industries. The countryside must reap the many benefits of electrification, especially by harnessing rivers to generate hydroelectricity. Rural higher education would encourage decentralisation and civic awareness. And a radically reformed constitution would institutionalise the Commonwealth–state cooperation required to work towards all of these goals. Sometimes Page spoke also of his commitment to more conventional interests such as a secure banking system, tariff reform and free trade throughout the British Empire.

Page's grand goals were so intertwined they cannot be readily separated out. Planning was a means of developing rural infrastructure, including hydroelectric power schemes, which would provide a productive basis for regional governance and decentralisation; rural higher education could help build civic cultures supportive of development; and 'cooperative federalism' was a basis for implementing policies nationally, such as an Australia-wide transport system servicing decentralised industries. Many of the specific issues that he engaged with so tirelessly are still very much with us today – the state–Commonwealth power balance, tensions between countryside and city over the allocation of public resources, attempts to forge a coherent national economic policy, and an energy policy for the nation.

Page's Country Party has been said to be hard to classify using the conventional left–right political spectrum. Even for a regionally based party, it is *sui generis* as a conservative party that upholds public invention to aid its favoured industries. The man himself is every bit as puzzling. A cursory survey of his career could lead to political biographer David Marr's comments about 'knights on horseback' – 'attractive bit players' in politics who see the everyday world 'not quite as the rest of us do', while 'what drives them is always a little opaque'.[5] Marr wrote with Tony Abbott foremost in mind, but his comments could also be directed at less central political players such as Frederic Eggleston, Bert Kelly, Barry Jones and others. Such figures were often thoughtful individuals who challenged

---

5   David Marr, *Political Animal: The Making of Tony Abbott*, Quarterly Essay no. 47, Black Inc., Collingwood, Vic., 2012, p. 110.

fundamentals and occasionally nurtured ideas that grew into mainstream policy, including private investment in public infrastructure (Eggleston), free trade (Kelly) and innovation (Jones). Even if they achieved less than they hoped to, their very mixed political fortunes helps define what was and was not politically possible at various times in Australia's past and suggests much about Australian history and the basis of current debates.

Applying Marr's very generic label to Page only partially captures the man and his significance. Far from being opaque, he made very clear what he wanted and why. As a career politician he certainly had a grasp of reality, strained as this was at times. Above all, he was not a bit player. Self-perceived visionaries are hardly rare but Page was different – a long-term holder of high office in a position to actually do something about shaping Australia. The man was not just seeking more resources for the countryside, keen on this as he was. This rare combination of the earthly and the dreamer saw himself as a statesman leading a grand cause that sat far above mere party politics.

A biographically based approach can be vital to understanding the past by providing a means to relate the particular to the general. In Page's case, seniority, tenacious advocacy and breadth of vision made for a life that enlivened many major public issues. He saw the nation as a tractable land of possibilities that a visionary like himself, dedicated to a very personal conception of the greater good, had a public duty to try to realise. His rich policy career and the reactions of those around him thus help map how the Australian political imagination was at least occasionally capable of stretching beyond conventional politics to consider how the nation could realise its potential. As has frequently been noted, visionaries often inadvertently tell us more about what they represent in their own present than the future they foresee.[6]

That Page's various policy triumphs and failures extended across six different decades makes him even more important. Such rare political longevity illuminates important changes in the wider policy environment around him. There were, for example, major changes in how policy was formulated within government, notably a post-Depression dominance of economic precepts with which Page struggled. Over time, even his own Country Party gravitated towards very different ideas of national

---

6   Such as noted by Ian Turner (ed.) in *The Australian Dream: A Collection of Anticipations about Australia from Captain Cook to the Present Day*, Sun Books, Melbourne, 1968, p. ix.

development. Although Page saw himself as a dedicated party man, this was not in the tribal sense of unthinking loyalty. He was more consistently faithful to issues that he implored the Country Party to uphold. It is significant that at times he tried to work with the Australian Labor Party leadership, such as on national planning.

Exploring Page's policy initiatives also illuminates important social and political movements that he hoped would galvanise this campaigning. Such contexts as the early Country Party, new state movements and attempts to harness the business world and the engineering profession delineate what wider support or opposition his various causes elicited. Indeed, Page's career embodies an important ongoing tension in Australia's national history. On the one hand, he was broadly in company with ardent developmentalists who thought that direct action could readily realise the nation's potential. On the other, he confronted realists in government and business who stressed the limitations of the Australian natural environment and of government action. Competition between hopeful and more sober conceptions of national development was one of the great debates of twentieth-century Australia, with Page playing the role of an especially incorrigible optimist.

The distinctiveness of Page's policy vision further enhances his value as a basis for wider historical assessment. It has often been said that Australian politics has derived many of its animating ideas from European and American sources. Although Page made enthusiastic use of international exemplars, this was highly selective. Fundamentally, he synthesised home-grown and overseas-sourced ideas into his own distinctively broad yet prescriptive developmentalist vision of the nation, making him a major example of a thinker functioning in a very practical political context. Recent studies have sought to broaden conceptions of the importance of ideas in Australian public life. This includes work by James Walter and Tod Moore that touches on Country Party figures, notably Page himself, his energetic admirer Ulrich Ellis, and Page's confidant David Drummond. They call Page an 'inventive political strategist' and an 'intellectual' of the Country Party, and argue that other scholars have placed too much emphasis on the local absence of canonical figures of the stature of Edmund Burke or John Stuart Mill.[7] Australia has instead been rich in more applied thinkers such as the economist L.F. Giblin, the pioneering

---

[7] Tod Moore in James Walter with Tod Moore, *What Were They Thinking?: The Politics of Ideas in Australia*, UNSW Press, Sydney, 2010, pp. 155–6.

management theorist Elton Mayo and the public servant, economist and banker H.C. 'Nugget' Coombs (all of whom, incidentally, Page knew). Such figures can be ideologically ambiguous, including Page the anti-socialist who simultaneously advocated strong national government.

## The significance of Australian developmentalism

Developmentalism helps us understand Page, but just as importantly his career casts light on the place in twentieth-century Australia of this major but little-studied concept. Although the term developmentalism is not original to this book, it has only occasionally been widely used in the assertive, encompassing sense meant here.[8]

The sentiments it encompasses pre-date Page. The economic historian S.J. Butlin observed that 'development has, as it were, always been part of Australian religion since Arthur Phillip' and was identified with growth via 'geographical spread and quantitative increase'.[9] The political scientist J.D.B. Miller wrote in 1954 that 'Australian propaganda has traditionally represented it as a land of boundless resources, only waiting for people and capital to release its energies'.[10] John Gascoigne in his study of Australian exceptionalism wrote of how Australia came under European domination in 'an age energised by the possibilities of "improvement"' of the land, industry and of human nature itself. Australia was seen as 'a piece of waste land writ large requiring to be brought into productive use'.[11] Page himself in his first speech on a national stage indicated his central goal to be 'the

---

8   A partial exception is in Jillian Koshin's biography of Tasmanian Premier and hydroelectricity enthusiast Eric Reece. She defines developmentalism as 'The set of ideas which, in the name of progress, believes in, and promotes the establishment or growth of industry – particularly manufacturing and processing plants, power plants, and resource extraction'; *Electric Eric: The Life and Times of Eric Reece*, Bokprint, Launceston, Tas., 2009, p. 4. Quite differently, the term is also applied to economic theory advocating growth in developing economies through fostering strong internal markets and imposing high import tariffs.
9   S.J. Butlin, 'The role of planning in Australian economic development', *Economic Papers*, no. 15 – *Planned and Unplanned Development*, The Economic Society of Australia and New Zealand, Sydney, 1962, p. 12.
10  J.D.B. Miller, *Australian Government and Politics: An Introductory Survey*, Duckworth, London, 1954, p. 11.
11  John Gascoigne (with the assistance of Patricia Curthoys), *The Enlightenment and the Origins of European Australia*, Cambridge University Press, Cambridge, 2002, p. 70.

Development of Australia'.[12] National development was accordingly the foremost stated objective of the first government in which he held office. Prime Minister Bruce proclaimed himself 'managing director of the greatest company in Australia, the Commonwealth Government, and its duty is to develop Australia'.[13]

Developmentalism also has an important cultural dimension as an expression of national identity. Donald Horne described development as Australia's 'secular faith', amounting to 'a kind of patriotism'.[14] The historian John Hirst, in his riposte to Russel Ward's *The Australian Legend*, saw Australian nationalism as having a base in a pioneer legend that celebrates national development achieved through harnessing the land.[15] Faith in development stretched across the party political divide. Shortly after Page's death, Arthur Calwell wrote of development as 'a unique nationalism' and of the 'unanimity that exists on the *need* for national development'.[16] All twentieth-century Australian governments extolled development, albeit with significant differences of strategy between individual states. Tasmanian governments pursued industrialisation through hydroelectricity, Playford diversified the South Australian economy by offering financial incentives to attract manufacturing and post-war Western Australia beckoned private investment for the exploitation of mineral resources.

In Page's time there was little sense of a choice between material development and quality of life issues. There was also a general assumption for most of the twentieth century that government leadership was the way to incite development. Developmentalist sentiment extended into the business world and civic movements that Page tried to harness to his policy goals, attracting such varied contacts as industrialist and planner Herbert Gepp and the Tamworth-based journalist and new state devotee Victor (V.C.) Thompson. Developmentalism was especially strong in Page's milieu of rural-based politics as it was seen as favouring public investment in rural infrastructure and services that promoted equality

---

12   Earle Page, *A Plea for Unification: The Development of Australia*, Daily Examiner, Grafton, NSW, 1917, the published text of his speech to the Australasian Provincial Press Association conference of 13 August 1917.
13   Bruce speaking in 1928, quoted in Donald Horne, *Money Made Us*, Penguin Books, Ringwood, Vic., 1976, p. 134.
14   Ibid., pp. 133, 134.
15   John Hirst, 'The pioneer legend', in John Carroll (ed.), *Intruders in the Bush: The Australian Quest for Identity*, Oxford University Press, Melbourne, 1982, pp. 14–37.
16   A.A. Calwell, *Labor's Role in Modern Society*, Lansdowne Press, Melbourne, 1963, pp. 16, 134. Calwell's italics, used to draw a contrast with disagreement on *methods* for promoting development.

between city and bush. In the early twenty-first century, the eminent journalist Paul Kelly could still write of nation-building as 'a brand that resonates with Australia's political culture, where everybody thinks nation building equates with motherhood'.[17]

Peter Loveday and Lenore Layman have written perceptive articles on development as an ideology in Australia.[18] Yet most histories of modern Australia only fleetingly address the many and varied developmentalist goals dear to Page and many others. N.G. Butlin, Barnard and Pincus produced a strong survey of the twentieth-century economy, but stressed the interaction of the private and public sectors rather than ideas about national development.[19] Histories of Australian economic thought dwell on the policy revolution arising from Keynesian demand management theory, not such overtly applied concepts of national development as the regionalism, electrification and planning that so enlivened Page.[20] (One exception is Geoffrey Stokes, who sees standard portrayals of the Deakinite Australian Settlement – White Australia, industry protection, wage arbitration, state paternalism and imperial benevolence – as tending 'to overlook or reduce the significance of contesting traditions and political alternatives', and so argues for the addition of components including 'state developmentalism' in which the state has a central role in economic development.)[21] Ian Turner pointed out in a 1968 anthology that visions of a future Australia had been decidedly worldly ones but focused his selection on political radicals and nationalists, not developmentalists.[22] Geoffrey Serle surveyed Australian nationalism and nation-building in terms of high culture, such as Bernard O'Dowd's 1912 poem 'The Bush'. With lines such as 'She is the scroll on which we are to write / Mythologies our own and epics new', it promulgated a prophetic spiritual nationalism that is a far cry from the applied developmentalism of Page and others.[23]

---

17   Paul Kelly, 'Building from the base', *The Australian*, 28 October 2009.
18   Peter Loveday, 'Liberals and the idea of development', *Australian Journal of Politics and History*, vol. 23, no. 2, August 1977, pp. 219–26; Lenore Layman, 'Development Ideology in Western Australia 1933–1965', *Historical Studies*, vol. 20, no. 79, October 1982, pp. 234–60.
19   N.G. Butlin, A. Barnard and J.J. Pincus, *Government and Capitalism: Public and Private Choice in Twentieth Century Australia*, George Allen & Unwin, Sydney, 1982.
20   Such as Alex Millmow's otherwise highly informative *The Power of Economic Ideas: The Origins of Keynesian Macroeconomic Management in Interwar Australia 1929–39*, ANU E Press, Canberra, 2010.
21   Geoffrey Stokes, 'The "Australian Settlement" and Australian political thought', *Australian Journal of Political Science*, vol. 39, no. 1, March 2004, pp. 6, 14–15.
22   Turner, *The Australian Dream*, pp. ix–x.
23   Geoffrey Serle, *From Deserts the Prophets Come: The Creative Spirit in Australia 1788–1972*, Heinemann, Melbourne, 1972, pp. 69–71.

Broad as developmentalism is, it nearly always incorporates an assumption that government will play the decisive role in realising a truly remarkable national potential. Bruce, for example, said that Australia's natural resources 'if brought to full development would probably solve most of the economic problems that face the world today'.[24] Despite developmentalism's ideological nature, its advocates invariably disdained impractical abstraction and did not try to build theoretical constructs. Development was often also seen as a means of sustaining a bigger population more capable of defending such a large nation: 'unless we peopled Australia rapidly and developed our resources we should expose ourselves to physical assault' agreed Page.[25] At times this was linked to imperialist sentiments by being cast as improving capacity to absorb population overflow from the Mother Country, notably during the Bruce–Page era of the 1920s. How exactly all this would be successfully planned was often very unclear. Commenting just a year after Page's death, S.J. Butlin saw planning in Australia as merely 'the general acceptance of a rather vaguely defined line of advance ... with the "planning" only acquiring definite objectives and real content at the level of specific plans, commonly plans of limited scope and with limited time horizons'.[26]

Charting reactions over time to Page's developmentalist campaigning helps show how developmentalist thought changed. Early in his public career, the dominant form was centred on rural development and assumed that a nation as vast as Australia could surely exploit hitherto underutilised land. This encouraged assistance for migrants to settle on the land and related efforts to harness rivers for irrigation. Page drew from this practice of seeing water resources as a key to national development, but differed from most other 'water dreamers' by stressing ultimate goals of decentralisation, regionalisation and hydroelectricity rather than irrigation.[27] Reactions to Page also test the validity of assumptions that the Australian people and their governments long had a resolute – not to say heroic – commitment

---

24   W.A. Sinclair, 'Capital formation', in C. Forster (ed.), *Australian Economic Development in the Twentieth Century*, George Allen & Unwin Ltd, London, and Australasian Publishing Company, Sydney, 1970, p. 24.
25   Earle Page, *Truant Surgeon: The Inside Story of Forty Years of Australian Political Life*, edited by Ann Mozley [Moyal], Angus and Robertson, Sydney, 1963, p. 156.
26   S.J. Butlin, 'The role of planning in Australian economic development', p. 9.
27   The term is used by Michael Cathcart in his *The Water Dreamers: The Remarkable History of Our Dry Continent*, Text Publishing, Melbourne, 2009.

to nation-building. This supposedly took practical form through vast, visionary projects such as the Snowy Mountains Scheme, but somehow petered out during the late twentieth century.

Exploring Page's developmentalist campaigning during the peak years of his political career when he was part of the Bruce–Page Government also helps test an emerging perception that this was a period of policy innovation. Until recently, historians thought otherwise. Serle referred to a 'miserable decade' culturally, part of a wider 1900–30 period during which social experimentation stalled. Stuart Macintyre wrote of the Bruce–Page Government as having 'made little use of the new broom' as 'the lines of national policy were too firmly established'.[28] More recently, historians such as Frank Bongiorno have begun to identify major innovations during this period.[29] Intellectual debate on Australian development reached a high point in the interwar years, spurred on by concern that the nation was underperforming.

Much of this debate revolved around tariffs and dispute over limits to land exploitation. The most widely known developmentalist tract, Edwin Brady's 1918 *Australia Unlimited*, eponymously saw no such limits.[30] The controversial geographer Thomas Griffith Taylor responded by pointing to environmental constraints in central and northern Australia, while foresters such as Charles Lane Poole warned of continued deforestation. Daisy Bates saw Taylor as slandering British pioneers: 'Surely the spirit of the British adventurer is not dead; it is only doped in these times with the pabulums administered by faddists, jazzists, and other "futilities"'.[31] Intense policy and intellectual debates on land use, regionalism, electrification, planning and federalism continued right through the interwar period and beyond, with Page a leading participant.

Page's political status makes him also of inherent interest. Why, among would-be nation-shapers, did he constitute a rare exception by holding high office for decades as a party leader and minister? And how was it that he nonetheless failed to keep his own Country Party enthused for

---

28  Serle, *From Deserts the Prophets Come*, pp. 90–1, 102; Stuart Macintyre, *A Concise History of Australia*, Cambridge University Press, Melbourne, 1999, p. 167.
29  Frank Bongiorno, 'Search for a solution, 1923–39', in Alison Bashford and Stuart Macintyre (eds), *The Cambridge History of Australia*, volume 2, Cambridge University Press, Melbourne, 2013, pp. 65–8.
30  Edwin J. Brady, *Australia Unlimited*, G. Robertson, Melbourne, c. 1918.
31  In J.M. Powell, *Griffith Taylor and 'Australia Unlimited'*, the John Murtagh Macrossan lecture 1992, University of Queensland Press, St Lucia, Qld, 1993, p. 26.

his ideas, especially in the post–World War Two era? Page was involved in many initiatives that cast light on these questions and his modus operandi. This book examines in detail two that were toweringly ambitious even by Earle Page standards: the 1931–32 campaign to separate northern New South Wales unilaterally from the rest of the state and his 1938–39 attempt to establish powerful machinery for national economic planning. The latter, in particular, is only fleetingly mentioned in histories of the period. Page effectively took over the government from a stricken Prime Minister Lyons and briefly held the attention of the entire nation. It is the foremost example of his self-belief as a nation-shaper: its failure helps mark the start of his decline.

## Page's legacy

Aitkin's description of Page as the most under-regarded federal politician remains a decidedly minority view amongst historians. There has been no previous full-length book on Page other than his own memoir, *Truant Surgeon*. Chris Bowen, himself a former treasurer, considered the lack of such a study of Page to be 'a gap in the written historical record of Australia'.[32] Most assessments – or assumptions, in some cases – are at odds with Page's powerfully idiosyncratic persona and significance. Ross Fitzgerald wrote of Page's 'intellectual weaknesses' being exploited when in 1927 he found himself confronted on economic policy by the new federal Labor parliamentarian E.G. Theodore.[33] A.W. Martin described Page as having 'personified the limitations of a country surgeon and businessman', and as being 'a plodder at best'.[34]

Page's fleeting tenure as prime minister also influences assessments, usually to his detriment. Political scientist Malcolm Mackerras marked Page down in prime ministerial ranking on the grounds that unlike another Country Party caretaker in the office, John McEwen, he failed to successfully dictate to the majority party about his successor.[35] He is often summed

---

32  Chris Bowen, *The Money Men: Australia's 12 Most Notable Treasurers*, Melbourne University Press, Carlton, Vic., 2015, p. 81.
33  Ross Fitzgerald, *"Red Ted": The Life of E.G. Theodore*, University of Queensland Press, St Lucia, 1994, p. 200.
34  A.W. Martin, *Robert Menzies: A Life, Volume 1, 1894–1943*, Melbourne University Press, Parkville, Vic., 1993, pp. 123, 279.
35  Malcolm Mackerras, 'Menzies the Top Bob amid the greats', *The Australian*, 16 August 2008. In 2010 Mackerras rated Page as "low average"; see Malcolm Mackerras, 'Ranking Australia's prime ministers', *Sydney Morning Herald*, 25 June 2010.

up as canny – a 'born intriguer' wrote Barry Jones.[36] Historian Fred Alexander saw Hughes and Bruce rather than Page as leading promoters of applied science, despite Page's strong interest and his almost certainly being the first senior Commonwealth Cabinet minister with scientific training.[37] Even other prominent developmentalists have ignored him. The manufacturing industrialist Barton Pope in 1982 called for a national planning council, evidently without realising that Page tried to create such a body in 1938–39. Pope listed Australia's great developmental visionaries as including Alfred Deakin, John Forrest, Playford, John Curtin and Chifley – but not the less conventional Page.[38]

Another conspicuous gap is that histories of the Country Party do not address Page's full national vision or what his career implies for Australian history. Foremost of these is B.D. Graham's 1966 *The Formation of the Australian Country Parties*. This exhaustive account of the labyrinthine steps leading to the party's emergence is one of the great works of Australian political history. It addresses the role of rural ideology, but limits discussion of associated policy to accounts of new state movements and orderly marketing schemes for primary produce. Graham wrongly cast Page as one of a crop of Country Party leaders 'who prided themselves on being good administrators and conventional politicians'.[39] Ulrich Ellis's *A History of the Australian Country Party* is an important outline of events but is more descriptive than interpretative. His chapter-long profile of Page is a perceptive character study yet bears signs of Ellis having been his foremost follower, especially in its treatment of new states.[40] Ellis is nonetheless an important and underestimated source on twentieth-century Australian politics. Paul Davey's later Country Party histories provide invaluably clear overviews of party organisation and political events but are less comprehensive on the ideas held by party members, including Page.[41]

---

36   Barry Jones, 'Leadership: Ranking our prime ministers', *The Weekend Australian*, 12–13 June 1996, p. 25.
37   Fred Alexander, *Australia since Federation: A Narrative and Critical Analysis*, third edition, Thomas Nelson, West Melbourne, 1976 (first published 1967), pp. 65–7, 269.
38   Barton Pope, 'Planning for the next one hundred years', in Barton Pope, Macfarlane Burnet and Mark Oliphant, *Challenge to Australia*, Rigby, Adelaide, 1982, p. 10.
39   B.D. Graham, *The Formation of the Australian Country Parties*, Australian National University Press, Canberra, 1966, p. 290.
40   Ulrich Ellis, *A History of the Australian Country Party*, Melbourne University Press, Parkville, Vic., 1963.
41   Paul Davey, *The Nationals: The Progressive Party, Country and National Party in New South Wales 1919 to 2006*, The Federation Press, Leichhardt, 2006; Paul Davey, *Ninety Not Out: The Nationals 1920–2010*, UNSW Press, Sydney, 2010.

That Page has been largely ignored by historians is not of his own making. He wanted to leave a legacy of policy ideas, such as through *Truant Surgeon*. This book appeared posthumously in 1963, and it remains the most vibrant and purposeful of Australian prime ministerial memoirs (admittedly not a strong field). Its many messages are presented amid a cavalcade of anecdotes and other reminiscences. It is strongest as a source on his formative experiences, including as a young doctor and pioneering Country Party MP. Page relates his political career as a series of struggles to implement his ideas on hydroelectricity, new states and federalism, with other passages addressing health policy, central banking and wartime service. The title alludes to Page's patently misleading portrayal of himself as an apolitical figure who wandered into national politics by little more than chance. Historians have made only fleeting use of *Truant Surgeon*, most often for its account of Page's early years. Page also left voluminous bodies of largely untapped personal papers with the National Library of Australia and the University of New England.

This book presents a political life, but does cover all aspects of Page's long career equally. A biographical study should not impose such a mass of material as to obscure the significance of its subject. My focus is on Page's prescription for the nation and his distinctive role in national development debates – hence the emphasis on regionalism and decentralisation, electrification, cooperative federalism, planning and rural education. There is less detail on Page's more conventional contributions to health policy, national insurance, central banking and international trade negotiations. All were fields in which he played a prominent but less individually original role. National insurance schemes, for example, had wide support within coalition governments in which Page served. Coverage of Page as treasurer focuses on his contribution to shifting the balance of Commonwealth–state financial relations. Health policy is dealt with mainly to the extent that it reflected his ideas on cooperative federalism and establishes his place in the second Menzies Government.

This book also does not dwell on those few aspects of his career that are already well documented. Early steps towards central banking, with which Page had a significant involvement, have been addressed by L.F. Giblin and Robin Gollan.[42] Page's major role in establishing subsidised

---

42   L.F. Giblin, *The Growth of a Central Bank: The Development of the Commonwealth Bank of Australia 1924–1945*, Melbourne University Press, Parkville, Vic., 1951; Robin Gollan, *The Commonwealth Bank of Australia: Origins and Early History*, Australian National University Press, Canberra, 1968.

private health insurance in the 1950s has been critically analysed by James A. Gillespie.[43] Page's 1941–42 service in London was a dramatic career interlude that is best known for Page's involvement in Churchill's attempt to divert the Australian 7th Division to Burma. This unhappy episode for Page colours impressions of him today almost as much as his attack on Menzies of a few years earlier. Less well known is his wartime proposal for a new international trading regime and his hopes of guiding post-war reconstruction policies. Like so much else about Page, this has barely been written about and yet says a lot about the man.

---

43   James A. Gillespie, *The Price of Health: Australian Governments and Medical Politics 1910–1960*, Cambridge University Press, Melbourne, 1991; see Chapter 11, 'Private practice, publicly funded: The Page health scheme'.

# 1

# FAMILY, COMMUNITY AND METHODISM

## The Forging of Page's World View

Earle Page came from a remarkable family, one that instilled in him values that lastingly shaped his vision of a future Australia. Studies of political thinkers and players typically stress public careers, not private lives. 'None of us can enter into another person's mind', wrote Bernard Crick in his famed life of George Orwell.[1] But so driven a figure as Page invites resolving the question of why certain ideas took such firm root so as to better understand what fundamentally drove his public actions. Page's unwavering adherence to a rigidly prescriptive world view over decades points to indelible formative experiences. He remained resolutely undeterred by changes in the policy environment, the growing indifference of party colleagues and an increasingly mixed record of triumphs and failures. Despite picturing himself as a rationalist, Page's commitment was deeply emotional.

Page himself attested to powerful early personal influences: a family tradition of community service, particularly in education; a happy upbringing in Grafton that inspired his faith in small communities; rural isolation, which bred resentment of the big cities; and his exposure to exciting new technologies that promised social transformation. Page harnessed all of these drivers when in 1917 he seized upon his first venture onto the national stage to deliver a life-defining speech.

---

1   Bernard Crick, *George Orwell: A Life*, Penguin, Harmondsworth, 1982 (first published 1980), p. 30.

'NOW IS THE PSYCHOLOGICAL MOMENT'

# Alderman Page states his world view

Few senior Australian political figures have had the audacity to open their public career by proclaiming a comprehensive policy vision of the nation: even fewer remained largely faithful to it for decades. The occasion for Page was his speech to the Australasian Provincial Press Association at its conference held in the *Courier* newspaper building in central Brisbane on 13 August 1917. Page was present as the delegate of the Grafton-based *Daily Examiner*, of which he was part-owner. About 150 proprietors, editors and journalists reckoned to be representative of a total of 700 newspapers attended from Queensland, New South Wales, Victoria and South Australia. Amid a conference otherwise more preoccupied with wartime paper shortages and post office charges, they were presented with the singular sight of an unknown small-town alderman demanding the radical recasting of the governance of the entire nation. Page was the conference's first invited speaker and seized his opportunity by going far beyond his allotted half-hour to keep his audience's attention for a full 90 minutes. Over 40 years later, in *Truant Surgeon*, he rightly recalled his oration as 'an embodiment of my thinking on national aspects of development, the basic concepts of which I have upheld to this day'.[2] It reflects both a deep attachment to place of origin and a thrusting impatience with barriers to realising Australia's potential.

Page's stated premise in 1917 was that 'there is no doubt that the present system of government in this land does not make for its development'.[3] This arose from his foremost bugbear, the 'evil' of 'centralisation'. The concentration of government in state capital cities meant that 'public money is always expended in that corner where the seat of government is constituted'. Using infrastructure and social amenities to instead improve rural living standards would support the redistribution of population and industry into the countryside.

Underpinning this decentralisation was regional political control. This reflected Page's most fundamental belief, from which much of his wider thought derived – the inherent tendency of small-scale communities to foster civic cooperation and engagement that would lead social and economic development. Page was to become renowned as an advocate

---

2  Page, *Truant Surgeon*, p. 45.
3  This and all following quotes from this speech are taken from the text published as Page, *A Plea for Unification*.

of new states, but these were but a move towards smaller entities that he later dubbed federal units – the dullish moniker for the basic building blocks of the more thorough decentralisation of political and economic control. These federal units were to be 'big enough to attack national schemes in a large way, but small enough for every legislator to be thoroughly conversant with every portion of the area, and land settlement and proper development will naturally follow'.

The great paradox of Page in 1917 and later is that he simultaneously wanted a strong 'Central National Government' under which 'men will begin to think in terms of the continent of Australia as a whole, rather than of their state'. State parliaments were beset by an intolerably 'parochial outlook'. Page's national government could set Australia-wide policies but devolve their implementation to his federal units. It would also be better able to meet international obligations as a properly functional component of the British Empire. Although this 1917 speech was entitled 'A Plea for Unification', Page recalled in his memoirs that at that time unification signified a true federal system with a national government strong only in 'fields of common significance throughout Australia' – land policy, taxation, education, immigration and transport – leaving more regional entities to carry out major works locally.[4]

Page called for a two-stage reform process to realise his mixed regional and national vision: unification of the nation under a central government, followed by the 'consequent subdivision of the whole of this Commonwealth into small self-governing areas, with local legislatures of men who know well the needs and resources of their respective districts'. He linked this national regionalisation to the successful settlement of returned soldiers, a big selling point in 1917. The fired-up, still youngish Page was ready to strike a militant note in public. If the existing overlap between state and federal governments continued, 'there must be ultimately civil war'.

Conveniently, Page had a model ready at hand for the nation to follow. This was the northern portion of New South Wales, including his beloved Clarence Valley, undoubtedly the finest yet most disregarded part of the country. Page told the assembled press that although this region was nearly the size of Victoria, with 'millions of acres of fertile soil, power possibilities unsurpassed in Australia, and mineral wealth untold', it was denied such basic services as adequate schools and hospitals. Yet in Victoria, 'self-government has added everything that makes for physical,

---

4   Page, *Truant Surgeon*, p. 45 n.

mental and moral development ... cities, universities, well-equipped hospitals, technical schools and 5,000 miles of railways'. Properly administered, the northern region 'could easily maintain the whole of the present population of Australia'. But it was not unique, for 'many other areas in Australia could do the same thing under favourable conditions of self-government'.

Decentralisation Page-style was enlivened by his vision of rural electrification using hydroelectricity. This had been a Page policy passion for several years prior to his 1917 speech and was linked to his admiration for the Clarence River. This was 'the noblest stream flowing to the east coast of Australia' but where 'unique power waiting for development has been allowed to run to waste'. Page was to conduct a lifelong campaign to dam the Clarence as the first of a series of regionally controlled hydropower schemes stretching across the nation. In this, he was in good company: internationally during the early twentieth century, dams came to be seen as the epitome of progress by promising 'a renewable resource, furnishing power and water indefinitely'.[5]

As of 1917, Page's technological vision also encompassed railways under 'federal control, [which] with intelligent provincial advice, will ensure the proper linking up of the various provincial railway systems, and promote the opening up of all classes of land now absolutely unused'. Page's hopes for better rural services included education to support decentralisation and civic awareness. He decried the dearth of educational facilities in the northern region, where 'there is scarcely a technical school in the whole area ... [and] scarcely a secondary school'. In future years, Page was to vastly expand this interest in education by advocating a national network of small-scale rural universities.

National economic planning became Page's main means of initiating decentralisation. He only implicitly suggested planning in his 1917 speech by calling for a national government with a comprehensive development agenda, but over coming years became the foremost advocate of a plan to guide the nation. He most certainly never advocated a command economy, but instead a gentler indicative approach involving the planning of infrastructure and provision of incentives for new industries. This would help trigger what he called a self-sustaining 'reproductive process' of development.

---

5   Nick Cullather, *The Hungry World: America's Cold War Battle Against Poverty in Asia*, Harvard University Press, Cambridge, Massachusetts, 2010, p. 119.

Finally, Page spoke of reforming federalism to enable the Commonwealth and the states to together lead national policies that would put his vision into practice. His ensuing career was to be peppered with proposals to have these two main levels of government work in unison, the next best thing to outright national planning. In 1917 he spoke bluntly of 'a bastard Constitution … which has left the National Government continually at the mercy of the states'. It imposed 'such formidable cracks in the national edifice as to threaten its collapse'. Page attributed the Constitution's weakness to having been drafted in a time of peace, whereas those of the United States and of Canada reflected fear of war. Hence in Canada 'no doubt was left about the Federal Government alone being concerned with the ultimate power'. But the drafting of the Australian Constitution had been beset by 'petty ambitions of the state politicians'. Clearly, 'the only thing for Australia to do was to throw the whole Constitution into the melting-pot, and re-mould it in the light of the experience gained during the past 17 years'.

Page's 1917 speech also contained early harbingers of the specific policies on federalism that he later pursued in government. He anticipated 'the Federalising of State debts' as a step towards a new federal system, a key feature of the 1927 Financial Agreement between the Commonwealth and the states that is often touted as Page's finest achievement. In a series of press articles a few months after this 1917 speech, he opined that, unlike other Allied nations and Germany, in 'Australia alone has no attempt been made at national industrial organisation', due to 'the present chaotic system of seven different, overlapping and conflicting sets of laws and industrial tribunals' – foreshadowing the issue that felled the Bruce–Page Government 12 years later.[6]

Reactions to this speech would have readily given the ever-positive Page the impression of a receptive audience. The city press paid little attention, but his comments were reproduced across rural Australia in such publications as the *Singleton Argus*, the *Cairns Post* and the New South Wales–wide *Farmer and Settler*. A transcript was also helpfully distributed in booklet form by Page's own *Daily Examiner*.[7] The secretary of the Australasian Provincial Press Association and owner of the *Grafton*

---

6   *Daily Examiner*, 3 November 1917, p. 7.
7   Page, *A Plea for Unification*.

*Argus*, T.M. Shakespeare, was moved to advise Page to build a network of rural newspapers that would eventually 'have a far reaching effect upon future policies of the Commonwealth'.[8]

This speech stands as an early indicator that Page had a very distinct mind indeed, not at all constrained by the narrower agendas of the rural protest movements then emerging around him. Page's synthesis of ideas amounted to an ideology, an all-embracing doctrine that could draw on concepts of community, decentralisation and national leadership and that had sufficiently wide application to reach consistent conclusions on almost any political and social issue. This helps explain his persistence: Page was not advocating mere policies with conclusively achievable aims, but something that could be applied universally and endlessly. He judged most new ideas according to their compatibility with the basic principles of his 1917 speech. This far from unassuming small-town figure had produced a major variant on the theme of Australia as a social laboratory, 'in which the state was seen not as the enemy of individual freedom … but as the enabler of freedom'.[9] This concept is usually associated with Alfred Deakin and the early post-Federation era. Page had a vision just as Deakin had one that advocated arbitration, protectionism and White Australia, but his was based on the very different world view that he first presented to the nation in 1917.

Page spent the next four decades trying to implement this vision. Changes in his views were more of strategy than of fundamentals as he adopted new arguments for old positions to match the shifting political environment. How did Page's upbringing provide the basis for his remarkable persistence?

## Page's early life – the imprint of family and community

The Grafton of Page's birth was a rural town of about 2,250 inhabitants situated on the Clarence River. It provided services to local farmers, increasingly those running the dairy farms that emerged as the region's main industry during the 1880s and 1890s. The family from which he hailed was large, supportive and innately committed to civic engagement.

---

8   Shakespeare to Page, 21 August 1917, Earle Page papers, UNE Archives, A180, box 7, folder 4.
9   Cathcart, *The Water Dreamers*, p. 214.

Page was the fifth of the 11 children of Charles Page and Mary Johanna (Annie) Page, née Cox. He frequently reflected on the strength of his family tradition, writing in 1924 to his wife of how 'we are lucky to have forebears like this' and of 'their fibre which is in us'.[10]

The family's sense of community service is vividly enshrined in the symbolism incorporated into the Page Memorial Window, installed in 1957 at what is now Wesley and St Aidan's Uniting Church in Canberra. This commemorates a century of good works, with the choice of Canberra over Grafton implying a sense of commitment primarily to the entire Australian nation. It depicts four scenes from the life of Christ, each marking a particular family member. One is dedicated to Earle himself, quite regardless of his still being very much alive in 1957. This shows Jesus healing the sick and includes the Rod of Asclepius, the classical symbol of medicine, and the coats of arms of the University of New England and of the Commonwealth of Australia. The second panel is dedicated to Page's parents and the third to his missionary brother Rodger. But it is the top panel that dominates. This commemorates Earle's paternal grandfather James, along with his wife Susannah. James was the founder of the family in Australia and a powerful unseen influence on his famous grandson.

James Page had a strong Methodist background and commitment to education. Like his future grandson, James was drawn to the practical uses of science. He is even said to have on at least three occasions been saved from the effects of self-experimentation with drugs by the prompt application of a stomach pump. James subsequently switched from applied chemistry to teaching, for which he studied at the then new University College, London, which, unlike Oxford and Cambridge at the time, accepted students of all denominations. He was head teacher at the Great Queen Street Wesleyan Day School in London for 11 years and then headmaster of Wesleyan Lambeth School, as well as being secretary of the United Association of Schoolmasters of Great Britain. His work in education brought him into contact with such luminaries of Victorian science as T.H. Huxley and Charles Darwin (who lived near him in Kent).

---

10   Earle Page to Ethel Page, 23 October 1924, Earle Page papers, UNE Archives, A180, box 9, folder 72.

**Figure 2: 'He went about doing good': Earle Page panel, Page Memorial Window, Wesley and St Aidan's Uniting Church, Canberra.**

At far left is the entire window, headed by the panel dedicated to James and Susannah Page.

Source: Courtesy of Wesley and St Aidan's Uniting Church, Canberra. Photographs by Jennifer Wilks.

The Board of National Education of the New South Wales colonial government invited several qualified teachers to help implement its adoption of the Irish National System of education so to broaden access to education through new multi-denominational primary schools. James was asked to start a National School at Grafton. As his oldest son suffered from tuberculosis, he gladly accepted. He arrived in Sydney in 1855 and soon shifted north to Grafton to open the first such school – which under James also offered adult evening classes – north of the Hunter.

James set a daunting precedent for involvement in civic causes. He campaigned to establish local government in Grafton and became Grafton's first town clerk in 1860. He was secretary of the Grafton Schools Board from 1866, started a School of Arts, wrote newspaper leaders and served with other local bodies as diverse as the area's first building societies and the Grafton Hospital. James upheld his commitment to Methodism by also serving as treasurer and senior trustee of the local Wesleyan church. He died in 1877, three years before the birth of Earle, but Susannah, a Huguenot, lived until Earle was 18 years of age. Three of James's sons were mayors: Thomas in Grafton for several terms in the 1870s to 1880s, Robert in Casino, and Earle's father Charles in Grafton in 1908–9.

Charles Page was born in 1851 and initially worked as an apprentice to a local blacksmith, coachmaker and saddler; he later took over the firm. Annie was his employer's daughter; her family having moved from Melbourne to Grafton shortly after her birth in 1853. Her status as eldest child and thus as a co-carer limited her educational opportunities, but Earle recalled his mother compensating by being an avid reader and determined to secure university educations for her own children. This played a crucial role in sparking the careers of Earle and several of his siblings.

When Charles and Annie married in 1870, they settled at Chatsworth Island, 'a small and primitive downstream settlement on the Clarence'. They at once endeavoured to bring 'the benefits of education and the comforts of religion' to fellow settlers. This included teaching English to Gaelic-speaking Scottish immigrants brought out by James's friend, the Presbyterian clergyman and indefatigable political activist John Dunmore Lang.[11] This commitment continued after their return to Grafton, including an important role in establishing a local secondary school. Charles and other members of the Page and Cox clans feature prominently in local press reports as lay volunteers in the Grafton District Synod. For nearly 40 years Charles was superintendent of the Grafton Methodist Sunday School. On his death in March 1919, the local press reported that he and Annie's names were 'known in every Methodist household in New South Wales'.[12] Family life provided young Earle with great personal security. In the decades to come, even amid the tumult of

---

11  Page, *Truant Surgeon*, p. 4. The year of marriage is as advised by the Page family; Earle Page in *Truant Surgeon* gives the year variously as 1870 or 1871 and NSW government records state 1871.
12  *Daily Examiner*, 19 March 1919, p. 4.

politics, he bore few lasting grudges. As an elderly man he looked back fondly on 'a very happy boyhood and adolescence' amid his 'extraordinary clannish' family.[13]

Education owes more to family background than does any other component of Page's vision for Australia. High family expectations and three older brothers set him daunting examples to follow. His mother's determination resulted in five of her children studying at the University of Sydney, a remarkable outcome for the time. Page dwelt in his memoirs on the success of his siblings in professions that encompassed teaching, medicine, the public service, nursing and missionary work. Brother Reg held high appointments with the New South Wales Department of Education. Another brother, Will, turned from teaching to become a pioneering psychiatrist working with returned soldiers. Two of his sisters, Edith and Ella, married teachers. The Page family was also strongly engaged with technology: Earle's maternal grandfather and his brothers Cyril and Maund were engineers. Page's generation continued the family's involvement in local government, with two of his brothers serving as councillors.

Earle's older siblings were also his mentors. Page wrote of the particularly great influence of James, 'a born teacher' whose mathematics coaching helped him jump two forms at school.[14] In March 1938, prior to heading to Britain for trade negotiations, Page wrote a touching farewell letter to the then seriously ill James assuring him that 'giving bright boys their opportunity to reach the highest professional and commercial eminence' was 'the divine afflatus'. He attested to James's 'good comradeship, advice and help' as having been vital to his own 'early precocious scholastic development'.[15] James died late the next year.

Older sister Edith and her teacher husband crucially aided her siblings' studies by boarding them in Sydney when they were at secondary school. In adult life, Page was especially attached to his brother Harold, eight years his junior. One other member of the Page clan recalled that 'Earle thought more of Harold than himself'.[16] Harold subsequently joined the Commonwealth Public Service and then the New Guinea administration based at Rabaul. He rose to be deputy administrator but died in 1942 as a prisoner of the Japanese.

---

13   Earle Page to James Page, 27 March 1938, Earle Page papers, UNE Archives, A180, box 3, folder 25.
14   Page, *Truant Surgeon*, p. 5.
15   Earle Page to James Page, 27 March 1938.
16   Jim Page, *Great Uncle Harold: Harold Hillis Page 1888–1942*, privately published, no date, p. 1.

Page's awareness of 'the search for knowledge and the extension of educational facilities … [as] part of my family inheritance' featured prominently in his later writings. In his memoirs he celebrated his appointment in 1955 as first chancellor of the University of New England as placing 'the coping-stone of tertiary education on the structure begun by my forebears'.[17] Commitment to education and community service undoubtedly drew on his family's Methodism. Although Page's personal papers and public statements make only few references to religious belief, in 1902 he volunteered to become a Methodist medical missionary in the Solomon Islands before deciding to instead continue as a doctor at the Royal Prince Alfred Hospital in Sydney. Page's brother Rodger won fame as a missionary and adviser to the Tongan royal family and was a central figure in the rise to prominence of the Australian Methodist Church in Tonga.

Methodism in the nineteenth-century Anglosphere had a reputation not only for commitment to education and commerce, but also for challenging established hierarchies. Australian accounts testify to the fervour of this 'high-voltage religion' in the second half of the century, and the influence on colonial families of its work ethic and social conscience.[18] Political theorists have written of how Methodists and other dissenters encouraged Christian faith in earthly utopias and continuous progress, distinctly reminiscent of Page's ambitions for worldly improvement. Methodists have been strikingly well represented in Australian public life and include Garfield Barwick, Barry Jones, Brian Howe and John Howard.

None of this should be taken to imply that Page's family was especially wealthy. More impressive is its breadth of engagement with the Grafton community. In addition to serving in local government, Pages sat on the board of trustees of the public hospital, managed a canned meat works, ran a cinema and organised schools. Thomas Page and some of his brothers founded the *Grafton Argus*. Charles included Earle and his siblings in an active and welcoming social life, exposing them to an impressive array of future contacts. Earle recalled that through his church work his father welcomed strangers to Grafton, especially the young, and invited them to their home to partake at 'an elastic dining table round which I made many friends'.[19]

---

17  Page, *Truant Surgeon*, p. 11.
18  Historian Graeme Davison provides a rousing account of this in *Lost Relations: Fortunes of My Family in Australia's Golden Age*, Allen & Unwin, Crows Nest, NSW, 2015, pp. 165–6, 180–2.
19  Page, *Truant Surgeon*, p. 4.

**Figure 3: Charles and Annie Page with their family, c. 1890.**
Back row – Edith (Cissie) and James; middle row – Rodger, Charles, Annie, Maund, Earle; front row – Reginald, Harold, William, Ella. Cyril and Daphne were yet to be born. Note the evident damage to one of Annie's eyes, treatment of which influenced Earle Page's later decision to study medicine.
Source: Courtesy of the Page family.

Political discussion, in particular, was often 'the order of the day' for the Pages.[20] Charles was a close friend of John See, later Premier of New South Wales 1901–4, who as member for Grafton naturally took a strong interest in local development, especially transport infrastructure and harnessing the Clarence. Earle later recognised his remarkable family as a political asset. In his main campaign speech for this first run at parliament he spoke of how he had 'at his disposal the knowledge gained by his family in three generations of public service on the river', especially that of his grandfather, father and uncle. This drew applause from his audience of Graftonians, who clearly knew the Page family well.[21]

---

20  Ibid., p. 39.
21  *Daily Examiner*, 23 October 1919, p. 3.

1. FAMILY, COMMUNITY AND METHODISM

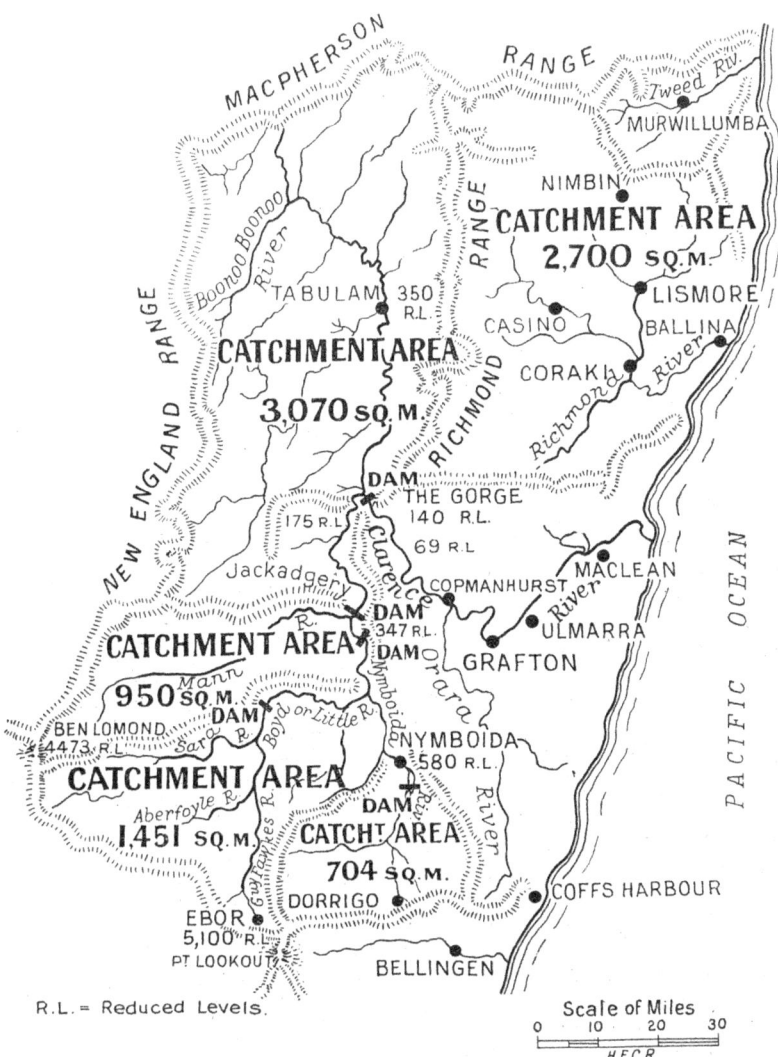

**Figure 4: Page's beloved Clarence Valley region.**
This depiction is from his 1944 booklet *Clarence River Hydro-Electric Gorge Scheme* and shows proposed dam sites.
Source: Courtesy of Hardie Grant Travel.

Page's other great formative influence was his idealisation of the small community in which he spent his childhood. This was powerful enough for him to give up a burgeoning medical career in the big city to return home. In his memoirs he proclaimed that 'the main inspiration … of my political life, and indeed, the predominant influence throughout my eighty-one years has been the Clarence Valley where I was born'.[22] A visiting journalist described the Grafton district at the start of the twentieth century in strikingly similar terms to Page's August 1917 speech: 'one of the most fertile and interesting in the colony,' with 'marvellous and extensive resources'.[23] Yet the town was deprived of a proper water supply, a telephone service, railway links and even a bridge across the Clarence.

Page particularly recalled Grafton's inclusiveness. To this day, Grafton is a welcoming town, attractively set amid the greenery of the Clarence Valley. Page the parliamentarian would have noted the contrast with the plainer countryside around both Melbourne and Canberra. In his youth, Grafton was 'a small and friendly community lacking entirely in any sense of class or party' where 'the broad Clarence … bound us in a fraternity'.[24] Even in the midst of the 1890s depression, he had 'never in my recollection seen people so happy or so cooperative in realms of mutual help'.[25] The 'loyalty and understanding' of school chums provided 'the continually renewed inspiration which enabled me to persevere in my quest for national balance and a place in the sun for the country dweller'.[26] Page's enthusiasm for the role of community overshadowed what little sense he had of social class: to him, social division was more a matter of the gap in living standards between town and country. There is some basis for his fond recollections, as Grafton indeed seems to have had a flatter social structure than many other country towns. Unlike Armidale in New England, also well known to Page, the Grafton hinterland was dominated by small selectors rather than large pastoralists.

22  Page, *Truant Surgeon*, p. 36.
23  *Australian Town and Country Journal*, 30 June 1900, pp. 30, 34. The author is described only as 'Beri'.
24  Untitled draft for Page's memoirs, Earle Page papers, National Library of Australia, MS 1633 (hereafter EPP), folder 1855, pp. 5–6.
25  Ibid.
26  'Chapter Two – Schools + Student Days', EPP, folder 1855, pp. 5–6.

Page's commitment to his community included an absolute faith in the potential of the Clarence River, the basis of his great hopes for hydroelectricity. The Clarence is the focus of a watershed that is mainland Australia's second-largest river system south of the Tropic of Capricorn. It is fed by high rainfall, and in Page's lifetime supported an unusually wide range of primary industries that stretched from dairy to also include beef, maize, sugar and subtropical fruits. But it is also prone to flooding. Page as a boy witnessed a series of major floods between 1887 and 1893, recalling his excitement as rescue boats plied the flooded town but later mourning the damage to local farming. Later, he saw the river as a personal inspiration: 'my own autobiography owes much to the river which had formed such a vivid backdrop to my stage of operations'.[27]

The Clarence, family and community all nurtured Page's lifelong commitment to new states and regionalism. In a speech marking his retirement from the Menzies Ministry in 1956, he began his list of lifetime goals with 'to sub-divide the larger states of Australia in order to get government on the spot and to accelerate the development of our natural resources', and stressed that this idea had been firmly planted well before he ever entered parliament. He recalled not only the Grafton area's dearth of public amenities but also the artificiality of the New South Wales–Queensland border to his hometown's north. This 'imaginary line' had 'caused extraordinary discrimination', most obviously an 18-mile gap between state railway systems.[28] To Page, existing state boundaries were too arbitrary to deserve reverence.

Agitation for equality in regional entitlement, the realignment of colonial and state boundaries, and the creation of new states were all part of the Australian political landscape decades before the advent of Earle Page. Early in the development of the colonies it was clear that the uneven spread of population and production had fostered divergent interests and imbalances in the distribution of wealth and power. The only successful separation movements were three of the earliest: Van Diemen's Land in 1825, Victoria in 1851 and Queensland in 1859. Queensland was itself prone to demands to align political representation with regional identities. Most of what later became Queensland was included in the short-lived colony of North Australia created in 1847. During the 1850s there was

---
27  Page, *Truant Surgeon*, p. 36.
28  See 'Australian Country Party Complimentary Dinner to Sir Earle Page, Sydney 22nd June 1956, Address by Sir Earle Page', EPP, folder 2358.

an expectation among settlers in northern and central areas of the future Queensland that they would eventually have their own colonies. This was encouraged by John Dunmore Lang, who had 'thought all government from a distance was bad government'.[29] To the south, Lang also called for the separation of New South Wales between the Murrumbidgee and Murray rivers as early as 1856 (at the same time coining the name Riverina for this area).

Other separation movements of varying degrees of longevity appeared across the Australia of Page's youth as far away as the Western Australian goldfields and Albany. There were also early British proposals in the 1830s and 1840s for the creation of local governments in the Australian colonies that would have been much stronger than the local councils that did eventually appear.[30] Most of these early campaigns were short-lived, but were harbingers of the more determined regionalism that Page so zealously supported. The northern New South Wales separation movement was the one that mattered most to him. Its history stretched back intermittently to the 1840s. This was partly a matter of distance from Sydney, but also reflected the tendency for new statism to arise in areas prosperous enough to spawn ambitions of fulfilling a great potential. New England, adjacent to Page's coastal north-east, is widely seen as having had a particularly 'strongly articulated perception of its "difference" and destiny'.[31] By the 1880s the Glen Innes Separation League alone reportedly had 1,400 members.

Page was directly exposed to new statism from an early age. He frequently referred to it as being in his blood by virtue of campaigning by his grandfather James and two of his uncles. James variously agitated for the transfer of the Clarence Valley to Queensland or the creation of an entirely new colony, and once organised a petition to the British parliament. In 1948 Earle proudly told a conference on new statism that as a Page he stood at the head of 'almost a century of fighting for our political

---

29   D.W.A. Baker, 'Lang, John Dunmore (1799–1878)', *Australian Dictionary of Biography*, National Centre of Biography, The Australian National University, adb.anu.edu.au/biography/lang-john-dunmore-2326/text2953, published first in hardcopy volume 2, Melbourne University Press, Parkville, Vic., 1967.
30   A.J. Brown, 'Regional governance and regionalism in Australia', in Robyn Eversole and John Martin (eds), *Participation and Governance in Regional Development: Global Trends in an Australian Context*, Ashgate, Aldershot, 2005, pp. 6–8.
31   J.S. Ryan, 'Prelude – Uplands always attract', in Alan Atkinson, J.S. Ryan, Iain Davidson and Andrew Piper (eds), *High, Lean Country: Land, People and Memory in New England*, Allen & Unwin, Crows Nest, NSW, 2006, p. 3.

freedom through self-government and our economic freedom through the fullest provision of modern invention and amenities for the outback people'.³² He remained impressed by his grandfather's association with Lang. Page was particularly drawn to Lang's belief that self-governing territories would provide the building blocks for a federated nation-state encompassing the entire continent. Lang had told the people of Port Phillip District in 1841 that separation from New South Wales would match the subdivision of the United States into the small democratic states that had driven that nation's development. There is evidence that early Australian colonial settlers expected separation to eventually lead to a federal nation and that such an outcome also influenced British policy towards the Australian colonies.³³

Young Earle and his family would have been very aware of incessant local appeals for the Sydney-based government to provide transformative infrastructure – hydroengineering, railway links and harbour works – which spawned such protest groups as the Clarence Railway and Harbour League. The *Clarence and Richmond Examiner* of his youth routinely editorialised on 'the feeling which widely prevails outside the Metropolitan area, that the interests of the country are made subservient to those of the great metropolis and its immediate surroundings'.³⁴ Page later bluntly told his wife in 1918 that as a city person, she did not know 'the absence of opportunity' that resulted in 'the degradation and atrophy from disuse of the finest material that goes on in the country that I had hoped it would have been my province to have helped remove'.³⁵

The press of Page's youth was also full of reportage on the campaign to federate the colonies, especially the closely associated free trade versus protection debate. (The state parliamentary seat of Grafton returned the

---

32   'History of Decentralisation: Speech by Sir Earle Page', in Decentralisation and New State Movement Convention, *Decentralisation and New State Movement: Armidale Convention, June 1948*, Armidale, NSW, 1948, pp. 25–6.
33   This has been explored by legal scholar A.J. Brown: 'Constitutional schizophrenia then and now: Exploring federalist, regionalist and unitary strands in the Australian political tradition', in K. Walsh (ed.), *The Distinctive Foundations of Australian Democracy: Lectures in the Senate Occasional Lecture Series 2003–2004*, Papers on Parliament No. 42, Department of the Senate, Parliament House, Canberra, 2004, especially pp. 41–9; also his 'The Constitution We Were Meant to Have: Re-examining the Origins and Strength of Australia's Unitary Political Traditions', *Democratic Experiments: Lectures in the Senate Occasional Lecture Series 2004–2005*, Papers on Parliament No. 44, Department of the Senate, Parliament House, Canberra, 2006, especially pp. 54–9.
34   *Clarence and Richmond Examiner*, 22 April 1890, p. 2.
35   Earle Page to Ethel Page, 14 November 1018, Earle Page papers, UNE Archives, A180, box 7, folder 71.

Protectionist See from 1880 until 1904; the adjoining seat of Clarence returned the same Protectionist and later Liberal member for 28 years from 1887, John McFarlane.) The adult Page frequently quoted the foremost New South Wales federationist of these times, Henry Parkes, as linking new states to national prosperity. The early drafters of the Australian Constitution readily accepted the need to provide for the creation of new states, but only after intense debate on the precise mechanism for doing so.

Queenslanders such as John Murtagh Macrossan and Samuel Griffith were especially outspoken. Macrossan was the parliamentary leader of the Queensland northern separation movement. Griffith was initially hostile to separation but as premier proposed in 1892 to divide Queensland itself into a federal structure. Such ruminations indicate the conceptual strength of new statism at the time and how open an issue was the basic shape of the still putative Australian nation. The debate was to extend well into the twentieth century, generating receptive audiences that encouraged the young Earle Page. The drafters of the Constitution eventually included section 124 on new states, based on a provision in the United States Constitution. This enabled the Australian Commonwealth to admit new states formed out of an existing state or states, but 'only with the consent' of the parliaments of the mother states. This crucial requirement was to dog Page and his fellow new state campaigners for decades to come.

## Young Earle sets out: School, university and the wider times

Formal education enabled Page's professional success and entry into public life. He attributed his youthful determination to 'become a doctor and give the country people a fair deal' to a family calamity during his childhood.[36] His mother had been using a cold chisel to remove an iron hoop from a barrel when a steel splinter flew up into her left eye. Treatment was unavailable in isolated Grafton, and as an adult Page bitterly recalled accompanying her on agonising, costly trips to distant Sydney in a vain attempt to save the eye. At a very young age he became aware of a Faculty of Medicine at Sydney University in which a fellow townsman – Grafton

---

36 'Australian Country Party Complimentary Dinner to Sir Earle Page', EPP, folder 2358; 'Notes for Country Party Complimentary Dinner 22/6/56', EPP, folder 2358.

Elliot Smith, later an eminent anatomist – had enrolled after winning the only scholarship for medicine then available, the Struth Exhibition. Page organised his studies over the next several years around an ambitious plan to secure this lucrative scholarship, awarded only at five-year intervals on the basis of results in first-year Arts. Passing the first-year examination in Arts was then one of the standard means of entry into Medicine at Sydney University.[37]

The Struth, some lesser academic prizes and the proceeds of coaching other students were critically important as Page's family had suffered major financial losses in the 1890s depression. As a boy visiting Sydney during the May 1893 bank smash, he saw panicked cable car passengers offer to swap pound notes for nominally less valuable gold or silver coins, soon to be followed by the banks foreclosing on properties. Page 'knew my father would be ruined'.[38] He realised he would have to depend on his own resources to secure an education – significantly, he appreciated this even as a 12-year-old. This unhappy episode also provided an emotional basis for his lasting commitment to establishing central banking in Australia. (That said, Page in his memoirs added more conventional motivations such as difficulties the early Commonwealth Bank had in coping with shortages of foreign exchange and the Genoa Economic and Financial Conference of 1922 that advocated that all countries have a central bank.)

At the age of 11, Page won a bursary to Sydney Boys High School, flagship of the colony's public education system. But as his parents considered him too young to leave home, he instead began his secondary studies at Grafton Public School. There he prospered under talented mathematics and languages masters and built friendships with future local leaders such as Alf Pollack, later a Grafton solicitor and state member for Clarence. In 1895 Page switched to Sydney Boys High for his final year of school. The school's then location in inner-urban Ultimo gave him his first taste of city living. The school principal was a fellow Methodist, Joseph Coates, another of the teachers that the adult Page paid grateful tribute to in his memoirs. He studied simultaneously for honours in matriculation and the first-year Sydney University Arts exam and, again with the support of gifted teachers, duly secured the Struth Exhibition. As his family

---
37  See John Atherton Young, Ann Jervie Sefton and Nina Webb (eds), *Centenary Book of the University of Sydney Faculty of Medicine*, Sydney University Press for the University of Sydney Faculty of Medicine, Sydney, 1984, p. 178.
38  'Australian Country Party Complimentary Dinner to Sir Earle Page', EPP, folder 2358.

was unable to afford the fees required to sit for both the Senior and Matriculation examinations, he only formally passed the latter: Sydney University declined a decidedly hopeful offer of three tons of potatoes in lieu of the Senior Examination fee. Page commenced classes in medicine at Sydney University in early 1896 aged all of 15, an achievement he modestly recalled as the culmination of a 'series of events which savoured to me of the miraculous'.[39] It actually reflected magnificently precocious purposefulness and intelligence.

Page thus spent a highly unusual adolescence as a medical student. He described his first years of study as 'inspiring, absorbing and happy'.[40] It provided him with a small store of anecdotes he would happily draw on for years to come: picking for his fellow students the winners of four Melbourne Cups in a row, before unforgivably faltering in his last year of study; snakes brought in to be milked of their venom for research being let loose in the lab; and, as a raw young pathologist, being roasted by the Sunday papers when corpses he had examined were subsequently found in the wrong graves. His studies also owed much to the 1890s being a decade of great advances in medicine. The microbial causes of such deadly diseases as tuberculosis and plague were discovered, new surgical methods for compound fractures were developed, X-rays began to be taken and advances in aseptic surgery expanded scope for abdominal operations (later a Page speciality). No senior Australian politician, even Barry Jones, spent formative years so enlivened by direct exposure to the fruits of science.

But university also provided Page with a new and lasting focus for his anger. He recalled in his memoirs of how 'former ignorance and current prejudice' had to be overcome 'before the fruits of the medical and technical revolution could be obtained'. All too typical was the reluctance of 'the older professional men' to accept that antidiphtheritic vaccine could save thousands of children.[41] This was an early and powerful manifestation of Page's lasting self-image as a courageous innovator battling the forces of reaction. Page the student was also excited by Federation-era political debate. He was impressed by such members of the University Senate as Edmund Barton and Andrew Garran (father of Robert), and

---

39  Page, *Truant Surgeon*, p. 12.
40  Ibid., p. 17.
41  Ibid., p. 18.

by the University Chancellor Normand MacLaurin (another doctor, and a Federation opponent). Page participated in the Federation debates 'to some extent myself', probably his first political engagement.[42]

Page's final year of study was his most challenging. Although yet to graduate, he was appointed superintendent of the Royal Alexandra Hospital for Children for a month to cover for absent medical residents, a clear sign of a burgeoning professional reputation. He was 21 when he received his degree in 1902, equal top of his class of 18 fellow students (albeit in a year when no firsts were awarded). Page attached significance to the fact that the two other honours students that year were also from the north coast. The eminent surgeon Alexander MacCormick offered him a position as his house surgeon at the Royal Prince Alfred Hospital. Glowing references from professional colleagues confirm that he was a fine young surgeon indeed. Dr Joseph Foreman, lecturer in gynaecology, later described Page as 'one of the best men the Sydney University has turned out – an exceptionally good surgeon and sound practitioner'.[43] Page never undertook any other formal studies, such as in economics or other social sciences relevant to his policy interests, perhaps unfortunately for him. But he later asserted that training as a surgeon was invaluable for politics. In wartime London nearly 40 years later he declared himself to be still at heart a 'truant surgeon', convinced that by applying the surgeon's 'combination of early diagnosis, quick decision and immediate action, half the political and international troubles would never arise'.[44]

Page did not directly write about the impression of city life he gained as a young surgeon. But his unremitting sense of its many failings suggests that he never felt settled in Sydney and at its hospitals routinely witnessed some very ugly scenes indeed. His disdain was not salved by his later maintaining city residences, including at suburban Strathfield and Wollstonecraft, and was often expressed using medical analogies. As a first-term parliamentarian he diagnosed that 'when a city becomes over a certain size it loses its manufacturing value, because workmen have to travel too far to work, and departs from its proper functions, involving degeneration and ill-health of its population'.[45] Medical metaphors were to enliven numerous other Page pronouncements, such as in March 1929

---

42   Ibid., p. 39.
43   Reference by Dr Joseph Foreman, 3 September 1915, Earle Page papers, UNE Archives, A180, box 11, folder 87.
44   Page, *Truant Surgeon*, p. 372.
45   *Commonwealth Parliamentary Debates*, 7 April 1921, p. 7282.

when he likened a parliamentary attack by Billy Hughes to 'the bursting of a long accumulating abscess of jaundice, spite and venom, with all the after effects of poison, that had turned into a running sore'.[46] This became one occasion when the instinctively combative Hughes appealed to Page for a truce.

The influence on Page of the wider context of his youth is also important but harder to chart. Social optimism was abundant in late colonial Australia. The 1880s and early 1890s spawned confidence in utopias of reason, 'where the destructive habits of human society are corrected by good design and clear thinking'.[47] There was an accompanying distinct sense in this young country of an 'absence of history and a corresponding freedom to invent the future'.[48] Optimistic developmentalist calls to arms pervaded Page's early years. The journalist and historian A.W. Jose in the 1909 edition of his widely read *History of Australasia* implored the nation to 'take seriously in hand the developing of the country's natural resources', for which 'young Australians cannot serve their country better than by preparing themselves with zealous study to take their share in the task directly they become men'.[49]

Did much of this utopian and developmentalist thought percolate through to provincial Grafton to be directly imbibed by the young Earle Page? Or was it absorbed when he was studying in Sydney? Some certainly reached Grafton, for his family remained very aware of its legacy of contact with that aforementioned great optimist John Dunmore Lang. Although Page was widely read, his writings and speeches do not appear to mention utopian or like-minded writers active during his formative years. Page instead acknowledged his early attraction to ideas of an Imperial federation. In London in 1942 he told Lionel Curtis, leading theorist of Empire federalism and of world government, that his writings had drawn him to politics 25 years earlier – yet another account by Page of why he entered public life.[50]

---

46  Page, *Truant Surgeon*, p. 181.
47  Helen Irving, *To Constitute a Nation: A Cultural History of Australia's Constitution*, Cambridge University Press, Cambridge, 1997, pp. 38, 44.
48  Stuart Macintyre, *A Colonial Liberalism: The Lost World of Three Victorian Visionaries*, Oxford University Press, South Melbourne, 1991, p. 12.
49  Quoted in Horne, *Money Made Us*, p. 133.
50  Page's wartime diary, entry for 15 January 1942, EPP, folder 2787 (part 3). Page wrote here of *The Empire on the Anvil* as being by Curtis, but it is actually by W. Basil Worsfold; he may have meant Curtis's 1916 *The Problem of the Commonwealth*.

Less abstract forces transforming rural Australia during Page's youth might have more directly influenced his faith in technology and progress. In a prepublication synopsis of his autobiography he reflected how as a youth he had witnessed a transformation from the 'primitive position of the era in which I was born to improvement of the whole social order', with the result that 'my outlook, my character, my ways of thought and action are a palimpsest of all these changes'.[51] Amongst these would have been the spread of exciting new household and consumer goods during the second half of the nineteenth century. These included kerosene lamps, electricity, bicycles, tap water, telegrams, new ways of weighing and packaging, paper money, matches and much else.[52] Perhaps their visibility added to rural fears that industrial manufacturing was surpassing agriculture and that the benefits of new technology were not being equally shared out by the big cities. This contributed to a late nineteenth-century rural culture embittered by growing anti-urbanism, alienation and loss of status. Such stress was most obviously reflected in population and economic drift to the cities. The percentage of the Australian population living in metropolitan areas rose steadily from 32 per cent in 1881 to just over 38 per cent in 1911: that of primary industry workers out of total breadwinners plummeted from 44 per cent in 1871 to just 26 per cent in 1921.[53]

The late nineteenth and early twentieth centuries also saw a rapid rise of small-scale wheat and dairy farming in regions such as the Mallee, the Riverina and Page's north-eastern New South Wales. Simultaneously, the 1895–1902 Federation Drought, arguably the most notorious Australian drought of all, and a dwindling supply of new viable land constrained population growth and production more widely across rural Australia. Don Aitkin links the rise of rural political activity around this time to a growing shortage of unoccupied land, the impact of railways on small-town industry and the increasing difficulty of dividing farms so as to keep children on the land. The protectionism and industrial arbitration central to what became known as the Australian Settlement of the early Federation era seemed deliberately designed to favour the cities over the country. But new railways and the telegraph also connected rural

---

51  Earle Page to Ethel Page, 23 October 1924, Earle Page papers, UNE Archives, A180, box 5, folder 7.
52  See Geoffrey Blainey, *Black Kettle and Full Moon: Daily Life in a Vanished Australia*, Penguin, Camberwell, Vic., 2003, pp. 424–5.
53  Graham, *Formation of the Australian Country Parties*, p. 133.

communities and helped spread awareness of their common interests.[54] Faith in farming as the backbone of the nation stayed strong, and new regional and sectoral associations aided the formation of the first political country parties during the early twentieth century.[55] Within an overall pattern of rural decline during the twentieth century there were sufficient variations between regions and periods to keep rural hopes and dreams very much alive.[56]

These rural anxieties and reactions were so pervasive they must surely have made an impression on an alert young man like Earle Page. In his memoirs he wrote of how the recovery of the Clarence Valley from flood, drought and the financial insolvency of the 1890s was frustrated by decade-long low prices for farm products. He recalled farmers who were already struggling to meet transport and handling costs sometimes being forced to pay for the dumping of unsaleable produce at sea, and that 'practically everyone on the northern rivers lived more or less within a barter economy'.[57] Such bitter reflections raise the question of the extent to which Page's views were a manifestation of the celebrated ideology of countrymindedness that arose during this time of rural hardship.

'Countrymindedness', says Aitkin, is 'physiocratic, populist and decentralist'. It holds that rural traits such as community cooperation bring out the best in individuals, and that country life is the ennobling basis of the national economy. By contrast, urban life is parasitical and corrupt. But as power resides in the cities, there is a need for a political party for country people 'to articulate the true voice of the nation'.[58] Aitkin postulates that Page might have originated countrymindedness as a term, but this does not appear to be backed by clear documentation from a man who tended to repeat favoured words and phrases. The term dates back to at least the early 1930s, although it was often used in the narrower sense of sympathy for rural causes.

---

54  Don Aitkin, 'Countrymindedness – The spread of an idea', in S.L. Goldberg and F.B. Smith (eds), *Australian Cultural History*, Cambridge University Press, Cambridge, 1988, pp. 52–4.
55  Graham, *Formation of the Australian Country Parties*, pp. 38–54.
56  Graeme Davison and Marc Brodie (eds), *Struggle Country: The Rural Ideal in Twentieth Century Australia*, Monash University ePress, Clayton, 2005, p. xii.
57  Page, *Truant Surgeon*, p. 9.
58  Aitkin, 'Countrymindedness', in Goldberg and Smith, *Australian Cultural History*, pp. 51, 52.

Countrymindedness added a stridently discordant note to the Australian Settlement by dwelling on its exclusion of an entire sector of the nation. This cut clean across the expectation that all citizens had the opportunity to fulfil their potential, an important feature of 'state developmentalism'.[59] It was also a very flexible predisposition that ranged from agrarian romanticism to progressive social and economic ideas such as decentralisation, and from praising farmers alone to casting the denizens of small towns as fellow upholders of rural values. Countrymindedness certainly overlapped with many of Page's early ideas. He agreed that the nation depended on primary producers, that rural pursuits brought out the best in people (though he would have stressed small communities more than farming) and that decentralisation was vital.

But Page went well beyond the defensiveness of countrymindedness to embrace assertive developmentalism for the entire nation. He did not advocate such strands of agrarian romanticism as common ownership of land or the perceived virtues of the peasant lifestyle. Page had seen enough of rural isolation to be more interested in alleviating poverty. He was more excited by the opportunities that modernity presented rural Australia and the wider nation, such as through electrification. Conventional countrymindedness provided only a partial foundation for his wider beliefs. Page may have bridged countrymindedness and developmentalism, but development was his priority.

Page probably also derived inspiration from American agrarian thought. Debate in late nineteenth-century Australia about rural education was heavily influenced by accounts of agricultural colleges in the United States.[60] Page had sufficient interest in American development to undertake a wartime trip there in 1917. The most prominent American rural improvers of these years were the scholars and journalists who led the famed Country Life Movement. Foremost was the renowned Cornell professor Liberty Hyde Bailey, who advocated environmental conservation, rural education, new technology (including electrification) and decentralisation. Although this movement had an intellectual base, it had much in common with more populist concerns held in Australia about rural decline. Like Page, Bailey thought that urbanisation sapped naturalness and spontaneity. John Wesley Powell, another outspoken

---

59  Stokes, 'The "Australian Settlement" and Australian Political Thought', pp. 13, 15.
60  Greg Logan, 'An urban revolution for rural Australia: The genesis of agricultural colleges in colonial Australia', in R.C. Petersen and G.W. Rodwell (eds), *Notes from Essays in the History of Rural Education in Australia and New Zealand*, William Michael Press, Casuarina, 1993, pp. 203–4.

American, proposed the regional control of watersheds. Although there appears to be no direct evidence of Page avowedly emulating Bailey or Powell, his travels and reading on the United States (such as the writings of James Bryce, then a famed British interpreter of the US) most likely exposed him to their thoughts and reinforced his own ideas.

## Page returns to Grafton: Poverty and technology

Page's early experiences as a medical professional powerfully reinforced and refined his ideas about rural development. He did not last long as a city-based doctor. At the end of his first year as a house surgeon he accepted an invitation to stay on as a pathologist. This nearly ended his life. Post-mortems were conducted without rubber gloves, the pathologists instead simply smearing their arms with vaseline. When Page conducted a post-mortem on a patient who had died of peritonitis following perforation of the bowel after typhoid, the application of smelling salts failed to kill the infectious microbes. Page's arms became so severely infected that friends and colleagues solemnly 'bid me farewell from this life'.[61] Unexpectedly, he recovered after a colleague made a series of incisions on both arms, administered without anaesthetic. He ended his hospital employment and, as soon as he was well, returned to Grafton, where early in 1903 he joined a local practice as junior partner to another general practitioner.

Page later reflected that this experience left him with a fatalism that removed his fear of death but also made him determined to use each day to the full. He moved quickly to establish himself as a local doctor. In April 1903 he purchased an existing practice in South Grafton. This was a somewhat marginalised community of about 1,300 inhabitants on the southern side of the Clarence, pointedly isolated by the lack of a bridge across the river. By September 1904 he had raised enough capital to open his own small private hospital, Clarence House, also in South Grafton. Page recalled in his memoirs how he was motivated by the need to extend modern medicine across the Clarence Valley region, an idea he had harboured since his student days.[62] Working as a rural doctor added a very practical sharp edge to his appreciation of the city–country contrast:

---

61  Page, *Truant Surgeon*, pp. 24–5.
62  Ibid., pp. 25–6.

> A patient 70 or 80 miles away in the bush who was seriously ill had very little chance of recovery. It took 12 to 15 hours to ride for a Doctor and it took 12 to 15 hours for the Doctor to ride back – more often than not only to find that his patient had died hours before his arrival.[63]

One constituent testified that a seriously injured person's chances of survival were a matter of how quickly Page could reach them.[64]

Page added that the deciding factor in his decision to stay in his home town was the need to overcome hostility to new medical practices. In September 1903 local doctors denied him use of the Grafton Hospital to conduct a radical hysterectomy using the latest techniques, despite his being on the honorary staff. So Page instead proceeded to do so before their very eyes using a makeshift operating room in his mother's house 'as a contribution to their education'. He wrote with equal satisfaction of inviting members of the hospital board to inspect Clarence House, with the result that they installed 'similar indispensable facilities'.[65] Such triumphs consolidated Page's self-image as a visionary pitted against reaction, but who ultimately had history on his side. Open contempt for blinkered elements of his profession was to be carried over into his political career as a persistent disdain for sceptics of his plans for the nation. The intensity of young Dr Page led him into some righteous exchanges. In November 1905 he helped publicise a dispute over the employment of medical officers by local friendly societies by placing a long, angry letter in the press. He rambled through the minutiae of the case and ended by accusing the societies of making statements 'calculated to mislead both the medical profession and the public'.[66]

Page's outwardly rationalist, almost deterministic, approach to public policy and technology owes much to his training in medicine and early successes in introducing innovations into his small-town practice. His X-ray machine was the first in New South Wales outside Sydney, but as the Grafton region still lacked an electricity supply it had to be modified to use bichromate batteries. He acquired what was said to be the first car on the north coast of New South Wales, a Rover that his

---

63 'Speech by Hon Earle Page MP, Acting Prime Minister, Motor Trades Show Sydney, 14–1–27', EPP, folder 1784.
64 'Earle Christmas Grafton Page', a profile written by Denning, c. 1947, Warren Denning papers, NLA, MS 5129, p. 3.
65 Page, *Truant Surgeon*, pp. 26, 27.
66 *Clarence and Richmond Examiner*, 4 November 1905, p. 12.

brother Maund converted into a prototype ambulance, and also installed a hospital telephone. Both were important acquisitions for a rural practice that stretched 100 miles along the coast and 50 inland. Electricity was the technology that had by far the greatest impact on Page's ambitions for the nation. His hospital's pressing need for reliable power helped convince him of its wider importance:

> The problem of securing good lights in our modern hospital to permit surgery to be performed at all hours of the day and night ultimately led me to one of my life's objectives. This was to make electricity available in ample quantities at a uniform price in country and city alike and especially to secure the harnessing of all our latent water power and the conservation of all our waters.[67]

This was truly innovative thinking for the time – gas still predominated even in the big cities and electricity was first used in the Royal Prince Alfred Hospital only in 1912. Page was to retain a ready faith in the ability of technology to catalyse regional equality and liberate the individual.

In September 1906 Page married Ethel Blunt. They had met when she was a senior staff nurse at the Royal Prince Alfred. Five years older than Earle, she was the daughter of a Sydney building contractor. He recalled first encountering her rather abruptly during a medical procedure involving an archaic cupping process to draw inflammatory fluids from the patient. This necessitated setting alight pieces of paper saturated with methylated spirits so as to create vacuums within glass tumblers. Page became 'conscious that something unusual was happening behind me' and discovered that a discarded bit of burning paper had set Nurse Blunt's dress ablaze: 'I decided that she must be kept under observation'.[68] Perhaps Page was also attracted by Ethel having topped her training year. He later persuaded her to join Clarence House. They had five children: Mary, Earle junior, Donald, Iven and Douglas.

Although there is little indication that Ethel played a direct role in forming Page's policy ideas, their private correspondence affirms his description of her as his foremost political and personal confidante, who supported the family and his medical practice during his frequent absences.[69] (The next closest was David Drummond, the long-serving state and federal Country

---

67 Untitled draft for Page's memoirs, EPP, folder 1855.
68 Page, *Truant Surgeon*, p. 27.
69 Ibid., p. 29.

Party MP with whom Page shared northern New South Wales and Methodist origins.) Ethel joined him in public campaigning and was described by her husband as the better public speaker of the two: this is very plausible, given testimony by Ellis and audio recordings that suggest that Earle was only a competent orator. She was a founder of the Women's Country Party, and served with the Australian Red Cross Society, the Country Women's Association and the National Council of Women.

Over many years, Page sent Ethel a stream of affectionate and discursive letters, frequently writing of private goals and stresses. She appears to have been influential in Page's decision not to become a missionary and instead devote himself to more earthly pursuits. In May 1906 he wrote that she had helped in 'bringing back to me, altered and changed beyond recognition my loftier ambitions and desires; different they are from the old ones of four years ago; with more thought of my work in this life and my beneficial influence on men's welfare here than on my own salvation and other men's salvation hereafter'.[70] Soon after, he assured Ethel that he would 'long for your sympathy and communion and counsel at every critical time of my life'.[71] Ethel maintained a discernibly separate persona from that of her husband. She often spoke in public on women's participation in politics, in which her husband showed little interest. After a 1925 trip to the United States and Europe, she observed that American women were 'far ahead of us with regard to the number of women taking part in public affairs'. By contrast, Australian women 'do not seem to be alive to the necessity of organisation and the benefit of the effect in political life'.[72]

Following his marriage, Page began to display a distinct business bent that he retained for the rest of his life. In 1908 he invested £2,100 in land for dairy farms and a sawmill in southern Queensland near Kandanga, 'a property that is sure to grow in value and more than double in a few years', he told Ethel.[73] By 1912 his combined assets stood at £10,000. Page developed a wide portfolio of interests in farming, timber, the share market and newspapers, as well as a faith in the potency of the private sector. In policy pronouncements he invariably portrayed private investment in development projects as inherently preferable to public money.

70  Page to Ethel Page, 5 May 1906, Earle Page papers, UNE Archives, A180, box 11, folder 90.
71  Page to Ethel Page, 17 June 1906, Earle Page papers, UNE Archives, A180, box 11, folder 90.
72  *Sunday Times*, Sydney, 9 August 1925, Social and Magazine Section, p. 5.
73  Page to Ethel Page, 25 November 1909, Earle Page papers, UNE Archives, A180, box 7, folder 71.

'NOW IS THE PSYCHOLOGICAL MOMENT'

## Page's first policy campaigns: 'The dull roar of the flooded stream'

In November 1952 Ulrich Ellis presented Page with a draft prologue for a projected book on water resources. Even allowing for the drafter's propensity for overwriting, this testifies to the early influence the Clarence River had on Page. Ellis wrote that for Page 'the dull roar of the flooded stream has always stirred his blood' and so he 'set himself the task of achieving the marriage of electrical power and water as a prime factor for the advancement of the Valley'.[74] For his entire life, Page was inspired by the Clarence as the defining physical feature of his home territory, and a source of sustenance, floods and potentially transformative electric power.

Page did not originate the idea of damming the Clarence, but he was primarily responsible for nurturing this goal. Page became convinced, early in his adult life, that the Clarence presented immense potential for hydroelectricity. It surely had all the necessary ingredients: reliable water supply, water flow over distance and potential dam sites. Page was particularly interested in a 10-kilometre segment known as The Gorge. This sits about 130 kilometres upriver from the mouth of the Clarence, just down from where the Mann River joins it. At The Gorge, the Clarence passes through a deep rocky gap bounded by mountains, providing a possible basis for a dam.

Page grew up in an era of much-publicised progress globally in the generation of electricity that made hydroelectricity commercially viable. This raised hopes for its ability to transform whole societies, including by easing rural poverty. A new electrical generator, the dynamo, was developed in the 1870s to produce continuous electrical current in commercial quantities. From 1891, the use of alternating current in the transmission of electricity from the point of generation to that of consumption mitigated hydroelectricity's drawback of usually being generated in locations remote from end users. (Alternating current involves transmitting electricity at high voltage from the point of generation to near the place of consumption, then using a transformer to reduce the voltage to a level safe for usage.) Dynamite and new air rock drills reduced the cost of building hydroelectric power stations, and there

---

74  'A Man and His Valley – Prologue', document by Ulrich Ellis, 17 November 1952, EPP, folder 2369.

were also improvements in turbines and penstocks (used to channel water to turbines). A modest hydroelectric scheme commenced at Godalming in England in 1881. The internationally publicised large-scale use of hydroelectricity turbines in 1895 at Niagara Falls is generally taken to mark the start of modern commercial hydroelectricity, along with other pioneering projects in the Sierra Nevada mountains of California and the Appalachians in the US south-east. Faith in electricity spread worldwide. In the United States, it was 'invoked as the panacea for every social ill', that 'promised to lighten the toil of workers and housewives, to provide faster and cleaner forms of transport, and to revolutionise the farm'.[75]

Early Australian advocates of hydroelectricity were conscious of greater progress being made overseas. This included the pioneers of Tasmanian hydroelectricity James Gillies, a metallurgist who proposed its application to zinc refining, and Alexander McAulay, a mathematician at the University of Tasmania. Page was probably very aware of early hydroelectric facilities in northern New South Wales – at Tamworth in 1888, the Gara River near Armidale in 1895 and at the Styx River in 1906 – part of a number of small, tinkering developments across the nation. Australia's first sizeable facilities appeared in the 1910s in Tasmania, at the Mt Lyell copper mine and at Great Lake in the state's central region. Power generation and supply in Australia was then mostly in the hands of private companies and local councils. Reports of new electrical technologies featured in the Grafton press of Page's early adulthood, from one on how the new apparatus of the transformer could render powerful currents 'harmless and agreeable', to an account of steps towards installing electric street lighting, a sure sign that 'Grafton is on the move of progress'.[76]

Page was particularly aware of past proposals to harness the Clarence system. Early suggestions focused on port operations and flood control: in 1887–88 the engineer Sir John Coode reported to the New South Wales Government on unblocking the mouth of the Clarence, and in 1894 J.W. Archibald and D.W. Campbell proposed a dam at The Gorge for flood prevention. In 1908 the system's impressively reliable flow attracted mainland Australia's first major hydroelectricity proposal. William Corin, chief electrical engineer in the New South Wales Public Works Department, put to local councils a joint water supply and power scheme based on the Nymboida River,

---
75   David E. Nye, *American Technological Sublime*, MIT Press, Cambridge, Massachusetts, 1994, p. 143.
76   *Clarence and Richmond Examiner*, 25 August 1903, p. 2, and 11 December 1913, p. 4.

which flows into the Mann River. Only the water supply component was taken up at the time. Family tradition again contributed to Page's interest: he recalled that his father as mayor of Grafton in 1908 was 'the driving force' in providing the town with a permanent water supply from the Nymboida.[77] The Nymboida River was later the temporary focus of Page's hydroelectric campaigning. Corin was to become hydroelectricity's most prominent supporter within the engineering profession and a pioneering proponent of a national electricity grid.

Page was sufficiently aware of international developments to use his first overseas trip, to attend the 1910 Australasian Medical Conference in New Zealand, as an opportunity to 'visit and study new water-power developments … especially their progressive improvements in extending electricity to country homes and farms in the vicinity of the projects'. This 'stimulated my ambition to secure the installation of similar schemes in Australia, especially on the Clarence'.[78] It also marked the start of a lifelong penchant for seeking out overseas exemplars for his policy ideas that eventually stretched to Egypt, North America, Africa, Japan and the Indian subcontinent. Another notable early trip came in 1922, when during the parliamentary recess he visited Java, Singapore and Malaya with the entrepreneur and Nationalist MP H.E. Pratten, another fellow Methodist. Page was dismayed by the inept marketing of Australian goods overseas.

His medical practice well established, Page became increasingly involved in local civic movements and politics. He later credited a local mining engineer and surveyor called W.J. Mulligan with first proposing to dam the Clarence River itself for power. Page took the idea up as combining his attraction to regionalism and new technology, and claimed that this led to his being 'persuaded to enter South Grafton Council to sponsor proposals for such development for the Clarence River'.[79] His first experience of public office came in 1913 when he was elected to South Grafton Council.[80] Alderman Page made a name for himself by extolling ambitious civic improvements, ranging from conventional schemes for a secure town water supply and public electric lighting, to the more transformative damming of the Clarence. When he became mayor in 1918, his own *Daily*

---

77   Page, *Truant Surgeon*, p. 3.
78   Untitled draft text on Page's early medical career prepared for his memoirs, EPP, folder 1855; see also similar published text at Page, *Truant Surgeon*, p. 37, from which the latter quote comes.
79   Page, *Truant Surgeon*, p. 37.
80   Grafton Council was created in 1859, but South Grafton split off in 1896. The two were reunited in 1957 and incorporated into Clarence Valley Council in 2004.

*Examiner*, in extolling his many virtues as an alderman, made particular mention of how the electrical lighting of South Grafton 'will always stand as a monument to his ability, thoroughness and progressiveness'.[81] Page in 1913 also made early forays into parliamentary politics by chairing campaign meetings for the local candidate for state parliament endorsed by the New South Wales Farmers and Settlers' Association (FSA), the state's main representative body for primary producers.

In 1914 Page accompanied Corin to The Gorge, then accessible only on horseback. The following year Corin produced the first fully professional study of a dam at that location. This proposed a 2-mile tunnel to supply a power station sited below The Gorge, but Corin lacked Page's propensity for attracting the public and political eye. Alderman Page wrote articles in the *Grafton Argus* in August–September 1914 – not a good time to be trying to capture the public imagination – and included Mulligan in a delegation seeking the agreement of the Labor state Minister of Works to have the area properly surveyed. The idea was pigeonholed for the duration of World War One. When the engineer H.G. Carter assessed the Clarence in 1929 he credited Page as having first 'so ably sponsored' the hydroelectric harnessing of the Clarence to the wider public, not Mulligan or Corin.[82] Corin, undeterred, produced in December 1918 a fuller proposal involving four distinct stages of construction, beginning with damming the Nymboida and culminating in a 200-foot-high dam at The Gorge.

Page's early campaigning to dam the Clarence, however heartfelt, gave him only a certain amount of publicity and little tangible success. It was the new state movement that contributed most to building his local profile. Early engagement with new statism was vital to the rise of Page and decisive in his lasting commitment to decentralisation and regionalisation.

Nationwide, new statism had died away for several years after Federation in 1901, attributed by Page to a ready assumption that the new Commonwealth would support local projects.[83] In 1908 a petition from north Queensland containing over 58,000 names was presented to the Commonwealth Parliament. Two years later, T.J. Ryan, a future Labor premier, secured the passage of a motion through the Lower

---

81   *Daily Examiner*, 14 February 1918, p. 4.
82   H.G. Carter, 'Report on the Hydro-Electric Development of the Clarence-Mitchell Rivers', 8 March 1929, EPP, folder 1046.
83   Page, *Truant Surgeon*, p. 40.

House of state parliament to divide Queensland into three. In 1915 the issue re-emerged in the Riverina and northern New South Wales, including a proposal that the Riverina follow its economic ties by being incorporated into Victoria. The northern revival reflected a continuing sense of being ignored by Sydney, but there is disagreement over what exactly the precise grievances were. The failure of the state government's 1911 Decentralisation Commission to deliver observable outcomes seems to have been one factor, but Page and others have written also of drought; wartime legislation that fixed butter and wheat prices at artificially low levels; and demands for public projects as various as a bridge linking Grafton and South Grafton, rail links, ferry services across the Clarence and removal of a dangerous reef from the river mouth.

More importantly, all accounts agree that Page led this 1915 resurgence. On 7 January 1915, 250 locals, including the mayors of Grafton and South Grafton, gathered at Grafton Town Hall to discuss a dispute over the payment of costs for the Clarence ferry service. Alderman Page altered the meeting's direction by successfully raising a motion for northern separation, either to form a new state or to merge with Queensland. He proposed that an investigative committee confer with communities across the north of New South Wales and in southern Queensland in preparing a full report. Page sat on this eight-member 'Literary Committee', which included both mayors. In April it duly presented to a further public meeting a document articulating local grievances. The document bore characteristic Page references to The Gorge's hydroelectric potential and 'the psychological moment', possibly his first public use of this shorthand for a receptive political and public mood.[84] This and a second April meeting resulted in the formation of the Northern New South Wales Separation League, with Page prominent on its nine-member executive. Page also emerged as the movement's leading propagandist, including through articles in the *Daily Examiner* cast as a debate between Page and a supposed new state sceptic dubbed Rocky Mouth.[85]

Page had no doubt that it was he who relaunched the movement, and in his memoirs detailed how he followed up the January 1915 meeting. He began by consulting with local lawyers and journalists to draft a case for separation

---

84  *A New State: Proposed Separation of Northern New South Wales: A Statement Compiled and Published by the Committee appointed at a Public Meeting Held in Grafton, in January 1915*, Grafton, 1915, no author given, copy at EPP, folder 1889 (part 2). The references to The Gorge and 'the psychological moment' are at pp. 18 and 22.
85  See for example the *Daily Examiner*, 9 October 1915, p. 4, and 15 October 1915, p. 4.

# 1. FAMILY, COMMUNITY AND METHODISM

and described the April forum as 'one of the most representative meetings ever held in Grafton'. This was all well covered by the *Daily Examiner* ('twelve and a half columns' on the statement to the April meeting, he recalled). He travelled with local lawyer Fred McGuren to regional centres including Kyogle, Lismore, Casino and Ballina to address public meetings and form new branches of the Separation League. This is all an early instance of the modus operandi that Page was to employ for decades to come – approach selected influential figures for support, follow up with appeals to the wider public and, throughout, keep proselytising through the local press. Less successfully, Page led a party inland to Tamworth, where he was rebuffed by V.C. Thompson who thought that concerted campaigning should await the end of the war. (There was a distinct Tablelands–North Coast rivalry.) In December 1915 Page was one of 'a band of keen local enthusiasts' who bought the *Clarence and Richmond Examiner* to recast it as the *Daily Examiner* and appointed McGuren as chairman of directors. This purchase was overtly strategic: Page told his wife in 1916 that the newspaper would be 'the medium for having our views carried into effect'.[86] Four *Daily Examiner* board members sat on the Literary Committee: Page, McGuren, W.F. Blood and E.G. Elworthy.

Pushing for such a massive realignment of government was indeed hardly likely to gain momentum during a major war. The northern New South Wales movement faded as leaders like Page enlisted and the state government finally completed a highly visible local project, the Glenreagh to South Grafton railway. Despite this, new statism had secured the commitment of figures such as Page, and it gave him both wide exposure and a network of influential local contacts that was to be invaluable when he sought to enter national politics.

## Page's war: 'Some distinctly military surgery'

In January 1916 Page joined the Australian Imperial Force's (AIF) Army Medical Corps. The inquisitive, striving Page approached war service as a chance to broaden his skills. He wrote to his wife from Cairo looking forward to 'some distinctly military surgery' after which 'I would be

---

86  Page to Ethel Page, 13 September 1916, Earle Page papers, UNE Archives, A180, box 7, folder 72; also Page, *Truant Surgeon*, p. 41.

content to go home'.[87] Captain Page was initially posted to the 3rd Australian General Hospital and remained on active service for just over a year in Egypt, England and France. During a frustratingly inactive period in Egypt, he took up the suggestion of his commanding officer Neville Howse, who Page had known since his student days, that he visit the new Aswan Low Dam. In France he spent five months at a casualty clearing station, where during heavy fighting over 1916–17 Page and eight surgeon colleagues together dealt with as many as 900 cases a day. Two of Page's brothers also served – Harold as an infantry officer and Will as a medical officer.

From November 1916, Page sought to return to Australia, if necessary by arranging a direct swap with Will, then still in Australia. In March 1917 he was finally permitted to return for family and financial reasons that he claimed threatened personal ruin, with the understanding that his remaining partner at Clarence House would enlist in his place.[88] Page's intention to return before war's end was quite open and not exceptional. In December 1916 he approached Howse, by then director of medical services for the AIF, and corresponded with the Defence Department accordingly. The official history of Australia in the Great War notes that out of a total of 1,242 AIF medical officers, some 300 returned to Australia in line with AIF practice of releasing those 'due for a rest and employment in Australia'. Howse himself had by 1916 a policy of releasing medical officers who wanted to return on urgent family or financial grounds.[89] Later, Howse became a rural Nationalist MP and Page's colleague in the Bruce–Page Cabinet.

Page's early return does not seem to have raised public opprobrium. Mention of his then former war service in his 1917 speech to the Australasian Provincial Press conference still elicited applause. In his memoirs Page fleetingly referred to returning due to illness.[90] Page arranged to travel back via North America, at his own expense, so as to study major hydroelectric developments. This, he told Ethel, would also fulfil an 'overpowering desire to see the American states and Canada', which he

---

87  Page to Ethel Page, 28 July 1916, Earle Page papers, UNE Archives, A180, box 7, folder 72.
88  Earle Page papers, UNE Archives, A180, box 9, folder 71 (part 1) and (part 2), including Earle Page to Ethel Page of 24 November 1916.
89  A.G. Butler, *Official History of the Australian Army Medical Services, 1914–1918, Volume II – The Western Front*, first edition, Australian War Memorial, Canberra, 1940, pp. 830–3 (the foregoing quote is at p. 831).
90  Page, *Truant Surgeon*, p. 44.

expected to be unlike 'staid and too stiff' Europe where 'conditions are bitterly unequal'.[91] Indeed, an officer's batman is said to have assumed Page's first name to be a title.[92]

Page had a proverbial good war – relatively short and personally rewarding, without direct involvement in combat. He would surely have been deeply affected by his exposure as a surgeon to the immediate results of battle: perhaps memories of this influenced his later attack on Menzies. But he said little about the human cost of war in letters to Ethel or in the short account in his memoirs, possibly reflecting a mixture of tact and wartime censorship. His letters are more focused on the professional benefits of wartime doctoring. Even when still in France he wrote of 'an experience that one would not have missed'. Page concluded that 'the best thing of all is the meeting men from every school of medicine in the world finding them with similar ideas and measuring oneself by their standards and getting a true comparative estimate of his ability + capacity'.[93]

Foreshortened as it was, Page remained proud of his war service. In the speech to the Australasian Provincial Press Association he did not hesitate to use wartime anecdotes, declaring for instance that 'unification' so possessed him that 'during the long nights in France he had thought of little else'.[94] Looking back on his public life much later, he reflected on how wartime collaboration 'firmly inspired my belief in the ideals and benefits of Commonwealth co-operation, which later I was able to carry forward in my political career'.[95] During his service and trip back to Australia, Page noticed that in 'the small states of the United States of America and of Europe … railways are built to encourage, and not discourage, trade'. This, he said, was when he 'realised that no true nation could be welded together until there were more partners with small enough states to realise their inter-dependence and give complete interstate free trade that was the real reason for our federal union'.[96]

---

91  Page to Ethel Page, undated but probably late 1916, Earle Page papers, UNE Archives, A180, box 9, folder 71.
92  George Bell, Henry Newland, W.F. Simmons and D.A. Cameron, obituary of Sir Earle Page, *The Medical Journal of Australia*, 12 May 1962, p. 733.
93  Page to Ethel Page, undated but probably late 1916.
94  Earle Page, *A Plea for Unification*, p. 5.
95  Page, *Truant Surgeon*, p. 64.
96  'Australian Country Party Complimentary Dinner to Sir Earle Page', EPP, folder 2358.

'NOW IS THE PSYCHOLOGICAL MOMENT'

## Page the person: Ideas, cunning and singleness of purpose

Page's early life imparts a strong sense of a remarkably purposeful and energetic individual. Considering what sort of person emerged from the formative experiences that shaped his approach to policy is essential to understanding how he conducted his political career.

Ulrich Ellis, a highly skilled journalist, first met Page as a member of the press gallery when federal parliament sat in Melbourne. He subsequently worked with him between 1928 and 1961 variously as a personal secretary, Country Party scribe and tireless new state campaigner. Ellis wrote extensively on Page, most tellingly in his history of the Country Party. He portrayed Page as conducting politics 'with reckless energy, native cunning and a certain contempt for the orthodox rules of the game'.[97] Above all, 'his main driving force was ideas, and they were legion', such that 'singleness of purpose – or purposes – was perhaps his predominant characteristic'.[98]

Page himself reflected to his wife that politics 'was a battle of ideas and ideals' and that the winners were those who were able to 'lay down the principles that will endure'.[99] Though Page was rarely ill, Ellis recalled that 'his longest spells in bed were the results of occasional accidents precipitated by absent-minded driving while haranguing his passengers'.[100] This may explain such incidents as in late 1917 when Page was thrown from the car in which he and two others were travelling: Page was knocked unconscious and the others pinned under the overturned vehicle.[101] A Country Party MP from Queensland, Charles Russell, perceived also a 'ruthlessness' behind Page's 'generally gay and debonair personality', which he thought typical of Country Party leaders.[102] Such comments, the 1917 speech and many other public and private statements suggest that Page thought of himself as being on a very special mission, far more important than anything he could achieve as a mere surgeon.

---

97    Ellis, *A History of the Australian Country Party*, p. 324.
98    Ibid., pp. 322, 323.
99    Earle Page to Ethel Page, 2 May 1927, Earle Page papers, UNE Archives, A180, box 7, folder 71.
100  Ellis, *A History of the Australian Country Party*, pp. 322, 323.
101  *Brisbane Courier*, 29 December 1917, p. 6.
102  Charles W. Russell, *Country Crisis*, W.R. Smith & Paterson, Brisbane, 1976, p. 83.

1. FAMILY, COMMUNITY AND METHODISM

**Figure 5: Ulrich Ellis.**
Source: Courtesy of John Oxley Library, State Library of Queensland, neg: 195159.

Although Page spoke clearly enough before large audiences, some of his listeners had difficulty with his often gushingly enthusiastic style of conversation. Even as staunch an admirer as Ellis reported that Page's recollections for the preparation of *Truant Surgeon* 'rarely contained verbs and often no subjects and predicates, and … he seldom finished a sentence or a thought'.[103] But Page could moderate this when required. The parliamentary officer Frank Green, no great admirer of Page, wrote that this 'tough individualist' had such a facility with words that 'the only way to conduct an argument with Page with any hope of success was in writing'.[104] Ellis added that Page sometimes used his verbosity with deliberate tactical intent to confuse.[105] Innumerable formal speeches and writings show that he was very capable indeed of well-ordered argument. He became an indefatigable user of mass communications – radio, film, self-published booklets and particularly the rural press.

Ellis also dwelt upon Page's self-centeredness. That 'the very universe revolved around him and his plans' tended to determine his personal interactions. Page 'had no reluctance in impressing the services of any person from a Prime Minister to a journalist or a humble messenger'. Ellis generously added that 'if he seemed selfish or unduly demanding, he could feel that he was obeying the dictates of his destiny which impelled him to push forward regardless'.[106] It is telling that Page did not respond to humour of which he was the object.[107] The long-serving press gallery journalist Warren Denning found Page to be 'fidgety, impatient, sometimes almost incoherent', but with 'more "going power" than any other person I had seen in parliamentary life'.[108] Arthur Fadden recalled Page as 'sometimes an irritating and exasperating colleague', leading to such outbursts as that mentioned in the introduction. But he also remembered Page as being 'like a father to me from the time I entered the House', and producing 'a veritable flood of ideas on every conceivable subject'.[109]

---

103 Account provided to journalist Cecil Edwards and reported in Edwards's *The Editor Regrets*, Hill of Content, Melbourne, 1972, p. 182.
104 Frank C. Green, *Servant of the House*, Heinemann, Melbourne, 1969, pp. 35, 103.
105 Ellis, *A History of the Australian Country Party*, p. 324.
106 Ibid., pp. 323, 326, 327.
107 Ellis quoted in J.B. O'Hara, 'The Entry into Public Life of Sir Earle Christmas Grafton Page (1915–1921)', BA (Hons) thesis, Department of History, University of New England, 1969, p. 6.
108 'Earle Christmas Grafton Page', profile by Denning, Warren Denning papers, NLA, MS 5129, pp. 3, 19.
109 A.W. Fadden, *They Called Me Arty: The Memoirs of Sir Arthur Fadden*, The Jacaranda Press, Milton, 1969, pp. 81–2.

Page's intense approach to policy issues greatly coloured how he worked as a party leader and minister. He felt compelled to leave a lasting legacy, reflecting powerful emotions derived from a mixture of family tradition, replication of the harmonious community of his childhood and the Methodist commitment to earthly progress. Ellis touched on Page's fundamentally emotive approach to issues – and inadvertently identified his foremost weaknesses – by adding that 'he rarely worked from premise to conclusion but proceeded from the original idea to its justification, arguing the case in reverse before he allowed it to burst upon the public'.[110]

That Page saw himself as working towards a higher purpose was also reflected in his being undeterred by failure, to which he typically responded with a long, patient wait before trying again. When another opportunity finally arose, he simply announced his specific goal and proceeded to push ahead regardless, especially when not constrained by a strong prime minister. He invariably applied his trademark energy and inventiveness but also his tendency to perceive ready solutions to complex problems. At some crucial moments he imprudently dismissed his critics as sadly misguided, such as on the inevitability of new states.

Unlike many other self-styled visionaries, Page was a cultural conservative who admired the British Empire as a force for international stability. But his reading, education and sojourns in Sydney and overseas gave him a broader perspective than the typical rural activist. Page read very widely. In July 1935 the parliamentary librarian recorded him as having borrowed a work on economic planning by the English socialist G.D.H. Cole, a biography of Czech President Edvard Beneš, studies of Franklin Roosevelt's New Deal and of Japan's role in the Pacific, as well as some unspecified 'mystery stories'.[111] That part of his personal library which survives at his former residence at Heifer Station includes very serious tomes on current affairs, ancient and modern history, and economics that range from Plutarch's *Lives* to the observations of the American foreign correspondent John Gunther. Yet Page's interpretation was frequently narrow, aided by creative use of selected statistics. He habitually seized upon whatever seemed to justify his existing views, such as taking writings by the historian and philosopher of urban life Lewis Mumford to be confirmation of the inherent evil of big cities.

---

110 Ellis, *A History of the Australian Country Party*, p. 325.
111 Parliamentary Librarian to Page, 19 July 1935, Earle Page papers, UNE Archives, A180, box 1, folder 3.

Page's policy forays invariably reflected faith in the power of political action. He continued to believe, with only minor qualifications, in the ready ability of government to create conditions that would develop both economy and society along the proper decentralised and regionalised lines. This faith exceeded his confidence in politicians and public servants as individuals, hence a consistent preference for utilising outsiders from private industry to help implement his policies. In this, he conspicuously lacked the early Country Party's distrust of banks and other big business.

Page had some self-appreciation of his unconventionality in democratic politics. Although a highly respected local member, he was not a populist who looked to the masses for guidance or sought to use their supposed will as backing for his actions. Contrary to the early Country Party's egalitarian mores, Page was convinced of the prime role of the leader. As something of a historicist, he spoke of natural laws having driven all societies, notably the decisive role of bold leaders and the superiority of compact, homogenous states. In personal notes, Page reflected on how the historian Arnold Toynbee 'points out fundamental basis of successive civilisations been saved and transmitted to posterity by virile minority', no doubt a reflection of how he saw himself.[112]

Page often felt it necessary to package a rarefied goal with something more publicly acceptable, such as linking economic planning to defence preparedness. In private he bemoaned the reluctance of the citizenry to see at once the merits of his appeals to action. In 1921 he told the editor of the *Coff's Harbour Advocate* that the closure of local public works by the state government was due to 'the supineness and apathy of the North, in not unanimously and enthusiastically getting behind the separation movement', as he had 'urged them to do for many years'.[113] But as will be seen in following chapters, he nonetheless foresaw public opinion as eventually catching up, particularly if the public was gradually acclimatised to be ready for a well-timed initiative and a visionary leader who seized the psychological moment.

---

112 Notes for a speech, Earle Page papers, UNE Archives, A180, box 4, folder 41 (part 1). Page's own underlining; undated, but from late in his career.
113 Page to editor of the *Coffs Harbour Advocate*, 25 January 1921, Earle Page papers, UNE Archives, A180, box 1, folder 1.

# 2

# 'WE WERE DETERMINED TO USE OUR OPPORTUNITIES TO THE FULL'

Page's Rise to National Prominence

Earle Page had luck, as all politicians need. He entered politics at a formative time that made possible his astonishing rise to national prominence. Rural activism led to the appearance of the Country Party and a reshaping of the party system. Page liked to modestly portray his sudden rise as entirely the result of lucky accidents, but in fact his electoral success in his native Grafton and transformation into a national figure also owed much to his unremitting determination. Strategic leadership of the resurgence of new statism helped Page build a personal network of rural elites associated with this cause, while his closely related advocacy of regionalism and decentralisation became his first distinctive contribution to national political debate.

This all culminated by February 1923 in Page reaching a near ideal position from which to attempt to influence national policy. Suddenly, he was Commonwealth treasurer, de facto deputy prime minister and leader of a party that held almost half the positions in Cabinet. Page was not interested in high office for its own sake. The Bruce–Page Government, as it chose to call itself, took office during a resurgence of national optimism and unhesitatingly accepted responsibility for reinvigorating economic progress. It did not simply resume policies interrupted by the war but sought to rationalise Australian governance so as to provide a more efficient basis for national development. This helped make the 1920s an era of innovative policies conducive to Page's personal plans for shaping a still formative nation, starting with ambitious attempts to shift the nation towards a comprehensive system of cooperative federalism.

## Page's return from war and entry into public life, 1917–19

When Page returned to Australia in June 1917, his personal world was brimming with promise. He had undertaken war service, built a career as a surgeon and was locally prominent for his political activism. New statism, however, was still in a lull in the Grafton area. The war was continuing, a north coast drought had just broken and the state government was showing interest in a major new local project, the Nymboida hydroelectric power scheme. Page soon re-established himself as a prominent local figure. Throughout the remainder of 1917 he wrote for the *Daily Examiner*, delivered public lectures, lobbied MPs and harried newspaper editors, later reflecting in a draft of his memoirs that 'policies must be hammered continually into the minds of the public'.[1] He drew on his travels to produce long and earnest press articles on how hydroelectricity in Canada amounted to 'Lightening the Farmers' Lot'.[2] Page particularly recalled how the parents of children he had delivered years before still bemoaned the dearth of educational opportunities around Grafton. The parliamentarians he accosted 'seemed to have no thought-out remedy', but Page had no doubt that 'my own ideas of local development and sub-division of the large states and harnessing the water powers of Australia would give those opportunities'.[3]

Immediately after the war ended, new statism revived in several regions of Australia. This overlapped with the wider rural agitation that was the basis for the most enduring political development of the time, the appearance of the Country Party. The particularly strong revival in northern New South Wales has been attributed to the onset of regional drought in New England and to the state government's failure to provide new rail and port facilities.[4] Proponents shared a sense of rural marginalisation: a booklet

---

1   Quoted in Sally Collier, 'Earle Christmas Grafton Page: A doctor for the nation', *Armidale and District Historical Society Journal*, no. 39, 1996, p. 9.
2   *Daily Examiner*, 23 June 1917, p. 4, and 30 June 1917, p. 4.
3   'Australian Country Party Complimentary Dinner to Sir Earle Page', EPP, folder 2358.
4   Graham, *Formation of the Australian Country Parties*, p. 154.

issued in 1920 as the movement's 'first real text-book' warned that 'where political power is combined with commercial supremacy the danger will always be that the political power may be used to advance the commercial interests of the centre at the expense of the remainder'.[5]

New statism's local appeal and wide network of supporters made it an excellent basis for launching a political career. Proponents collectively provided a milieu in which Page was at home – a preponderance of town-based figures drawn from the professions, the rural press, Chambers of Commerce and local government, along with farmers' and graziers' associations. New statism in the north appears to have had a socially narrower and more elite base than in other parts of New South Wales.[6] This helped him build a diverse range of influential personal contacts that included the New England–based Thompson, Drummond, and the Tamworth lawyer and MHR for New England over the period 1913–19, P.P. Abbott. Page also began to forge ties with like-minded figures from further afield such as F.B.S. Falkiner, a prominent sheep-breeder from the Riverina who was elected to the House of Representatives in 1913 with FSA sponsorship.

Page's political rise was also propelled by rural protest finally starting to organise itself into an Australia-wide political movement. Rural activism already had a long but sporadic history of 'political experiments', such as post–gold rush land reform leagues and the Victorian-based Kyabram movement's post-Federation demands for smaller government. These were typified by sudden emergence followed by rapid dissipation or merger with urban-based groups. But during the 1910s continuing rural insecurity led to 'a cultural reaction to the dominance of the big coastal cities on the one hand and the pastoralist establishment on the other' that decisively strengthened moves to form rural-based political parties.[7]

---

5   Northern New State Movement, *Australian Subdivision, Effect on Development, The Case for Northern New South Wales*, Glen Innes, NSW, 1920 (also known as *Australia Subdivided: The First New State*), p. 8; textbook quote by Ulrich Ellis, *New Australian States*, The Endeavour Press, Sydney, 1933, p. 153.
6   See Grant Harman, 'New state agitation in northern New South Wales, 1920–1929', *Journal of the Royal Australian Historical Society*, vol. 63, no. 1, June 1977, pp. 26–39, for an outline of support for new statism in this region; on the social base for northern new statism, see Nancy Blacklow, '"Riverina roused": Representative support for the Riverina New State Movements in the 1920s and 1930s', *Journal of the Royal Australian Historical Society*, vol. 80, no. 3–4, December 1994, pp. 176–94.
7   Graham, *Formation of the Australian Country Parties*, p. 139.

Rural-based protest during the period 1910–20 was being fuelled by such unwelcome government intrusions as compulsory wartime marketing, tariffs and arbitration, and referenda conducted in 1911, 1913 and 1919 that sought unsuccessfully to greatly expand Commonwealth economic powers. The organisational skills necessary for political parties were fostered by rural community entities that ranged from farmers' associations to annual agricultural shows, cooperative companies and masonic lodges.[8] (Page's membership of the Grafton Freemasons from late 1917 would have added to his range of local contacts.) Wheat farmers were especially prominent in providing early rural political leadership. This reflected the added challenges faced by export-focused producers vulnerable to international price fluctuations and who were often based on small holdings in such drought-prone regions as Victoria's Mallee.[9]

Wheat was also the target of the first comprehensive wartime regulation of a primary industry. A compulsory wheat pool was instituted in 1915 that covered price control and shipping, jointly administered by the Commonwealth and the states. Regulation was later extended to other primary producers, including dairy farmers and graziers. Producers' reactions were mixed, ranging from resentment of government control to finding comfort in centralised purchasing and guaranteed prices. Page later testified that the problem was not the existence of such schemes per se, but rather the levels of prices they set for wheat, sugar and butter.[10] These were wartime schemes only; their extension into peacetime would require legislation that needed the collaboration of the states in order to overcome significant constitutional problems. Over time, producer demands came to focus on a direct role in managing state-supported regulation and its post-war continuation. When combined with deeper currents of countrymindedness and small producers' perceptions of exploitation, the broad political outcome was to encourage rural pressure groups to directly enter parliamentary politics.

The first rural political parties were tentative and ill-organised, but significant for their being spread right across the nation. They included the appearance in 1912 of a country faction of the governing Liberal Party in Victoria that challenged the authority of Premier William Watt, and

---

8   Ibid., pp. 292–4.
9   Ibid., p. 28.
10  Page, interview by B.D. Graham, 22 February 1956, Bruce Desmond Graham papers, NLA, MS 8471.

a faltering effort in 1913 by the FSA of New South Wales to foster a state country party. The New South Wales FSA and the Queensland Famers' Union endorsed candidates for the 1913 federal election but the eight elected did not go on to form a distinct party. A stable rural parliamentary party first appeared in Western Australia in 1914 when the local FSA and Country Party won 10 state seats at separate elections that year for the upper and lower houses of state parliament. In Queensland the following year the Queensland Farmers' Union won five seats. In 1915 a similar group also appeared in New South Wales, based on the FSA and calling itself the Progressive Party. The Queensland and New South Wales parties in particular were anti-Labor, but concern to remain independent made all of the early rural parties reluctant to seek portfolios in Liberal ministries. The problem that this raised of how to otherwise wield influence was to be decisively addressed by Page.

The Victorian Farmers' Union (VFU), founded in the Mallee in 1916, rejected alignment with established parties in favour of seeking concessions from them: these parties would become 'putty in the hands of an organisation' said Isaac Hart, one of the VFU's founders. It sought to reform the wheat pool and also attracted support from dairy farmers who resented Commonwealth fixing of butter prices, and from Goulburn Valley irrigation settlers seeking the repeal of barriers to acquiring the freehold of their leases.[11] Page, however, showed from the outset little personal or policy empathy with wheat-farming militants. The VFU later became the main power base for several of his parliamentary colleagues and rivals, including Percy Stewart, Thomas Paterson and Albert Dunstan. Stewart in particular made an early impression on Page as 'weather beaten … a typical wheat farmer, accustomed to the tough conditions of a difficult industry in a hard climate' and who delivered speeches 'ornamented with bitter invective'.[12] Another important early step towards a federal parliamentary Country Party was the formation of the Australian Farmers' Federal Organisation (AFFO) as a national body in 1916. This was an initiative of four major state bodies, the VFU and the FSAs of New South Wales, South Australia and Western Australia, in response to the wartime regulation of primary industry. The AFFO's platform included new states, the first time this issue had been adopted by a national organisation.

---

11   Graham, *Formation of the Australian Country Parties*, pp. 110–11, 112–13.
12   Page, *Truant Surgeon*, p. 54.

Page's final stepping-stone to parliament was his February 1918 election to the mayoralty of South Grafton by his fellow councillors, attributed by Page's own *Daily Examiner* to the eminence of his family mixed with his advocacy of 'unification' and of local government.[13] He immediately signalled that his interests were more national than local by placing a long article in the *Daily Examiner* on the 'Case for Unification'. Mayor Page told his constituents that:

> the early rapid development of the United States was largely due to the comparatively small size of the subdivisions permitting true local self-government in the widest sense, giving the people a personal knowledge of their public men, and permitting these to have an intimate and intelligent grasp of the whole area they were administering.[14]

He built on his August 1917 speech by observing that as the Australian states lacked historical tradition and respective unifying features they were ripe for 'the unification of the whole country', prior to 'the localisation of local powers in small, compact inexpensively governed provinces'.[15] In April 1918, he won statewide attention by using a local dinner in honour of Premier William Holman to attack the state government's lack of commitment to the north coast, drawing cheers from other diners. The district, Page said, needed electricity from the river, proper harbours and better communications with adjacent regions. Compared to the mighty Clarence, many of the streams carrying much of the world's commerce 'were only muddy ditches in comparison'.[16]

In his memoirs, Page attributed his decision to run for national parliament to his commitment to the new state cause and local public works, especially 'water development'.[17] Regional patriotism was a strong motivator, but Page recalled that he also wanted to 'introduce the fight throughout the whole of Australian politics' for national subdivision and development.[18] He usually claimed to be acting on his own initiative, but in his June 1956 speech to the dinner marking his retirement from

---

13  *Daily Examiner*, 14 February 1918, p. 4.
14  *Daily Examiner*, 16 February 1918, p. 3.
15  Ibid. An example of his statements on hydroelectricity is in the *Glen Innes Examiner* of 7 July 1919, p. 5.
16  *Daily Examiner*, 29 April 1918, p. 3.
17  Page, *Truant Surgeon*, p. 47.
18  Page speech to the Annual Convention of the New England New State Movement, Grafton, 23 October 1961, New England New State Movement, Armidale, UNE Archives, A547, box 33.

the frontbench Page also recalled 'a petition from more than half of the people' as the trigger. In a 1961 speech he added a reference to 'the leader of the movement' (unnamed, but probably Abbott) having pressed him to nominate. Page announced on 8 October 1919 that he would stand as an independent at the forthcoming federal election for the north-eastern New South Wales seat of Cowper, running against the incumbent John Thomson.

Page's long-standing support for a new state and local development provided a ready basis for a campaign that played on local resentments. His own *Daily Examiner* offered unabashed support, assuring electors that Page had 'the ability, means and time to give to his country, and that the interests of the electorate would be safe in his hands'.[19] The more detached *Sydney Morning Herald* assessed Page to be 'a very popular resident' who had Thomson 'caught at a severe disadvantage'.[20] Page in campaign mode used his private car to traverse the entire electorate twice, usually speaking in public three times a day, six days a week.[21] Despite his early return from active service, campaign advertisements featured him in AIF uniform.[22] Page maintained a studied independence from established party politics: although 1919 was the first national election to use preferential voting, he did not instruct his supporters on second preferences.[23]

Page's keynote speech for the campaign was delivered at Grafton's Theatre Royal on 22 October. It reaffirmed his August 1917 address and was the first prominent instance of a personal trademark – trying to marry the immediate interests of a local audience with his national vision. He ranged from local telephone services and the hydroelectric potential of the Clarence up to nationwide regional self-government, the dangers of state enterprises and the greater good of a more ordered national economy. The people of Grafton were told that their local postal services 'were starved in order that the Melbourne Post Office might be made the finest in the Southern Hemisphere'. Page presented as a committed fiscal conservative, calling what became known as vertical fiscal imbalance – whereby the Commonwealth collected excess revenue that it promptly transferred to the states to spend – 'one of the prime causes of this orgy of extravagance'. He attacked the fundamentals of Australian governance by describing the

---

19   *Daily Examiner*, 24 September, 1919, p. 4.
20   *Sydney Morning Herald*, 2 December 1919, p. 6.
21   O'Hara, 'The Entry into Public Life of Sir Earle Christmas Grafton Page', pp. 79.
22   Such as in the *Daily Examiner* of 11 October 1919, p. 6.
23   O'Hara, 'The Entry into Public Life of Sir Earle Christmas Grafton Page', p. 83.

'whole Federal system [as] made for wastefulness, as almost everything was duplicated'. A revised Constitution 'would enable national affairs to be controlled by a National Parliament' and shift regional matters to 'local subdivisions of Australia that should be made according to community of interests'. Page foreshadowed his still developing interest in planning by raising the careful use of tariffs 'to establish secondary industries that the primary industries demanded', and so 'make the country self-contained'. He also proposed national insurance, an essentially contributions-based scheme to deal with the deprivations of unemployment, sickness and old age.[24]

There is a significant omission from Page's 1917 and 1919 speeches. No reference was made to agricultural support schemes of guaranteed prices, produce pools, production quotas or export bounties – often collectively dubbed orderly marketing. These were already issues of debate and are widely regarded as having been the Country Party's raison d'être. Page certainly supported such schemes, particularly for the wheat industry. But unlike many of his political colleagues, orderly marketing was not the foremost focus of his policy activism. Part of the reason is that over the period 1918–21 Australian dairy farmers opposed market regulation as having artificially depressed prices. During the 1919 campaign Page, seeking to represent a dairy-producing area, declared himself against 'government interference with the dairying industry, and more especially with the price-fixing of primary products'.[25] But more fundamentally, he had frequent misgivings that the widespread subsidisation of industries would include those that were inefficient. Orderly marketing did become important to Page's conception of how the national economy should be managed and to his party's political strategies – he, for example, praised a new Dairy Produce Control Board when it was created in 1924.[26] But it was never the dominant feature of a much broader personal world view that saw salvation for primary producers as more likely to be found in regionalism, technology and planning. (Page, incidentally, sometimes used the phrase orderly marketing to instead describe the efficient overseas marketing of Australian goods.)

---

24   All quotes in this paragraph are from the *Daily Examiner*, 23 October 1919, p. 3.
25   See Graham, *Formation of the Australian Country Parties*, pp. 151–2; Page quote from *Daily Examiner*, 23 October 1919, p. 3.
26   On Page and the Dairy Produce Control Board, see the Lismore *Northern Star*, 23 October 1924, p. 4.

Page proceeded to win Cowper with over 52 per cent of the primary vote, an impressive result for an independent in a diverse electorate that stretched from his native Clarence Valley southwards to the Manning River and Taree. Thomson received a mere fifth of the primary vote, behind not only Page but also the Labor candidate. Page topped the poll in 15 of Cowper's 16 major population centres and won nearly 60 per cent of the primary vote in its biggest district, Grafton. The only major centre where he failed to top the primary vote was Kempsey in the south, and even there Thomson secured a mere 48 votes more than Page.[27] The victorious Page was paraded through the streets of South Grafton and serenaded by an apparently surprise gathering of a local band and schoolchildren.[28] Why did Page triumph so readily and proceed to hold this seat as a local power base for the next 42 years?

First, Page had built a very broad personal profile in the Grafton region. During the 1910s he had made his own additions to his family's reputation for conspicuous public service, particularly by serving on South Grafton Council. Although a town-dweller, his medical practice gave him exposure throughout Grafton's extended hinterland. By contrast, the sitting member was, according to Page, rarely sighted in the electorate, not helped by his being ill in hospital for part of the 1919 campaign. Thomson was used to little opposition, having been returned unopposed at the previous two elections. Page strengthened his ties to his electorate and credentials as a man on the land when in 1923 he was part of a syndicate that purchased Heifer Station on the Clarence River, a beef cattle property about 50 kilometres north-west of Grafton. Page bought out the other owners in 1932.[29] Ellis later described this property as Page's 'pride of his personal possessions', where 'he returned at every opportunity to renew his energies and his inspiration in close contact with his beloved river'.[30]

Second, Page had strong ties to the local press. Newspapers were extremely important in rural Australia for providing regular communication across dispersed communities and asserting local identities.[31] In northern New South Wales they enthusiastically supported the local political movements and new state campaigns with which Page was engaged. Page and his

---

27  O'Hara, 'The Entry into Public Life of Sir Earle Christmas Grafton Page', pp. 85–6.
28  *Daily Examiner*, 16 December 1919, p. 4.
29  See Jim Page, *The History of Heifer Station*, privately published, no date.
30  Ellis, *A History of the Australian Country Party*, p. 323.
31  Graham, *Formation of the Australian Country Parties*, p. 142. See also Blainey, *Black Kettle and Full Moon*, pp. 104–9.

business colleagues positioned the *Daily Examiner* as an agent for other northern papers. Page wrote of how the *Daily Examiner*, the Lismore *Northern Star*, the Tamworth *Northern Daily Leader* and the Tweed River *Daily* 'developed a uniform policy on decentralisation and became the vehicles for our campaign'.[32] In June 1921, he also became an owner of the *Northern Star*, while fellow new staters formed a powerful network by controlling other regional publications. Thompson edited newspapers in Tamworth from 1911, while E.C. Sommerlad edited the *Inverell Argus* and, from May 1918, owned the *Glen Innes Examiner*.

Third, and most fundamentally, Page rode the nationwide and local rise in rural protest politics. In October 1918 a North Coast Development League was formed to promote local public works, notably Page's scheme to dam the Clarence. Page was elected league president, and the following year led a public roadshow along the north coast and then inland to the Tablelands. Ellis later commented that Page would have used such speaking tours to gauge public support for a run at federal parliament.[33] In April 1919 alone, he addressed meetings at Inverell, Glen Innes, Armidale and Tamworth.[34] Drummond was impressed when he heard Page speak at Inverell, marking the start of his admiration of Page.[35]

## Page's transformation into a national figure, 1919–23

Page, the nationally unknown new rural MP – intense, well-educated and more 'townie' than farmer – later claimed that he had entered parliament with few personal ambitions. He was supposedly subject to just three years leave of absence agreed to by his medical partners in Grafton. Page later reflected that his three partners 'displayed a touching faith in the speed of parliamentary process whereby I would achieve constitutional

---

32  Page, *Truant Surgeon*, p. 42.
33  J.B. O'Hara, 'A doctor in the house: Earle Page 1915–1920', *Armidale and District Historical Society Journal*, no. 14, April 1971, p. 95.
34  John Joseph Farrell, 'Bones for the Growling Dog?: The New State Movements in Northern New South Wales 1915–1930', MA (Hons) thesis, Department of History, University of New England, 1997, p. 30.
35  Jim Belshaw, 'Decentralisation, Development and Decent Government: The Life and Times of David Henry Drummond, 1890–1941', PhD thesis, University of New England, submitted but subsequently put aside by its author; see newenglandhistory.blogspot.com.au/2010/06/decentralisation-development-and-decent.html, Chapter 2, 'Entry into politics 1907–1920'.

reform, carve out some New States, and inspire the development of water conservation and electric power on the Clarence and on other Australian rivers'.[36]

In his maiden speech he assured the House of Representatives, rather disingenuously, that 'it was almost by accident that I strayed into the by-paths of politics', then proceeded to propose the complete overhaul of the national Constitution and Commonwealth Budget.[37] Looking back in 1955, he added that he entered national politics only as he had been unable to get results outside it.[38] But there is little doubt that Page had harboured grand ambitions. His obituary in the *Medical Journal of Australia* reported that during the 1910s members of his local community spoke of him as a future prime minister and that early in 1917 Page told his commanding officer he aspired to that office.[39] Ellis also thought that Page entered parliament with such hopes of high office, only to find that lesser ministerial rank was sufficient for pursuing the policies that were his primary interest.[40] As a new MP, Page proceeded to build a public profile far exceeding that of any other rural-based politician. A mere 16 months after being elected, he was a national figure, leading the Country Party and issuing demands to a formidable prime minister.

Page's rise was helped by post-war policy debates. One of these was a revival of popular interest in developmentalism. Proponents saw the young nation as now ready to realise its potential, aided by a keen sense of entitlement for rural Australia. The appeal of such optimism was marked by the reaction to Brady's 1918 *Australia Unlimited*. This illustrated book for the popular market was physically heavy but lightweight in content, yet was reviewed effusively by the press. Brady asserted that Australia's farmlands, 'highly fertile and unlimited in area', were capable of supporting a population of 200 million. Contrary to the obvious, he doubted 'if there are a hundred square miles of true desert within the whole area of the Australian continent'.[41] Boosters such as Brady drew forth articulate critics, including the geographer Thomas Griffith Taylor,

---

36  Page, *Truant Surgeon*, p. 49.
37  *Commonwealth Parliamentary Debates*, 4 March 1920, p. 194.
38  Page speech on being granted life membership of the Country Party, 24 June 1955, quoted in Collier, 'Earle Christmas Grafton Page: A doctor for the nation', *Armidale and District Historical Society Journal*, p. 5.
39  Bell et al., obituary of Sire Earle Page, pp. 731–4.
40  Ellis, *A History of the Australian Country Party*, p. 328.
41  Brady, *Australia Unlimited*, pp. 37, 57.

the science administrator David Rivett and the pioneer environmentalist James Barrett. Taylor was particularly outspoken about environmental limitations and 'could not resist ridiculing every sacred cow'.[42] Hostile public and media reactions to such critics reflected how ideas of national development had come to overlap with wider Australian patriotism.

Page's continuing advocacy of unification and new states was aided by his entering parliamentary politics at a time of decisive evolution in Australian federalism. Ongoing sparring between the Commonwealth and the states created a debate for him to join. The Australian nation was still formative, with many basics of national governance highly contestable. In particular, the Commonwealth was seeking to increase its financial and other powers well beyond what the states had agreed to in 1901, encouraged by the war having boosted the role of central government. The Commonwealth takeover of customs and excise in 1901 deprived the former colonies of a quarter to a third of their total revenues. As the Commonwealth initially collected far more than it spent, section 87 of the Constitution – the 'Braddon clause' – required it to return three-quarters of these receipts to the states for the first 10 years after Federation. In 1908 the Deakin Government's *Surplus Revenue Act 1908* provided for the Commonwealth to retain remaining surplus funds rather than automatically also grant these to the states. The growth of national responsibilities imposed stress on these early fiscal arrangements, and in 1910–11 the Commonwealth fixed its payments to the states at 25 shillings per capita. These were provided with no guarantee of longer-term continuation and were eroded by price inflation. In 1915 the Commonwealth's introduction of estate duties and a progressive income tax brought it into direct competition with the states for revenue.

Increased Commonwealth activity elevated one of Page's main passions to the forefront of debate: state–Commonwealth policy cooperation. Although the constitutional debates of the 1890s assumed a clear division between these two main levels of government, it became evident soon after 1901 that they had essentially concurrent powers that necessitated close consultation. The earliest formalised mechanisms for this were post-Federation premiers' conferences, convened by the states rather than the Commonwealth. In 1915 complementary legislation enacted by the Commonwealth, South Australia, New South Wales and Victoria

---

42   J.M. Powell, *Griffith Taylor and 'Australia Unlimited'*, pp. 25, 39–40.

created the first significant intergovernmental agency, the River Murray Commission, empowered to regulate use of the river's waters. Despite these early forms of cooperation, 'tension had begun to develop between the legally restricted responsibilities of the federal government, as set out in a specific list of transferred powers, and the need for increased activity suggested by the Commonwealth's growing importance in the overall governance of the country'.[43] This was inevitable in a federation that commenced with a small central government but then had to meet the growing needs of a new nation. Increasing Commonwealth assertiveness was exemplified by its convening a premiers' conference on post-war reconstruction in September 1919, just three months before Page was elected to parliament.

The means of constitutional change was also evolving. By 1919 it was widely recognised that High Court judgments generally favouring the Commonwealth were more important than referenda to amend the Constitution or the voluntary surrender of powers by the states. The court rejected a challenge to Deakin's Surplus Revenue Act, and in 1920 the famed Engineers' Case largely removed the concept of implied immunity of the states from Commonwealth law. This amounted to ushering in 'the primacy of the Commonwealth, a primacy which was to develop in the next half-century into dominance'.[44]

Debates on federalism acquired added impetus from high hopes engendered by the end of the war and a related widening of perceptions of the potential of national government. Wartime planning of industry and American-sourced concepts of industrial management encouraged a swing away from laissez-faire policies and towards ideas of efficiency in government and the planning of the economy. Duty-focused, collectivist views of society were promulgated by a bevy of policy thinkers, who although marginal to conventional politics were outspoken in their belief that the nation could be engineered for the better. They included historian and adult educator G.V. Portus, Frederic Eggleston and Elton Mayo, as well as organisations such as the Workers' Educational Association (WEA). The year 1915 saw, for example, publication of the proceedings of a wartime conference on industrial planning as *National Efficiency: A Series of Lectures* by the economist R.F. Irvine and others. In 1919

---

43   W.G. McMinn, *A Constitutional History of Australia*, Oxford University Press, Melbourne, 1979, pp. 134–5, 192.
44   Ibid., pp. 130, 138.

Portus produced *An Introduction to the Study of Industrial Reconstruction* and *The Problem of Industry in Politics* that enthusiastically cited British exemplars for industrial planning.[45] Page read widely in search of ideas and supporting arguments, and by the early 1920s he began to show an interest in concepts of national planning and efficiency that later became prominent in the Bruce–Page Government.

For Page, the most significant of these new intellectual figures was F.A. Bland, an associate of Portus who became an increasingly voluble advocate of political decentralisation and efficient public administration. Bland wrote in a 1923 WEA publication of a shift of emphasis from traditional 'negative' government functions of external security and internal order towards more positive functions 'arising out of the social, intellectual, artistic and economic conditions of modern times'. These included education, public health, 'public utility schemes' and 'the fostering and development of economic resources'.[46] Bland was to become a prominent admirer of many of Page's ideas, especially on planning and related cooperative federalism.

Most fundamentally for Page, he entered parliament when tension and change in the established political parties created openings for the emergence of a national Country Party. Without this, he might indeed have returned to Grafton after just one term. The party system had already begun to assume a recognisably modern form with the 1909 Fusion of the Free Trade and Protectionist Parties to form the first Liberal Party, and the continued rise of the Australian Labor Party (ALP) to form a majority government in 1910. The war had heightened political tensions generally by sharpening social divisions, such as between ex-servicemen and those who stayed at home, Catholics and Protestants, and capital and labour. Post-war, continuing internal tensions weakened the two major parties and left neither well-placed to respond forcefully to growing support for rural candidates.[47]

In the run-up to the 1919 election and after, the main anti-Labor party was beset by continuing difficulties in assimilating discordant elements. Some of this discord arose from the Fusion having brought together two formerly rival parties. But much was attributable to the unexpected

---

45  See Moore in Walter, *What Were They Thinking?*, pp. 137–8, 158.
46  F.A. Bland, *Shadows and Realities of Government: An Introduction to the Study of the Organisation of the Administrative Agencies of Government with Special Reference to New South Wales*, Workers' Educational Association of N.S.W., Sydney, 1923, p. 3.
47  Graham, *Formation of the Australian Country Parties*, p. 294.

need to also accommodate ex-ALP leader Hughes. In November 1916 he and his immediate supporters had stormed out of the ALP over the conscription issue. They briefly formed a Cabinet of their own before joining the Liberals in February 1917 to create the Nationalist Party as the basis of a united ministry. The ALP split in every state except Queensland, resulting in the Nationalists easily winning the federal election of May 1917. The advent of peace the following year released tensions in a government that had primarily been unified by the exigencies of the war effort. In December 1919 Hughes's instinctive economic interventionism saw him lead his government into an unsuccessful referendum conducted simultaneously with the federal election that sought greatly increased Commonwealth powers over trade and commerce, trusts, combinations, monopolies and industrial affairs. There was further unease within his own party over its leader's support for state-owned enterprises, such as the Commonwealth Shipping Line and ventures into radio and oil refining. The prime minister was also widely distrusted for his autocratic style. The Hughes problem was to present Page, during his first term in parliament, with a unifying target for his early leadership of the Country Party.

He also gained from perceptions that Hughes was anti-rural. Although Australia's gross domestic product actually diminished by almost 10 per cent between 1914 and 1920, many rural industries did well. Pastoralism was buoyed by British wartime acquisition of wool, and prices for most rural products remained high after peace was declared. But a strong perception that the Nationalist Government increasingly favoured urban over rural interests helped give Page and his political confreres purpose and prominence. All major farmers' organisations other than the VFU supported the Nationalists during the war. This support rapidly dissipated from 1918 as the Hughes Government signalled its intention to extend regulation and protection. Its mid-1918 decision to fix the price of meat sold in metropolitan markets outraged graziers. In March 1919, Commonwealth plans to greatly increase tariffs to shield manufacturers drew the ire of farmers' organisations. Fears that a federal parliamentary rural party would divide the non-Labor vote largely evaporated when the Hughes Government introduced preferential voting after the May 1918 by-election for the seat of Flinders, at which a VFU candidate had threatened to run. (This candidate's withdrawal enabled Stanley Bruce to enter politics by winning this seat.) Farmers' organisations opposed the December 1919 referendum, again with the notable exception of the VFU.[48]

---

48    Ibid., pp. 115–16, 118–19.

The main mover in organising such rural unrest into a federal Country Party was the AFFO and its constituent state bodies. Initially, it demanded that the Australian Wheat Board, formerly an object of resentment for wartime management of the wheat pool, be made a permanent body offering secure purchasing. The state organisations convened a series of joint meetings that culminated in the AFFO in August 1919 adopting a new federal platform in good time for the forthcoming federal election. This document effectively marks the start of the early Country Party's characteristic support for both free markets and selected state intervention. It called for tariff reform, rationalisation of federal and state functions and freedom from excessive regulation, but also for producer representation on the various boards and commissions regulating their interests. The AFFO platform also overlapped with Page's sentiments by calling for 're-arrangement of the functions of the Federal and State Governments to enable the Commonwealth effectively to carry out national functions'. But by not incorporating his full national vision on regionalism and electrification it is also evident that Page differed from the emerging mainstream of rural agitation. Nor did the AFFO yet amount to a united nationwide political party: its four member bodies proceeded to issue their own manifestos, albeit each based on the AFFO's platform.[49]

In October the Graziers' Association of New South Wales accepted an invitation from the FSA to declare its support for the new rural-based Progressive Party, helping to broaden it beyond small wheat farmers.[50] Good showings at by-elections by candidates endorsed by farmers' organisations led them to endorse a total of 27 candidates nationwide at the 1919 election. One of these was Page, who gladly accepted the FSA's apparently unsolicited support as it 'provided the very machinery I sought and appropriate allies should I be elected to parliament', a further indication of his intention to pursue a program of change.[51] This came so late in the campaign that he undoubtedly would still have won without the FSA imprimatur. Many of the other 26 ran as candidates for a state farmers' organisation or as rural-oriented Nationalists. Page was already a convert to the idea of a national Country Party. He later wrote that

---

49   Ibid., p. 130; Ellis, *A History of the Australian Country Party*, pp. 47–8. The full text of the platform is reproduced in *The Land*, 29 August 1919, p. 11.
50   Don Aitkin, *The Colonel: A Political Biography of Sir Michael Bruxner*, Australian National University Press, Canberra, 1969, pp. 42–3.
51   Page, *Truant Surgeon*, p. 48. Page here mistakenly refers to endorsement by the AFFO instead, an error he did not make in a 1956 interview with Graham; see Graham, *Formation of the Australian Country Parties*, p. 131.

his opening campaign speech owed much to Falkiner, now running for the Senate, who had called for 'a solid Country Party that will vote as such'.[52] The term Country Party was already well established, though not yet standard; it was in use in New South Wales as early as 1893.[53]

The 1919 election produced a strange set of results. They were indicative of the still formative nature of the Australian party system, especially the lack of a clear focus for the rural protest vote. Out of a House of 75 members, the election returned 30 Nationalists, 26 ALP members, 8 'Farmer-Nationals' endorsed by the Nationalists or farmers' organisations, 3 Liberals from South Australia, 5 VFU representatives, 2 members of the Western Australian FSA and 1 independent Nationalist.[54] This nonetheless amounted to a historic breakthrough for rural political movements at the national level. Page was one of 11 who agreed to a proposal by the member for the Victorian electorate of Grampians, Edmund Jowett, to meet. At their first meeting, on 22 January 1920 in Parliament House, Melbourne, they unanimously resolved 'that this party shall be known as the Australian Country Party, and shall act independently of all other political organisations'.[55]

All of the 11 had gone to the election without the backing of a dedicated party structure or platform other than what was provided by a farmers' organisation. They had few agreed policies beyond generalities concerning support for rural Australia, cutting taxes and opposing socialism. Yet the press reported that the new Country Party expected 'to be able to exert a considerable influence on the Government's actions, especially in such matters as the proper exercise of economy in public expenditure'.[56] Although six of the 11 had some parliamentary experience, Page recalled them as 'untried cohorts' who were 'fortified by our political innocence and backed by an indestructible optimism'.[57] His colleagues were: three VFU members, W.G. Gibson, W.C. Hill and Stewart; a Victorian grazier, Jowett; a Victorian dairy farmer, Robert Cook; a Tasmanian newspaper proprietor, William McWilliams; a Western Australian parliamentarian, Harry Gregory; a wheat farmer and former mayor of Perth, John Henry Prowse; a Queensland pastoralist and parliamentarian, Arnold Wienholt;

---

52　Page, *Truant Surgeon*, p. 69.
53　Graham, *Formation of the Australian Country Parties*, p. 57.
54　Ibid., p. 132.
55　Melbourne *Argus*, 23 January 1920, p. 6.
56　Melbourne *Age*, 23 January 1920, p. 7.
57　Page, *Truant Surgeon*, p. 61.

and a New South Wales dairy farmer and pastoralist, Alexander Hay. The only state not represented was South Australia. Page had a near fully national parliamentary network to work with.

Contrary to what is widely assumed today, Page was not their first leader. McWilliams, one of only two with appreciably long parliamentary experience, was chosen to lead on a one-year trial basis with Jowett as his deputy. Page became party secretary and whip. At a meeting in Melbourne in February 1920 the AFFO formally approved the new party styling itself as the Australian Country Party. This federal example encouraged the appearance of state counterparts. By the end of 1920 avowedly rural parties had been established in every state except Tasmania, and those in Victoria and in New South Wales had been consolidated by good showings in state elections. AFFO delegates and Country Party federal parliamentarians met in Sydney in March 1921 where they adopted a platform more reminiscent of Page's own national agenda. This provided for constitutional reform via a convention, subdivision of the states, decentralisation, planned marketing by producers and consumers, and the 'scientific investigation, complete survey and tabulation of the resources' of the nation.[58] But the AFFO still soon became more preoccupied with more conventional issues. Its June 1922 conference focused on new markets for wheat, representation on the Tariff Board, dairy and sugar prices, non-European labour, taxation reform and duty on sulphur.[59]

McWilliams lost the party leadership in April 1921. Page attributed this to the leader's 'increasing tendency to vote against the majority' and added that his own ascension was entirely at the behest of his parliamentary colleagues. He even claimed to have been the only party room member not to vote for a Page leadership.[60] An important factor in his rise within the Country Party was the fluidity of its policies and strategies. The early rural parties – the Progressive Party in New South Wales, the VFU, the federal Country Party and others – were each united only by their generalised fear of rural decline. They attracted and accommodated rural interests ranging from small wheat farmers to town-based professionals and large-scale graziers, all with differing expectations of the new party. Graham described the rural political movement of 1914–19 as characterised by

---

58   Ellis, *A History of the Australian Country Party*, pp. 69–70.
59   *The Land*, 23 June 1922, p. 11.
60   Page, *Truant Surgeon*, p. 66.

'sudden changes of direction, muddled strategies, and confused aims'.[61] The historian W.K. Hancock, in his classic and influential *Australia*, saw the Country Party of the 1920s as 'a coalition of diverse interests'.[62] Supporters espoused causes as varied as new states and soldier settlement, and were divided on orderly marketing and free trade.

Such a formative new party provided just the sort of inclusive political and policy environment that could accommodate Earle Page. So singular a figure would not have been as nearly as successful within a more established party, whether the Nationalists or the ALP. Page also had the advantage of not being identified with any one rural class or producer group, an important element in sustaining his leadership. He was quite distinct from the rural radicals associated with small wheat farming, notably the outspoken and inflexible Stewart, and from wealthier pastoralists such as Jowett. Working day-to-day as an equal partner in a wider movement was not Page's instinctive preference: this was to become evident in his engagement with fellow new staters during the early 1920s.

A string of issues with wide rural appeal helped the Country Party consolidate itself under Page's leadership. In July 1921 the government finally approved the Massy-Greene tariff, named for the Minister for Trade and Customs. This established a broad and high tariff structure as a basis for manufacturing-led development, and was consolidated over the next few years by the Tariff Board's responsiveness to appeals from individual manufacturers for protection. Manufacturing accordingly increased its share of gross domestic product from about 13 per cent to 18 per cent between 1920 and 1931. This marked shift in development policy away from rural industries amounted to a major provocation of country interests. They saw tariffs as affirming the urban bias of the Hughes Government by imposing costs on such capital equipment as reapers, binders and wire.

The new tariff, continuing debates over decontrolling wheat, wool and dairy production, and demands for rural credit for farmers as prices started falling from late 1921 all gave the nascent Country Party a firmer sense of purpose. (Hughes announced in April 1921 that wheat pooling would end – but following some complicated political manoeuvres agreed to

---
61  Graham, *Formation of the Australian Country Parties*, p. 96.
62  W.K. Hancock, *Australia*, Jacaranda Press, Brisbane, 1961 (first published 1930), pp. 200–1.

guarantee voluntary pools formed by the states.) There was also a widely shared belief that parliament had lost control of government expenditure, with the result that high taxation was constricting industry. In a speech to the VFU in Ballarat in September 1922, Page won headlines and coined a resonating phrase by likening the Hughes Government to a burglar and sternly demanding that it 'drop the loot'.[63] The issues that featured in Page's election policy speech of the following month, his first as party leader, mark the growing breadth of his party's interests. They included decentralisation, government expenditure (we are 'the watchdog of the public interest, and a break on waste', said Page), public debt, arbitration, tariffs, rural credits, constitutional reform and the future of wartime marketing arrangements. 'Australia', he said, 'has reached the period in her history where her greatest need is sound government upon an organised plan'.[64]

Another major factor in Page's success is that turbulent relations with the Hughes Government earned him national attention. The early Country Party saw itself as honourable and apolitical – quite unlike how it perceived Prime Minister Hughes. It took pride in its undisciplined, slightly chaotic ways. Consider the following statement by Page soon after he became party leader:

> The Country Party is essentially a party distinct from any other, and decides to remain so, because it is suspicious of the influences behind the other parties. It has its own organisation, its own offices, its own party rooms; but has not a signed party discipline that compels its representatives to vote for principles they disapprove of simply because another party or the Government advocates them. It supports good government and good legislation. It does not seek office, but it will not refuse to take the responsibility for its actions if called upon to do so.[65]

Page as party leader at once launched attacks on Hughes. He benefited from the prime minister's instinctive habit of publicly counterattacking, recalling that 'within six months his attitude had made me one of the best-known members of the House and recognised throughout Australia almost as readily as himself'.[66] Page's 1922 election speech assailed the prime

---

63  Page, *Truant Surgeon*, p. 84.
64  *Sydney Morning Herald*, 27 October 1922, p. 9. Page explained in his memoirs that rural credits were foremost to assist farmers when their sales are spread over a long period; see *Truant Surgeon*, p. 119.
65  Sydney *Sun*, 17 April 1921, p. 5.
66  Page, *Truant Surgeon*, p. 57.

minister as a breaker of promises with a 'total disregard of the financial position of the country' and made veiled references to the ex-Laborite who must surely be behind the creeping socialism and extravagance enveloping the nation.[67]

The political uncertainty of the time made the stance of Page and his party a matter of national significance. Following the 1919 election, the Hughes Government did not quite hold a secure majority in the House of Representatives. With the support of four 'Farmer-Nationalists', as Page called them, the new Country Party held the balance of power between the Nationalists and the ALP, a position he found 'both exhilarating and sobering'.[68] The Country Party's search for a political strategy at first appeared to be a choice between a coalition with the Nationalists or preserving its independence by instead freely bargaining for concessions from either larger party. It settled on trying to influence the government without bringing it down, Labor being a worse alternative. But mixed messages that gave the strong impression of unpredictability enhanced the Country Party's influence. Page publicly refused to grant Hughes immunity from a vote of no confidence and even pointedly declined to provide any guarantees when the prime minister went abroad on official business.

Uncertainty was heightened by the Country Party's unpreparedness to vote solidly in the House. A motion on 19 October 1921 to reduce the size of the 1921–22 Budget came within a single vote of defeating the government. Hughes was saved by Alexander Hay deciding not to vote with his Country Party colleagues as he feared a Labor government would result. It is a measure of the Country Party's still formative political skills that most of its MPs did not share Hay's realisation that they were effectively moving a censure motion.[69] It also appears that the dissident Tasmanian Nationalist MP George Bell accidentally missed the Division in the House as he happened to be visiting the Senate at the time: Page suspected he had been literally led astray by his party colleagues.

Finally, the hyperactive Page established a widely recognised persona with a special strategic place of his own. Unpredictable as the new Country Party was, most of its MPs' contributions in parliament were limited to

---

67  *Sydney Morning Herald*, 27 October 1922, p. 9.
68  Page, *Truant Surgeon*, p. 62.
69  See Hay's own account in the *Sydney Morning Herald*, 8 December 1922, p. 12.

workaday matters. Amid prosaic debates on returned servicemen, tariffs, expenditure on a new capital city and public service salaries, Page had an unusually broad and clear sense of direction. Page's speeches read well in Hansard and helped make him the effective leader of debate on many national issues. His speech to the House of 7 April 1921 in response to the Massy-Greene tariff is a fine example of his pushing discussion in new directions. He only briefly addressed the agricultural marketing issues then preoccupying most of his colleagues, saying more about amenities in the countryside that would aid decentralisation, targeted tariffs to support selected industries, 'thoroughly comprehensive power schemes throughout the Continent', railway freight rates that were constricting industry in country towns, the 'degeneration and ill-health' of city dwellers, greater constitutional powers for the Commonwealth and 'subdividing the present big states'.[70] Although cautiously worded by Page to match his status as the new leader of his party, this speech is highly reminiscent of the expansive national vision of August 1917.

## Regionalism and decentralisation: The basis of Page's vision

During this first term in parliament, Page expressed his policy persona foremost through his commitment to regionalism and decentralisation. The shift of industry and population away from big cities, and the related regionalisation of government structures, remained his most fundamental policy goals after he had been elevated to the Country Party leadership. This was far more than an incarnation of the yeomanry–closer settlement ideal that already had a long history in Australia. Summarising his case for new states in 1924, Page said that the 'higher civic spirit' arising from giving people 'complete power of controlling their own local development' would 'provide opportunities for the mobilisation of the local knowledge of local resources which do not exist under the present large states of Australia'.[71] He stressed that this should not merely be an extension of existing local government, but rather the 'creation of a new self-governing administration' not beholden to a distant capital city.[72]

---

70  *Commonwealth Parliamentary Debates*, 7 April 1921, pp. 7282, 7284.
71  Page's evidence to the Cohen Royal Commission published in Earl Page, *The New State in Northern New South Wales, Resources, Finance, Government: Statement of the Case*, Northern New State Movement, Tamworth, 1924, p. 2.
72  Ibid., p. 26.

In presenting decentralisation and regionalism so ideally, Page was undoubtedly projecting his personal memories of the Grafton community onto the entire nation. On new states, as on almost any given issue, Page had broader goals than most of his peers. He treated each proposed new state, including northern New South Wales, as a possible step towards a nationwide network of self-governing bodies. Most new staters were reacting to a specific local grievance and so sought a simple two-way breakup of their state to create a single new entity, such as a New England or a North Queensland. Page signalled his preference for considerably smaller and multiple entities by his pointed use of such terms as 'federal units', 'local subdivisions', 'provinces' or 'small self-governing areas', rather than new states.[73] He also laced his statements on regionalism with populist references to how these new entities would relieve the 'grossest extravagance both in national and State affairs', such as through leaner local legislatures.[74] Page's regionalist and decentralist vision animated much else that he pressed for as a new parliamentarian, including hydroelectricity and constitutional reform.

Page was also an early advocate of a link between decentralisation and the provision of the social amenities and infrastructure needed to sustain rural populations. He used his fresh memories of country doctoring in arguing that the difficulty of retaining settlers on the land was as much due to lack of basic facilities as to the failure to pay a fair price for their produce. In his first term in parliament, he portrayed railways as much as hydroelectricity as his favoured means of easing 'the monotony and drudgery of country life', drawing on his observations in North America.[75] Even after telephones were installed in his South Grafton practice, it remained torturously difficult to contact patients in outlying areas. In one case, it took two days for word to reach him by horse and buggy of a critically ill patient in the Guy Fawkes district 130 kilometres from Grafton and the same amount of time for Page to arrive, by which time she was dead.[76]

Unusually among federal parliamentarians of his time, Page welcomed plans for Canberra. He interpreted the new national capital as a model for decentralisation based on small cities.[77] Conversely, he saw centralisation

---

73  See for example Page's August 1917 speech, p. 3, his article in the *Daily Examiner* of 16 February 1918, p. 3, and his 1919 election speech as reported in the *Daily Examiner* of 23 October 1919, p. 3.
74  *Daily Examiner*, 23 October 1919, p. 3.
75  *Commonwealth Parliamentary Debates*, 19 November 1920, p. 6760.
76  Page, *Truant Surgeon*, p. 31.
77  See for example an untitled typed note at EPP, folder 1624, undated but appears to be pre-1927; also Page's comments about Canberra's founding in *Truant Surgeon*, Chapter 18.

in big cities as the root of much evil and was prepared to state this bluntly, if a little wordily at times. E.C. Mumford, secretary of the Taxpayers' Association of New South Wales, must have been taken aback by a Page letter of February 1921 informing him that:

> your Association will never get anywhere except it starts at the root of the problem, and the fundamental difference which has caused Australian development to lead to the possession of a series of states in which the capital is practically one-half of the total, is due, in my opinion, to the operation, first, of the unwieldy size of the states, which contributes most largely to the development of the professional politician, and the embarkation into government enterprises which gives to that politician enormous and uncontrolled patronage at his disposal.[78]

This all amounted to a remarkable personal vision of Australian governance cast in spatial terms to achieve social and economic ends. There are three intertwined specific themes here: decentralisation, nationwide regionalisation of governance and creation of new states. Although the first two are the more fundamental, with new states essentially Page's means to them, new statism was his second most important political platform during his early years in parliament, after the Country Party itself. It was also vitally helpful to the early Country Party that, lacking its own strong formal organisation, drew upon new statism and related rural-based civic movements.

From a twenty-first-century perspective, the new state cause may seem outlandish. Yet in the early 1920s, it was a very serious issue indeed, supported by a powerful mix of intellectual and popular support. V.C. Thompson's *New State Magazine* ran maps of the nation divided into an array of new states and territories, and cartoons portrayed each big Australian city as an insatiably greedy top-hatted toff, perhaps influenced by Labor Party iconography. Advocates drew on long-standing resentment of the urban concentration of public works and social services. Persistent demand for new states was 'practically unique' to Australia due to the internal diversity of the larger states and the continuing sharpness of contrast between a few big cities and a sparsely settled countryside.[79] Also, Australia's system of government has long accorded only a minor role to local councils as against that of the metropolitan-based state governments.

---

78  Page to Mumford, 24 February 1921, Earle Page papers, UNE Archives, A180, box 1, folder 1.
79  R.S. Parker, 'Why new states?', in R.S. Parker, J. Macdonald Holmes, J.P. Belshaw and H.V. Evatt, *New States for Australia*, Australian Institute of Political Science, Sydney, 1955, p. 8; see also R.G. Neale, 'New States Movement', *Australian Quarterly*, vol. 22, no. 3, September 1950.

CANTANKEROUS OLD GENT: What, you want to set up in business on your own account? You'll make a mess of it, my boy!

DETERMINED YOUNG CHAP: I'll risk that. At anyrate I shan't have your finger in all my affairs.

**Figure 6: Sydney and the North, *New State Magazine*, June 1923.**
Source: Cartoon by J.C. Bancks.

Most accounts of new state movements portray them as products of commonplace resentments about government resources. This does not do justice to the deeper reasoning of thinkers like Page. Since Page saw new states as steps towards Australia-wide regionalism, he encouraged advocates to campaign as a united movement working to a national agenda. 'The new state movement is not a local movement', he insisted in June 1924.[80] Supporters of a national approach were usually policy-oriented intellectuals such as Bland and the barrister and constitutional lawyer John Latham. New statism was also a major basis of early challenges to the fundamental wisdom of the Constitution of the still young Commonwealth.

There was considerable variation in the strength of specific new state movements. When Page entered public life, the best organised was that in his native northern New South Wales. It remained so over the next several decades, partly due to the strategic leadership he provided. (It was often called the New England movement, although it included the north coastal region.) Similar movements persisted, to varying degrees, in the Riverina, the Monaro, western New South Wales, and central and northern Queensland. New statism was weaker in the more compact Victoria and Tasmania, and in South Australia and Western Australia it was constrained by the paucity of population outside the capital cities. Exceptions were short-lived movements on the Western Australian goldfields in the 1890s and later in the same state's south-west.

Decentralisation, regionalisation and new statism together form a long, complex story that waxed and waned throughout Page's career. While a true believer, he nevertheless suspended his new state campaigning whenever he needed to instead give priority to the Country Party's coalition with its urban-based partner. But his personal commitment never dissipated, signalled by the alacrity with which he would seize an opportunity when success appeared feasible. After the Great War, there emerged two main schools of thought on reorganising governance to implement regionalism. One proposed a unitary system under which all sovereign power would lie with a national government that delegated authority to regional governmental units at its own pleasure. But true new state advocates invariably favoured a genuine federal system in which sovereign regional entities were guaranteed a high degree of autonomy. They were very conscious of the distinction between regional*ism* that enabled local political control, and a nominal regional*isation* based on a top-down system that merely delegated to regions. Page agreed that it was critically important that regions have sufficient authority to guide their own development.

---

80  Dubbo *Western Age*, 27 June 1924, p. 2.

Page welcomed support for his cause from whatever source, including from across the party divide. The ALP rivalled the early Country Party in perceiving deficiencies in Australian federalism, but with the fundamental difference of proposing a national government fully empowered to implement the ALP's wider program. From 1918 the replacement of state governments with regional authorities beholden to the Commonwealth featured at ALP conferences. In 1920 the ALP issued a pamphlet dividing Australia (with Papua–New Guinea) into 31 provincial legislatures, all entirely dependent on the national government for revenue.[81] Labor support was thus of limited use to most bona fide new staters. Yet Page managed both to condemn the ALP proposals as supporting unification of the wrong sort and to welcome them as an affirmation of his own views. In a November 1920 letter to the *Daily Examiner*, he cast them as evidence of 'a widespread awakening to the necessity shown by our new state propaganda of alterations of the present state boundaries'.[82]

Page's regionalism and decentralisation raised obvious tensions that detracted from his effectiveness as an advocate. Foremost was his continued insistence on a strong central government and consequent difficulty in defining a suitable balance with his autonomous federal units. In his maiden speech to parliament in March 1920, Page proposed the Commonwealth's 'complete control of all national activities', only to be queried by a Labor interjector as to why he did not support outright unification.[83] For decades, Page's stance has understandably puzzled scholars. In 1950, R.G. Neale miscast him as being close to the ALP's stance on a strong central government that delegated to regions.[84] In 2005, A.J. Brown commented that the August 1917 speech illustrated 'the mysterious way in which Earle Page held to both unification and new states as a goal'.[85]

Characteristically, Page was not overly troubled by this evident contradiction. A strong central government suited his deep-seated inclination to impose his own agenda. Page's attempts to resolve this were only stated in the broadest of terms. In October 1923 he spoke to a new state convention in Rockhampton of a national government that

---

81   Ellis, *New Australian States*, pp. 140–2; *New State Magazine*, August 1921, pp. 4–5.
82   *Daily Examiner*, 8 November 1920, p. 3. (This page is missing from Trove but a copy of the letter is in the Earle Page papers, UNE Archives, A180, box 1, folder 1.)
83   *Commonwealth Parliamentary Debates*, 4 March 1920, pp. 195, 196.
84   Neale, 'New States Movement', pp. 22–3.
85   A.J. Brown, 'The constitution we were meant to have', p. 52.

was 'able to plan, but will not be able to execute the details of the plan', and by concentrating purely on 'high policy' would leave 'the spade work of development and settlement' to 'local self-governing authorities'.[86] Whether Earle Page – schemer, planner, driver – would in practice have sat back in a national government to give local authorities such freedom remains decidedly doubtful.

Demands for new states recurred over decades, suggesting a long-term underpinning of regional and community sentiment that intellectual activists like Page, Drummond, Thompson and Ellis could draw on. Even if new states were always improbable, the considerable emotional energy they generated reflected some deep-seated perennials of Australian life – rural protest based on a keen sense of equality in entitlement, awareness of the burden of geographic isolation, local patriotism, and ready assumptions about a nexus between government and economic development. This all gave Page a receptive platform outside the political mainstream for most of his career. But he was to face a major challenge in his attempts during the 1920s and early 1930s to unite inherently localised new state activism into a nationwide force capable of establishing his federal units across Australia. Even Page, with his unique standing among new state activists as a major national figure, would remain strongly identified with the north-east of New South Wales.

## Page's national leadership of new statism: His rallying cause 1920–23

The early 1920s were the heyday of new statism. This provided Page, as a rising new MP, with a ready rallying point for attempting to instil his spatial concepts of regionalism and decentralisation into national policy. The issue passed through two distinct stages: a strong revival in 1920–23 associated with the emergence of the Country Party, but then unexpected failure before the 1924–25 Cohen Royal Commission into new states that was convened by the New South Wales Government. Against a background of continuing anxiety about accelerating urbanisation – the Australian metropolitan population grew by over 37 per cent between

---

86  Earle Page, *New States: Why They Are Necessary in Australia – Speech by Dr Earle Page*, delivered at the New State Convention, Rockhampton, October 1923, Northern New South Wales New State Movement, Tamworth, 1923, p. 3.

1921 and 1933, the rural by 20 per cent and the urban provincial by a mere 8 per cent – energetic new proponents vied among themselves and with Page for attention.[87]

Northern New South Wales became the nation's driver of new statism. Although the movement claimed to be non-political, it was strongly linked to the upper echelons of the Country Party for all to see. In addition to Page, prominent supporters included Drummond (a Progressive and Country Party MLA 1920–49, and MHR for New England 1949–63), Michael Bruxner (a Progressive and Country Party MLA 1920–62, and state party leader 1922–25 and 1932–58), P.P. Abbott (Country Party MHR for New England 1913–19, and a Senator 1925–29), Thompson (Country Party MHR for New England 1922–40) and Sommerlad (a Country Party MLC 1932–52). Thompson's organisational contribution shifted the movement's hub to his home town of Tamworth. In January 1920 he published a series of newspaper articles on new states that later appeared as a booklet with a foreword by Page.[88] In March 1920 a New State Press League was established at a local newspaper conference at Glen Innes that Thompson organised.[89] Two months later, over 5,000 people attended the inauguration of the campaign in Tamworth called by the local council.[90] At Glen Innes in August, the Tamworth and Inverell New State leagues formed a united Northern New State Movement, with Abbott as president and Thompson as general secretary.[91] Thompson took temporary leave from editing the *Northern Daily Leader* to devote himself full time to the cause and to personally produce *New State Magazine*.

This all proved more durable than the short-lived 1915 Grafton-based movement. New statism now had the dedicated Thompson active on the ground and the firm support of the local press, encompassing a larger, more viable region. Perhaps, too, it was propelled by the release of aspirations bottled up by the immense distraction of war. Page spoke later of his entering parliament at a crucial 'psychological moment to get

---

87   Heather Radi, '1920–29', in Frank Crowley (ed.), *A New History of Australia*, William Heinemann Australia, Melbourne, 1974, p. 359.
88   The booklet was Victor C. Thompson, *The New State, Embracing Northern New South Wales: A Series of Articles Published in the Daily Observer, Tamworth, and Addenda*, Daily Observer, Tamworth, 1920.
89   Ellis, *New Australian States*, pp. 152–3.
90   *Sydney Morning Herald*, 27 May 1920, p. 10; Harman, 'New State agitation in northern New South Wales', p. 30.
91   Ellis, *New Australian States*, p. 153.

results' when 'the First World War was just over'.[92] As major causes for the early Country Party, new statism and decentralisation briefly provided him with a more comfortable fit with his party peers than at any other stage of his career.

Page provided new statism with strategic leadership. *New State Magazine*, to which Page contributed the foreword to the inaugural issue, records how he tried to rally the new state faithful across the nation. He addressed the May 1921 meeting of the Riverina movement and travelled on to Western Australia twice that same year where he spoke to the Great Southern New State League in Albany.[93] He was not alone in this nationwide proselytising – Thompson accompanied him to Queensland, Drummond went to the Riverina and Bruxner travelled to Western Australia – but Page held a unique status as leader of the federal Country Party. New statism also enlivened Page's public jousting with the prime minister. Unable to get the existing states to act, Page and other activists turned to trying to amend section 124 of the Constitution to shift the decisive say on new states from state parliaments to local referendums. Over 1920–22 the parliamentary Country Party called repeatedly for a constitutional convention as a prelude to a referendum on this at the 1922 election. Page wanted every state divided into four electorates that would each provide three convention delegates, thereby producing a northern New South Wales delegation.[94]

Prime Minister Hughes promised action, then dallied. In November 1921 his government introduced a Bill for the election of convention delegates from House of Representatives seats, but withdrew this following strong and varying objections from MPs of all three major parties. During a May 1922 visit to Grafton, Hughes flickeringly raised hopes by commenting that 'if by a New State you mean the opportunity of helping yourselves I am with you to the end'. The visit was cut short when Hughes, 'proud of his horsemanship', asked Page to help provide him with a mount, only to break a collarbone when his horse reared and to find himself as Dr Page's patient.[95] Hughes almost immediately denied that his comments meant he supported a new state. Two months later, he concluded that the

---

92  'Australian Country Party Complimentary Dinner to Sir Earle Page', EPP, folder 2358.
93  *New State Magazine*, July 1921, p. 17, and August 1921, p. 27.
94  Ellis, *New Australian States*, p. 162.
95  Page, *Truant Surgeon*, pp. 74–5.

Commonwealth could not act ahead of state government support. This reversal contributed decisively to Page's determination following the 1922 election to remove Hughes from office.

The new state movement benefited greatly from the growing public reputation of the new member for Cowper. Although Thompson remained prime organiser, he never matched Page as a strategist or for prominence. This became central to public perceptions of Page. Newspapers in April 1920 wrote of him as 'the possible future Prime Minister of Pacifica', formed out of the New South Wales north.[96] Hancock called Page 'the apostle' of the new state movement.[97] Other major political figures who engaged with new statism were dabblers by comparison. Premier Ted Theodore of Queensland, for example, proposed in 1922 the creation of new states but only after unification had been achieved, in line with ALP policy.[98] There was a parliamentary consensus in Queensland that the state was too big, but less agreement on how to rectify this. A few prominent non-parliamentary figures, such as the Anglican Bishop Radford of Goulburn, approached Page's breadth of vision, but lacked his persistence and national profile. There are hints of tension over Page's prominence, such as a short but sharp reference in *New State Magazine* to his not being part of the movement's rank and file.[99] Thompson publicly attributed the formation of the Northern New State Movement to the efforts of his newspaper, and pointedly referred to Page as instead covering the federal parliament.[100] Page preferred proselytising and high-level political manoeuvring to the tedious detail of organising and fundraising.

Page's strategy included an ambitious attempt to organise a national new state movement. This was first seriously signalled at the April 1921 convention of the Northern New South Wales Movement at Armidale, which also attracted delegates from as far as central Queensland and Albany in Western Australia.[101] Page took a leading role at the important All-Australia Conference on new states held at Albury in July 1922. This was the first time that new state enthusiasts had met on an expressly national basis, and it was used by Page to endorse a broad strategy. Delegates came from northern New South Wales, the Riverina, Queensland and

---

96   Such as the *Kyogle Examiner*, 28 April 1920, p. 4.
97   Hancock, *Australia*, p. 201.
98   Ellis, *New Australian States*, p. 172.
99   *New State Magazine*, August 1921, p. 30.
100 Thompson, *The New State*, pp. 48–50.
101 Ellis, *New Australian States*, pp. 154–5.

the Western Australian goldfields. Attendance also reflected intellectual interest in decentralisation by including the Decentralisation League of Victoria; the Australian Legion, a Melbourne-based body that endorsed the Country Party and counted Latham as a member; and the Sydney-based Australian New States League.

Page led the convention's discussions on strategy. As a constitutional convention now seemed doubtful, he suggested that all new state organisations could bring the issue before their respective state parliaments so as to test the possibility of success under section 124. The anticipated negative results would help clear the way for seeking a referendum to shift the basis of approval to local votes.[102] But Page was not in full control of proceedings. His proposal that a preliminary convention of 'skilled technical advisers' produce tabulated data prior to any constitutional convention was defeated, presumably for fear of delegates being effectively sidelined. (A heavy reliance on data was a feature of much of Page's new state proselytising.) The conference instead appointed Page as president of the 10-member executive of a new All-Australian New States movement.[103] This body seems to have done little beyond proposing new state boundaries and making overtures to the ALP, but the Albury convention did help spark debate that led to the only occasion that the New South Wales Parliament endorsed a new state. In September 1922 it agreed to a motion moved by Bruxner supporting a northern new state but only after the Nationalist Secretary for Mines and Forests, F.A. Chaffey, a new state sympathiser from the north, had this amended to focus on the federal government and the still hoped-for constitutional convention.

The wider Northern New South Wales Movement attached greater importance than did Page to building what Thompson dubbed 'a people's movement'.[104] It circulated petitions, organised public meetings and tried to build a hierarchical structure around a central executive, district councils and local leagues.[105] By October 1921, 197 local leagues had been created.[106] But popular support fluctuated with specific local grievances. Protest such as over the lack of a Tablelands to north coast

---

102 *New State Magazine*, September 1922, p. 4.
103 Ibid., pp. 5–7; see also Harman, 'New State agitation in northern New South Wales', p. 32; Adelaide *Register*, 11 June 1923, p. 11.
104 *New State Magazine*, November 1921, p. 16.
105 V.C. Thompson, 'Why I think the New State Movement is a winner', *New State Magazine*, July 1921, pp. 4–5.
106 Farrell, 'Bones for the Growling Dog?', p. 134.

railway provided too narrow a base to sustain interest. In 1921 a petition expected to gather about 200,000 signatures instead managed an estimated 30–40,000. According to William Green, a former mayor of Tamworth who had dropped out of the new state movement, a 1922 appeal to raise £25,000 for a fighting fund generated less than £500. The number of local leagues had dwindled to 12 by March 1923, probably as they had long since served their immediate purpose of electing delegates to the 1921 Armidale convention.[107]

## Page creates a power base: Forging the coalition with the Nationalists

The 1923 creation of a coalition between the Country Party and the ruling Nationalists elevated Page to the forefront of government and raised his hopes of reordering the nation. Page's decisive role in creating this lasting feature of Australian politics, by itself, secures for him an important place in political history. It also earned him a unique standing within the Country Party by identifying him with a political strategy that helped ensure its long-term survival.

Page sensed early an opportunity to benefit from Nationalist Party disunity. He signalled to its growing anti-Hughes element the possibility of a mutually productive alliance. In mid-1922 he spoke of how the Nationalists' 'more sober element was getting very tired of the thinly disguised socialism and the theatrical posturing and extravagance of the Prime Minister'. Hence 'the Country Party must with the assistance of some party whose ideals were framed on the same lines, get into power, otherwise the Commonwealth Parliament would decay and would not rise to its destiny'.[108]

Although Page was central to the creation of a coalition at the national level, he was more chief proponent than originator of this strategy. There was a precedent at the Commonwealth level in the form of the Reid–McLean Government of 1904–5 that shared out portfolios between Free Traders led by George Reid and conservative Protectionists led by Allan McLean. The Western Australian Country Party joined an anti-Labor

---

107 Ibid., pp. 117–18, 134, 158.
108 *Townsville Daily Bulletin*, 26 May 1922, p. 4; Melbourne *Argus*, 15 June 1922, p. 9.

coalition as early as June 1917. Federally, Hughes suggested a coalition in November 1921 in the wake of the parliamentary vote on the Budget that nearly toppled him, part of a wider offer that also proposed massive cuts to Commonwealth expenditure. In September 1922 the president of the Western Australian Primary Producers' Association (formerly the FSA), Alex Monger, became the first Country Party leader to propose specific terms for the Country Party's willingness to continue the state coalition it had joined in June 1917. This included demands that Country Party representation in Cabinet be proportional to its numerical strength in parliament, and that it hold all portfolios directly affecting primary industries.[109]

Hughes again offered a federal coalition in the run-up to the December 1922 election. This election resulted in the Country Party winning 14 seats to the Nationalists' 26 and Labor's 29. Now unambiguously holding the balance of power, the parliamentary Country Party met at Parliament House, Melbourne, on 16 January 1923. It, at first, had no agreed strategy other than a vague preparedness to consider an understanding with the Nationalists provided that Hughes quit the ministry altogether. The Nationalists met the same day and delivered a message to the Country Party proposing that their respective party leaders meet on 22 January. Page was so keen on a modus operandi that he suggested they instead meet the following afternoon. The Nationalists appointed a negotiating team of six that included Hughes and Stanley Bruce. Page was one of three Country Party negotiators, along with Stewart and W.G. Gibson, but his own account makes clear that the negotiations were predominantly his own show.

Page kept the exact nature of any Country Party–Nationalist collaboration an open issue. The Country Party was prepared to support a wholly Nationalist government 'with a policy generally approved by the Country Party', or else could join a coalition that shared out portfolios. Hughes in canvassing options indicated that he did not entirely reject the possibility of a Country Party–led government with Page as prime minister, possibly as he thought this would not last long. Although newspaper reports suggested that Page was initially interested in this, as the negotiations continued he and the Country Party instead increasingly favoured joining a coalition with the Nationalists.[110] Page's terms for

---

109 Graham, *Formation of the Australian Country Parties*, pp. 179, 215.
110 Ibid., pp. 188–90; Page, *Truant Surgeon*, pp. 91–2, 95.

a coalition insisted on a separate identity for the Country Party and such a 'distribution of portfolios as will give the Country Party power as great as its responsibility'.[111] He was clearly keen to acquire a say in power, and worked away at the Nationalists to make this acceptable to the Country Party by dropping Hughes from the front bench. (In the terminology of the time, Page spoke of a 'composite government' to refer to what is today commonly called a coalition. To him, a composite government was one in which the participating parties retained their distinct identities, as against a coalition in which they were effectively merged.)

Centrally involved in the Country Party's manoeuvrings was John Latham, who had just been elected as an Independent Union Liberal MP. Latham attended Country Party meetings, primarily as he could not on personal and policy grounds countenance sitting as a Nationalist while Hughes, who he had unhappily accompanied at the 1919 Paris Peace Conference, still held office. This is a further indicator of the openness of the early Country Party. Page recalled this 'honoured guest' providing 'the benefit of his practical wisdom and his sage legal advice', motivated by an attitude to Hughes even 'more virulent than our own'.[112] Ellis, a witness to these events, noted how the Country Party's exchanges with the Nationalists owed much to 'Latham's clarity of style and forceful expression'.[113] Latham only joined the Nationalists in November 1925 and became attorney-general the following month. He continued advising the Country Party, including on the constitutional dimensions of new states, before serving as Opposition leader in 1929–31 and subsequently as chief justice of the High Court.

Page's detailed account in *Truant Surgeon* of the negotiations is vague about his own ambitions, despite his otherwise very evident determination for a major say in government. Negotiations and exchanges of letters went on inconclusively and by the end of January had reached deadlock, mainly due to Hughes's refusal to resign. Page then proceeded to release all the written exchanges for public scrutiny. The press warned that if the Nationalists and the Country Party could not reach an agreement there

---

111 From Page's 'Memorandum for Nationalist Party Managers', 24 January 1923, reproduced in Page, *Truant Surgeon*, p. 388.
112 Ibid., p. 90.
113 Ellis, *A History of the Australian Country Party*, p. 94.

was a possibility of a minority Labor government: the hostility between Hughes and Page should not be allowed to lead to such 'a travesty of government by the people'.[114]

Hughes finally resigned on 2 February. Page proceeded to deal directly with Bruce, marking the start of a working relationship that became central to his career. Bruce had only been a minister since December 1921 when he was unexpectedly appointed treasurer. Prior to entering parliament, he was managing director of a Melbourne importing firm. As a wounded veteran – of the British army at Gallipoli – he made such an impression at recruitment meetings that the Nationalists invited him to stand for Flinders. One of Bruce's major strengths was the contrast that his measured, stately demeanour presented to Hughes's intensity and abrasiveness. Bruce rejected the idea of a Nationalist government supported by the Country Party but readily agreed to a coalition as a more stable option.

On 6 February, Page arrived in Melbourne to negotiate with Bruce on the terms of a coalition. With Hughes gone, progress was swift and a result was announced late on 7 February. The formal agreement was set down in Bruce's spindly handwriting and released the following day. It is one of Australia's most important political documents and is preserved in the Earle Page papers in the National Library of Australia. The two parties were to retain their separate identities and the Country Party would hold five portfolios in a ministry of 11 members. Page would take precedence after only the prime minister. Not unimportantly, the new government was to be called the Bruce–Page Ministry. The agreement allocated specific portfolios between the parties but did not set out any agreed policies, a sign that the two leaders were comfortable with each other's stances.[115] Ellis later wrote that Page 'regretted' being unable to consult all Country Party members.[116]

When the Country Party party room belatedly met on 9 February, Page came under attack for not consulting it earlier. Party uncertainty about a coalition reflected a fear of loss of autonomy, the fate of some state parties such as in Queensland. Just 14 months earlier, the Progressive Party in New South Wales had split over the issue of coalition with the

---

114 *Sydney Morning Herald*, 17 January 1923, p. 12.
115 Graham, *Formation of the Australian Country Parties*, p. 193.
116 Ellis, *A History of the Australian Country Party*, pp. 98–9.

state Nationalists. Page countered that the terms of the coalition clearly provided for a distinct Country Party – indeed, this was their first article. Although two federal members later told the House that they had not wanted a coalition, at the time the party room satisfied itself with a motion on maintaining its identity.

It was clear to most that Page had secured a very good deal indeed, one that gave the Country Party nearly half of all ministerial positions. As Graham later wrote, 'nothing showed his skill in leadership as much as his efforts, in the months following the formation of the coalition, to persuade the Country Party movement to accept it'.[117] This forging of a coalition is further affirmation of Page's resolve to achieve substantial change, not just to lead a marginal protest party. 'We were determined to use our opportunities to the full', he later said.[118] As it became clear that the coalition constituted a balanced formula for maintaining the Country Party's independence while giving it great political influence, state country parties began exploring coalitions of their own, notably the New South Wales Progressives. Victoria remained the exception, where VFU radicals challenged the coalition concept for years to come.

Transition to a Bruce–Page Government proceeded remarkably smoothly, a tribute to the two men's desire to build a successful government. Page's choice of the Treasury portfolio for himself no doubt reflected the priority his party gave to reining in public expenditure (and was one of the portfolios he proposed for the Country Party when Hughes mooted a coalition 15 months earlier).[119] In his first speech to the House as treasurer, he stressed the need for the government 'by its handling of the finances and by its general administration … to improve the public credit in order to permit of the conversion on the best possible basis for Australia of the huge war loans that are to fall due during the ordinary life of this parliament'.[120]

---

117  Graham, *Formation of the Australian Country Parties*, p. 193.
118  Page, *Truant Surgeon*, p. 102.
119  Davey, *Ninety Not Out*, p. 21.
120  *Commonwealth Parliamentary Debates*, 8 March 1923, p. 243.

**Figure 7: The new Bruce–Page Ministry at its swearing-in ceremony, 1923.**
Standing (left to right): W.G. Gibson, Percy Stewart, Eric Bowden, Austin Chapman, R.V. Wilson, L. Atkinson; seated; G.F. Pearce, Bruce, Lord Forster (governor-general), Page, Littleton Groom. Missing is Thomas Crawford.
Source: Courtesy of the National Library of Australia, (nla.gov.au/nla.obj-136658156), photograph by T. Humphrey & Co.

Page's role over the next six and a half years as treasurer and de facto deputy prime minister gave him a say in most major decisions of the Bruce–Page Government. His conventional budgetary responsibilities were among the least distinctive of his achievements. There was little sense of demand management fiscal policy during this period. Governments did not feel that they could readily reduce unemployment, and public expectations were correspondingly limited. One historian, writing at the high point of Keynesianism, considered Page's budget speeches 'more like a Chairman's address to the annual meeting of a large public company than the nation's principal document on economic policy'.[121] But Page was the first Commonwealth Treasurer to introduce budgets on a regular basis and early in the financial year, and he also improved the form of budget papers. Page himself said that previously budget items had been

---

121  Boris Schedvin, *Australia and the Great Depression: A Study of Economic Development and Policy in the 1920s and 1930s*, Sydney University Press, Sydney, 1970, p. 88.

largely lumped together into uninformative totals, with the result that 'public criticisms tended to be directed towards the total amount rather than to the diverse items', which was 'not conducive to intelligent public surveillance of government expenditures'.[122]

Two years before becoming treasurer, Page had called deficit budgeting 'a Rake's Progress'.[123] Page's first budgets reflected his oft-stated commitment to relief from taxes, especially for primary producers, and to smaller government. They provided for reductions to land and company taxes, a single collecting agency for Commonwealth and state income taxes, a higher income tax exemption level, an expanded averaging system for income tax on primary producers (helping them manage profit and loss fluctuations), widened deductions for farm improvements and pest control, and reduced postage charges. His first budget speech added the need for a national insurance scheme. Page described existing welfare as failing to:

> remove that sense of cruel insecurity which haunts great masses of our people through the whole of their life – the fear that accident or temporary sickness may break up their home, the continual fear of unemployment due to causes entirely beyond their control, and finally the fear of a destitute old age after a life of toil.[124]

Attempts to introduce national insurance were to feature in Page's parliamentary career, especially at the end of both the Bruce–Page and the Lyons governments.

Most importantly, Page drew on his policy visions to become the first Commonwealth Treasurer to explore the wider possibilities of this office. When visiting London in 1925 he invited the British science administrator Frank Heath to visit Australia and report on imperial cooperation in research. This led to the replacement the following year of the Institute of Science and Industry with the Council for Scientific and Industrial Research (CSIR), funded by a special trust fund so as to help long-term research planning. Another important initiative was banking reform that reflected Page's hopes for a central bank 'with power to control and save shaky banks and restore them to solvency without destruction of

---

122  Page, *Truant Surgeon*, p. 135; see also J.R. Nethercote, 'Liberalism, nationalism and coalition 1910–29', in J.R. Nethercote (ed.), *Liberalism and the Australian Federation*, The Federation Press, Leichhardt, 2001, p. 130.
123  Ellis, *A History of the Australian Country Party*, p. 64.
124  *Commonwealth Parliamentary Debates*, 26 July 1923, p. 1653.

their customers', an echo of his childhood memories of the 1893 bank smash.[125] When Page became treasurer, national policy on banking and currency was still very basic. The Commonwealth only started issuing coinage in 1909, and the Commonwealth Bank was created in 1911 purely as a trading bank in competition with the private banks. Concerns grew about the autocratic powers of the Commonwealth Bank's governor, its failure to provide credit for primary industry and its not acting as a central bank.

After the war, banks were unable to transfer to Australia funds they held in London due to a British embargo on the export of gold and the refusal of the Australian Note Issue Board, an autonomous department of the Commonwealth Bank, to buy London funds and issue notes against them for fear of sparking inflation. The tying up of bank funds in London limited the provision of advances to finance Australian exporters. In his October 1922 election policy speech, Page spoke of placing the Commonwealth Bank under an independent board that would reorient it towards supporting national development, especially rural projects including hydroelectricity and rural credits for primary producers. The new directors would be 'men of the broadest outlook', empowered to make the bank's resources available 'for development of the primary and secondary industries in Australia'.[126] Legislation in 1924 duly created an independent board with control of the note issue and also empowered the bank to fix and publish its discount rate. Following a trip to North America in 1925, Page created a rural credits department within the Commonwealth Bank to provide low interest loans to primary producers on the security of their produce.[127] Page recalled his efforts to place 'Australian public and private finance and development on a sound footing', including the *Commonwealth Bank Act 1924*, as 'the legislative enactments which, in retrospect, give me the greatest satisfaction'.[128]

Yet the 1924 legislation was just a partial step towards a true central bank. A proposal to require private banks to hold 5 per cent of their funds with the Commonwealth Bank was dropped after opposition from the banks. In 1927, Page as treasurer introduced legislation to completely separate the Commonwealth Bank's savings bank functions from its central bank functions as 'an ideal safeguard for the whole banking

---

125 'Australian Country Party Complimentary Dinner to Sir Earle Page', EPP, folder 2358.
126 *Sydney Morning Herald*, 27 October 1922, pp. 9–10.
127 Page, *Truant Surgeon*, pp. 118–20.
128 Ibid., p. 112.

system', but this was also strongly opposed by the private banks and not fully implemented.[129] Page remained an advocate of an independent Commonwealth Bank. In 1931 he opposed an unsuccessful attempt by Theodore, now Commonwealth Treasurer, to assert political control over the bank by legislating to sell off its gold reserve so as to meet government debts.[130] Important as Page's measures were, a central banking role for the Commonwealth Bank was only effectively assumed during World War Two, and was shifted to the new Reserve Bank of Australia in 1960.

For all the rural development rhetoric that characterised the Bruce–Page years, the Country Party from the outset found it politically difficult to reduce tariffs that increased the costs of manufactured products used by farmers. The burden that tariffs imposed on primary industries remained a major, if inconsistently pursued, concern. The federal parliamentary party and state party associations were not united on the tariff issue: V.C. Thompson, for example, was a protectionist.[131] In his memoirs, Page makes clear that the Country Party was opposed to the levels of protection imposed by the Massy-Greene tariff but was willing to countenance duties recommended by the Tariff Board for 'any worthwhile industry which could satisfy local needs and ultimately enter export markets'. Various marketing crises and a reluctant realisation that tariffs were here to stay led the government to implement an array of subsidies and pricing schemes for rural producers 'to enable the survival of primary industries, to provide them with reasonable conditions, and to assist the expansion of export markets'.[132] Despite his reservations about industry support by government, Page famously called on primary producers to 'get into the vicious circle themselves' by seeking protection and compensating support through government organised marketing schemes.[133]

Over the period 1923–24 new legislation provided for dairy produce and dried fruit export control boards made up of government nominees and producers' representatives, for government-arranged bank advances to dried fruit growers, for an Australian Meat Council, for bounties on beef and cattle exports, for government guarantee of bank advances to voluntary wheat pools and for a specific advance to the Tasmanian

---

129 Ibid., p. 125; Giblin, *The Growth of a Central Bank*, pp. 120–1.
130 Schedvin, *Australia and the Great Depression*, p. 238.
131 Graham, *Formation of the Australian Country Parties*, pp. 153–4, 229–31.
132 Page, *Truant Surgeon*. p. 65.
133 Quoted in Ellis, *A History of the Australian Country Party*, p. 115; see also Page, interview by B.D. Graham, 9 May 1956, B.D. Graham papers, NLA, MS 8471.

hop growers pool. What became known as protection all round was accepted as a means of reconciling urban and rural interests at a time when Country Party support was essential to the government's survival. (The appointment of a primary producer representative to the Tariff Board also helped to soothe the Country Party.) Less well known is that in a 1924 speech, which appears to be one of the first where he used the phrase 'vicious circle' before a major audience, Page also spoke at length about helping primary producers improve their competitiveness. This included the better marketing of exports, collaboration to end 'suicidal competition' on export markets, new power sources and standardising manufacturing to reduce costs.[134]

One ALP Senator observed of all this that 'having a medical man in the ministry, the government is dealing out small doses of socialism – say a half-teaspoonful every twenty-four hours'.[135] Country Party members admitted a certain parallel, but rationalised such orderly marketing as a regrettable necessity that compensated for the tariffs and arbitration that served urban interests. Even Stewart referred to how 'we are compelled to accept the results of that system and hop into the ring to secure our share along with the rest'.[136] But this public–private symbiosis was predicated on private ownership of the means of production: Page remained a stalwart opponent of state enterprises and the nationalisation of industry.

## The Bruce–Page Government signals its intentions: Commonwealth–state cooperation

Page took his place in the new Bruce–Page Government determined to reform the federal system and the Constitution. As he wrote in an early draft of his memoirs:

> In the first decade [after Federation] parliamentary activity was largely devoted to the formal initiation of the constitutional provisions by the establishment of the practical framework. In the second ten years parliament, dominated by the necessities of war,

---

134 Page was speaking at the annual conference of the New South Wales FSA; *The Land*, 22 August 1924, pp. 2–4.
135 Senator Albert Gardiner, *Commonwealth Parliamentary Debates*, 25 September 1924, p. 4727.
136 Stewart, *Commonwealth Parliamentary Debates*, 25 September 1924, p. 4778.

operated for the most significant period under the defence powers of the Constitution in the process of which significant weaknesses were revealed by experience. It therefore fell to the parliament in the third decade to profit from the experience of the previous periods and to apply the lessons learned in an effort to make the Constitution work in the manner visualised by the architects of the Federal system.[137]

Bruce and Page were Australia's first national leaders to grapple comprehensively with coordinating policy with the states and the related correction of unbalanced fiscal relations. Their efforts reflect the tensions arising from an inelastic constitution that inspires developmentalist policy-makers to try either to change its provisions or manoeuvre around it. In doing so, Page worked under his prime minister's leadership, but still distinguished himself as a determined strategist with a discernible agenda of his own. He was to apply lessons from this early experience to many later ventures into cooperative federalism and economic planning.

Page, a self-declared 'lifelong advocate of constitutional reform', once claimed to have also been 'spurred into Federal politics by my interest in the principles of Federation'. This encompassed a conviction that such issues as electrification and transport could only be 'dealt with on a Federal or interstate level, and by a process of constructive national thinking'.[138] Federal ideas have deep roots in Australia's past but, as scholars of federalism have long observed, the Commonwealth–state balance has never been settled.[139] Page entered this debate as the leading proponent of the view that the federal system and the Constitution on which it was based were barriers to national development that were in dire need of reform. This led him as treasurer to pursue cooperative federalism, with the Commonwealth leading the development of national policies in collaboration with the states, but using its fiscal and other powers to remain firmly dominant.

Page considered himself a committed federalist. He described the classic series of American essays on constitutional federalism *The Federalist Papers* as his 'constant companion' and saw it as pointing to a model of a united

---

137 Draft for *Truant Surgeon*, EPP, folder 1860. A similar but less eloquently worded sentiment appeared in the published *Truant Surgeon*, p. 102.
138 *Commonwealth Parliamentary Debates*, 8 March 1944, p. 1071; also Page, *Truant Surgeon*, p. 102.
139 See for example A.J. Brown, 'Federalism, regionalism and the reshaping of Australian governance', in A.J. Brown and J.A. Bellamy (eds), *Federalism and Regionalism in Australia: New Approaches, New Institutions?*, ANU E Press, Canberra, 2006, pp. 11–32.

British Empire organised on federal principles.[140] Here he was reflecting a long tradition of a 'compound republic', which 'added the natural advantages of largeness to the local advantages of smallness'. The effective dual citizenship that this provides of respective states and of the nation helps explain the durability of Australian federalism.[141] That federalism made the Australian nation possible by reconciling local loyalties with nationalism makes it a vital concept in Australian history, one that is illuminated by Page's policy campaigns.

Much of the written history of federalism in Australia consists of detailed technical accounts of Commonwealth–state financial relations, with only fleeting references to competing ideas and political drivers. Cooperative federalism appears frequently as a broad term encompassing various means by which Commonwealth and state governments jointly managed overlapping interests. In 1952 the political scientist S.R. Davis observed that the 'unmistakable trend in Australian government is in the direction of extensive inter-governmental co-operation and co-ordination under the impetus and leadership of the Commonwealth', yet 'there is no systematic account of it'.[142] This has not greatly changed. W.G. McMinn added that the various cooperative mechanisms that appeared over time became important means of effectively limiting the states' power and increasing that of the Commonwealth. He listed four types of cooperation: use of state or Commonwealth bodies to implement the other's programs; joint agencies such as the River Murray Commission; the pooling of legislation, such as to create a national aviation regime; and more informal executive cooperation through such bodies as the Australian Agricultural Council.[143]

Starting in the Bruce–Page years, Page played a major role in the development of such cooperative mechanisms. Just a few years after his 1917 call to scrap the existing Constitution entirely, Page found himself advocating cooperation between the states and the Commonwealth. The Bruce–Page Government tried to pioneer a move away from change forced by High Court decision and the Commonwealth's growing fiscal power by offering a voluntary alternative based on Commonwealth-led cooperative federalism. This broadly matched Page's developing ideas on unification and national approaches to policy and was one of the reasons why he and

---

140  Page, *Truant Surgeon*, p. 257.
141  Brian Galligan, *A Federal Republic: Australia's Constitutional System of Government*, Cambridge University Press, Melbourne, 1995, pp. 39, 43, 53.
142  S.R. Davis, 'Co-operative federalism in retrospect', *Historical Studies*, vol. 5, no. 19, 1952, p. 215.
143  McMinn, *A Constitutional History of Australia*, pp. 191–4.

Bruce worked well together. He sought to fill the Constitution's lack of provision for collaboration between the two main levels of government by institutionalising means by which they could together develop national policies – effectively forms of nationwide planning. This became Page's way of attempting to drive policy fields over which the Commonwealth lacked constitutional authority. An outline of early measures to encourage intergovernmental cooperation reads like a roll-call of initiatives that he either led or contributed significantly to, most famously the Financial Agreement of 1927 that realigned Commonwealth–state financial relations and gave the Loan Council binding status. Page had a major hand in negotiating this arrangement, a career highlight that influenced his wider approach to federalism and constitutional reform. More specialised cooperative bodies also appeared under the Bruce–Page Government and in following years, covering fields as diverse as food and drug standards, immigration, road construction and primary produce marketing.

An important consideration here is that despite the difficulty of amending the Constitution, during Page's career it was decidedly not a revered document. Throughout his Bruce–Page heyday it still lacked any claim to have been especially successful by virtue of longevity. It attracted strident criticism for not preventing vertical fiscal imbalance. Both Page and Bruce strongly ascribed to the widespread view that such separation of revenue-raising from expenditure weakened accountability and the responsible use of public funds. Page had no qualms about correcting this and other anomalies, thereby 'making the constitutions of our states and Commonwealth our servants and not our masters'.[144] To him, the Commonwealth Constitution was at once a feckless impediment to progress and a potential basis for enshrining his policies. Either way, he frequently found himself pushing against what was already part of the received wisdom of Australian governance – that the wording of the Constitution is very hard indeed to change.

Also significant was the strength of what the political scientist Hugh Emy called 'the federal bargain' – Australia's '*sine qua non* of political co-operation and even of political integration'.[145] This holds that all Australian governments are formally equal in status and sovereign in nature, and has proved highly resistant to unilateral challenge. Instances

---

144 Speech 6 January 1927 to the Constitutional Club, Brisbane, EPP, folder 417.
145 Hugh Emy, *The Politics of Australian Democracy: Fundamentals in Dispute*, second edition, Macmillan, South Melbourne, 1978 (first published 1975), p. 72.

of the Commonwealth and the states working together, such as on orderly marketing, were thus necessary political accommodations, not the results of preference. Page was one of the first prominent political figures outside the ALP to openly challenge this bargain. Despite his protestations to the contrary, Page was never a true federalist who equally respected both tiers of government. As he had clearly stated in 1917, the national government should be dominant in setting policy. He approached federalism as, at best, a means of combining nationally determined policy settings with local expertise in implementation. Tension between the rational importance he attached to strong central government and his emotional attachment to regionalism persisted throughout his long engagement with issues of federalism.

Page's essentially national perspective was made stridently clear in his early public statements as treasurer, no doubt to the unease of his new state confreres. Just five months after becoming treasurer, he told the new state convention in Rockhampton that as Federation had failed there was a need for an 'intense NATIONAL FEELING that will override all parochial considerations, disregard the existence of imaginary state boundaries, and prevent the continuation of that system of pitting one capital city against another, which has proved so detrimental to the BALANCED AND PROPORTIONATE DEVELOPMENT of Australia as a whole'.[146] Yet most published assessments of Page underplay this commitment to strong national government via such means as collaboration with the states and instead focus in isolation on his engagement with new statism. Geoffrey Sawer very plausibly suggested that most Country Party MPs opposed Page's proposed constitutional convention as they felt that what he really wanted was greater Commonwealth powers. Sawer and A.J. Brown are among the few scholars to have commented that Page was essentially a centralist who wanted greater Commonwealth powers.[147]

Debate on Commonwealth–state relations during the Bruce–Page years initially centred on the fiscal balance. The Commonwealth's wartime introduction of its own direct taxation contributed greatly to the states' collective share of all government revenue tumbling from 93 per cent

---

[146] Page, *New States: Why They Are Necessary in Australia*, p. 2; Page's own capitalisations in this published version of his speech.
[147] Geoffrey Sawer, *Australian Federal Politics and Law 1901–1929*, Melbourne University Press, Parkville, Vic., 1956, p. 203.

in 1901–2 to 55 per cent in 1918–19.[148] Commonwealth expenditure declined after the war, and many federal parliamentarians advocated eliminating the heightened vertical fiscal imbalance that resulted by ending the per capita grants still being made to the states. Proposals for fiscal reform also included a cooperative council to reduce the cost of loans by coordinating borrowing by both levels of government. The Commonwealth had long favoured this and made it a condition of related proposals that it take over state debts. At the Premiers' Conference of April–May 1908 Deakin had proposed a finance council under which the Commonwealth would arrange all loans, acquire the states' debts and establish a debt sinking fund – all foreshadowing what Bruce and Page later implemented.[149] The states were conflicted between being attracted to offloading their debts and their well-founded suspicion that coordinated borrowing would increase Commonwealth dominance.[150]

The case for coordinated borrowing grew after the advent of peace in 1918. Australian governments resumed competing for loans locally and internationally, the Commonwealth sought to convert old loans into new obligations so as to service war debt, and the states wanted to finance soldier settlement and public works. Australia's net external debt continued to rise, reaching £419 million in mid-1923 and £570 million in mid-1928, largely related to rural development. The states were continually in deficit, as wartime inflation had eroded the real value of their per capita grants. The 1920–23 Royal Commission on Taxation recommended ending the per capita grants and all income tax being collected by the Commonwealth.[151]

Leadership in intergovernmental cooperation, financial or otherwise, had by the early 1920s shifted to the Commonwealth. This was driven by the imperatives of the war and the centralism of Prime Minister Hughes, hence his government's taking the initiative in convening the 1919 Premiers' Conference. The distinction between levels of government was

---

148 Nicholas Brown, 'Government, law and citizenship', in Bashford and Macintyre (eds), *The Cambridge History of Australia*, volume 2, p. 409.
149 R.S. Gilbert, *The Australian Loan Council in Federal Fiscal Adjustments, 1890–1965*, Australian National University Press, Canberra, 1973, p. 37. S.R. Davis records a Loan Council as being proposed as early as 1903; see S.R. Davis, 'A Unique Federal Institution', *University of Western Australia Annual Law Review*, December 1952, p. 355.
150 R.L. Mathews and W.R.C. Jay, *Federal Finance: Intergovernmental Financial Relations in Australia since Federation*, Thomas Nelson (Australia), Melbourne, 1972, p. 105.
151 R.C. Gates, 'The search for a state growth tax', in R.L. Matthews (ed.), *Intergovernmental Relations in Australia*, Angus and Robertson, Cremorne, 1974, pp. 165–6.

shifting from differing policy responsibilities to different organisational functions in dealing with increasingly shared issues. The Commonwealth began assuming a role as a central planner, especially of economic policy, with state governments handling implementation.

The new Bruce–Page Government sought to resolve these issues of federal finance and policy cooperation by asserting a leading role for the Commonwealth. Bruce led and Page provided crucially important encouragement and support. These efforts, says A.J. Brown, resulted in 'Australia's first real system of co-operative intergovernmental relations'.[152] The 1922 Premiers' Conference, the last presided over by Hughes, had a comparatively limited agenda of proposed cooperation in uniform railway gauges (even then a decades-old issue), export promotion, immigration and land settlement. The May 1923 conference presided over by Bruce and Page was very different indeed.

Its 'number of proposals to secure national co-operation', as Page rather casually described this effort to recast national governance, amounted to an attempt to comprehensively shape the Australian federation in a way broadly compatible with what he had called for in 1917.[153] The premiers were presented with a powerful signal of the new government's commitment to national efficiency in the form of an unprecedentedly ambitious agenda for Commonwealth-led policy coordination. This covered 25 specific issues, each with an accompanying paper for the premiers to ponder. They included the coordination of government borrowing; the application of science to industry, notably hydropower; Commonwealth grants to the states for main road development; uniform railway gauges for the Port Augusta to Hay and Kyogle to Brisbane lines; rationalisation of industrial relations powers; joint electoral rolls; coordination of the collection of statistics; and, as detailed in Chapter 3, the planning and standardisation of electricity generation. The Commonwealth also proposed an Australia-wide stocktake of economic resources to assess what capital and labour the nation needed for 'successful development'.[154]

---

152 A.J. Brown, 'Subsidiarity or subterfuge?: Resolving the future of Local Government in the Australian federal system', *Australian Journal of Public Administration*, vol. 61, no. 4, December 2002, p. 37.
153 Page, *Truant Surgeon*, p. 146.
154 A full set of agenda papers is at EPP, folder 1730; reports of proceedings are at folder 2663 (part 2). See also accounts of the conference in the Melbourne *Argus*, 24, 28, 29 and 30 May 1923; and in Michael Roe, *Australia, Britain, and Migration 1915–1940: A Study of Desperate Hopes*, Cambridge University Press, Cambridge, 1995, p. 49.

## 2. 'WE WERE DETERMINED TO USE OUR OPPORTUNITIES TO THE FULL'

It was clear that this new Commonwealth Government was set on enlisting the states in a radical rationalisation of the federation. It saw national efficiency as both means and end, leaving no place for intergovernmental duplication. The May 1923 Premiers' Conference was also the Bruce–Page Government's first attempt to overhaul Commonwealth–state financial relations. Bruce, in opening the conference, signalled that this was the foremost issue and led for the Commonwealth throughout the ensuing conference debate. He described existing duplication between the levels of government and double taxation as intolerable, 'the gravest inconvenience to taxpayers'. Page spoke late in proceedings, when his grasp of the proposed reforms – thorough and confident, despite his lack of ministerial experience – drew him into sparring with the states on important details.[155]

Negotiations quickly became intense and complex. Bruce and Page proposed to limit Commonwealth income tax to incomes of over £2,000 per annum in exchange for the abolition of the per capita grants.[156] Although the states agreed that fiscal relations were out of kilter, they objected to this implied focusing of their own taxes on lower income earners. They countered that the Commonwealth should instead withdraw from income tax altogether, and the states make compensating grants of their own to the Commonwealth – which Bruce and Page promptly declined because of continuing defence obligations. The Commonwealth's final offer, to limit its direct tax to company tax while also abolishing the per capita payments, narrowly failed due to rejection by New South Wales. The premiers, except the Western Australian premier, accepted only the joint collection by the states of Commonwealth and state taxes.

More significant was that the states agreed at this 1923 conference to create a loan council, albeit a voluntary one limited to seeking agreement on the timing and terms of loans. The raising of loans remained with each government, including decisions on amounts. (New South Wales withdrew from this Loan Council when Jack Lang became premier in 1925 but rejoined in December 1927 following his defeat.) This was the

---

155 Melbourne *Argus*, 26 May 1923, pp. 9, 21–2.
156 Mathews and Jay, *Federal Finance*, p. 119, say this was first proposed by Bruce and Page at a treasurers' conference; however, R.S. Gilbert, historian of the Loan Council, and Page himself both state it was at this premiers' conference; see Gilbert, *Australian Loan Council*, p. 75, and Page, *Truant Surgeon*, p. 130.

first practical step towards the 1927 Financial Agreement and the recasting of the Loan Council as a powerful entity that was to influence lastingly Page's conception of cooperative federalism.

Page's sudden rise in national politics had been propelled by a powerful mix of complementary issues, especially new statism, continuing rural demands for equal entitlement with the big cities and the organisation of rural protest into the early Country Party. Despite his idiosyncratic and striving nature, Page felt comfortable in the new Bruce–Page Government, exemplified by his enthusiasm for its early efforts to realign the federation. He quickly established himself as a forceful policy leader within a still formative parliamentary Country Party, most members of which were still feeling their way on issues. This all put him in a strong position to pursue his more personal policy agenda of hydroelectricity, new states and Commonwealth intervention to improve rural roads.

# 3

## THE USE OF POWER
### Treasurer Page Pursues His National Vision

Page took his place in the Bruce–Page Government in February 1923 with characteristic self-assuredness. The press quickly sensed a very singular Commonwealth minister of state. Journalists were bemused by his continuing to practise as a surgeon: just three months after being sworn in as treasurer, Page was reported to have operated on his brother James, then headmaster of a public school near Maitland.[1] Shortly before the 1928 election, he drew nationwide headlines for performing an emergency appendectomy on the Labor Member for Hume ('Doctor Fights for Life of Political Foe: Canberra Drama').[2] Ethel Page also began to make a name for herself, telling the Women's Section of the VFU that 'country women's organisations without politics … remind me of those rivers in Central Australia which … lose themselves here, there and everywhere in the sands of the desert'.[3]

Page signalled his intent to shape Australia by using his new status as a senior minister to pursue personal visions in three related policy areas: hydroelectricity, new states and rural roads. In each, the change he sought went well beyond what was proposed by most other rural-based civic movements and advocates, including those in his own Country Party. This made him a major influence on what policy ideas were current.

---

1 *Cessnock Eagle and South Maitland Recorder*, 11 May 1923, p. 2.
2 Melbourne *Herald*, 18 September 1928, p. 1.
3 *Farmers' Advocate*, 28 September 1923, p. 3.

The perception that the early Country Party was more 'a pressure group concerned wholly and solely with the wallets of rural producers' than a true political party is an overstatement, but has a degree of validity; its leader's vision, however, was far broader indeed.[4]

## Page's vision of hydroelectricity

Geoff Page wrote in his poem 'The River' of his grandfather Earle 'dreaming of the Gorge' – of how 'New wires are swooping over the farms / the sixty watt bulb with conical shade / a kind of enlightenment / equal to Voltaire's'.[5] Electrification was the most pronounced manifestation of Earle Page's faith in technology. This 'potent decentraliser' enlivened his vision of a regionalised and decentralised nation. He championed hydroelectricity above other forms of power generation as it could be based on the regional harnessing of river systems by local authorities. Hydroelectricity also had an emotional resonance for Page as it drew on his devotion to his home region. Damming The Gorge section of the Clarence River was to be the first step in a nationwide harnessing of Australia's rivers. His inspiration quite literally ran past his own front yard at Heifer Station.

Electrification also neatly bookends Page's career. It provided a focus for his early activism in Grafton and was his foremost cause after he left the federal ministry in early 1956. Page was one of a number of prominent Australians who in the nineteenth and early twentieth centuries looked overseas for ideas about development, especially in the United States. Most famously, Alfred Deakin studied irrigation in California and India; Page's fascination with hydroelectricity drew on his trips to New Zealand in 1910 and to North America in 1917. He became the foremost Australian devotee of the most cogent technological cultural phenomenon of this time: faith in the socially transformative power of electricity, or 'electrical triumphalism'.[6]

---

4   Quote from L.L. Robson, *Australia in the Nineteen Twenties: Commentary and Documents*, Nelson, Melbourne, 1980, p. 70.
5   Geoff Page, 'The River', *Collected Lives*, Angus and Robertson, North Ryde, NSW, 1986, pp. 45–58.
6   The term is used by Bill Luckin in *Questions of Power: Electricity and Environment in Inter-War Britain*, Manchester University Press, Manchester, 1990, pp. 1–22.

Page's campaign to dam the Clarence is also a good indicator of his thought processes: doggedness, commitment to place and a tendency to focus on a single developmental trigger from which much else would undoubtedly flow. He succeeded against professional doubts and political indifference in having hydroelectricity debated from the 1910s onwards. Yet Page only occasionally used the exultant rhetoric of American and European technological visionaries or their metaphors of a higher cause of conquering nature. One historian of technology described this as 'an essentially religious feeling' that sought 'to reinvest the landscape and the works of man with transcendent significance'.[7] Page was far more focused on immediate practical benefits.

Page's perception of these benefits differed from such other Australian hydroengineering enthusiasts as the engineers William Corin and John Bradfield by stressing electricity more than irrigation or flood control. Although these latter applications were not unimportant to him, hailing as he did from a flood-prone region, his main interest in 'water conservation' was the potential of hydroelectricity to power his social and economic vision. This went well beyond easing the harshness of rural life, a common policy aspiration in Australia and elsewhere. (One of Franklin D. Roosevelt's most important New Deal agencies was the Rural Electrification Administration.) Page saw electrification as crucially important to decentralised national development by enabling 'reproductive' investment in rural-based industries and by supporting social amenities. Hydroelectricity flowed through most elements of his distinctive approach to development – local autonomy, transformative technologies, planning, cooperative federalism, franchises for foreign investors and enshrinement in the Constitution.

Electrification and hydroelectricity also provide evidence of Page's trait of either ignoring cautious technical advice that deigned to thwart his goals, or liberally interpreting it as affirming them. This again marks him as more an instinctive thinker than the consummate rationalist he took himself to be. Tracing Page's electrification campaigns also helps build a picture of how he operated at different times. In the 1910s his appeals to local governments and state ministers were heavily influenced by exemplars in North America and New Zealand. But in the 1920s he worked through

---

7   Nye, *American Technological Sublime*, p. xiii.

the Commonwealth Government of which he was a senior member and, late in the decade, a robustly independent Development and Migration Commission that he expected to validate his vision of the Clarence Valley.

Although Page first became interested in hydroelectricity in the early 1910s, his ideas about its application only reached a settled form a decade later, when he successfully led local governments to establish a power station on the Nymboida River. In an April 1922 article in the *Daily Examiner* entitled 'Cheap Power: Australia's Greatest Need', Page neatly summarised the centrality of electrification to development and modernity itself:

> In the economy of the world today the most marked characteristic is the admission of the necessity for cheap power. It is everywhere recognised that progress and development are largely dependent upon a constant and adequate supply that will be always available, widely distributed and easily applied. The ideal would be a power available in every home, on every farm and in every factory, in the country not less than the town, and supplied at a price within the reach of all.[8]

Electricity, he concluded, was the best way to achieve this, as it could be widely distributed, stored and 'easily applied to everyday use'. Indeed, electricity consumption was a strong indicator of a nation's 'standard of comfort if not of civilisation', by which benchmark 'Australia occupies a position with the most lowly civilised races'.[9] One of the main barriers was centralisation. He complained that the 'excessive centralisation of industry' was largely due to state government control of power production and neglect of water power. State governments had been 'like the wolf in the fable of the wolf and the lamb – they have neither used the water nor allowed others [to] use it for power development'.[10] Page's vision was to use electricity as a 'potent decentraliser' to help create a more productive and united Australia that was decentralised yet efficient, ordered yet egalitarian.[11]

---

8   *Daily Examiner*, 14 April 1922, p. 3.
9   Ibid.
10  'Power Production', 1925, EPP, folder 2088; unsigned but format and characteristic references to the Clarence River and North American exemplars indicate that it was prepared by Page and apparently for Cabinet.
11  Notes for speech 'Electrical Standards', no date but c. 1925, EPP, folder 1053.

## The Nymboida and Jackadgery: Page and regional hydroelectricity

During his 1917 travels, Page was greatly impressed by how electrification was managed in Ontario and British Columbia. In a 1919 booklet produced through the North Coast Development League, *The Clarence Gorge Hydro-Electric Scheme*, he presented the Ontario Hydro-Electric Power Commission as a model for regional control of power production and evidence of the transformative power of regionalism. Page reported that it was successfully managed by local governments, made good use of private contractors by issuing debentures backed by the provincial government and encouraged electricity use by keeping charges to manufacturers and farmers low.[12] He concluded that the commission had 'secured intelligent and harmonious co-operation among local bodies' and 'developed a national outlook throughout the whole area'. Page felt 'a pang when one contrasts the more favourable conditions of our climate' with 'our entire failure to manufacture our own necessities, quite apart from providing munitions or manufactures and the lack of the comforts of life that prevails here'.[13]

Once home, Page continued to seek lessons from overseas. He studied closely, for example, a January 1918 article in the *New Zealand Journal of Science and Technology* on the economics of electrification, heavily underlining passages on how widely distributed power could help establish new industries.[14] His interest was reinforced by rapid development in electricity use in Australia. The 1920s saw a fourfold increase in Australian electricity consumption, faster than most other countries (but similar to Canada). By 1927, mainland Australia's electricity production of about 300 kWh per capita was approximately half as big again as Britain's.[15] In 1921 the State Electricity Commission (SEC) of Victoria became mainland Australia's first statewide electricity public utility. Following a vociferous technical debate over the relative merits of brown coal and

---

12   North Coast Development League for the Grafton Chamber of Commerce, *The Clarence Gorge Hydro-Electric Scheme: Harnessing 100,000 Horse-Power*, The League, Grafton, NSW, 1919, pp. 35–43.
13   Ibid., pp. 54, 58.
14   E. Parry, 'The economics of electric-power distribution', *New Zealand Journal of Science and Technology*, vol. 1, January 1918, pp. 49–55. Page's copy is at EPP, folder 1762.
15   There is contemporary evidence that Australia lagged behind the United States and Canada in the production and industrial use of electricity, but the picture becomes more mixed if European nations and Tasmania are also considered: See H.R. Harper, 'Presidential Address', *The Journal of the Institution of Engineers, Australia*, vol. 6, no. 2, February 1934, p. 86.

hydroelectricity, it proceeded to aggressively exploit Gippsland's brown coal reserves. There was also a jump in the local manufacture of electrical goods, albeit mostly consumer items produced by foreign subsidiaries while most more complex manufactures continued to be imported. But electrification remained heavily orientated to meeting urban rather than rural demand, much of which was made possible by British loans to state governments.

Page in the early 1920s drew on the status of office, his local prestige as the Clarence region's most famed citizen and the results of his travels to promote three closely related strategies for electrification – the harnessing of the Clarence River system as the first of a series of regional initiatives; the planning of power utilisation by a national commission that would begin its task by surveying Australia's water resources; and greater efficiency via the standardisation of the means of electricity production and distribution. His first attempt at harnessing the Clarence system, the Nymboida River project of 1923, was also his foremost success in implementing a hydroelectric power project. Widely considered a triumph at the time, Page saw it as just an encouraging first step for the wider Clarence and the nation.

Page's efforts on the Nymboida centred on the regional control and low charges that had so impressed him in Canada. In 1912, W.J. Mulligan had drawn attention to the electricity potential of the Nymboida, 'which he had raised some years previously', and two years later forwarded a proposal to the Grafton and South Grafton councils.[16] This led to a conference of the two councils in April 1914 that involved Page in his capacity as an alderman of South Grafton. The councils duly carried Page's motion to ask the state government to undertake an assessment of the Nymboida for power generation. But, as with parallel efforts to harness The Gorge, little of substance happened until Page's return from the war, when he used his positions as vice-chairman of the Lighting Committee of South Grafton Council and subsequently as mayor to revive the idea.

---

16  This and most following details on the origins of the Nymboida project are based on 'Story of hard fight for modern methods: Genesis of Nymboida scheme', *Daily Examiner*, 2 November 1938, p. 41; North Coast Development League, *The Clarence Gorge Hydro-Electric Scheme: Harnessing 100,000 Horse-Power*; Ulrich Ellis, 'The Story of Nymboida, notes for Sir Earle Page', 12 December 1952, Earle Page papers, UNE Archives, A180, box 3, folder 34; and an undated document in EPP, folder 1855, p. 23, evidently prepared for the drafting of *Truant Surgeon*.

In December 1918, Corin produced a more ambitious plan for the Nymboida and The Gorge than his vision of 1915. He pointedly commented that to meet the power needs of the Grafton neighbourhood the Nymboida alone would do, but if the goal was to develop new industries then The Gorge must also be harnessed. In February 1919 Page convened a meeting in Grafton of councils from the Clarence and Richmond regions to promote the plan, telling them that the Nymboida was not an alternative but a preliminary to The Gorge as part of the wider development of the Clarence. In December the state parliament legislated for hydroelectric works at the Nymboida, at Burrinjuck and on the Tumut River and its tributaries. But little came of this and so Page continued lobbying along with his valued local supporters Roy Vincent, a state MLA from 1922, and Alf Pollack. Pollack became general secretary of the Northern New South Wales Separation League and of the Joint Electricity Committee of Northern Municipalities and Shires, and was Country Party MLA for Clarence over the period 1927–31. They lobbied for the creation of a confederation of local councils to form a county council with powers approximating those of the Ontario Commission, including to raise money and manage electricity production. Page later claimed that the state government acted only after he publicised its delays. The Clarence River County Council (CRCC) was duly proclaimed in May 1922.

A contract was finally let early in 1923 for a power station of 4,800 kW capacity. This was funded under the Migration Agreement with Britain, which provided for joint British–Australian funding of rural development projects that supported emigration from Britain: another idea, as we will see in Chapter 5, that Page keenly supported. Treasurer Page featured on the cover of the printed program for the 'switching on' ceremony of 26 November 1924 as 'The Father of the Scheme'.[17] The project marked the success of his strategy of using his influence over local governments in his home region to forge a united approach to the state government. The CRCC and the Richmond River County Council amalgamated in 1952 to form the Northern Rivers County Council, later described as occupying 'pride of place in rural electrical enterprise' in the state.[18]

---

17  Booklet commemorating the switching on, dated 26 November 1924, EPP, folder 1046. There was a small council-run hydroelectric scheme at Dorrigo shortly before the Nymboida scheme; see the *Daily Examiner*, 25 November 1924, pp. 4, 5, cutting at EPP, folder 1044.
18  Guy Allbut, *A Brief History of Some of the Features of Public Electricity Supply in Australia: And the Formation and Development of the Electricity Supply Association of Australia, 1918–1957*, Electricity Supply Association of Australia, Melbourne, 1958, p. 28.

The Nymboida project became the template for Page's concept of the electrification of Australia, especially the localisation of control. Even before generation commenced, Page announced his hope that the Nymboida scheme 'might prove a turning point in the history of Australia'.[19] He often recalled how he and Pollack had 'induced nearly sixty councils to combine for the gradual harnessing of the Clarence waters for power', thereby providing a 'shining example of what can be done with electricity'.[20] One of the most important issues in electricity use is price setting and its impact on consumption. Fundamental to electrification, Page-style, was a common flat rate subsidised by the taxpayer. Although contrary to most tenets of commercial sustainability, this would encourage the uptake of electricity in the countryside. As he later said, 'our experience of the flat rate at Nymboida has been that the consequent rapid expansion of rural demand makes power cheaper for every user and unthought of use and advantages are continually turning up'.[21] On switching-on day, he assured a conference in Grafton of local governments that 'the psychological moment had arrived for the people of the North'. The conference minutes recorded that 'while in America he had been struck with the fact that government had been from the bottom up', it was sadly the case that 'the very opposite prevailed in Australia, where government was from an unwieldy top which bore down and crushed the lower controlling bodies'.[22] Page even called his Sydney home Nymboida.[23]

For all Page's pride, the Nymboida scheme only serviced adjacent shires. He at once sought to expand regionally based hydroelectricity, starting with a power station at Jackadgery on the Mann River. This briefly had state government support. Two days before the Nymboida commencement, Page led a delegation of local councillors and MPs to Premier George Fuller, who agreed to pay part of the interest bill for Jackadgery and to seek support under the Migration Agreement.[24] Page set out to create

---

19   *Sydney Morning Herald*, 20 September 1923, p. 8.
20   Typed summary of facts and figures on the Clarence, no date but appears to be late 1950s, EPP, folder 2333; *Commonwealth Parliamentary Debates*, 14 September 1944, p. 838.
21   'Dr. Earle Page's Prescription for National Health and Development', February 1946, EPP, folder 2295.
22   This and the preceding quote are from 'Minutes of the Proceedings of the Conference, with other Papers and Information Relative to the Proposed Jackadgery Hydro-Electric Scheme' at Grafton of 'The Electricity Committee of Northern Municipalities and Shires', 26 November 1924, EPP, folder 1046, pp. 21, 26.
23   Earle Page papers, UNE Archives, A180, box 7, folder 62.
24   Ibid., p. 4.

a yet larger local government structure as the basis for the regional management of Jackadgery. He exhorted councils to form a North Coast and Tablelands county council encompassing Casino, Inverell, Grafton, Byron, Tweed and other local governments. The *Daily Examiner* duly reported that although the total area was enormous, the compactness of settlement within each component district made the proposal 'of especial advantage in connection with a scheme for the distribution of electricity' and a distinct prospect for Migration Agreement funding.[25] A much more ambitious project than the Nymboida, Jackadgery fell foul of changes of state government from Fuller's Nationalists to Jack Lang's Labor in June 1925, and in October 1927 to T.R. Bavin's Nationalists.[26] Page had great power at the local and Commonwealth levels, but dealing with state governments was a very different matter.

## Planning the electrification of the nation

Page also sought to build on the Nymboida success by directing the Bruce–Page Government towards planning the electrification of all Australia. The ambitious agenda for policy coordination that they presented to the May 1923 Premiers' Conference included a strategy for national electrification, the first of a long series of Page-inspired overtures to the states to join him in shaping the economic and social landscape. But Australia's small population, distances between population centres, and interstate rivalries worked against planned electrification and in favour of the absence of ultimate national purpose that Page so abhorred.

National organisation and standardisation were widely recognised as important for electrification. Standardisation was a major issue for the United States electrical industry throughout the 1910s and 1920s as part of a wider standardisation movement. In Britain, it was known that the division of generation between local governments hampered nationwide electrification. In Australia, Page attempted to take the lead by using his status in the Bruce–Page Government as a powerful platform for appeals to the Australian public and state governments, on a scale quite unlike his

---

25   Letter by Page to local councils, 4 December 1924, EPP, folder 2083; note also his speech at Glen Innes of 15 February 1924 on an enlarged County Council, folder 1050; *Daily Examiner*, 5 September 1925, cutting in Earle Page papers, UNE Archives, A180, box 6, folder 57.
26   See for example a letter from The Port of the Clarence Advisory Board to Premier Bavin, 16 February 1928, in NAA, CP211/2, 34/13.

earlier efforts as an alderman. He saw standardisation as leading to lower costs, more reliable services and a national grid that could carry surplus power between local production systems.

Since the Commonwealth lacked a direct constitutional role in power generation, Page added to the Bruce–Page Government's advocacy of cooperative federalism the Commonwealth-led coordination of a national power grid implemented by the states. At the May 1923 Premiers' Conference he exhorted state power ministers to accept this approach, assuring them that the absence of a body akin to the US Federal Power Commission helped explain Australia's backwardness in power production. He proposed a federal–state commission that would 'determine prospective power needs in Australia over a period of twenty years' and put all electricity production on a planned 'co-operative Commonwealth–State basis'.[27] The new commission would lay down common standards for equipment and transmission, and survey the nation's power resources before issuing 'a comprehensive power-scheme for the whole of Australia' that identified sites for new power stations. The stridency of the language employed in the agenda paper strongly suggests that it was drafted by Page himself. It provocatively concluded that 'the only advantage in Australia's backwardness is that practically a virgin field lies before us for development on the right lines'.[28]

During the conference debate Page at first tried to be tactful, carefully presenting the Clarence as merely one of several potential power centres. But state ministers still reacted with hostility to what they saw as an unwarranted intrusion by the Commonwealth. The Victorian minister, Arthur Robinson, quoted his state's electricity commissioners as describing the Commonwealth proposal as 'utopian and certainly not within the legitimate range of Federal co-operation for at least another generation', especially given Australia's population distribution. Page was nonplussed by such an 'ostrich-like' attitude: 'future generations will rue our short-sightedness', he decried. He, for one, 'did not look forward to the six capital cities of Australia simply continuing to grow larger and larger without the institution of large civic centres elsewhere'.

---

27  Page, *Truant Surgeon*, p. 142.
28  This and following comments are from the official report of the conference, 'Standardisation of Electrical Power Schemes', pp. 71–9, EPP, folder 1045.

A major gap between Page and the state ministers was his conviction that industrial development would surely follow the provision of electrical power. He rhetorically challenged them on 'whether power follows population and industries, or whether it is not the other way about', and then supplied the answer himself – that 'the history of development throughout the world is that where the power is you also have population and industries'. Hence zinc was mined at Broken Hill but sent to Risdon in Tasmania where hydroelectricity was used in producing zinc ingots. The electrification of Australia 'will induce other industries to come here, and so the whole thing will proceed in a beneficial circle, enabling us to grow up, not only a contented people, but also in sufficient numbers to hold this continent for the Empire'. Yet in the end the assembled ministers reluctantly agreed merely to share information on their respective state's power resources and to work with a new advisory board on standardisation.

This was a prominent early instance of Page seriously misreading state governments, and a formative encounter with their sensitivity to any loss of authority to the Commonwealth. On this occasion it was the Commonwealth's presumption that they resented more than the idea of efficient electrification. The Victorian minister pointed out that the states were already working towards standardisation of production and transmission. Page was only ever to get his way with the states by bluntly applying the Commonwealth's growing fiscal power in a federal system that he had openly disdained.

Page continued to press for the planning and standardisation of national electrification by whatever other channels seemed available. This was typical, means never being as important as his grand ends. The Bruce–Page Government was very receptive to policy advice from industry leaders, including in electricity. The year after the unsuccessful premiers' conference, it readily agreed when the Australian Commonwealth Engineering Standards Association, a semi-private body that advised the Commonwealth and state governments, proposed using its existing work on standardisation as the basis for being entrusted with some of what Page had intended for his federal–state commission. The Commonwealth provided financial support for the association's 'complete survey of the Power Resources of Australia, with a view to their development and more economical and efficient use'.[29] Although Page later held this up as

---

29 'Opening Remarks' by Chairman of the National Committee of Australia of the Australian Commonwealth Engineering Standards Association, 6 May 1924, EPP, folder 1053; *Quarterly Bulletin*, The Institution of Engineers, Australia, Sydney, April 1924, p. 51.

an outstanding example of industry-led national coordination, it never amounted to effective national planning of electrification.[30] In 1925, he proposed to Cabinet the revival of his idea for a national electricity body.[31] In July that year he directly contacted the SEC to propose that if the state government legislated on standards for voltage and frequency, the Commonwealth would ban the importation of non-compliant equipment. The SEC's chief engineer responded that all this would be costly and should be limited to new projects only, with the Commonwealth merely promulgating standards for which it invited the states to legislate.[32]

## New states: Star witness before the Cohen Royal Commission

Page's engagement with the new state issue when serving in the Bruce–Page Government was very different from his efforts on federalism and hydroelectricity. He played a much more individual role, without the support of his prime minister. His elevation to national office in 1923 had raised the hopes of his new state followers. In fact, membership of federal Cabinet restricted Page to a very selective engagement with the cause, conducted mainly on his own terms as a senior minister whose first loyalty was to his government. He became more cautious in his public statements, curbing his allegations of urban-based conspiracies of greed. But when in 1924 the New South Wales Government convened the Cohen Royal Commission to inquire into new states, Page seized the opportunity to assert himself as national leader of the new state movement with a gusto that helped to ensure its survival.

Although Bruce supported new states in principle, his new government signalled caution by affirming Hughes's constitutionally correct line that they needed to be initiated by existing state governments. Bruxner's successful 1922 resolution in the New South Wales Parliament elicited the very proper response from the prime minister that he would not act until the state government came up with a solid proposal – a factor in the subsequent appointment of the Cohen Royal Commission.[33]

---

30  Page, *Truant Surgeon*, pp. 142–5.
31  'Power Production', EPP, folder 2088.
32  H.R. Harper to Page, 27 July 1925, EPP, folder 1053.
33  Aitkin, *The Colonel*, pp. 78–9; also Ellis, *New Australian States*, pp.168–9.

Page at first largely toed the Hughes–Bruce line on new states. He opened the second Armidale convention of the Northern New State Movement in June 1923 by announcing that it was up to state governments to make the first move.[34] Other parliamentary new staters were less restrained. V.C. Thompson, a backbencher, became the most ardent parliamentary agitator. In 1923 he formed a Federal Parliamentary New State League of 21 members, presided over by the unrelated W.G. Thompson, a Nationalist senator from the Queensland new state stronghold of Rockhampton. Latham sat on its executive. It was Thompson who led a delegation to Bruce in July 1923 to propose amending the Constitution to replace initiation by state parliaments with a less onerous process based on a petition of at least 20 per cent of local electors triggering a local referendum. In 1924 and again in 1925 Thompson introduced private member's motions on a referendum to amend section 124: neither was put to the parliamentary vote.[35]

High ministerial office inhibited Page because of the tension new states raised with his coalition partners. Ellis, a member of the parliamentary press gallery in those years, later wrote of the Bruce–Page Cabinet having in 1925 examined various options for amending section 124, including a constitutional session of parliament and a royal commission, before its eventual proposal to conduct a referendum was blocked by Nationalist MPs.[36] As his foremost means of implementing a pressing agenda to improve rural living standards, Page needed to make the coalition work. He had limited opportunity, especially at first, for the luxury of focusing on a personally favoured issue like new states. Calls to provide such basic rural amenities as phone services and roads permeated his speeches. Speaking in December 1923 on the introduction of radio to the bush he reflected, with atypical eloquence, on his hope that 'that word "lonely" will be eliminated from Australian life'.[37]

So Page made a strategic judgement that the time was not yet ripe for his new state–regionalist agenda. His caution drew criticism, such as in parliament in July 1926 from Frank Forde, a Queensland Labor new stater,

---

34  Ellis, *New Australian States*, p. 176.
35  Ibid., pp. 166, 181–2; Graham, *Formation of the Australian Country Parties*, p. 231.
36  Ellis, *A History of the Australian Country Party*, p. 111; Ellis, *New Australian States*, pp. 199–200.
37  Page at the opening of the Wireless and Electrical Exhibition, Sydney, 3 December 1923, quoted in Sally Warhaft (ed.), *Well May We Say…: The Speeches That Made Australia*, Black Inc., Melbourne, 2004, p. 540, originally reported in *Radio*, 12 December 1923.

and Hughes, still with a personal score to settle.[38] But Page was prepared to momentarily re-enter the new state fray when a singularly promising opportunity suddenly materialised at the state government level. The 1924–25 Cohen Royal Commission was the most comprehensive of three formal inquiries into new states conducted during the inter-war period. Far from staying focused on federally initiated constitutional reform, Page and the other new staters put enormous effort into trying to win over the royal commission, and, by extension, the government of New South Wales. As a willing witness, Treasurer Page resumed his persona as an unconventional nation-shaper to produce the fullest case for new states yet seen.

A royal commission into new states was first proposed at the June 1923 Armidale convention. Four months later, the Fuller State Government decided against constructing a Northern Tablelands to north coast railway. This led to such protests from the True Blue Progressives – who had split from the Progressive Party in protest against a coalition, but whose support in parliament now kept the Nationalists in office – that in December Fuller agreed to review this decision. Late in 1923 he acceded to Bruxner's request for a royal commission as part of a deal to maintain support for his government. The royal commissioner, Judge John Cohen, was a Grafton native, presumably coincidentally (perhaps less coincidental was that he was a former Nationalist state MP).[39] Crucially, the Cohen Royal Commission had a very wide brief that included assessing the fundamental question of whether new states in New South Wales were 'practical and desirable' and whether the ends they would supposedly achieve could be more readily secured by restructuring local government.

Cohen and his fellow commissioners deliberated for over a year, from April 1924 to May 1925. This included four lengthy tours of the state's north to gather evidence from over 200 witnesses (including a minority hostile to new states), encompassing professionals, business figures, councillors, farmers and state government officials. Page was the new state movement's star witness, the foremost national advocate of the allied concepts of new states, regionalism and decentralisation. He was not queried when he described himself to the royal commission as 'leader of the general movement for Australian subdivision'.[40] Page's evidence was

---

38 *Commonwealth Parliamentary Debates*, 24 June 1926, pp. 3481–8 and 3492–4.
39 Aitkin, *The Colonel*, pp. 76, 78–9.
40 Page, *The New State in Northern New South Wales*, p. 1. This is the published version of Page's Cohen evidence.

typically confident and wide-ranging, but the sceptical, clinical dissection that followed was not a happy experience for him. By casting his evidence as the starting point for a strategy to regionalise the entire nation, Page also highlighted how he differed from most of the new state movement.

Page gave evidence to the royal commission in two long sessions, the first on 19–20 May 1924. As something of a historicist, he asserted that throughout world history, compact, homogenous entities were the form of government 'which lends itself most readily to good government and intensive development'. In Australia, this would solve problems of defence, population and public finance, a typical Page conflation of disparate issues. By drawing on 'a higher civic spirit' to marshal their resources and develop efficient transport, self-governing regions could encourage manufacturing far more effectively than would tariff protection.[41] Responding to probing by counsel for the royal commission, Page added that any 100,000-square-mile area with natural resources and a population of at least 70,000 had potential to be successfully self-governing.[42] In attempting to persuade that beyond a certain point there was an inverse relationship between the size of a state and its production per square mile, he quoted figures comparing the relatively compact Victoria with Western Australia, ignoring differences in basic geography.[43] Page frequently held up Victoria as being of the approved size, particularly when berating New South Wales audiences.

As ever, Page dwelt on possibilities, not foreseeable limitations. Conscious as he was of the paucity of connections between existing state rail systems, he still argued that regional control of railways would result in local networks eventually adding up to an effective national system. Nor did Page have in mind the simple replication of the existing form of state governance on a smaller geographic scale. He instead proposed to restrain government expenditure by a model based on diminutive legislatures (dubbed councils, not parliaments), unpaid MPs and a mere four ministers each. He pointedly added that 'I would like to see the States called "Provinces" and not "States", because that would properly indicate

---

41   Ibid., pp. 1, 2, 7.
42   Royal Commission of Inquiry into Proposals for the Establishment of a New State or New States, *Evidence of the Royal Commission of Inquiry into Proposals for the Establishment of a New State or New States, formed wholly or in part out of the present territory of the State of New South Wales, together with the List of Exhibits and Printed Exhibits*, Government Printer, Sydney, volume 4, 1925, p. 2215.
43   Page, *The New State in Northern New South Wales*, pp. 1, 6.

to the public the fact that they are to deal with the local problems of the local development of their areas and not to encroach on the domain of national policy'.[44]

Naturally, Page focused his evidence on northern New South Wales. This region, he said, had the population, the natural resources and the overall ability to finance itself. It boasted an 'exceptionally fertile' coastal belt 'where drought – that spectre that haunts the balance of Australia – is practically unknown'. Unalienated land was plentiful and on the Clarence River alone '100,000 HP is possible' if a hydroelectric scheme was built. Inland, hydropower and wool could together support a textiles industry on the fertile New England Tablelands.[45] But when Page confidently predicted an annual revenue surplus for the new state of £416,064, state Treasury officials responded with their own calculation of a deficit of over £1.3 million.[46] In his second bout with the royal commission, over 19–21 November 1924, Page replied to Treasury's item-by-item dissection of his cost and revenue estimates by disputing the assumption that the new state would spend public funds at the same rate as when it was a component of New South Wales. Treasury's estimate reflected the 'unnecessary circumlocution and consequent grave overstaffing' that characterised the existing New South Wales public service, not the slimmer apparatus Page envisaged.[47]

Page's 'advanced text-book of Constitutional reform', as Ellis described his evidence, attracted press attention in both city and rural newspapers.[48] Yet Page and his fellow advocates made a poor impression on the royal commission. The commissioners looked carefully and critically at the new state case to reach their central conclusion that proposals to carve three new states out of New South Wales – the north, the Riverina and the Monaro – were 'neither practical nor desirable'.[49] They were not at all persuaded by data supposedly demonstrating that new states stimulated

---

44   Ibid., pp. 19–22, 29.
45   Ibid., pp. 3, 8.
46   These figures are taken from Royal Commission of Inquiry into Proposals for the Establishment of a New State or New States, *Evidence*, volume 3, 1925, pp. 1440–1. Page estimated total expenditure by the northern new state at £2.85 million. Both sides subsequently amended their estimates, but the net difference was still approximately £1.47 million.
47   Royal Commission of Inquiry into Proposals for the Establishment of a New State or New States, *Evidence*, volume 4, 1925, p. 2173.
48   Ellis, *New Australian States*, p. 195. For press coverage see, for example, *The Land*, 23 May 1924, p. 5; and the *Sydney Morning Herald*, 20 May 1924, p. 5, and 22 November 1924, p. 16.
49   Quoted in Ellis, *New Australian States*, p. 195.

population growth. New state witnesses had, for example, pointed to the rapid growth of the American state of Iowa without realising that much of this actually pre-dated its statehood.

The royal commission found that new states would actually increase the cost of government and that the alleged benefits of decentralisation could be obtained by less irrevocable means. Treasury figures contradicted assertions that the regions proposed as new states made net contributions to revenue. The port of Sydney had such spare capacity that there was little need for new regional ports. The state rail system was not, as alleged, designed to favour the metropolis over the countryside. Above all, population movement to cities was a worldwide phenomenon likely to continue in new states. Cohen added that it was beyond his terms of reference to consider whether a referendum on new states should be held, but the implication was clear. Page and the wider new state movement also failed to address convincingly the immense practical difficulty of creating a new state, the constitutional formula being far simpler in principle than in practice. As Hughes had opined, creation of a new state required threshold issues such as the drafting of a widely acceptable new constitution and the division of assets with the parent state to have 'assumed a very concrete shape' before substantive action could be taken.[50]

The royal commission findings dampened new state agitation until another trigger arose when the economy deteriorated in the late 1920s. Although the royal commission experience demonstrated that new statism had not gained broad traction amongst opinion-makers beyond provincial elites and their circle of activists, it nonetheless suggested a wider acceptance of the allied concept of decentralisation. The royal commission recommended the reform of administration and the strengthening of local government to address what it considered to be the actual problem facing rural New South Wales – the centralisation of public works and social services. The need for regional teachers' colleges and better public health services was especially pressing. It proposed that shires and municipalities elect district councils to plan and manage health services, education, land settlement and public works (other than railways and large-scale irrigation). The royal commission also recommended that the state government resolve some specific grievances, notably the Northern Tablelands–north coast railway.

---

50  Ibid., p. 160.

Page's criticisms of the Cohen Royal Commission's findings drew on his nationwide perspective. He complained of an 'absence of the consideration of the larger view which ultimately connects the new state issue with the urgent problem facing Australia, that of the National Development and Effective Occupation of the Continent'.[51] Page cast the royal commission as having instead adopted a provincial New South Wales outlook, hence such conclusions as that unified nationwide railway gauges would disadvantage Sydney.[52] Even at this still early stage of his political career, Page saw himself as habitually battling blinkered outlooks. He may not have won the royal commission over, but the attention he attracted had enhanced the status of the new state movement when it could otherwise have faded for good in the face of the royal commission's withering criticisms – a deputy prime minister and treasurer had lent it his authority as a national issue. The publication of his evidence as a book by his own Northern New State Movement proudly depicted Page on the cover as 'Treasurer of the Commonwealth'.[53] Page's effort to impress the royal commission significantly qualifies Graham's portrayal of the new state cause as one of several that the Country Party largely shelved during the Bruce–Page years.[54]

Page also contrived to interpret the royal commission's support for the localisation of administration as amounting to endorsement of his fundamental ideas. With some justification, he saw the recommended district councils as an admission of the validity of his argument that the entirety of New South Wales could not be effectively administered from Sydney. Indeed, the creation of these councils could lead to their spread across the nation, and serve as a step towards the formation of new states. History remained on his side – 'the present New South Wales Parliament seems to be doomed', he said, for surely the existing state would eventually be superseded.[55]

Immediately after the royal commission, however, Page reverted to a watchful passivity on new states, consistent with his habitual preparedness to await the psychological moment. His Country Party policy speech for the 1925 election made but the briefest of references to new states

---

51 Comments by Page on Cohen's findings, New England New State Movement, Armidale, UNE Archives, A1, box 14.
52 Ellis, *New Australian States*, p. 198.
53 Page, *The New State in Northern New South Wales*.
54 Graham, *Formation of the Australian Country Parties*, pp. 231–2, 283–4.
55 Comments by Page on Cohen's findings, UNE Archives, A1, box 14.

and planned development.⁵⁶ The advent of the Bavin–Buttenshaw Nationalist–Country Party State Government in October 1927 weakened the new state movement yet further. This was the first long-term urban–rural coalition in New South Wales and included David Drummond as education minister. (There had been two earlier Nationalist-Progressive governments, one of which lasted only a day.) It commenced new public works in the north, notably the Armidale Teachers' College and the Guyra–Dorrigo railway. The effectiveness with which these very visible projects deflated new state agitation says much about the shallowness of public support for the cause. Page's lifelong commitment to new states resurfaced resoundingly when circumstances turned again in 1931–32.

Page's commitment is also evident in his enthusiastic engagement with some fleeting new state initiatives by his own government. The Bruce–Page Government twice attempted to create new states in northern and central Australia, even in the 1920s long a focal point for hopes and assumptions about Australian development. The government was willing to pursue new states when this did not risk a major confrontation with its own Nationalist MPs or the existing states with whom it had much else to negotiate.

In 1923, George Pearce, minister for home and territories, proposed new federal territories of Northern and Central Australia, with parts of Western Australia and Queensland to be included if their governments agreed. In 1926 the Commonwealth responded to recommendations of the Royal Commission on Western Australian Disabilities Under Federation by proposing to annex the state's territory north of the 26th parallel. (The 1910s and 1920s were the high point of Commonwealth use of royal commissions as a means of addressing difficult policy issues: 56 Commonwealth royal commissions were held from 1911 to 1929, but after that only 10 up to the early 1970s.) The state government would be relieved of all liability from loan monies spent on the north and the Commonwealth would spend £5 million on the region's development annually for 10 years, from which a new state could be created. Page later commented that at this time his immediate interest in this region was the 'balanced representation in the federal parliament' of the western half of the nation, and only eventually a new state. The plan foundered

---

56   1925 Country Party policy speech, EPP folder 2331.

over the conditions of the proposed federal expenditure: Page refused to guarantee this allocation until there had been a full assessment of the region's needs.[57]

The following year the Bruce–Page Government divided the Commonwealth-administered Northern Territory into North Australia and Central Australia. During debate on the legislation, Bruce referred to their eventually becoming 'States of the Commonwealth'.[58] Each was endowed with a government resident and an advisory council, and a North Australia Commission was created to oversee the development of both regions. Neither survived the fall of the Bruce–Page Government and a united Northern Territory was re-established in 1931.

## Tied grants for rural roads: Page helps alter the federation

Page had more practical success in furthering his national vision via the narrower but more widely acceptable field of tied Commonwealth grants for the construction of rural roads. As a fiscal conservative, he professed to be affronted by vertical fiscal imbalance. But his national development agenda, especially for rural Australia, and his impatience with state governments were more immediately important to him. This order of priorities led to his imposing these grants on the states.

Page was motivated by his regionalist vision and long-standing commitment to improved rural roads. He recalled vividly how as a young doctor he was 'no stranger to the primitive and gruelling transport system which served most parts of Australia' and the results of this for critically ill patients.[59] Commonwealth-tied grants for roads did not entirely start with Page. In 1922 the Commonwealth distributed £250,000 between the states on a per capita basis that it insisted be directed to rural roads that would improve market access by soldier settlers. This was a historic step in Commonwealth–state financial relations, yet the parliamentary

---

57   Ellis, *New Australian States*, pp. 185–6, 266–8; Earle Page, *Commonwealth Parliamentary Debates*, 12 October 1961, p. 1985.
58   *Commonwealth Parliamentary Debates*, 10 February 1926, p. 824.
59   Page, *Truant Surgeon*, p. 146.

debate on the legislation – a wide-ranging Act on the expenditure of Commonwealth loans – barely addressed these inter alia grants.[60] They are not mentioned in Page's memoirs.

Page became the first federal minister to systematically use section 96 of the Constitution to make tied Commonwealth grants to the states. The 1923 Royal Commission on Taxation briefly noted that this Commonwealth power to 'grant financial assistance to any State on such terms and conditions as Parliament thinks fit' included specifying end uses. The introduction of such grants for road construction over three years from 1923 marked the effective start of what constituted the main form of tied grants for the next 30 years. This 'interesting exception to the general philosophy of the Commonwealth concerning grants to the states' was an important early instance of the Constitution being interpreted according to its literal wording to get the desired result instead of honouring the intentions of its drafters. Over succeeding decades, tied grants gradually became central to Commonwealth–state financial relations.[61] As such, this constitutes an important part of Page's legacy.

Tied grants for roads were first mooted at the Premiers' Conference of May 1923, leading to the *Main Roads Development Act 1923*. The Commonwealth directed £500,000 to the states to construct rural main roads, to be matched pound for pound by each state up to their prescribed share of the total (based on a mixture of population and geographic size). Proposals for specific projects had to be approved by the Commonwealth Minister for Works and Railways, then Percy Stewart.[62] Similar arrangements were repeated in 1924, and again in 1925 when funding was greatly increased. The Commonwealth was clearly signalling a lack of trust in state willingness to pursue national development vigorously, a characteristic Page concern.

That the Commonwealth's concurrent negotiations with the states over wider federal financial relations never seem to have jeopardised these tied grants is a measure of their importance to Page. His action as the initial scheme approached expiration at the end of 1925–26 is a fine example of his commitment and rationalism. During his 1925 trip to the United

---

60   Bureau of Transport Economics, *Road Grants Legislation in Australia: Commonwealth Government Involvement, 1900–1981*, Bureau of Transport Economics Occasional Paper no. 48, Australian Government Publishing Service, Canberra, 1981, p. 5. The legislation was the *Loan Act 1922*.
61   Mathews and Jay, *Federal Finance*, pp. 98–9. Page's *Australian Dictionary of Biography* entry states that he acquired the idea of tied grants from the Royal Commission on Taxation.
62   Draft agenda paper 'Proposed National Main Road Development', in NAA, CP103/11, 818.

States and Canada he had studied federal and local government road policies, and on his return proposed the creation of a new federal highways commission of senior Commonwealth and state engineers to plan out a national road network, and for it to be empowered to apportion monies for works accordingly.[63] Following its re-election in November 1925, the Bruce–Page Government moved to fund its increased road grants by higher customs duties on petrol. Page said that this would protect locally owned refiners (then essentially the Commonwealth-owned Commonwealth Oil Refineries) and make up for tax avoidance by larger foreign-owned oil companies.[64] The Commonwealth also argued that using petrol duties to generate the revenue required was equitable in that the cost was borne by road users.

The result was the *Federal Aid Roads Act 1926* (1926 Act). This was widely recognised as having quite different implications for federal–state relations than previous legislation. It allocated £2 million annually to the states for an unprecedented 10-year period and imposed a far greater degree of Commonwealth control. Despite Page's pleas that 'good roads, and an efficient transport system, are an essential part of our machinery of national development', the legislation met with objections ranging from the threat road transport posed to railways to denunciations of the petrol duty.[65] It was not only opposed by oil companies but also was the subject of unsuccessful legal challenges by Victoria and South Australia that eventually reached the Privy Council. (A young Robert Menzies appeared as a counsel for Victoria. He argued that section 96 referred only to the strictly financial terms of Commonwealth grants to the states and was not intended to effectively broaden Commonwealth powers. Menzies did not deign to mention Page in his published account of the origins of tied grants.)[66]

The importance of this legislation to Page is reflected in his vitriolic ripostes to criticism from the oil companies, calling them 'monopolistic foreign importing interests' bent on 'the scotching of any development whatever

---

63   Page, *Truant Surgeon*, p. 147; see also 'Roads', an undated memo reporting on the US and Canadian systems of road funding that recommended an Australian Federal Highways Commission, EPP, folder 1775.
64   Page, *Truant Surgeon*, p. 148; see also draft of this part of *Truant Surgeon*, 'National Transport System', at EPP, folder 1857.
65   *Commonwealth Parliamentary Debates*, 6 August 1926, p. 5030.
66   See Robert Menzies, *Central Power in the Australian Commonwealth: An Examination of the Growth of Commonwealth Power in the Australian Federation*, University Press of Virginia, Charlottesville, 1967, pp. 76–7.

in the Commonwealth that will tend to make us more independent of them'.[67] The government's justification remained simple. The Minister for Works and Railways (now W.C. Hill) spoke of roads as 'a problem of national importance, and of too great magnitude for the various State Governments to handle without the aid of the National Government'.[68]

The 1926 Act's funding was mostly for rural roads, including 'main roads which open up and develop new country'.[69] Following the American example, the Commonwealth imposed detailed specifications for road construction. The states had to submit proposals covering a five-year period for approval by the Commonwealth minister, and add 15 shillings for every pound they received (equating to 75 per cent of the Commonwealth grant). All roads built using these grants were to be maintained by the states out of other funds and to the satisfaction of the Commonwealth, or else grants could be suspended. Page's powerful federal highways commission did not come to pass, but a Federal Aid Roads Board served as a consultative body of ministers and engineers. This 1926 model survived until just 1931, when the Scullin Government gave the states much more autonomy in the use of the grants.

Over a decade later, Page looked back on the 1926 Act as having 'revolutionised in many respects the whole of the roads problem of Australia'.[70] In his 1956 evidence to a New South Wales inquiry into local government boundaries, he spoke proudly of having been personally responsible for this scheme, 'the main defence against shire bankruptcy, under which the road user pays his fair share of road construction and upkeep in addition to the contributions of the local residents and ratepayers'.[71] Despite the challenges from the states, Page did not see himself as using the roads scheme to impose unreasonable control. When the Chifley Government tightened road funding arrangements in 1947, Page complained of the Commonwealth becoming 'the controller instead of the partner'.[72]

---

67  Draft speech by Page, undated, c. 1926, EPP, folder 417.
68  *Commonwealth Parliamentary Debates*, 27 July 1926, p. 4590.
69  Section 5 of the *Federal Aid Roads Act 1926*.
70  *Commonwealth Parliamentary Debates*, 30 June 1937, p. 753.
71  'Local Government Enquiry Commencing at Grafton on 10th September 1956 on Proposed Redivision of Local Government Boundaries – Evidence of Sir Earle Page, MP', EPP, folder 1798.
72  'Memorandum on Federal Aid Roads', an undated history of road funding prepared by or for Page, c. 1947, EPP, folder 2577.

There is support for Page's claims of a decisive personal role in these early tied grants. In 1950 the Australian Automobile Association attributed the 1923 legislation to 'crusading countrymen' in the federal parliament. It added that the 1926 legislation, 'derived from American and Canadian practice', had 'exerted a revolutionary influence on road patterns, construction, administration and finance'.[73] In a 1952 speech Sir John Kemp, chairman of the Queensland Main Roads Board and delegate to a 1926 national conference of roads ministers and engineers on the Commonwealth's then forthcoming legislation, credited Page with creating the roads grants and having 'inaugurated what until recently was the greatest scheme of public works Australia had yet seen'.[74] (The Bruce Highway in Queensland is, incidentally, named not for Stanley Bruce but for one Henry Adam Bruce, a Labor state and federal parliamentarian.)

Tied grants eventually became a staple of Commonwealth–state financial relations that to this day enable the Commonwealth to use its fiscal power to impose control and reap kudos. They were most famously used in the post-war era and beyond as the main basis for Commonwealth funding of higher education. Page's contribution to institutionalising tied grants alone gives him a significant place in the evolution of the Australian federation. He later became an advocate of all Commonwealth grants to the states being tied to a specific purpose, particularly for hydroengineering. In a speech of May 1956, Page told parliament that 'it is absurd that we in this parliament should be raising enormous sums of money, and making ourselves most unpopular throughout Australia, simply to hand the money to the states without any tag on it at all; without any suggestion that there should be co-ordination'. With no small degree of overstatement, he said that the Commonwealth should re-establish how 'in the 1920s there was a most cordial co-operation with all the states'.[75]

Page was more successful with roads than he was with national railway unification: a notable exception was the unification of the Sydney–Brisbane line that included construction of a bridge over the Clarence at Grafton. The bridge was completed in 1932, well after the Bruce–Page

---

73 Australian Automobile Association, *A National Roads Policy for Australia*, issued as a submission to the Commonwealth Government, Wynyard, c. 1950, pp. 8–9, copy at EPP, folder 1238.
74 Sir John Kemp speech, 'Some Aspects of Modern Transport and their Relation to Road Construction', 20 March 1952, EPP, folder 1238; see also Kay Cohen, 'Kemp, Sir John Robert (1883–1955)', *Australian Dictionary of Biography*, adb.anu.edu.au/biography/kemp-sir-john-robert-10717/text18987, published first in hardcopy volume 15, Melbourne University Press, Carlton, Vic., 2000.
75 *Commonwealth Parliamentary Debates*, 22 May 1956, pp. 2321, 2322.

Government had lost office. Page used Commonwealth funding to do much for his electorate, including legislation in 1924 for the Grafton to Brisbane rail line and the sealing of the road from Grafton to the coast.

Page never saw himself as being absolutely bound by obligations to the governments in which he served. Bruce allowing him latitude to pursue some of his personal goals was perhaps due to the prime minister privately reasoning that this was part of the price of a successful partnership. Page accepted many of the inevitable strictures of high office, but remained alert to how his status as a senior government minister presented him with opportunities to pursue his personal policy vision, then and always his ultimate interest.

# 4

# GOVERNMENT AND PARTY
## The Basis of Page's Power

Page's standing as the second most senior minister in the Bruce–Page Government and leader of the Country Party was central to his ability to pursue his developmentalist agenda. Page the personality was a singular holder of high office, and the dynamics and priorities of government and party provided him with both confidence and opportunity. His policy influence was based on his compatibility with Stanley Bruce's and his government's commitment to national development; the maintenance of the Country Party–Nationalist coalition; and on the effective consolidation of policy authority within the Country Party with the leader of the federal parliamentary party. Events in the mid-1920s were critically important: Page decisively defended the coalition from internal challenges and shifted the locus of power in his party away from farmers' organisations and towards himself.

## Treasurer Page in office

Page was a confident treasurer and party leader, imbued with a striving sense of personal purpose. He was conspicuously different from other politicians, not least through his continuing to live up to the truant surgeon tag by, as Ellis put it, being willing to 'as cheerfully minister to a violent opponent as to a firm political friend'.[1] Recollections of peers and adversaries alike give a strong impression of an assertive minister who ranged far beyond his portfolio responsibilities in pursuing his national

---

1   Ellis, *A History of the Australian Country Party*, p. 326.

vision. Jack Lang recalled how as a newly elected premier of New South Wales in 1925 he was the subject of a visitation from the Commonwealth treasurer. Page 'bustled in, full of energy and assurance', and 'seemed to think that ... my agreement was only a matter of form'. Lang, hardly a shrinking violet, was affronted that Page 'was lecturing me as if I was a young medical student'.[2] Page's high standing in the Bruce–Page Government lent him to expect a say in almost every major decision and a vantage point from which to survey the direction of the entire nation.

As treasurer, Page's agreement in principle with the need to restrict government expenditure was never allowed to obstruct his developmentalist agenda. He took little interest in a Commonwealth public service that was then oriented to process and administration, as against substantive policy. Page's personal papers and official records contain scant evidence of reliance on his own department for support of any sort. His memoirs make only passing reference to just one of the two secretaries of the Treasury who worked under him: James Collins, for his assistance in 1924 with legislation on central banking.[3] At the day-to-day level, Page 'brought despair to secretaries, public servants and fellow ministers bearing neat files of papers and impeccable records' by dismembering the files in question. Exchanges with senior officials gave the superficial illusion that he lacked purpose as conversation leapt from topic to topic and were at risk of termination by a sudden Page decision to break for a game of tennis or a nap on his office couch.[4] Frank Green noted with distaste Page's habit of assuming that a partner in conversation agreed with him and concluding the matter under discussion by simply moving on to another issue.[5]

Yet even if the public service had been strong on policy advising, Page would not have let it intrude on this agenda. He habitually preferred outside experts to help him pursue his goals. Page, conspicuously, did not conform to the early Country Party's suspicion of big business and so sought the counsel of such figures as Herbert Gepp, general manager of the Electrolytic Zinc Company, and F.B. (Tim) Clapp, chairman of Australian General Electric. Page the incorrigible optimist assumed that a policy case presented clearly and logically to people of influence was bound to win

---

2   Jack Lang, *I Remember: Autobiography*, McNamara's Books, Katoomba, NSW, 1980 (first published 1956), p. 239.
3   Page, *Truant Surgeon*, p. 116. The other was James Heathershaw.
4   Ellis, *A History of the Australian Country Party*, pp. 326–7.
5   Green, *Servant of the House*, p. 103.

their support. This attitude survived repeated disappointments that would have discouraged a less persistent individual. By contrast, Page made few attempts to reach out to organised labour.

His attraction to robust business leaders was leavened by ongoing dalliances with progressive intellectual figures such as Griffith Taylor and the pioneering sociologist C.H. Northcott. Page's sporadic dealings with these figures were conducted through correspondence, perusal of their publications and occasional meetings. The emphasis was more on validation of his ideas than openness to new concepts. Northcott, for example, who also hailed from the Clarence River region, corresponded with Page on their shared interest in population distribution and a proposed expert commission to assess new legislation.[6] Page drew on whatever written authorities and exemplars seemed to offer support. One of his favourite sources was a 1922 study of the economic history of the United States by the British trade diplomat John Joyce Broderick. Page interpreted this authoritative text very liberally and highlighted in his personal copy its passages on assistance to farmers and hydroelectricity. He found Broderick especially handy for making the case that new states would of themselves spark development. Page was still referencing Broderick as late as his April 1957 speech to the Country Party Annual Conference.[7]

What influence such progressive thinkers had on Page was to the not inconsiderable extent that during the 1920s he became an advocate of national efficiency. This very broad concept was in practice 'synonymous with whatever was virtuous in progressive eyes', but was taken by Page to mean government structures that could further his national vision through such means as economic planning, coordination between levels of government and the selective nurturing of industries – not efficiency as imposed by rule of the free market.[8] In 1926 the Adelaide *Register* dismissed a characteristic Page speech as being of 'prodigious length, disarmingly egotistical and generously studded with references to national development, orderly marketing, improved distribution and all else that may be summed up in the blessed words National Efficiency'.[9]

---

6  See Northcott's farewell letter to Page, 5 September 1928, as he returned to England, Earle Page papers, UNE Archives, A180, box 10, folder 80.
7  John Joyce Broderick, *Report on the Economic, Financial and Industrial Conditions of the United States of America in 1922*, Department of Overseas Trade, HMSO, London, 1923; see Page's copy and his April 1957 speech at EPP, folders 2723 and 2607 respectively.
8  Quote from Michael Roe, *Nine Australian Progressives: Vitalism in Bourgeois Social Thought 1890–1960*, University of Queensland Press, St Lucia, Qld, 1984, p. 11.
9  Editorial in the Adelaide *Register* of 22 June 1926, p. 8.

In private, Page occasionally complained of the pressures of political life and contrasted the ugliness of party politics with his own higher values. In August 1922, amid his harrying of the Hughes Government, he shared with Ethel his despair that politics brought out 'the lowest in human nature'. Amid the 'fighting with tooth and claw', both 'H & M.G.' (Hughes and Massy-Greene) were 'unscrupulous to a degree', as against the 'clear thinking and straight acting' that Page saw himself upholding. Page feared that he was 'just too soft for this work'.[10] Such dark reflections were to reappear in the late 1930s. Page kept his personal fears to himself and to his wife: others rarely sensed any doubts. Late in 1924, he proceeded on what was publicly described as a 'health trip' to North America as 'Dr Page's health has for some time been unsatisfactory, due largely to the strenuous time he had last year'.[11] Yet even on this trip Page immersed himself in United States and Canadian development policy and so returned home brimming with ideas concerning roads and much else.

## Page and Bruce: Not so odd a couple

The Bruce–Page Government almost immediately established itself as Australia's most self-consciously developmentalist administration since Federation. Although the 1920s was a decade of widespread optimism about Australian development, the shared determination of Bruce and Page was needed to translate this into policy. These two inexperienced party leaders did not move as stealthily as has sometimes been claimed. From the outset they tried to alter fundamentals, strongly signalled by the comprehensive overhaul of federalism that they proposed at the 1923 Premiers' Conference just three months after coming to office. Staley and Nethercote, in their account of Australian liberalism, considered Bruce and Page to have headed a government of 'active interventionism'.[12] They did more than any of their predecessors, and most of their successors, to define and consolidate the role of the Commonwealth in promoting national development. This was by asserting its leadership of policy fields where it shared responsibilities with the states, by overhauling federal

---

10   Page to Ethel Page, 13 August 1922, Earle Page papers, UNE Archives, A180, box 9, folder 71.
11   *Daily Examiner*, 27 December 1924, p. 3. The term 'health trip' is used for example in the Perth *Daily News*, 15 December 1924, p. 7.
12   A.A. Staley and J.R. Nethercote, 'Liberalism and the Australian Federation', in J.R. Nethercote (ed.), *Liberalism and the Australian Federation*, The Federation Press, Leichhardt, NSW, 2001, p. 8; see also in this source Nethercote, 'Liberalism, Nationalism and Coalition 1910–29', especially pp. 128–33.

financial relations and, later in the decade, through promoting economic planning. Page's later view of the 1920s as a creative period when the coalition with the Nationalists 'permitted enormous strides to be made in Australian progress' celebrates the alacrity with which he and Bruce sought to reorganise the nation to developmentalist ends.[13]

The rapid forging of the coalition by Bruce and Page and the largely effective collaboration that followed was made possible by their being closer in broad policy outlook than is often realised. At the personal level, Page seemed scattergun alongside the stately, measured Bruce, but this was more stylistic than substantive. They shared a national outlook underpinned by faith in efficient, rational governance firmly under Commonwealth leadership. Unusually for party leaders of their time, neither had served in a state or colonial parliament. Ellis wrote as a witness of 'a unique partnership between these two complementary personalities imbued with similar broad objectives'.[14] Page thought that his working relationship with Bruce had been 'from the outset … intimate and cordial', and so he had 'few qualms about walking down the passage to see him, with or without knocking on the door'.[15] He recalled that 'Bruce and I had no difficulty in agreeing on the principle that a Government and the members of the Government should always express one opinion, and one voice only, on matters of government policy', and that it was rare for the Bruce–Page Cabinet to resort to a vote.[16]

Fundamental to their ability to work well together was the broad compatibility of the two men's respective visions of economic development. Bruce's was less fully defined than that of Page, and so remains open to wider interpretation. The prime minister's approach emphasised increasing the scale of the economy via immigration based on the more extensive and intensive use of rural land. He told an Imperial Conference in 1924 that 'Australia's aim above everything else is to populate her country and advance from her position of a very small people occupying a very vast territory'.[17] This goal was closely linked to a larger vision for the economic development of the Empire, with Britain supplying manufactures and finance to Dominions that in return provided foodstuffs, raw materials

---

13  'Australian Country Party Complimentary Dinner to Sir Earle Page', EPP, folder 2358.
14  Ellis, *A History of the Australian Country Party*, p. 100.
15  Ibid., p. 129.
16  Page, *Truant Surgeon*, p. 101.
17  Quoted in W.H. Richmond, 'S.M. Bruce and Australian economic policy 1923–9', *Australian Economic History Review*, vol. 23, no. 2, 1983, p. 239. Richmond does not discuss Page's views.

and outlets for excess population. Page recalled having also long seen a bigger population as essential for the nation's ability to 'save enough to provide the amenities and developments for future generations' and 'to defend it against outside foes'.[18] The very mixed economic circumstances of the 1920s also helped Page, in that the Bruce–Page Government felt it had a duty to enliven a generally sluggish economy. This 'deeply disturbed course of economic activity' included a slight recession in the early 1920s and a dip from 1925 to 1926 that heralded the Great Depression.[19]

Like Page, Bruce saw natural resources as key to the nation's future: the economic historian W.H. Richmond classified him as a 'rural optimist'. Bruce did not advocate a fully laissez-faire economy and accepted arbitration and tariffs as important, though not central.[20] He also accepted that rural industries needed government assistance to secure better access to British markets, notably through imperial preference and marketing support. But he greatly preferred that primary producers improve their international competitiveness by more efficient management and promotion than by reliance on continued government support. Like Page, Bruce was more interested in improving efficiency than in protecting rural producers through orderly marketing.[21] He agreed with Page that protection should favour efficient industries so as not to unduly handicap those rural producers who had to compete internationally. But he struggled to find a logical basis for determining tariff levels and for identifying exactly which industries should be protected. A major gap between the two was that Bruce remained only a tepid advocate of new states and regionalism, as Thompson's 1923 delegation discovered. Like Hughes, Bruce put much of the onus for new states back onto state governments.[22]

Both men thought of themselves as essentially apolitical. As one of the few Australian national political leaders with a personal background in commerce rather than party politics, Bruce claimed that 'we were guided not by ideological motives, but by strict business principles'.[23] He and Page shared a lack of faith in the capacity of established government departments to implement developmentalist strategy. They instead tried

---

18  'Australian Country Party Complimentary Dinner to Sir Earle Page', EPP, folder 2358.
19  Butlin, Barnard and Pincus, *Government and Capitalism*, pp. 77–80.
20  Richmond, 'S.M. Bruce and Australian economic policy', pp. 238–40, 256.
21  Ibid., pp. 244–6.
22  Ellis, *New Australian States*, pp. 168–9.
23  Quoted in Judith Brett, *Australian Liberals and the Moral Middle Class: From Alfred Deakin to John Howard*, Cambridge University Press, Cambridge, 2003, p. 80.

to institutionalise rationalism and efficiency through a string of boards and commissions led by forceful, technocratic business leaders such as Gepp, their epitome of a modern manager. This included the 1926 creation of the CSIR, Australia's first effective national science agency, chaired by the mechanical engineer George Julius. Bruce's speech to parliament on the legislation for this was a fine encapsulation of his commitment to national coordination and efficiency. His objective was 'not to create a great new centralised institute of research, but, for the benefit of both the primary and secondary industries, to bring about cooperation between existing agencies and to enlist the aid of the pure scientist, the universities, and every other agency at present handling scientific questions'. The CSIR was to be structured so as to involve the states and avoid duplication with them. Like Page, Bruce was impressed by the United States, and hoped Australian could emulate its business culture where 'individual employers are expending vast sums of money in attempts to improve their methods and generally to advance their efficiency'.[24] Page attributed his own strong support for the CSIR to 'my country background and scientific training'.[25]

The Bruce–Page Government also established, at about the same time, the Development and Migration Commission. This planning and advisory body was to reinforce efficiency and population growth by guiding the placement of the greatest number of migrants on the land at the lowest cost.[26] It was of great importance to Page and is described in more detail in the following chapter. Such strong commitment to national efficiency under Commonwealth leadership did not readily appeal to state governments wary of Commonwealth intrusions, with the result that at premiers' conferences Bruce considered it necessary to exhort them to place national duty above politics. The Bruce–Page Government just before its fall also sought to create a bureau of economic research, which did not eventuate.

Page also largely matched his prime minister on the wider public issues that defined the party divide with the ALP. He often spoke of the deep divisions between the government and a Labor Opposition that was both highly protectionist and opposed to large-scale migration. Page strongly supported private control of the main means of production, declaring himself during the 1922 election campaign in favour of

---

24   *Commonwealth Parliamentary Debates*, 26 May 1926, p. 2330.
25   Page, *Truant Surgeon*, p. 138.
26   Richmond, 'S.M. Bruce and Australian economic policy', p. 247.

'the strictest limitation of Government enterprise to developmental works and public utilities'.[27] He preferred voluntary commissions to compulsory arbitration, and producer-led voluntary cooperative pools over compulsory government-managed arrangements. As treasurer, Page agreed to the sale of public enterprises such as the Commonwealth Harness Factory, the Williamstown Dockyards, the Commonwealth Woollen Mills and the Commonwealth Shipping Line, and also supported the termination of Commonwealth control of the sale of sugar.[28] Yet, as Page saw himself as more practical than ideological, he had few qualms about simultaneously supporting creation of a publicly owned central bank. Page also fully backed, but did not lead, Bruce's and the Nationalists' reactions to industrial turmoil. He recalled of the shipping strike of 1925 that the government had gone to the election of that year 'on the issue of a mandate to enforce constitutional law against mob rules [sic] and strikes'. The government's whole record 'depended on a united resistance to Labour [sic] doctrine and industrial anarchy'. He saw no prospect of a rapprochement with the ALP on these matters.[29]

The priority that Page attached to maintaining the coalition meant that he was usually at pains to work well with Bruce. But Page appears to have overestimated the depth of their relationship and at times inadvertently tested the prime minister's tolerance. Bruce's comments to his first biographer, Cecil Edwards, imply that he saw their closeness as more political than personal. Although it was 'a more or less happy combination', Bruce's recollection of Page's daily 'new brainwaves' that 'were nearly always half-baked' indicates wariness on his part.[30] He once told Robert Menzies that 'the working of Page's mind is still a complete mystery to me notwithstanding my very considerable experience of its vagaries'.[31]

Bruce's attitude to Page remained necessarily different from that towards other ministers, as their ability to work together was essential to the government's survival. The prime minister's tolerant (if patrician) nature helped. Edwards recalled Bruce as being 'kind and helpful' to him when a novice member of the press gallery in the early 1920s, and invariably

---

27 Melbourne *Argus*, 27 October 1922, p. 10.
28 Page, *Truant Surgeon*, pp. 108–11.
29 Ibid., p. 172.
30 Quoted in Edwards, *Bruce of Melbourne*, p. 82.
31 Bruce to Menzies, 4 October 1939, quoted in Martin, *Robert Menzies: A Life, Volume 1*, p. 279.

'courteous and dependable' thereafter.[32] Bruce's appreciation of Page's strengths and weaknesses was the basis of his ability to productively channel his deputy's enthusiasms. He recognised Page's creativity but doubted his ability to persuade – 'Page could have the most brilliant idea on earth, but he couldn't put it over'.[33] Hence Bruce's practice of opening premiers' conferences himself with long statements of intent that left Page with a subsidiary role in later debate.

Most historians correctly picture the Bruce–Page Government as a genuine partnership, but one led by Bruce. They were not equals in government. Page often initiated proposals, but Bruce retained final say. Bruce himself commented that regardless of the impression given in *Truant Surgeon* about who usually originated ideas, he was 'not frightfully concerned which of the things we did originated with him or with me, because in the long run it was my responsibility'.[34] As their ministerial colleague George Pearce observed, Bruce ultimately ran his own administration and frequently saw advantage in letting Page think he was in charge.[35] Page's own recollections are broadly consistent with this image of Page initiating but with the prime minister having authority to veto. He recalled that Bruce 'would cross-examine me for hours on every phrase; ruminate on the problem for a day or two, expound its details with the greatest clarity, and often suggest modifications or amendments which would strengthen its foundations'.[36] One of the most detailed studies to touch on the policy interaction of the two concerns Australia's support for a British return to the gold standard: it is evident that Bruce had final authority and issued guidance to his treasurer accordingly.[37] Similarly, when Bruce departed overseas in 1926, he presented Page with detailed written instructions on how he wanted outstanding business managed in his absence, ranging from War Service Homes to an offer from Sidney Myer to act as an Australian trade representative, hardly the act of a prime minister not in full charge.[38]

---

32   Edwards, *The Editor Regrets*, p. 35.
33   Edwards, *Bruce of Melbourne*, p. 82.
34   Ibid., p. 82.
35   Peter Heydon, *Quiet Decision: A Study of George Foster Pearce*, Melbourne University Press, Carlton, Vic., 1965, p. 94. See Edwards, *Bruce of Melbourne*, p. 82.
36   Page, *Truant Surgeon*, p. 103–4.
37   Kosmas Tsokhas, 'The Australian role in Britain's return to the gold standard', *Economic History Review*, vol. 47, no. 1, February 1994; see especially p. 134.
38   See Bruce to Page, 5 September 1926, EPP, folder 2368.

In recording the Bruce–Page Government's achievements, Ellis implied that most were driven by Page alone. His history of the Country Party, for example, lists initiatives that Page proposed in a flurry of memoranda prepared after returning from his travels in North America and Britain during 1925 – creation of a federal department of agriculture, rural credits, a national health council, and tied grants for water and sewage in country towns (subsequently thwarted by the states) and for roads.[39] This is an impressive list and a testament to Page's creativity. If he did not lead the government, Page nonetheless marked himself as a more original thinker than Bruce by adding a regionalist dimension to national policy and by linking different policy fields to a wider purpose of shaping the nation accordingly. The rural bias of the Bruce–Page Government was not just crude pork-barrelling but also reflected Page's commitment to spatially based development.

Against this, Ellis's list consists mainly of matters of interest specifically to the Country Party. It does not include several Bruce–Page initiatives of this time that had broader national significance, such as the Financial Agreement, which have a mixed provenance that Page must share with Bruce. Nor did Ellis dwell on Page's inability to secure outcomes on decentralisation, hydroelectricity, new states and related constitutional change. Bruce remained far less interested in these than did Page. It is significant that where Page failed in an objective he lacked Bruce's wholehearted support. To achieve major change, the Bruce–Page Government needed the full engagement of both party leaders, particularly in the united application of Commonwealth fiscal power to overcome opposition from state governments.

## Page upholds the coalition

The foremost means by which Page enhanced his standing in government and party was his consolidation of the coalition with the Nationalists. The agreement that he and Bruce forged in 1923 faced periodic challenges from within both participating parties. Page withstood these by intervening decisively in potentially divisive internal Country Party debates on strategy.

---

39   Ellis, *A History of the Australian Country Party*, pp. 102–4.

Following a series of instances of Nationalist and Country Party candidates contesting the same seats at state elections, Bruce and Page in 1924 sought to reaffirm the coalition by devising a further pact. Its central feature was an immunity clause discouraging such contests at the forthcoming 1925 federal election. This provided for each party to refrain from running a candidate in an electorate where there was already an incumbent from the other, and that in Labor-held seats the candidate should come from whichever party was strongest locally. If for some reason a seat still elicited candidates from both non-Labor parties, they were to exchange preferences. In effect, the Country Party was agreeing to limit its expansion to what seats it could win from the ALP. Both Page and Bruce threatened to resign from their respective party leaderships rather than drop the new pact. Serious opposition still came from within the AFFO and its membership of farmers' organisations, especially the radical faction of the VFU and associations in South Australia and Western Australia. One of the main complaints was that, by upholding the coalition, Page was endangering the separate identity of the Country Party and committing it to an anti-Labor role.[40] The agreement was therefore amended to make exceptions for individual seats, but this did not prevent the disputatious Stewart from angrily resigning from Cabinet in August 1924 on the grounds that the pact restricted voters' choice by protecting sitting MPs. Page – a little ironically – was to later describe Stewart as 'a brilliant man' who 'possessed the defect of being too egotistical for protracted teamwork'.[41]

The attacks on Page over the 1924 pact were the most serious test that he had faced as party leader. This opposition was attributable, in no small part, to his having engineered the pact personally with Bruce and then proceeding to insist that the party accept it without change, just as he had the 1923 agreement. Page as an autocratic party leader was determined to fight for the coalition as a basis for pursuing his goals. In his defence, Page could point to tangible gains that the Country Party had been able to deliver in coalition, such as abolition of federal land tax on Crown leaseholds, protection of rural industries, rural telephone services, the tied grants for roads and the Commonwealth Bank's Rural Credits Department. Page told a party conference in Adelaide that it was no coincidence that Labor was in power in states that lacked a coalition.[42]

---

40  Graham, *Formation of the Australian Country Parties*, pp. 223–6.
41  Page, *Truant Surgeon*, p. 174.
42  Port Pirie *Recorder*, 10 September 1924, p. 1.

His ability to see off challenges to his authority benefited fortuitously from sizeable budget surpluses from 1922–23 to 1924–25 arising from higher than anticipated customs and excise revenue during a rare inter-war period of buoyancy. Customs and excise constituted 66 per cent of total Commonwealth revenue in 1922–23 and over 70 per cent in 1924–25.[43]

That the coalition survived such challenges is remarkable given the fractiousness of the early Country Party. The still formative federal party lacked a solid institutional basis for constraining a strong parliamentary leader, leaving Page to manage the relationship with the Nationalists. (The state country parties were often more tightly organised.) This may help explain Page's power: opponents such as Stewart kept splitting away rather than having the option of organising opposition through an established party decision-making mechanism. Page also flourished because he successfully balanced his grander visions with concern to maintain the coalition, hence his caution about promoting new states and calculated acceptance of tariffs. The success of this first rural–urban federal coalition had a lasting impact on Australian politics and became a major factor in Page's long-term standing in the party.

More immediately, the scale of the government's win at the 1925 election helped Page consolidate his position as party leader and upholder of the coalition. The Nationalists won 11 extra seats and the Country Party one more. Page resisted lingering calls to end the coalition and did not object when the Nationalists took two more seats in an expanded Cabinet. He successfully maintained the federal coalition right up to 1929, despite splits over Country Party autonomy in the Victorian and South Australian parties in 1926 and 1928 respectively. The main point of contention that still could have ended the coalition – tariff policy – was left largely unaddressed.

Page also benefited in the eyes of the wider Country Party from the Bruce–Page Government's identification with orderly marketing programs. The protection this provided to primary producers included tariffs on some food imports (such as maize, hops and sugar); subsidies on the exports of high cost industries (such as dried and canned fruits); and Australian domestic parity prices for exports (notably dairy products). Some of these programs originated with the Hughes Government, including subsidies for beef exports and the embargo on sugar imports, or were the result of

---

43   Graham, *Formation of the Australian Country Parties*, p. 230.

concessions reluctantly made to pressure groups, such as subsidisation of canned fruit exports.[44] By early 1928, the Commonwealth Department of Markets was administering 15 federal Acts and nine producer boards and similar entities.[45] The sole major agricultural industry not receiving government support was wool, which by commanding a strong position in international markets had less need for bolstering. The inter-war period was to see the creation of a complex web of Commonwealth and state support schemes for farm industries, operating mainly through high domestic prices and with only the strongly export-oriented wool and wheat industries generally receiving less effective assistance.[46]

Page's ambivalence about orderly marketing schemes made him a less consistent originator and advocate of these arrangements than were other senior Country Party figures. Especially prominent was his future deputy leader Thomas Paterson, who in 1925–26 originated the earliest significant such program, the eponymous Paterson voluntary dairy scheme. Page could be economical in crediting others, but in his memoirs paid full tribute to Paterson for this initiative.[47] Page's ambivalence was the basis of his 1924 agreement with Bruce that industry-led cooperative marketing schemes should pay their own way, leading to the government's refusal to sponsor a compulsory wheat pool. Although the Rural Credits Department that Page had established in 1925 extended grants to various voluntary cooperative pools, he personally rejected a system of compulsory pools coordinated by a federal authority, pointing to the strictures imposed by section 92 of the Constitution guaranteeing free trade between the states. This may have also reflected Nationalist Party reluctance to keep indulging its junior coalition partner; if so, it again illustrates that maintaining the coalition took priority for Page over the demands of the Country Party's more radical elements.[48]

---

44   Ibid., pp. 228, 231.
45   'The Marketing of Primary Products: Statement from the Commonwealth Minister of Markets and Migration, Hon. T. Paterson', in *Supplement to The Economic Record*, February 1928, pp. 124–5.
46   A.G. Lloyd, 'Agricultural price policy', in D.B. Williams (ed.), *Agriculture in the Australian Economy*, second edition, Sydney University Press, Sydney, 1982 (first published 1967), pp. 359–60.
47   Page, *Truant Surgeon*, p. 105. The Paterson Scheme centred on dairy factories paying a levy on butter they produced, generating funds that were then paid back as a bounty on the approximately one-third of output that was exported. As the local market price was set during the export season at export parity, the scheme resulted in a rise in local consumer prices, i.e. the other two-thirds of sales, leading to a net gain. The scheme operated from 1926 to 1934. See Lloyd, 'Agricultural Price Policy', in Williams, *Agriculture in the Australian Economy*, p. 367. Paterson had felt that the domestic price for butter had been unfairly deflated by tending to be set at the London price less handling and other costs.
48   Graham, *Formation of the Australian Country Parties*, pp. 228, 244.

## Page and the Country Party: Shifting policy authority

In addition to successfully defending the coalition, Page consolidated his central role in policy formulation within the Country Party through changes to its national organisation. Bruce and Page's largely shared views on development made them politically closer to each other than to their respective parties. The stress in Page's memoirs on how well they worked together contrasts with the paucity of references to major policy being initiated by his own party colleagues. Both leaders formulated policy with only as much regard for their respective party rooms as was necessary. Page appears to have been frustrated by what he saw as the narrower visions of his colleagues, such as on new states and electrification. He was not especially close to his party deputy, W.G. Gibson, other than sharing an interest in rural communication and radio services. Drummond, who sat in the New South Wales legislature, remained his only real parliamentary confidant.

Yet, as Graham observed of Page, 'no other person in the party was as widely known and respected, and he demanded – and obtained – that unquestioning loyalty which Australian farmers are accustomed to give their leaders'.[49] Page used this status to play a decisive role in encouraging the state organisations to shift policy-making from the party's nascent national organisation to the federal parliamentary party. Page thereby became a great shaper of the Country Party, creating policy space for himself in the process. He had long held that major decisions on policy and strategy should be left to MPs, not the party organisation and outrider bodies. In 1924 he declared to the VFU that 'a leader must give a lead' and 'should not be expected to run to the rank and file for every little thing'.[50]

The main change that embedded Page's policy authority was the replacement of the AFFO as the party's foremost national body by the Australian Country Party Association (ACPA) at a national conference of the Country Party and allied organisations in Melbourne on 23 March 1926. Although the internal unity of all political parties was often tenuous in the 1920s – even an issue as seemingly innocuous as construction of a Sydney to Brisbane uniform gauge railway line led nine ALP parliamentarians and nine Nationalists to cross the floor of

---

49   Ibid., p. 287.
50   Ibid., p. 248.

federal parliament in opposite directions – the Country Party was at first especially loosely organised.[51] (There was also a split over the 1926 tied road grants legislation, which was opposed by some Nationalists and only passed with Labor support.) AFFO support for any particular position, such as the 1924 electoral pact, was not decisive as it was essentially a confederation that formulated recommendations for approval by state bodies, which were themselves bound by their respective constitutions.

As federal parliamentary party leader, Page did not have power over the AFFO, let alone the state organisations. In March 1925, for example, the AFFO demanded that the parliamentary party try to abolish high tariffs on agricultural machinery and introduce a compulsory wheat pool.[52] Page favoured a full reorganisation of the party and so at the March 1926 conference proposed an 'amended organisation of the Australian Country Party so as to form a political organisation to which all electors whose sympathies are with the policy of the organisation may belong' (thereby also seeking to widen the party to include rural-based secondary industry).[53] Page was reported as declaring it 'essential to separate the industrial from the political activities of the Country Party'.[54] Page told Graham in interviews conducted in 1956 that his main motivation in creating the ACPA was a clearer division between the party organisation and the federal parliamentary party. This would place the development of policy detail and parliamentary tactics firmly with the latter (while still allowing ACPA conferences a lead role in formulating the party's general policy platform).[55] In his memoirs, Page recalled that a stronger party organisation based on a federal structure would 'give balance to the Party's parliamentary policy', but added the more immediate motivation of managing the rural radicals on the coalition issue, especially Stewart who in March 1926 left the VFU to form a breakaway Country Progressive Party.[56]

Officials of state organisations had constituted the majority at AFFO conferences, but the constitution of the ACPA effectively institutionalised the dominance of the parliamentary party, especially in its provisions for the ACPA Central Council. These were drafted in 1926 and approved

---

51  Page, *Truant Surgeon*, p. 151.
52  Graham, *Formation of the Australian Country Parties*, pp. 284–5.
53  Ellis, *A History of the Australian Country Party*, p. 142.
54  *The Land*, 26 March 1926, p. 13.
55  Page, interview by B.D. Graham, 22 February and 7 March 1956, B.D. Graham papers, NLA, MS 8471.
56  Page, *Truant Surgeon*, p. 174.

the following year, creating a Central Council consisting of the federal parliamentary leader, two other federal representatives and 14 members elected from affiliated organisations. The role of federal parliamentarians was decisively enhanced by most of the organisations habitually appointing federal members as their representatives. Only eight delegates were needed to constitute a quorum, and the Central Council could appoint a smaller executive committee that needed only a quorum of three. The council was obliged to frame policy based on the party's platform in consultation with the federal parliamentary party. The ACPA met on average only annually in its first few years of existence, leaving the energetic Page a free hand to continue to build his extensive network of personal contacts and defend the coalition strategy.[57] Further, Page was appointed ACPA chair in 1927 and held this position until his death.

The growing dominance of Page and the parliamentary party was reflected in the federal Country Party's continued resistance to pressure from its supporting organisations and state bodies over tariffs. At a party meeting in February 1926 a motion on tariffs was put aside in favour of one calling for an inquiry into their effects, which Page was obliged to pass to the prime minister. (This led to the Brigden inquiry into tariffs, described in the next chapter.)[58] Similarly, in June 1927 the ACPA rejected a Western Australian motion for reduction of duties in favour of one calling for 'all-round protection' as advocated by Page.[59]

Page thus effectively made his own rules in the Country Party while it was still malleable. This was not to last. Over the next two decades the bulk of the party developed and consolidated its own priorities. There is one other concluding point in considering Page's role in government and party during the Bruce–Page years. After the government's fall in October 1929, it was Page, and not Bruce, who spent 1929–31 outside parliament and departed parliamentary politics for good in 1933, who maintained the principal developmentalist ideas that their government had upheld – Commonwealth-led coordination, an expressly national conception of development and planning, and the hope that development could be placed above party politics. An important aspect of Page's significance in Australian history is that he drew on his largely happy experience of the Bruce–Page Government to continue efforts to apply its precepts into the future.

---

57  Graham, *Formation of the Australian Country Parties*, pp. 285–7.
58  Ellis, *A History of the Australian Country Party*, pp. 119–20.
59  Graham, *Formation of the Australian Country Parties*, p. 246.

# 5

# PAGE AND THE FINAL THROES OF THE BRUCE–PAGE GOVERNMENT

Challenging the Nation through Planning and Federalism

During the latter 1920s and in the wake of the Cohen Royal Commission, Page shifted his attention from new states to trying to transform the nation through economic planning and the reform of federalism. This was enlivened by the Bruce–Page Government's creation of the Development and Migration Commission (DMC) and determination to finally resolve fiscal relations with the states. Historians widely recognise that Page played a major role in negotiating the Financial Agreement of 1927. Less well appreciated is that it was a time of consolidation of his own broader ideas about planning and federalism.

Page's commitment to national planning developed later than his other passions of regionalism, hydroelectricity and constitutional reform. He first expressed interest during the early 1920s, when, as a thoughtful new parliamentarian, he pondered ways to pursue the major themes of his August 1917 speech. This nascent interest only gelled when the Bruce–Page Government embarked on an institutionalised approach to planning by establishing the DMC in 1926. The principal task of this statutory authority was to appraise new development projects, but it also had a remarkably wide brief to investigate and attempt to guide the entire economy. Page upheld it as a working example of an expert agency that elevated development policy above party politics and used business leaders as advisers. Shortly after, Bruce and Page eliminated the vertical fiscal imbalance still dogging Australian federalism by using the Commonwealth's fiscal power to force the states to accept the Financial Agreement. They followed this success with a last concerted effort to have the states agree to the national coordination of policies on electricity, transport, health and other vital fields.

Page brought to each of these initiatives his characteristic energy and capacity for synthesis. For all his support for new states, he simultaneously advocated both national and regional scales of policy action. National economic planning, in particular, became one of his main means of trying to establish efficient new industries based on primary goods and of locating these to vitalise rural communities. In the final years of the Bruce–Page Government, Page was drawn to the DMC and planning amid related national debates over tariff policy. This attraction culminated in his attempt to have the DMC realise his hopes for regional development.

## Page champions planned national development and the DMC

The Country Party dabbled in planning as early as 1921 when it considered the 'complete survey and calculation of the resources of the Commonwealth', an idea that Page retained as the proper starting point for well-informed planning.[1] The following year he began the Country Party election policy speech with a declaration that 'Australia has reached the period in her history when her greatest need is sound government on an organised plan, recognising the stern necessity for economy without crippling the development of our primary and secondary industries'.[2] As treasurer, planning became a feature of his early speeches, such as in February 1924 when he told the citizens of Dalby in southern Queensland of the need for a 'national plan' for the development of 'power, roads, borrowing and finance'.[3] These early calls for planning were vaguely articulated – a sign that he was still developing his thoughts, for Page was not one to hold back on a fully formed idea. From 1925 he was

---

1   Handwritten draft statement of Country Party policy (undated, but associated documents suggest 1921), Earle Page papers, UNE Archives, A180, box 1, folder 1.
2   *The Land*, 27 October 1922, p. 4, copy in EPP, folder 2623.
3   Speech by Page, 30 February 1924, EPP, folder 1624.

speaking ringingly of the 'supreme importance' of Commonwealth–state cooperation in developing 'a national plan of development' covering transport, water use and much else.[4] He needed a working model and so his interest settled on the DMC.

Page's thinking on planning was almost certainly stimulated by Cabinet deliberations over February to May 1926 on establishing the DMC. Although this unprecedented agency became involved in attempts to shape the domestic economy, it originated with Australia's need to be seen to be better managing its participation in the Empire-wide strategy by which Britain responded to post-war unemployment and loss of overseas markets through export of capital and population to the Dominions. Australia's receptiveness to this was encouraged during these post-war years by urbanisation, industrialisation and ambitions for rural development. Prior to World War One, Australian immigration was largely the responsibility of the states. Following the 1921 Imperial Conference on Immigration, the British Government's *Empire Settlement Act 1922* established cost-sharing migration arrangements with the Dominions. In Australia, the 1923 Premiers' Conference agreed that Bruce should approach the British to negotiate a nationwide assisted migration scheme, which he duly raised at the 1923 Imperial Conference. The resultant '£34 million' Migration Agreement signed with Britain in April 1925 aimed for 450,000 assisted British settlers within 10 years.

In its ambition, the Migration Agreement exceeded previous arrangements involving the Australian states or the Commonwealth Government. It centred on the provision of cheap loans to fund development and migration linked to land settlement schemes. The Commonwealth Government raised the loans, and shared interest costs with Britain and the states. Specific development projects proposed by a state – defined broadly to include public works, land purchases and subsidisation of farmers – required the approval of all three governments concerned before funding would be made available. This gave the Commonwealth effective control over hitherto state-led migration and more firmly linked migration to national development policy.[5]

---

4  Page's 1925 election Country Party policy speech, copy in Ulrich Ellis papers, UNE Archives, A811, box 12, pp. 13, 15.
5  The agreement's complex origins are surveyed in Roe, *Australia, Britain, and Migration*, pp. 48–58.

The DMC served an important means by which Australia fulfilled its agreement obligations. Its approval was an essential condition of the Commonwealth's preparedness to fund a project. This met British concerns that funds provided on often generous terms would be well used and not lead to over-borrowing. Page later wrote of how 'never in the history of Empire relationships were more liberal [financial] terms offered to the Australian people', which he was determined to honour and thereby maintain.[6] There may also have been a concern to formally distance immigration from party politics, especially as there were indications that support for high levels of intake risked being held against the government. DMC tutelage improved the likelihood of the Migration Agreement being extended by encouraging the well-informed use of land and public funds and so expanding capacity to absorb migrants. In doing so, it also provided a model for planning based on the rigorous assessment of economic viability, use of advisers external to government and cooperation between levels of government.

The DMC was not Page's creation. It owed more to Bruce, supported by suggestions from the newspaper proprietor Sir Hugh Denison and also from Australia's representative in the British Foreign Office, Richard Casey, who in turn referenced the British Committee of Civil Research.[7] Introducing the DMC Bill into parliament, the prime minister said that Australia had failed to face the problem of development, having 'never had a stocktaking of our resources with a view to determining the industries that, having regard to our natural advantages, should be promoted'. Hence, now 'there must be a thorough and impartial examination of every scheme before it is approved'.[8] To such ends, the DMC had a near limitless brief to report on the Australian economy. It could investigate the establishment of new primary and secondary industries and conduct negotiations for the development of existing ones. It even had legislated provision for 'such other powers and functions as are prescribed', that classic catchall.[9] Page no doubt approved: his sense of urgency invariably blunted his appreciation of checks and balances.

---

6   Page, *Truant Surgeon*, p. 157.
7   See Roe, *Australia, Britain, and Migration*, pp. 64–8, on the origins of the DMC.
8   Development and Migration Commission, *First Annual Report for Period Ending 30 June 1927*, Commonwealth of Australia, Melbourne, 1927, pp. 5–6, EPP, folder 2322; and Roe, *Australia, Britain, and Migration*, p. 67.
9   *Development and Migration Act 1926*, section 13(1)(a)(vi).

The DMC sat apart from the mainstream of the Commonwealth public service as a legislated body corporate. It made extensive use of expert advisers from the business world. Herbert Gepp was appointed DMC chair and C.S. Nathan vice-chair, both business leaders with strong reputations for innovation and vision. Gepp was an energetic, if enigmatic, figure whose wide-ranging engagement with public policy included a central role in establishing the CSIR. Balance and wider acceptability were provided by the other two commissioners, former South Australian Labor premier John Gunn and New South Wales public servant E.P. Fleming. The DMC worked closely with Australia's newly emergent coterie of academic economists such as D.B. Copland, despite their frequent doubts about migration and Australia's development potential.[10] Page's habitual hope that expert opinion would validate his plans led him to initially welcome the DMC's use of policy experts, only to be disappointed when their rigour was applied to his vision for the Clarence Valley.

The DMC stressed efficiency, especially the more productive use of land through improved technology and management, but not Page's regionalism or electrification. Although it required ministerial approval to investigate broad development issues (while being free to initiate inquiries into specific projects), its chair proclaimed an expansive interpretation of its role. Shortly after his appointment, the blunt, assertive Gepp had printed for distribution a memo in which he declared the DMC 'the national clearing house for all ideas and schemes bearing upon economic development', with a responsibility to 'co-ordinate the whole of the developmental activities of Australia'.[11] He shared the Bruce–Page enthusiasm for national efficiency. Late in his tenure he told a University of Melbourne audience that 'problems of organisation lie at the root of Australia's economic difficulties' and that 'the Commission plays its part by ascertaining and stating the facts' in 'the application of science to industry and the consequent increase in efficiency'.[12]

Page's own approach to planning owed much to a simple but strongly held model. In brief, he considered that as the secondary and primary sectors were interdependent, each should be managed so as to generate incomes that maintained demand for the other's output. The prices of

---

10  Roe, *Australia, Britain, and Migration*, pp. 91, 112.
11  Memo by Gepp on the DMC, 17 November 1926, NAA, CP211/2, 57/7.
12  'Address to the Public Questions Society, University of Melbourne, April 1929', reproduced in Herbert Gepp, *Democracy's Danger: Addresses on Various Occasions*, Angus and Robertson, Sydney, 1939, pp. 34–5.

secondary and primary products needed to be brought into an alignment that maintained this mutually supportive demand and so kept the whole economy in balance. Farm prices and profitability were critical to determining demand for secondary goods, placing primary industries at the crucial centre of the economy. There was also an important place for competitive manufacturing based on Australia's natural advantage in raw materials. Efficient secondary industry would also help support primary production by supplying capital equipment cheaply. This all owed much to Page's pronounced sense of economic and social orderliness, with everything playing its proper and reinforcing role.

Page's fullest statement of such views was his speech to the Chamber of Manufactures of New South Wales on 21 June 1926, just one month after the creation of the DMC. Published as *Australian Industries: The Interdependence of 'Primary' and 'Secondary'*, it set out the implications of Page's model for development policy and planning.[13] He thought the economy could be neatly driven by a few vital sectoral linkages to remain in perpetual motion, and tied together planning, decentralisation, electrification and industrial standardisation. He opened this talk by summarising how the economy's component sectors could support each other:

> Manufacturers are interested in the primary producers as the suppliers of their raw material and as the purchasers of their finished goods. The more efficiently the manufacturers fulfil their function of supplying the tools specially adapted for the producer's work and articles for the producer's use, the more readily and cheaply can be supplied the raw materials for manufacturing processes. The more profit there is in agricultural industries, the more readily can manufactured goods be bought.[14]

A sound home market was the basis for a manufacturing industry to become internationally competitive. Making use of abundant raw materials to produce competitive goods would lead to an even split in total exports between manufactured items and 'raw products', so that primary industry would not be left disproportionately supporting the nation's standard of living. Here lay the role of planning. Government failure to 'lay down a definite plan of development' along these lines was handicapping industry. Planning should start with transport and power production 'conceived on a national scale', and support decentralisation

---

13   Earle Page, *Australian Industries: The Interdependence of 'Primary' and 'Secondary'*, Simmons Ltd, Sydney, 1926, copy at EPP, folder 2331.
14   Ibid., p. 1.

by enabling the disposition of factories at strategic points. Page gave vent here to his impatience with federalism – Australians must stop 'blindly worshipping the fetish of State rights'. 'It is idle', he said loftily, 'for those who profess to believe that such action infringes State rights to try and put the hands of the clock back.'[15]

Page's brief coverage here of the orderly marketing of rural produce portrayed it as a means of maintaining demand for manufactured items. It would help 'create a continuous purchasing power of finished goods in the hands of the producer', so that 'both primary and secondary industries thus tend to be stabilised and a beneficial circle of regular employment in all callings is created'. To Page, orderly marketing did not constitute an absolute end in itself, but was a subsidiary policy tool with a place in his wider conception of the economy. Making the best use of factors of production of capital, labour and management was to Page reminiscent of the brain, heart, stomach and hands of the human body all 'performing different functions and yet vital to the efficient work of the whole'.[16]

One wonders what Page's audience of manufacturing executives thought as they were exhorted to ponder this very big picture of 'well-balanced national progress'. They probably saw more relevance in his comments about standardising industrial capital equipment to aid mass production. Page also expressed some of his prime minister's concern about the consequences of high wages for international competitiveness, but hastened to add that greater efficiency could overcome this problem and also lead to increased real wages. There should also be a rationalisation of parallel state and national arbitration into a single Commonwealth-led system – the very issue that was to fell the Bruce–Page Government in 1929.

Capital, transport, power, standardisation, tariffs, marketing, finance and regulation – 'a well-conceived plan of efficiency must consider the place of all these in the national economy'. Page did not specify in this 1926 speech how such planning would be conducted. But he made clear his confidence that he could work with business leaders 'to create the public opinion that would assist these desirable policies'.[17] Manufacturers should even be trusted to nominate what assistance they needed to obtain the best capital machinery. Press coverage of the speech was mostly supportive, but focused on Page's comments on federalism. The Adelaide *Register* saw

---

15  Ibid., pp. 5, 9, 10–11, 12, 19.
16  Ibid., p. 7.
17  Ibid., p. 12.

it as indicative of 'the orderly soul of Dr Page' and particularly noted his comment that in the distant past problems of government had been left to 'mediocrities' but that now, he declared, 'the time has come for the best minds to take a hand in governmental operations'. It described the audience of manufacturers as having listened 'dutifully'. The *Register*'s main objection was that Page's comments about efficiency were an attack on the rights of states.[18]

Tariffs occupied an especially important place in how Page saw the economy being planned: his views on this drew him into the main economic policy debate of the 1920s. Free traders foresaw a primary industry–oriented Australia that was robustly competitive on world markets. Protectionists envisaged a more self-contained nation that developed on its own social and economic terms, including by fostering a large (albeit costly) manufacturing sector. The 1920s was a protectionist decade: the average tariff rate rose from about 10 per cent in 1918 to about 27 per cent in 1927.[19]

Historians have frequently commented on Page's encouragement of primary producers to accept tariff increases on manufactures in the name of the broader economic and political benefits of 'all-round protection'.[20] What is less widely appreciated is that as an advocate of planning, he kept a foot in each of the free trade and protectionist camps by generally being critical of tariffs but also supporting their planned use to nurture carefully chosen industries in decentralised locations – 'picking winners', in latter-day parlance. He was neither free trader nor ardent protectionist. Page considered 'natural and essential' industries in which Australia was internationally competitive worthy of nurturing, mostly resource-based industries and related manufacturing such as of agricultural machinery, but also some orientated to mass consumption. Tariffs could be powerful tools if used in a 'scientific' way that reflected a comprehensive review of 'the whole national position and national resources'.[21]

---

18  Editorial in the Adelaide *Register*, 22 June 1926, p. 8. Coverage in other newspapers was more favourable, such as the Perth *Daily News*, 22 June 1926, p. 4; and the Adelaide *Advertiser*, 22 June 1926, p. 12.
19  William Oliver Coleman, Selwyn Cornish and Alfred Hagger, *Giblin's Platoon: The Trials and Triumph of the Economist in Australian Public Life*, ANU E Press, Canberra, 2006, p. 66.
20  Graham, *Formation of the Australian Country Parties*, pp. 231, 246–7.
21  Earle Page, *Australian Industries*, p. 17; see also 'Speech Given by Dr. Earle Page at the Constitutional Association 15/2/32 on the Tariff', EPP, folder 384. The term 'scientific tariffs' was widely used by economists of the time; see Joanne Pemberton, 'The middle way: The discourse of planning in Britain, Australia and at the League in the interwar years', *Australian Journal of Politics and History*, vol. 52, no. 1, 2006, p. 57.

Page's only very selective opposition to tariffs raised tension with some of his political allies. H.P. Williams, manager of the influential New South Wales–wide rural newspaper *The Land*, berated him in March 1923 for countenancing tariffs to support sugar manufacturing. (Williams wanted the sugar industry to first establish a voluntary pool.)[22] In a 1924 letter to the Sydney-based manufacturer George Hoskins, Page vented his disgust at 'the idiocy of protecting a lot of fourth rate industries instead of making sure that the essential and basic ones that we can properly develop and get a market for were thoroughly protected to begin with'. He disdained the Commonwealth Tariff Board for lacking a strong sense of which industries should be nurtured.[23]

Statements by Page such as his speech to the New South Wales manufacturers made him a participant in the growing policy debate over the use of tariffs that extended through the decade. Among Australia's increasingly vocal policy-minded economists, Copland and E.O. Shann were free traders while L.F. Giblin was more accepting of protection. Bruce broadly agreed with Page that a moderate tariff should be applied cautiously according to scientific precepts. To this end, he commissioned the celebrated 1929 inquiry into tariffs headed by the Tasmanian-based economist James Brigden that became the most comprehensive analysis of Australian protectionism to date.

The Brigden Enquiry arrived at a politically cautious conclusion that tariff assistance already stood at an optimal level, a compromise between its members who advocated free trade and those favouring protectionism. Brigden himself became the foremost proponent of tariffs as improving the overall standard of living by their promotion of employment in manufacturing at acceptable wage levels and by supporting population growth. Like Page, Brigden considered tariffs in the context of the interaction of primary and secondary industries, but from a far more scholarly and theoretical perspective than did the avowedly practical Country Party leader.[24]

Despite Page's disinterest in theory, it was still highly unusual then or later for a politician to view the tariff question in terms of such a full model of the economy and vision of the entire country. Page did not argue the

---

22   H.P. Williams to Page, 6 March 1923, EPP, folder 1151 (part 2).
23   Page to George Hoskins, undated but in reply to a letter of 17 May 1924, Earle Page papers, UNE Archives, A180, box 10, folder 80.
24   The Brigden Enquiry was formally titled *The Australian Tariff: An Economic Enquiry*. For a fuller account, see Coleman, Cornish and Hagger, *Giblin's Platoon*, Chapter 4.

pros and cons of tariffs wholly in terms that much later became standard – he made no reference, for example, to tariffs effectively imposing flat taxes on consumers. Yet as an early and relatively sophisticated tariff critic, Page went well beyond mainstream Country Party concerns about the added costs of capital equipment to arrive at a carefully nuanced vision of protection's place in national development. By raising what tariffs implied for national efficiency, he challenged his colleagues to consider the wider impact of protectionism and helped presage future nation-changing debates on industry restructuring.

Page was also ahead of his time from the mid-1920s by making private investment a major element of his thinking on implementing major public works, especially for electrification. (One of the few other prominent advocates was Frederic Eggleston in his 1932 *State Socialism in Victoria*, but for different reasons. Eggleston drew on his unhappy personal experience in Victorian state politics in concluding that publicly owned essential services were inefficient.)[25] For most of Page's career, important infrastructure was almost entirely built and operated by state governments, especially after the Great War. He advocated private investment as more likely to take a longer perspective than would typically characterise the choices of short-lived governments. Private investors could construct dams and power stations in return for charters and franchise arrangements that guaranteed their rights to operate these facilities for a specified long-term period. Page wanted 'a uniform continent-wide policy that will keep in mind the requirements of national development while at the same time provide every means and facility for private enterprise to carry out this work'.[26] He does not seem to have ever reconciled his proposal to charge all electricity consumers the same flat rate with attracting private operators. Page also frequently called for stronger constitutional guarantees of private property rights so as to encourage private investment in infrastructure.[27]

---

25   Frederic Eggleston, *State Socialism in Victoria*, P.S. King & Son, London, 1932, pp. 13–14, 304–5.
26   'Federal Power Commission', EPP, folders 1625 and 2088; no date, but wording and the inclusion of a copy among papers prepared for the May 1929 Premiers' Conference suggest it was prepared for this conference.
27   Section 51(xxxi) of the Constitution gives the Commonwealth power to make laws on 'the acquisition of property on just terms from any State or person for any purpose in respect of which the Parliament has power to make laws'. The High Court interpretation of 'acquisition' and of 'just terms' has limited this protection of property rights; and the requirement concerning a 'purpose in respect of which the Parliament has power to make laws' is taken to mean that legislation based on s51(xxxi) must be supported by at least one additional constitutional power.

## Page and planned development: Attempting to transform the Clarence

Soon after its creation, the DMC optimistically foresaw itself as a 'detached body', free to enter into 'full co-operation' with state governments. It would be their adviser as they worked together to populate the continent, and it urged the states to appoint counterpart development commissioners.[28] In practice, the states tended to view the DMC as a menace to their favoured proposals. The organisation became especially suspicious of ambitious irrigation projects: Queensland proceeded with the Dawson Valley Irrigation Scheme alone, with unhappy results.[29] The DMC did not directly enter into the fierce debates of the Bruce–Page years over union power and arbitration, but its association with high migration and calls for greater efficiency to counter rising production costs drew the ire of organised labour. The federal Opposition leader Matthew Charlton attacked it in parliament and spoke of migrants as 'largely responsible' for unemployment.[30]

The DMC nonetheless operated widely and confidently, undertaking studies ranging from the dried fruit and tobacco industries to transport costs, national employment and the outlook for Tasmania. Yet the DMC never entirely fulfilled a national economic planning role, the Commonwealth lacking the necessary constitutional powers and the Bruce–Page Government not wanting to dictate to private industry. The closest it came to a comprehensive stocktake of the economy was a listing in its 1928 annual report of Australia's main imports, intended as a first step towards identifying suitable new industries for development on the basis that a high level of importation was suggestive of a solid local demand. The DMC was in practice more productive in assessing promising new targets for assistance on a project-by-project basis.[31]

Bruce and Page's shared enthusiasm for the DMC suggests they were aware of the need to manage such constraints to growth as shortages of good land and dubious irrigation schemes. Soon after the DMC's

---

28  Development and Migration Commission, *First Annual Report*, p. 6; A.J. Davies, 'Australian Federalism and National Development', *Australian Journal of Politics and History*, vol. 14, no. 1, April 1968, p. 41.
29  Roe, *Australia, Britain, and Migration*, pp. 97, 112–13.
30  Charlton, 23 February 1928, quoted in ibid., p. 119.
31  Development and Migration Commission, *Second Annual Report for Period Ending 31st December 1928*, Commonwealth of Australia, Canberra, 1929, pp. 11–12, EPP, folder 2322. For a summary of the DMC's research see Roe, *Australia, Britain, and Migration*, pp. 91–3.

creation, Page became an advocate of its permanent enshrinement in national policy. He encouraged his own party to endorse planning, and at an ACPA meeting in June 1927 he lectured invited state Country Party leaders on state cooperation in 'the initiation of a national plan of efficiency in production and marketing that will ensure balanced development'. He credited the DMC and the CSIR with furthering state–federal coordination but 'the work is only just begun'. Tellingly, he failed to offer a convincing rationale of how to implement all of this beyond offering old ideas about national power and port development, uniform rail charges and flat electricity rates.[32]

Page's confidence in the DMC culminated in his attempt to use it to realise regional development and electrification in the Clarence Valley. The DMC agreed to his request to look closely at the Clarence region as a candidate for Migration Agreement funding of an entire package of linked projects – hydroelectricity at The Gorge and Jackadgery, and related flood prevention, road, rail, port, timber and mining initiatives. The resultant probing of Page's faith that electrification would create its own demand demonstrated that the DMC was every bit as rigorous as he otherwise wanted it to be.

Following the defeat of the first Lang Government, which had stood out of the Migration Agreement, Page's home state of New South Wales finally signed on in March 1928. That month he approached Gepp about his comprehensive plan to develop the Clarence Valley. The DMC chair responded that if preliminary investigations were favourable, the commission could work with the state government on what 'would be just the sort of scheme that he [Gepp] knew the British government would view favourably, as it would lead to large development and increased population'.[33] Page followed up by sending Gepp a copy of his 1919 booklet *The Clarence Gorge Hydro-Electric Scheme*, leading a DMC economist to caution the chair that it had clearly 'not been prepared by technical men'.[34] Pressure also came from The Port of the Clarence Advisory Board, chaired by Alf Pollack.[35]

---

32   Speech reproduced in *The Primary Producer* of 9 June 1927, p. 1, copy in EPP, folder 2666.
33   C. Tye (Under-Secretary of the New South Wales Department of Public Works), memo, 8 March 1928, NAA, CP211/2, 34/13. Tye was reporting on Page's approach to Gepp.
34   E.N. Robinson to Gepp, memo, 30 March 1928, NAA, CP211/2, 34/13.
35   The Port of the Clarence Advisory Board to Premier Bavin, letter, 16 February 1928, NAA, CP211/2, 34/13.

The DMC duly dispatched its new deputy chair W.P. Devereux, a former pastoral industry executive, on appraisal tours of the region in July and August 1928. Page telegrammed Devereux that although the various projects proposed for the region 'must be regarded as a whole', if there had to be a choice hydroelectricity should take priority.[36] Page, with Pollack and others, insisted on accompanying Devereux for part of his second tour, including a visit on horseback to The Gorge. Devereux's detailed on-the-road reports to Gepp show him to have been a cautious observer, well capable of resisting Page's pressure. He concluded that a power project at Jackadgery had some merit provided the state government was supportive, but that The Gorge would produce far more power than was needed locally and inundate too much good land.[37] The Bavin–Buttenshaw State Government accepted at this time a Commonwealth proposal that it should also investigate The Gorge, resulting in similar findings by its chief electrical engineer, H.G. Carter, that the project was too large for immediate development but had longer term potential.[38]

Premier Bavin soon agreed with Devereux that The Gorge project should not proceed.[39] In March 1929 the state government added that Jackadgery was also too costly and elected instead to explore more modest proposals such as extending the Nymboida facility.[40] Page made similarly fruitless inquiries with potential British investors. A contact of his reported back in December 1929 that they thought the thin distribution of the Australian population made new hydroelectric installations commercially unviable and would only consider projects securely backed by Australian governments.[41] The DMC meanwhile continued to assess the wider development of the Clarence Valley, but had not reached any final conclusion by its abolition in 1930.[42]

This episode was an early instance not only of technical advice constraining Page but also of the caution of state governments that would actually have prime responsibility for his various schemes. It was an early indicator of the direction in which policy advice on development projects was

---

36  Page to Devereux, telegram, 10 July 1928, NAA, CP211/2, 34/13.
37  Devereux to Gepp, memo, 23 July 1928, NAA, CP211/2, 34/13.
38  Page, *Clarence River Hydro-Electric Gorge Scheme*, pp. 17–18.
39  Devereux to Gepp, memo, 23 July 1928.
40  'Extract from Summary Report No 12, Dated 28th March 1929', NAA, A786, R22/1.
41  Fred Sandman (?, signature unclear) to Page, 1 December 1928, EPP, folder 2083.
42  'Clarence Gorge Development – History of Investigations and Offers of Assistance from Three Federal Governments and Seven State Governments', c. 1954, EPP, folder 1798.

shifting. Even in this decade of developmentalist optimism, there was a countervailing awareness of the limitations imposed by Australia's settlement patterns and natural environment that gestured towards concerns most clearly articulated by Griffith Taylor. As the foremost historian of assisted migration between the wars has concluded, the DMC's 'dominant message had been that by capitalism's own standards, Australia offered little scope for productive development'.[43]

Page also came under pressure via the equally dispassionate scrutiny of the engineering profession. Australian engineers in the early 1920s had been divided over the potential of hydroelectricity, with William Corin being its main protagonist. In a 1920 study he declared that the water resources of New South Wales were grossly underutilised, and that the growth of Tasmanian manufacturing showed what was possible if hydroelectricity was applied intelligently.[44] But as the decade progressed, a majority opinion emerged among engineers and economists that hydroelectricity was of marginal significance on the mainland.

This conclusion drew on debates such as that in Victoria over brown coal versus hydroelectricity. John Monash stated in 1924 that 'water power' was not necessarily cheaper than thermal generation and that Australian stream flows were unreliable.[45] W.H. Myers, chief electrical engineer for New South Wales Railways and Tramways (and Page's colleague at Sydney Boys High), made a thinly veiled attack on Page and Corin at the March 1929 conference of the Institution of Engineers. He assailed 'wild deductions' by 'recently-returned travellers from abroad ... that the salvation of the country depends upon the development of "hydroelectricity" or of "super-power" schemes', and of how 'even electrical engineers, including some of standing, occasionally are not immune from the same habit'. Myers deflated simplistic comparisons with the United States by pointing out that Australia's potential hydroelectricity sources were remote from major cities and that population dispersal inhibited the interlinking of power systems.[46] A September 1929 report to the Australian Government by consulting engineer Alex J. Gibson was particularly telling, for Gibson

---

43   Roe, *Australia, Britain, and Migration*, p. 137.
44   'Report of the Chief Electrical Engineer, Department of Public Works', 1920, EPP, folder 1046.
45   Monash, Presidential Address to the Australasian Association for the Advancement of Science, Adelaide, 25 August 1924, reported in the Adelaide *Advertiser*, 26 August 1924, p. 14.
46   Quoted in Alexander J. Gibson, *Report on Power Development in Australia*, Government Printer, Canberra, September 1929, p. 33; see also Walter Harold Myers, *The Supply of Electricity in Bulk*, The Institution of Engineers, Australia, Sydney, 1929.

was a decentralist who considered agriculture 'the ultimate wealth of any community'. He challenged assumptions that hydroelectricity was inexpensive and that power availability alone would create new manufacturing. It was not 'the panacea for all the ills from which the [agricultural] industry suffers', especially given the dispersal of farms. Gibson predicted, largely accurately, that Australia's future power development would be predominantly coal-based.[47]

None of these critiques altered Page's faith in hydroelectricity nor his hopes for his home region. He so habitually contrived to interpret expert findings positively that he took the DMC's and Carter's cautious conclusions to imply that inadequate local demand could be solved at a stroke by linking The Gorge to a Newcastle–Brisbane transmission system. Corin died in 1929, leaving Page as Australia's most prominent advocate of hydroelectricity and the main agent by which the concept lingered as a policy issue prior to its resurgence via the Snowy Scheme.

## Page and cooperative federalism: The triumph of the Financial Agreement

As the 1920s progressed, changes in external financial conditions strengthened the case for a stronger Loan Council than the existing voluntary arrangement. Britain's return to the gold standard in 1925 created obstacles to lending abroad and raised interest rates. Unease about public debt included a growing suspicion in international circles that Australia was an unreliable borrower.[48] Conversion activity and the ongoing quest for new loans meant that an Australian government was almost always active in the international loan market. More fundamentally, Bruce and Page continued to see vertical fiscal imbalance and the duplication of functions between Commonwealth and states as affronts to their sense of efficiency. Both were conscious of the failure of referenda as means of change – when they took office in 1923, only two of 13 referendum questions put to the voters since 1901 had been approved. The Bruce–Page Government only put three questions to the voters: two simultaneously in September 1926

---

47   Gibson, *Report on Power Development in Australia*, pp. 35, 37, 39.
48   C.G. Headford, 'The Australian Loan Council – Its origin, operation and significance in the federal structure', in W. Prest and R.L. Mathews (eds), *The Development of Australian Fiscal Federalism: Selected Readings*, Australian National University Press, Canberra, 1980, pp. 165–6 (article first published 1954).

on corporations and industrial relations powers that included giving the Commonwealth authority to deal with interruptions to essential services; and that of November 1928 on the Financial Agreement. The main strategy for the reform of federalism remained one of seeking cooperative agreements with the states.

This resumed with a new offer to the states at the May 1926 Premiers' Conference. Bruce and Page proposed that the Commonwealth withdraw from all forms of direct taxation and discontinue the per capita grants, in return for which it would take over state debts. As in 1923, Bruce led for the Commonwealth in debate, with Page supporting by answering the assembled premiers' numerous doubts about details. Page denied that he and Bruce were out to impose unification. Their aim was a rationalisation of intergovernmental finance that would be in everyone's interest, 'to secure federation to [sic] the Australian states for all time, and to insist that there shall be a proper Federal basis which will assuredly be brought about if there be a distinct separation of their finances'.[49] Yet the states again rejected the Commonwealth's proposal, being reluctant to levy unpopular direct taxes alone and foreseeing that a future Labor government could restore Commonwealth taxation.[50]

In June, Page with Bruce's support issued a final demand to the states that 'the vicious principle of one authority raising taxation for another authority to spend' must cease. Page added a more personal argument that the remission of direct taxation to the states would prevent them from being financially strangled by the Commonwealth and so at risk of de facto unification.[51] Legislation was enacted to reduce (but not quite eliminate) Commonwealth direct taxes and to abolish the per capita grants in favour of distributing only any remaining Commonwealth surplus on a per capita basis. The *States Grants Act 1927* was effectively an ultimatum that the states had one year to agree to a mutually acceptable formula or else have the Commonwealth impose its own resolution. Bruce acceded to state appeals to delay implementation, and a draft of what became the Financial Agreement was negotiated at further premiers' conferences before an agreed text was signed by all governments on 12 December 1927. The subsequent referendum of November 1928

---

49 'Conference of the Commonwealth and State Ministers Held at Federal Parliament House Melbourne, May 1926 to Consider the Financial Relations Between the States and the Commonwealth – Report of Debates', EPP, folder 2663 (part 3).
50 Mathews and Jay, *Federal Finance*, p. 120.
51 *Commonwealth Parliamentary Debates*, 4 June 1926, pp. 2680, 2682.

approved the insertion of section 105A into the Constitution to enable the Commonwealth to implement the agreement. There was an almost unprecedented 74 per cent vote in favour, evidently as the voting public was opposed to more government debt.[52] Despite a 'yes' result in every state, the Labor Party, Percy Stewart and the Nationalist E.A. Mann voted in parliament against the enabling Bill, and two Country Party MPs declared they voted for it only in deference to the referendum results.[53]

The Financial Agreement in its final form abolished per capita payments to the states in return for the Commonwealth taking over existing and future state debts, but with the states joining it in contributing to debt servicing. The Commonwealth withdrew from most direct taxation and the Loan Council was accorded binding authority over borrowing by both levels of government.[54] The states' assessment that their new borrowings would increase more than their populations had led them to conclude that Commonwealth contributions under such a repayment-based arrangement would exceed the old per capita grants. (This was indeed the case until 1944–45. The states in the interim still found themselves exposed to the budgetary impact of the Great Depression.)[55]

The most lasting reform, and that which Page took most to heart, was the change in status of the Loan Council. Page played a significant tactical role in the machinations that led to its elevation to a binding decision-making body dominated by the Commonwealth, marking a decisive shift in the locus of fiscal power. The council would henceforth control all new public borrowing by determining annually the total proposed loan programs of the Commonwealth and the states, and judging whether these could be met at reasonable terms and conditions. This total would be divided up

---

52  Mathews and Jay, ibid., p. 109. But see Chapter 8 for Page's later reflections on the basis for this vote.
53  Page, *Truant Surgeon*, p. 133.
54  The full Financial Agreement was a very complex document. In addition to taking over formal responsibility for the existing and future public debt of the states, the Commonwealth also agreed to make grants to the states for 58 years from 1927 of fixed amounts equal to the per capita grants to each state in 1926–27, but with the proviso that these were to be contributions to interest charges on the then existing public debt of the states. The Commonwealth would also make annual contributions to the National Debt Sinking Fund in respect of state debt. These contributions consisted of the equivalent of 0.125 per cent of existing debt as of 30 June 1927 for a period of 58 years, and 0.25 per cent of the face value of loans raised subsequently for 53 years from the date the debt was incurred (other than loans raised to meet revenue deficits). The states were also required to make contributions to meeting their debts, but at different rates (and somewhat different again for New South Wales). See Mathews and Jay, *Federal Finance*, pp. 108, 121, and the *Financial Agreement Act 1928*.
55  Gilbert, *Australian Loan Council*, p. 96; Mathews and Jay, *Federal Finance*, p. 121, and Gates, 'The search for a state growth tax', in Mathews, *Intergovernmental Relations in Australia*, p. 160.

between governments by unanimous agreement. The Commonwealth would arrange all borrowing including conversions, redemptions and debt consolidation. Crucially, the council's voting formula gave the Commonwealth a dominant say – it had two votes and a casting vote, as against each state's single vote. In the absence of unanimity on the division of amounts between governments, a formula would be applied of up to one-fifth to the Commonwealth and the rest to be divided between the states in proportion to their net loan expenditures during the previous five years. Lacking a secretariat, its deliberations were conducted in secret by heads of government, treasurers and officials.

The Financial Agreement was the most comprehensive reform of federalism to that date, and a testament to Bruce and Page's determination to rectify a gross inefficiency. In one move, they had addressed three major concerns – coordination of public borrowing, debt reduction and vertical fiscal imbalance.[56] Looking back in 1957, Page accurately described the agreement as still 'the single major substantial alteration in the Constitution'.[57] W.K. Hancock, writing four decades after 1927, called it 'an important landmark of policy' amid what he called the 'easy-going mediocrity' pervading Australian society in the 1920s.[58]

The Loan Council, in particular, was a major success in institutionalising Commonwealth–state cooperation. The contemporary economist R.C. Mills, not otherwise an admirer of the Financial Agreement, considered the council 'an eminently desirable feature of Australia public finance' that would secure better terms for loans and curb unnecessary borrowing.[59] (Mills was one of a minority of prominent economists untroubled by vertical fiscal imbalance: Giblin, Mills and Leslie Melville all felt that the per capita grants had promoted equity between the states.)[60] Although the Loan Council briefly served as an economic council of governments during the Depression of the 1930s, it did not constitute a planning body that controlled the ends to which loan monies would be directed. Page was to become determined to rectify this.

---

56   Mathews and Jay, *Federal Finance*, p. 108.
57   'Submission to Federal Parliamentary Constitutional Committee of Amendments Proposed by Sir Earle Page', January 1957, EPP, folder 1659.
58   W.K. Hancock, 'Then and Now', *IPA Review*, vol. 22, no. 4, 1968, p. 92.
59   R.C. Mills, 'The financial relations of the Commonwealth and the states', *The Economic Record*, May 1928, p. 11.
60   Mathews and Jay, *Federal Finance*, pp. 122–3. Vertical fiscal imbalance re-emerged with the introduction of uniform income taxation in 1942.

Some contemporary observers saw Page as the sole or at least main progenitor of the Financial Agreement. One was F.A. Bland, by now Australia's most prominent political scientist, writing in a December 1935 article on Page and cooperative federalism.[61] Lang, a major player in the negotiations, recalled Page as 'the real architect' of the Financial Agreement.[62] In fact, Page was neither the originator of the agreement nor its sole driver in the Bruce–Page Government. Bruce's statements soon after he took office clearly indicate that he did not rely on Page in reaching conclusions about the need to reform federalism. The prime minister was more publicly prominent in debates at the 1923, 1926 and 1927 premiers' conferences.[63]

But Page, under Bruce's ultimate direction, did contribute significantly to the crucial detailed negotiations that enabled the creation of the Loan Council. His assertive advocacy and tactical contribution in the final negotiations gave him a lasting political and public association with the council. Mathews and Jay, foremost historians of Australian federal financial relations, reflected that the slow, complex steps towards the signing of the Financial Agreement, which involved finding ways around fears of Commonwealth domination, state reluctance to assume responsibility for unpopular forms of taxation and Lang's hostility, 'owed a great deal to the negotiating skill of the Commonwealth Treasurer'.[64] Geoffrey Sawer wrote of Page's 'ability to modify his own ideas as the opinion of his parliament and negotiations with the states required; the final agreement was a triumph both for himself and for the long-term non-Labor policy of putting this matter on a stable basis'.[65]

Lang's memoir, *The Great Bust*, contains firsthand, if eclectic, recollections of Page as treasurer. He portrayed him as an arch conservative in 'one of the most determined anti-Labor governments this country has had', not least as it handed the Commonwealth Bank over to 'big business'. Lang wrote at length of his state's suspicions of the Loan Council, and

---

61  F.A. Bland, 'Inventing constitutional machinery: A study of Dr. Earle Page's proposals for national councils', *Australian Quarterly*, vol. 7, no. 28, December 1935, p. 16.
62  Jack Lang, *The Great Bust: The Depression of the Thirties*, McNamara's Books, Katoomba, 1980 (first published 1962), p. 65.
63  See for example the assessment of the 1923 Conference in the Melbourne *Argus* of 30 May 1923, pp. 10–11.
64  Mathews and Jay, *Federal Finance*, p. 110.
65  Sawer, *Australian Federal Politics and Law 1901–1929*, p. 284.

called Bruce and Page unificationists who sought 'deliberately to wreck the sovereignty of the states'. More specifically, and rather closer to the reality, Lang readily conceded that Page was 'very inventive':

> He was full of plans. He had a formula for every occasion. He was ready to dash them off like prescriptions. His political enemies had no chance of catching up with him, because before they could he had already started on a new path.[66]

He also praised Page as 'a tough politician' who could both absorb and hand out criticism, with 'much the better political brain' than Robert Menzies.[67]

Lang was not alone in casting Page as an inveterate centraliser. The Financial Agreement was one of several aspects of Page's advocacy in the late 1920s that led other senior figures to perceive him as a centralist. According to Lang, during the campaign on the 1926 referenda on corporations and industrial relations powers, premiers thought he was plotting to impoverish them and centralise power.[68] Such suspicions came to the fore again, over a decade later, when Page tried to persuade the states to support his National Council planning initiative. Page thought of himself quite differently, but there is much in what the states sensed. He showed little empathy with the fundamental principle that the Commonwealth and the states are formally equal in status and sovereign in nature. Yet Page would remain immensely proud of the reform of the nation's financial machinery through the Loan Council and the Financial Agreement, even arguing that they helped the raising of funds for Australia's defence in World War Two.[69]

## Unfinished business: The Bruce–Page Government's final efforts to overhaul federalism

So strong was the Bruce–Page commitment to efficient governance that even after the major triumph of the Financial Agreement, it continued with ambitious attempts to reform federalism. These involved three

---

66   Lang, *The Great Bust*, pp. 35–6, 65.
67   Lang, *The Great Bust*, pp. 33, 35–6, 61, 62, 65, 71. Lang was presumably referring to the 1924 legislation that placed the bank under an independent board of directors.
68   Aaron Wildavsky, 'The 1926 referendum', in Aaron Wildavsky and Dagmar Carboch, *Studies in Australian Politics*, Cheshire, Melbourne, 1958, p. 33.
69   *Commonwealth Parliamentary Debates*, 14 September 1944, p. 830.

quite different strategies, with Page playing a significant role in each. The May 1929 Premiers' Conference effectively repeated the 1923 effort to have the states agree to national coordination of policy. The Peden Royal Commission into the Constitution, handed down in September 1929, provided the most comprehensive stocktake of the federation to date. But more novel – and lasting – were attempts to create a series of Commonwealth–state coordinating bodies, in which Page had the major hand. All three strategies were pursued with an urgency born of a growing sense that the economy was deteriorating and could not afford the burden of an ill-functioning system of governance. The breadth of Page's involvement consolidated and lastingly shaped his commitment to cooperative federalism.

The prosperity that earlier in the decade had enabled such initiatives as tied road grants and the creation of the CSIR did not last. By 1927 the Commonwealth Budget had fallen into deficit, leading to the sobriquet for Page of 'the most tragic Treasurer Australia has ever known', courtesy of the Nationalist MP H.S. Gullett.[70] As unemployment jumped during 1927 from under 6 per cent to 10 per cent, Bruce began to publicly ponder the reasons for slower economic growth. Falling international wheat and wool prices were clearly contributing, but he became increasingly concerned by tariffs and the arbitration system. He feared that tariffs had gone beyond protecting only efficient and essential industries, thereby placing an unjustified burden on exporters. Bruce did not oppose arbitration per se but feared that the overlapping Commonwealth and state systems caused confusion and conflict.[71]

The Bruce–Page Government therefore approached the May 1929 Premiers' Conference with a special sense of urgency. In his opening address, Bruce lectured the premiers on past failures and 'an obligation on the shoulders of every one of us to state our views with the utmost frankness, forgetful of all political considerations, and mindful only of the duty we owe to the people of Australia'. He was convinced that 'the basic cause of all the economic troubles of Australia is the high cost of production', the result of exorbitant labour costs and tariffs. Part of the solution lay in more efficient government.[72]

---

70  John Hawkins, 'Sir Earle Page: An active Treasurer', *Economic Round-up*, Commonwealth Department of the Treasury, no. 4, 2009, p. 60.
71  Richmond, 'S.M. Bruce and Australian economic policy', p. 252.
72  Bruce's opening speech to the 'Conference Between Commonwealth and States', Canberra, 28 May 1929, EPP, folder 1625.

As in 1923, Bruce and Page proposed rationalisation across an array of fields that collectively amounted to an overhaul of federalism. Page's favoured subjects of electricity and transport were prominent, but the Commonwealth also put forward health, workers' compensation, observance of Anzac Day, Aboriginal reserves, voting procedures, registration of doctors, national insurance, child endowment and industrial legislation. The latter was presented as being especially important in eliminating duplication by either the states transferring full powers to the Commonwealth or the Commonwealth entirely withdrawing from arbitration. Page's national power commission was again raised, to which end each state was called on to establish its own 'authoritative body' to manage power development.[73] The conference also considered Gibson's findings on national power resources but could only vaguely agree in principle on coordination and standardisation, for which the states would 'give full consideration' to creating power authorities.[74] This premiers' conference, the last presided over by the Bruce–Page Government, was frustrated – as always, from Page's perspective – by the resistance of the states.

The Bruce–Page Government's other late attempt to comprehensively reform federalism was the Peden Royal Commission. In 1927, following the new state movement's failure to achieve change via a constitutional convention or a parliamentary inquiry, the Commonwealth instead appointed a wide-ranging royal commission on constitutional reform. John Latham had raised this idea as early as 1923 as an alternative to a convention, and later suggested Sir John Peden of Sydney University as chair.[75] The royal commission's report was submitted only the month before the Bruce–Page Government was defeated. It reported that most witnesses 'expressed satisfaction' with existing Commonwealth–state cooperation, albeit amid grumbles about the Commonwealth assuming too many responsibilities. Its majority findings noted with approval advances in cooperative federalism. Most were Bruce–Page initiatives – foremost the Loan Council, but also the Federal Aid Roads Board, the Federal Health Council, the new Federal Transport Council, the DMC and the CSIR.[76]

---

73  Conference memo on power, EPP, folder 416; see also 'Federal Power Commission', EPP, folders 1625 and 2088.
74  Report of conference results, copies at EPP, folders 1781 and 2577.
75  Ellis, *A History of the Australian Country Party*, p. 109; also Page, *Truant Surgeon*, pp. 238–9.
76  Royal Commission on the Constitution, *Report* ('Peden Report'), Parliamentary paper no. 16, Government Printer, Canberra, 1929. The copy at EPP, folder 2712, bears some highlighting by Page himself.

The royal commission also showed that new states had survived the Cohen Royal Commission as an issue (if not as an immediate likelihood) by recommending a liberalised process for their creation based on a petition from local electors followed by a referendum of the whole existing state. Unlike the Cohen Royal Commission, Peden only concerned itself with procedure for creating new states, not their desirability. No attempt was made by the Scullin Government to implement the Peden Royal Commission recommendations, which were compromised by wide differences between the commissioners: four favoured continuation of a federal system, but the other three produced a minority report calling for full power to the Commonwealth. This was another disappointment for Page and would not have restored his confidence in formal inquiries.

Page played a bigger personal role in promoting machinery for intergovernmental cooperation in specific policy fields. He saw such bodies as ideally not only coordinating the Commonwealth and the states but also being accorded constitutional authority to exercise executive power. In the late 1920s, Page pursued this particular cooperative concept across two very different policy fields dear to him and to the Country Party: health and transport. The results were very different.

On health, Page was centrally involved in creating the first enduring intergovernmental entity for policy coordination. 'The germs of disease have neither respect nor recognition for the artificial boundaries of the states', he said.[77] At the May 1923 Premiers' Conference the Commonwealth had failed to secure agreement from the states to a royal commission on the division of administrative responsibility for health between the national, state and local tiers of government. This instead led to a special conference on national health and only then to the 1925–26 Royal Commission on Health. This inquiry placed a strong emphasis on preventative medicine, recommending the national coordination of public health by the Commonwealth setting broad policy objectives that would be implemented by state health councils and regional district administrations. Little was done beyond the creation of a Federal Health Council consisting of the Commonwealth and the states in November 1926. This was a consultative body of respective chief health officers, not ministers as Page had hoped. In 1936 it was replaced by a stronger

---

77   Earl Page, *A Policy for the People*, Australian Country Party, Sydney, 1928, p. 13.

and better-resourced statutory agency, the National Health and Medical Research Council that still functions today as the Commonwealth's manager of medical research funding and adviser on health issues.[78]

Page was at least as determined to institutionalise the coordination of another policy priority, national transport. This was a far more difficult proposition than health policy, and one that readily raised state hackles about Commonwealth intrusion. Transport had long elicited earnest affirmations from all Australian governments of the need to work together, notably to unify railway gauges. It featured prominently in Page's 1917 speech to the Australasian Provincial Press Conference, but progress was so uneven that in January 1927 he found himself reminding the Constitutional Club in Brisbane of the basic case for a 'definite, continuous and comprehensive policy of transport development'. All three tiers of government needed to work towards 'a sane, continuous and well-directed plan'. As always, Page thought that the Commonwealth must play the catalysing role, as 'states are quite unable to raise the funds necessary for so vast an undertaking and their necessarily local outlook makes them ill-suited to plan'.[79]

Transport received its most significant airing under the Bruce–Page Government when the May 1929 Premiers' Conference considered a report by the Commonwealth Transport Committee chaired by Major John Northcott, director of Army Stores and Transport. Its very broad findings on national coordination supported Page by calling for a federal transport council of ministers and a Commonwealth transportation authority with power for 'taking executive action necessary to carry out policy decided by the Transport Council'.[80] The establishment of this council was one of the few significant outcomes of this premiers' conference, but it was an advisory body that met just once under the Bruce–Page Government, in August 1929.[81] Scullin also made attempts to build Commonwealth-led cooperation, proposing at the February 1931 Premiers' Conference a breadth of topics comparable to what Bruce

---

78   Gillespie, *The Price of Health*, pp. 44–5; Page, *Truant Surgeon*, pp. 373–4; also transcript of Page's evidence to the Joint Committee on Constitutional Review, 15 January 1957, Sydney, p. 52, EPP, folder 1660.
79   Page speech to Constitutional Club, Brisbane, 6 January 1927, EPP, folder 417.
80   Commonwealth Transport Committee, *Summary Report on the Co-ordination of Transport in Australia by the Commonwealth Transport Committee*, Canberra, 1929, EPP, folder 1625. The chairman, Major John Northcott, was governor of New South Wales (1946–57).
81   See NAA, A1, 1932/8838.

and Page had raised, including transport, finance, banking, electoral administration and a 'three year plan'.[82] Growing financial pressures on state transport systems were to draw Page back into this field during the early Lyons Government.

## The demise of the Bruce–Page Government

The climax that industrial conflict reached in the late 1920s contributed decisively to the fall of the Bruce–Page Government in October 1929, although for reasons that had much to do with its own political misjudgements. In 1929 some 4.4 million working days were lost through strikes, approximately four times the annual average for the decade.[83] The period 1928–29 saw major and acrimonious strikes on the wharves, in the timber industry and on the New South Wales coalfields, all concerning issues of wages and conditions as the economy stalled. These drew robust responses from the Bruce–Page Government. In September 1928 it legislated to open up the nation's wharves to non-union labour and to require waterfront workers to submit to a licensing system that gave the government power to cancel their employment. The government lost nine seats at the November 1928 election, leaving it vulnerable to defeat in the House at the hands of what Page called 'an irregular Opposition' of dissident Nationalists and rural independents.[84]

Page's last major legislative initiative was to introduce a National Insurance Bill into parliament in September 1928, in attempted fulfilment of the goal he had announced back in his 1922 election policy speech. The Bill followed the recommendations of a long-running royal commission on national insurance. This provided for sickness, old age, disability and maternity benefits, mainly paid for by compulsory contributions by workers and employers, along with smaller payments to parents of children under 16 and to orphans. Page wanted a scheme based not on charity but on personal thrift and self-reliance, 'a scheme for encouraging, enabling, even compelling all workers to make some provision for their dependants'.[85]

---

82   'Conference of Commonwealth and State Ministers', 6, 7, 9, 10, 13, 25 and 26 February 1931, EPP, folder 1105.
83   Robert Murray, *The Confident Years: Australia in the Twenties*, Allen Lane, Ringwood, 1978, p. 216.
84   Page, *Truant Surgeon*, p. 181.
85   *Commonwealth Parliamentary Debates*, 14 September 1928, p. 6754.

The government faced opposition from within its own ranks, criticism of its trespass of such state responsibilities as workers' compensation and growing unease amongst employers. Insurance companies and friendly societies feared that their customers would choose to insure themselves through compulsory insurance alone. The scheme was strongly promoted during the 1928 election campaign only to be postponed indefinitely the following year. 'We missed the psychological moment for its passage in an attempt to make the legislation all-embracing', reflected Page in his memoirs.[86]

The May 1929 Premiers' Conference triggered the sequence of events leading to the defeat of the government. When the states rejected the proposed transfer of state industrial arbitration to the Commonwealth, Bruce declared that instead his government would withdraw from arbitration in most industries. In August 1929 he introduced into parliament a Maritime Industries Bill that sought to establish a new industrial tribunal to cover workers in interstate and overseas maritime transport, but also to leave most other federal industrial jurisdiction to the states alone. Unions representing the 700,000 workers subject to federal awards opposed any such shift to state coverage. The Bill was defeated on the floor of the House on 10 September 1929 by a single vote at the hands of Nationalist dissidents Hughes, Mann, W.M. Marks and G.A. Maxwell, along with erstwhile Country Party members Stewart and William McWilliams. The vital shift in Marks's vote arose from his objection to Bruce failing to consult parliamentary colleagues when he declared that a motion by Hughes to postpone the Bill until a referendum or an election amounted to a motion of no confidence in the government. (Page thought that Marks and McWilliams were additionally influenced by their objection to an unpopular new tax on foreign films.)[87] Also crucial to the government's defeat was the refusal of the Speaker, Littleton Groom, to vote in its favour.

The Bruce–Page Government was resoundingly defeated at the ensuing 12 October election. It lost 18 seats, including Bruce's own seat of Flinders and three held by the Country Party. Popular fear that a recast arbitration system would degrade living standards readily overrode ideals of co-operative federalism and national efficiency. Writing in his memoirs, Page reflected on other, less immediate, causes: the coalminers strike, for

---

86   Page, *Truant Surgeon*, p. 266; see also Ellis, *A History of the Australian Country Party*, p. 107.
87   Page, interview by B.D. Graham, 9 May 1956, B.D. Graham papers, NLA, MS 8471.

which he largely blamed the employer, John Brown; the government's decision not to proceed with prosecution of the same employer over a breach of federal law, seen as unfairly discriminating against organised labour; and his own 1929–30 Budget, which responded to falling customs revenue with increases in income and entertainment taxes, higher customs duties including on spirits and beer, and the duty on foreign films. Page admitted that the stress of continued opposition from both outside and within the government had made it a relief to lose.[88]

One of the first major policy moves of the new Scullin Government was to act on the long-standing ALP hostility to the Migration Agreement. In early November 1929 it announced the cessation of most assisted migration, citing rising unemployment and falling commodity prices, and followed this the next year with the abolition of the DMC. Page's angry speech to the House on the repeal of the DMC legislation shows how centrally it had lodged in his thinking. The DMC had used 'some of the best brains in the country' and was able to tackle 'the main factor in Australia's present economic sickness [which] is the lack of co-ordination in all those activities of government which have to do with the development of this country'.[89] The government responded on the plainer grounds of a need to economise and the lack of jobs for immigrants, as well as concerns over government control of development policy. Page's anger was no doubt sharpened by his seeing the demise of the DMC as extinguishing – for the time being – his hopes for The Gorge project. Bruce commented many years later that the Scullin Government's abolition of 'my' DMC denied the nation 'a clear-cut picture of the development of Australia' with 'no colour of politics'. Indeed, he considered this 'his deepest regret' after leaving office.[90] This heavily qualifies later suggestions that the Bruce–Page Government had operated in an 'atmosphere not conducive to the careful estimation of costs and benefits'.[91]

The DMC was extinguished as an organisation but the ideas it had embodied were to linger, mainly due to Page. The DMC model of co-opting business leaders, formalised coordination with the states, expert assessment of projects and the attempted distancing of national

---

88   Page, *Truant Surgeon*, pp. 182–5; see also Dagmar Carboch, 'The fall of the Bruce–Page Government', in Wildavsky and Carboch, *Studies in Australian Politics*, pp. 139–40.
89   *Commonwealth Parliamentary Debates*, 17 June 1930, pp. 2767, 2752.
90   Edwards, *Bruce of Melbourne*, pp. 440–1.
91   Sinclair, 'Capital formation', in Forster, *Australian Economic Development in the Twentieth Century*, p. 24.

development from party politics was, along with the Loan Council, the inspiration for Page's proposed national council of 1938–39 and a string of later planning proposals. Page tried to keep ideas of planning and cooperative federalism on the national political agenda for over three decades beyond the demise of the Bruce–Page Government. Yet for all his admiration for the DMC, both it and the Brigden Enquiry marked the start of increasing reliance on economic expertise in public policy. Brigden, in particular, was 'an enduring landmark in Australian economic history' by marking 'economists' first prominent step on the stage of public life in Australia'.[92] This shift was in future years to prove increasingly problematic for Page.

Scepticism concerning Page's developmentalist ambitions was clearly discernible even in the optimistic 1920s. He had not dominated the Bruce–Page Government, but was its most fecund generator of new policies. Page and the Country Party had habitually steered the government towards their various favoured policy initiatives but were often constrained by Bruce's caution, the resistance of the states, and the misgivings of experts in the DMC and the engineering profession. Despite this, and the comprehensiveness of the government's eventual defeat, the Bruce–Page experience gave Page a lasting sense of possibilities. Service as treasurer confirmed him as a major national figure and provided a stable platform for combining his official and more personal goals. He routinely alluded to these years when talking of what governments could and should do, the Bruce–Page Government being his benchmark for a sound developmentalist-oriented administration.

---

92  Coleman, Cornish and Hagger, *Giblin's Platoon*, pp. 65–6, 72.

# 6

# **PAGE AUDACIOUS**
## The 1930s

Page was out of ministerial office until November 1934 when the Country Party, belatedly, again formed a coalition with the urban-based conservatives, now recast as the United Australia Party (UAP). As a minister over 1934–39, Page successfully advocated fewer new policies than he had in the 1920s, but was as ambitious a visionary as ever. He was not restrained – but nor, for that matter, enabled – by a strong prime minister. The result was his two most audacious initiatives of all: attempts to unilaterally separate northern New South Wales from the rest of the state and, later, to establish governmental planning machinery for the shaping of Australia as a decentralised, regionalised nation.

Page faced a very different political landscape in this decade. The early 1930s was an unusually febrile time in Australian party politics. Under the stress of the Great Depression, most national and state governments were defeated at the polls. The ALP underwent splits involving both its right and left wings, and the new UAP absorbed elements of the Labor right. The Country Party sat on the cross-benches in parliament, but under an expectation that the coalition would be reinstituted once the Scullin Labor Government had been defeated. The strident rhetoric of Premier Lang and the perception that his government had rendered itself illegitimate by repudiating interest payments to British bondholders inspired a loyalist, middle class–based countermovement of such organisations as the All for Australia League.

Much of the tension over Lang was alleviated by the success of the UAP, led by the affable Tasmanian Joseph Lyons, at the national election of December 1931 and the premier's sudden removal from office by the state governor the following May. Lyons had been a senior minister in the Scullin Government but emerged as the leader of party dissidents who rejected Treasurer Theodore's proposal to expand credit as a response to the Depression. Lyons finally broke with the ALP in March 1931 when he supported a motion of no confidence in the government. His electoral appeal of restraint and personal modesty encouraged a coterie of Melbourne business and political figures to entice him into becoming the UAP's first parliamentary leader.

The UAP united the Nationalists, former ALP members who favoured strict economic austerity and some more populist movements including the All for Australia League. The new party emerged from an economic and political crisis unprecedented in the short history of the Australian Commonwealth – 'cobbled together out of political expediency, it was a party of action without elaborate party rules or even a mission statement'.[1] Lyons was a very different personage from Page. His instinct was 'to delegate and to manage rather than command'.[2] Frank Green, who had known Lyons since they played football and cricket together in Tasmania before World War One, recalled that 'the vitriol of Hughes, the aloofness of Bruce, the ascetic reserve of Scullin, were replaced in Lyons by a warm friendliness, courtesy and kindness, which never failed even at times of great stress'.[3] Prime Minister Lyons kept the UAP sufficiently united to reassure the public that stable government had been restored. It is a tribute to his ability to handle trenchant colleagues that, despite limited policy ambitions of his own, he eventually won Page's support and even admiration.

Page also expected to form a coalition immediately after Scullin's defeat. A joint party conference and policy statement for the 1931 election campaign even raised the possibility of the Country Party amalgamating with the UAP. Immediately after the election, Lyons offered the Country Party three portfolios (despite the UAP having won a parliamentary majority) but with the proviso that he alone would select ministers.

---

1 Anne Henderson, *Joseph Lyons: The People's Prime Minister*, NewSouth Publishing, Sydney, 2011, p. 319.
2 Ibid., p. 315.
3 Green, *Servant of the House*, p. 98.

This proved unacceptable to the Country Party, and so Page and his colleagues elected to stay on the cross-benches. Privately, Page feared that Lyons was a 'muddler'. He did not want to expose his Country Party to the 'big Melbourne manufacturers and stockbrokers' who had 'buried alive' John Latham, Lyons's predecessor as Opposition leader.[4]

Once in office, Lyons's reluctance to accede to Country Party demands for lower tariffs kept the two parties apart. Lyons did, however, cut many tariffs in early 1933 following advice from the Tariff Board, easing the path to reconciliation. Page received no shortage of advice from party members and farmers' organisations on whether to attempt to resume the coalition but hesitated on the grounds that 'the Country Party can do more in government than out of government'.[5] The coalition was finally restored in November 1934, after the UAP lost its majority at the election of two months earlier and failed in an attempt to continue governing alone.

Lyons provided an assurance that future decisions on tariffs would be acceptable to the Country Party. Although the Country Party soon scored a success when the new coalition government duly cut tariffs on a large number of items of machinery, its overall status was weaker than in the Bruce–Page Government. It held only four positions in a ministry of 14, two of which were without portfolio. Page became minister for commerce and was again de facto deputy prime minister. Commerce was a lesser portfolio than that of treasurer, but it did give him responsibility for agriculture and overseas trade policy. Thomas Paterson, Page's deputy until 1937, became minister for the interior.

During the 1930s, policy priority shifted from the national and rural development that had so suited Page in the 1920s to recovery from the Depression. Lyons maintained the deflationary policies of the Premiers' Plan agreed between Scullin and the states in June 1931 that imposed a shared sacrifice through higher taxes, less public spending and reduced interest payments to local bond holders. His government set out to restore business confidence by balancing budgets and lowering costs, including through cuts to public service salaries and social service benefits.

---

4   'Muddler', Earle Page to Ethel Page, 27 December 1931, Earle Page papers, UNE Archives, A180, box 7, folder 4; 'big Melbourne…', Page to A.G. Cameron, 29 April 1931, EPP, folder 810.
5   Page speech to the Riverina Division of the United Country Party, Wagga, 2 November 1934, Earle Page papers, UNE Archives, A180, box 7, folder 4.

Some emergency Depression taxes were also cut, while Stanley Bruce, back in parliament and now assistant treasurer, negotiated for reduced interest payments to British holders of Australian bonds.

Mid-1932 marked the start of a slow five-year period of recovery. Cheaper currency assisted export sales and the 1932 Ottawa Imperial Economic Conference gave Australian farmers greater access to British markets in return for lower tariffs on manufactures from Britain. Rural industries, particularly pastoralism, began a slow revival. Manufacturing recovered more strongly to become a mass employer, aided by the high tariffs imposed by Scullin and a devalued currency that made imports dearer. From 1933 unemployment began to fall but so gradually that it took until 1938 to reach 8 per cent, a middling rate for the previous decade.[6] Page himself suffered personal financial stress, especially during the depths of the Depression early in the decade and again in 1936–37, but kept this quiet. He stayed as active as ever in public life.

Rural policy was much less ambitious than in the 1920s. The focus was on wheat and dried fruits, each driven by different pressures. The wheat industry was afflicted by low prices and debt acquired from overexpansion in the 1920s. Although over the period 1930–36 growers received bounties and relief payments from the Commonwealth, it was only following a fall in wheat prices that a home consumption price was introduced in 1938, financed by a flour tax. The 1934–36 Royal Commission on the Wheat, Flour and Bread Industries (chaired by Herbert Gepp) favoured a central marketing authority and continued Commonwealth Government assistance. Although it supported a home consumption price only as a strictly temporary relief measure, by adding that wheat farmers were entitled to the same benefits available to other industries it effectively opened the way for ongoing home consumption pricing. Policy on dried fruit was driven by unwelcome constitutional challenges to the regulation of interstate trade that came to occupy much of Page's time late in the decade.

More positively for Page, the 1930s offered a far richer intellectual discussion on policy than had the 1920s. The journals *Australian Quarterly* and *Public Administration* first appeared in 1929 and 1937 respectively, and the Australian Institute of Political Science (AIPS) was established

---

6   Macintyre, *A Concise History of Australia*, p. 180; J.R. Robertson, '1930–39', in Crowley, *A New History of Australia*, pp. 435–6, 438.

in 1932. Widened debate drew forth reflections on Page's policy visions, especially planning and cooperative federalism. Economic thought began in the mid-1930s to turn to averting future depressions, leading many policy intellectuals towards a new openness to planning and welfarism that resulted in such publications as *Economic Planning*, the proceedings of a 1934 AIPS conference. Although these ponderings had an urban basis far removed from Page's native small-town habitat, they encouraged him to resume his interest in planning.

But the overall trend for Page during this decade remained one of growing difficulty in anchoring his personal initiatives in mainstream politics. The policy priorities of the Commonwealth Government narrowed, and the Country Party itself progressively offered Page less basis for pursuing his vision. There were also further signs that policy-making was building on the Development and Migration Commission and the Brigden Enquiry of the previous decade by continuing to shift towards greater reliance on economic expertise, eventually to provide a fertile basis for the acceptance of Keynesianism. The 1937 Royal Commission on Monetary and Banking Systems, for example, recommended that the Commonwealth Bank work to reduce fluctuations in the economy.

Page in the 1930s therefore found himself having to be keenly alert for opportunities to pursue his developmentalist agenda. His focus shifted as different opportunities appeared, making him the leading national advocate of change in five related elements of his national vision in sequence. Each arose from very different circumstances. Regionalism and new statism were revived by dramatic events in New South Wales, foremost being Lang's interest payment repudiation in 1931–32. From 1934 Page became directly involved in the campaign to establish a university in New England, led by new state advocates and providing a focus for his long-standing interest in rural-based education. His renewed engagement with cooperative federalism via Commonwealth–state policy councils was driven by the need to respond to challenges to Australia's trade interests and orderly marketing, leading to the creation of the Australian Agricultural Council in 1934. In 1936, electrification re-emerged briefly via Page's alertness to opportunities linked to trade policy and to collaboration with New South Wales.

Finally, Page became Australia's foremost political proponent of national planning. This was aided by the threat of war and led to his extraordinary 1938–39 attempt to create a National Council of Commonwealth and state ministers. This policy venture involved an effective hijacking of the government from the ailing Lyons. It encompassed all the objectives of Page's preceding policy campaigns on decentralisation, electrification, rural services and Commonwealth–state cooperation. Its abject failure was to be a factor in Page's dramatic attack on Robert Menzies and fall from political power.

## Page's freedoms as a private member, 1929–34: The resurgence of new statism

The defeat of the Bruce–Page Government restored the federal Country Party to a freedom it had not experienced since the pioneering days of the early 1920s and its challenges to the Hughes Government. Page described the five years that followed 1929 as a period that 'sharpened our wits and enabled us to prepare public opinion for the policies we hoped to implement when the next opportunity came'.[7] Characteristically, it was Page who took greatest advantage of this release from ministerial office and coalition to become outspoken on issues dear to him.

An early instance arose from Scullin's almost desperate attempt to counter the Depression via trade barriers. This was a cue for Country Party MPs to resume public attacks on tariffs after years of strained silence and for Page to revive his more finely balanced ideas on how tariffs should be applied. In July 1930 he spoke of the nation having gone 'tariff mad', especially as hampering the importation of electrical equipment retarded electrification across the economy. Page delighted in bold international comparisons, and so cast this as a reason why Australia was developing more slowly than Canada. He made clear his willingness to protect Australian manufacturing, but only where this concentrated on internationally competitive products based on primary inputs such as wool and flour. Lack of such targeting resulted in Australia having 'built up many exotic industries that are non-essential and unsuited for the natural environment of the country'.[8]

But the issue Page pursued most energetically was new statism, for the first time since his disappointment before the Cohen Royal Commission. In the wake of the Bruce–Page Government's defeat, Page's erstwhile

---

7 Page, *Truant Surgeon*, p. 227.
8 *Commonwealth Parliamentary Debates*, 17 July 1930, pp. 4252–4, 4260.

friend Percy Stewart accurately predicted to Hughes that 'no doubt Page will bring out his New State hobby horse and mount him again'.[9] New statism demonstrated its capacity to readily flare up as a focus for rural resentment by broadening markedly in the late 1920s and early 1930s, energetically fanned by Page. He rapidly became its central figure, including a largely successful effort to unite the various New South Wales new state movements. The main underlying cause of the revival was the impact of the Depression on rural Australia, but Lang's first repudiation in March 1931 provided a galvanising issue for Page and his followers to demand the separation of the state's north. To them, Lang's actions justified dispensing with constitutional formalities in favour of rebellion against a government that had rendered itself illegitimate, casting themselves as they did so as upholders of the federal Constitution. The defeat of the Bavin–Buttenshaw State Government in October 1930 helped by releasing New South Wales Country Party figures of the calibre of Bruxner and Drummond to join this campaign.

New state agitation strengthened in three very different ways. First, there was a marked geographic widening of campaigning beyond northern New South Wales. From 1931, the movement acquired an added base in the Riverina, drawing on the precedent of the Riverina New State League that had been active in the early 1920s. Agitation briefly matched that in the state's north, invigorated by the charismatic leadership of the Wagga Wagga timber merchant Charles Hardy. The course of events in this region was to have great implications for Page. There were also lesser revivals in the west and south-east of New South Wales, and in northern Queensland.

Second, new intellectual proponents and political movements added non-rural strands to new statism and decentralisation. New states became a beacon for agitation for constitutional change and creative responses to the Depression, overlapping with the more parochial agendas of older school new staters. This included movements that proffered themselves as avowedly anti-political alternatives to conventional party politicking. The outspoken decentralist civil engineer Alex Gibson, for example, was prime mover in the All for Australia League.

---

9   Letter from Stewart to Hughes, 30 October 1929, quoted in Graham, *Formation of the Australian Country Parties*, p. 284.

Page dallied with these more rarefied advocates in the early 1930s and again during the post-war era. Some responded by openly recognising him as the pre-eminent political advocate of new states and decentralisation. Bland, increasingly outspoken from his base at the University of Sydney on all kinds of issues, often wrote in support of Page initiatives. In the early 1930s Bland was an advocate of decentralisation and regionalism but not of the new states that had been so far proposed, which he thought would still be so large as to pose problems of remoteness. He dismissed northern New South Wales agitation as merely seeking a bigger share of public expenditure, and proposed amalgamating local councils into larger district councils, reminiscent of the Cohen recommendation.[10] The geographer J. Macdonald Holmes thought it opportune to create new states now that the geographic limits for agriculture were being reached, helping delineate natural boundaries for settlement.[11] More marginal but still outspoken figures included Dr Norman Pern, a Sydney general practitioner, who in his 1932 booklet *Australia Speaking!: Is Earle Page Right?* wrongly asserted that Page was interested only in splitting up New South Wales. Pern's own vision was of a 'United Federation of Australia' based on self-governing regions united by a national railway system.[12] A few new state advocates tried making use of broader interest in constitutional reform. In April 1933 Ulrich Ellis established (apparently at his own behest) a Constitution League in Canberra, a short-lived discussion group which attracted Solicitor-General Fred Whitlam and Labor-leaning journalist Warren Denning.[13]

Third, the wider regional base and engagement of articulate intellectuals encouraged a more national approach to new states, reminiscent of what Page had advocated at the Albury convention of July 1922. As the seasoned campaigner V.C. Thompson later recalled, there was an 'enlarging of the movement's sphere of political interest on the national plane'.[14] The Northern New South Wales Movement's 1929 convention at Armidale unanimously adopted a resolution calling for 'a national

---

10   F.A. Bland, 'The Abolition of States and the Increase of Local Government Bodies', reprinted from *The Shire and Municipal Record*, November 1932, copy in Ulrich Ellis papers, NLA, MS 1006, box 15, folder 55.
11   J. Macdonald Holmes, *The 'New States' Idea and Its Geographic Background*, New Century Press, Sydney, 1933.
12   Copies of Pern's publications are in the Ulrich Ellis collection, UNE Archives, A811, box 13.
13   See Ellis's account of the league's meeting of 11 April 1933, Ulrich Ellis papers, NLA, MS 1006, box 22, series 7B, folder 97.
14   From a historical account of the new state movement written by Thompson for Page (untitled), January 29 1958, p. 1, EPP, folder 2146.

movement for a new Federal system with a new distribution of powers and a new distribution of territory'.[15] Another national convention was held in Canberra in May 1930 against the background of the Scullin Government's attempt to liberalise mechanisms for constitutional amendment, and called for adoption of the Peden formula for new states.[16] Page became directly involved in the two main groups to emerge from this revival, bolstering his claim to national leadership of the new state movement: the Sydney-based Federal Reconstruction Movement (FRM), and the United Country Movement (UCM), which was to merge with the Country Party in 1931.

The FRM arose from the preference intellectual supporters of new states and decentralisation had for broader bodies than individual regional movements. It was formed in July 1932 with Stanley Kingsbury as first honorary secretary, a professional publicist who Page had once engaged to advise the new state cause.[17] Kingsbury advised the new state campaign to form a Sydney reform league to build urban-based support in anticipation of a statewide referendum. The FRM now proposed replacing the states with smaller federal units, and shared Page's interest in transferring many state powers to a strong national government.[18] The FRM's other leading lights included Bland, educationalist and state public servant H.L. Harris and Sydney barrister Richard Windeyer.

But the UCM was the most important organisation to arise from the 1931–32 spike in new state agitation. It was the closest the new state movement ever came to a united structure. The UCM was also the main basis for Page's resumption of active leadership of the movement. It emerged from a chain of events that began with the rise of the United Australia Association, led by Hardy to promote the Riverina cause. Hardy at his peak portrayed himself as offering a full alternative to the Country Party.[19] His impassioned calls for direct action to free the Riverina from the grip of Lang's Sydney led to his being cast as that rarest of species in the Australian political pantheon, the demagogue. Robert Clyde Packer – Frank's father – dubbed him the Cromwell of the Riverina.

---

15   Ibid., p. 1.
16   *The Canberra Times*, 20 May 1930, p. 2, and 21 May 1930, p. 5.
17   See Kingsbury to Page, 13 June 1932, EPP, folder 1020.
18   See Ellis, *New Australian States*, p. 224; and 'Report to Annual Meeting by the Provisional Executive Committee' of the FRM by R. Windeyer and Stanley Kingsbury, 28 September 1932, David Henry Drummond papers, UNE Archives, A248, V3010, folder 6.
19   Ellis, *A History of the Australian Country Party*, p. 171; Aitkin, *The Colonel*, pp. 136–7.

Hardy's speeches included oblique references to a secret paramilitary force supposedly at his disposal. His threats of unilateral secession attracted the attention of the New South Wales Police and the Commonwealth Investigation Branch. Andrew Moore in his history of right-wing agitation of the time concluded that paramilitary movements of the early 1930s, especially the Old Guard, had a distinct rural element. Some members were prominent in the Country Party and new statism, notably Aubrey Abbott, member for the federal seat of Gwydir and minister for home affairs in the final year of the Bruce–Page Government. They shared an avowed readiness to assume control should there be a breakdown of the Lang Government.[20] It was through Abbott that Page was introduced to the leader of the breakaway and more publicly prominent New Guard, Eric Campbell. Campbell found that Page 'expressed himself as being enthusiastically behind the New Guard, but his counsel was much more militant than I was prepared to accept'. The problem was presumably the proposed breakaway of New England, as Campbell recollected that 'our conversation was mainly directed to the New State Movement and water conservation' and claimed that his New Guard was 'purely a defensive organisation and could and would do nothing unless there was a breakdown too extensive for the police to control'.[21] There is no indication from Campbell or elsewhere that Page ever joined the New Guard, hardly a likely action by someone so accustomed to seeing himself as leader.

Hardy envisaged the secession of the Riverina as ushering in a regime of local authorities that would, rather incongruously, be led by a strong national parliament. He was Page's only serious rival as the new state movement's foremost public figure, and he thought that devious northerners were misusing new statism as a means of promoting the Country Party. He was even suspected of having designs on the national leadership of the Country Party. In May 1931, Hardy publicly challenged Page accordingly:

> If Earle Page refuses to co-operate with the Riverina and Western Movements, our intention is to go to the north coast to test whether the people want Dr Page or the Riverina Movement. Watch out, Dr Page, that you do not get out of step with the country people.[22]

---

20  Andrew Moore, *The Secret Army and the Premier: Conservative Paramilitary Organisations in New South Wales 1930–32*, New South Wales University Press, Kensington, NSW, 1989, pp. 93–9, 103–6.
21  Eric Campbell, *The Rallying Point: My Story of the New Guard*, Melbourne University Press, Carlton, Vic., 1965, pp. 97–8, 100.
22  Ellis, *A History of the Australian Country Party*, p. 178.

**Figure 8: Charles Hardy, c. 1931: Regional demagogue pictured in respectable mode.**
Source: Courtesy of National Library of Australia, nla.pic-an24716332, Lorne Studio.

Page wrote in his memoirs of the Riverina movement's attempt, backed by unspecified 'influential Sydney personalities', to take the place of the state Country Party. He drolly called all these pressures 'diverse undercurrents', which were successfully neutralised by the creation of the UCM.[23] 'Sydney personalities' may have been an oblique reference to the city-based All for Australia League, which had strong ties to the protectionist Chamber of Manufactures of New South Wales and had made overtures to Hardy. Some Country Party figures suspected the League of plotting to eventually absorb all non-Labor parties. But Hardy presented only a passing challenge. As a long-standing party leader with a good prospect of shortly returning to government, Page in 1931 was a firmly established national figure. Hardy soon displayed the typical limitations of the demagogue by outstripping his capacity for substantive action. He did not have a firm platform beyond the Riverina movement and lacked grounding in practical politics. His contempt for established politicians and suspected interest in the party leadership drew the disdain of more accomplished rural leaders such as Bruxner.

During 1931 Hardy slowly entered into alliances with other new staters and the Country Party. Over March to August he attended a series of four conventions of New South Wales new state movements. By June he had publicly reclassed Page, Bruxner and Drummond as colleagues to be thanked for having 'helped the new movements over the hurdles of constitutional difficulties'.[24] At the August convention Hardy called for all four regional movements in New South Wales to be moulded into one organisation, leading to the creation of the UCM with himself as chair. In October he led a Riverina delegation to the prime minister, only to find that Scullin not only opposed new states but favoured an all-powerful federal parliament that at its pleasure delegated powers to provinces and could amend the Constitution effectively at will. This prospect so unnerved Hardy that he switched to favouring more fully sovereign new states, bringing him yet closer to Page.[25]

Hardy wholly entered the Country Party fold when elected a senator in December 1931. He became representative of the malleability of so much new state agitation and its tendency to lack sustainable strategies. The UCM was soon effectively absorbed within the Country Party by being given

---

23  Page, *Truant Surgeon*, p. 207.
24  Aitkin, *The Colonel*, p. 138.
25  Ellis, *A History of the Australian Country Party*, pp. 180–1; *Sydney Morning Herald*, 12 October 1931, p. 9.

a place on the Central Council of the redubbed United Country Party (UCP) of New South Wales. The UCP supported the division of New South Wales along the lines of its new state movements – the Riverina, the north, the west, and the Monaro–south coastal–metropolitan region. Hardy's earlier calls for expanded local authorities had aroused such suspicions he was a mere unificationist that the UCM–UCP union was only consummated after he underwent searching questioning by Drummond. Hardy's response that 'he was utterly opposed to unification' and that 'his position as chairman did not mean that he was the Leader of the Movement' effectively marked his surrendering of any lingering pretensions to national leadership of new statism.[26]

Although Page declined an offer to lead the UCM, he became its main driver. He had the public status and political skills to tie it to his own northern wing of the movement, and soon outshone Hardy. He supported the UCM's de facto union with the Country Party and successfully proposed that it broaden its platform to advocate continued subdivision into 'new federal units', the shift of selected powers from the states to the Commonwealth and a national transport authority.[27] Almost uniquely among new state organisations, the UCM proclaimed criteria for delineating the boundaries of new states, albeit broad ones – political and economic balance, 'community of interest', facility of communications, diversity of production and natural outlets for trade.[28]

Page was also central to the UCM's entering into an alliance with the FRM. Soon after the UCM was formed, he and other UCM figures met with the FRM leadership, including Bland. The FRM was relieved to find that 'no difference exists between the objectives as we understand them of the Federal Reconstruction Movement and the ultimate objectives of the United Country Movement', including the transfer of transport and industrial powers to the Commonwealth prior to subdividing New South Wales. So reassured was it that Page and Drummond were elected as FRM vice-presidents.[29]

---

26   Ellis, *A History of the Australian Country Party*, p. 179.
27   Minutes of joint meeting of the New England, Riverina, Monaro–South Coast and Western movements, 13 August 1931, Ulrich Ellis papers, NLA, MS 1006, box 14, folder 45.
28   Ellis, *New Australian States*, p. 227.
29   Letter to the Secretary of the FRM from Bland, H.L. Harris and R.W.G. MacKay, undated but internal evidence suggests August 1932, David Henry Drummond papers, UNE Archives, A248, V3010, folder 6; the *Armidale Express* of 18 November 1932, p. 3 reported on the UCM conference in Armidale and the election of FRM vice-presidents.

A nominally united new state body assembled from multiple geographic and sectoral bases was always at risk from regional rivalries and conflicting motivations. Northern New South Wales disagreed with other regional movements over the configuration of its proposed new state, such as where its deep-water port should be sited. At the August 1931 convention western New South Wales objected to being bracketed with Sydney. It was felt by Drummond and Holmes that the metropolis needed a hinterland.[30] Drummond remained uneasy over the FRM and warned Page in November 1933 that Bland's plan for non-sovereign provinces 'somewhat along the lines of the English County Council' was bound to fail given 'the centralising influence which is bred in the bone of the people of this state'.[31] The importance that leaders of the Riverina and Northern movements attached to simpler and cheaper governments must have sowed unease among many grassroots supporters hoping for more public funding. But the 1929–32 revival did show that new statism and an elite-led sense of rural grievance had not only maintained a place in Australian political culture but also had grown to acquire urban-based adherents. Page played a central strategic role in this, not least by successfully resisting Hardy's short-lived bid to become national leader.

## Page militant: Leading the attempted secession of New England

Page's campaigning for new states reached its most militant phase in 1931–32. While dealing with Hardy, the FRM and the UCM, he simultaneously led the most remarkable of all new state campaigns, premised on the outright condemnation of the government of New South Wales as illegitimate. Page and his followers responded to their fear of the complete breakdown of government by plotting the unilateral separation of the state's north. Although this effort at secession evaporated almost immediately Premier Lang was removed from office, the episode is arguably Australia's greatest political conspiracy. It reveals much about the broader climate of ideas of the time and Page's unique ability to lead the new state movement.

---

30   Neale, 'New States Movement', *Australian Quarterly*, p. 16.
31   Drummond to Page, 29 November 1935, Drummond papers, UNE Archives, A248, V3010, folder 8, part 5.

The rural dimension to anti-Lang agitation drew on some basic mores of rural community culture – thrift and the belief that paying one's debts is an important matter of personal honour. This was so strong that it outweighed resentment of the large banks. It reflected a deep sense of a 'moral economy' as being essential to the nation's financial stability and made financial repudiation by a government highly suggestive of unfitness to rule.[32] This moral reinforcement of calls for northern secession was a central feature of Page's public campaigning.

On 9 February 1931 Lang announced his intention to repudiate the payment of interest due to foreign bond holders. (Lang subsequently twice defaulted on overseas interest payments, in March 1931 and again in January–February 1932). Page at once proposed to his 'closest colleagues' an entirely new and radical strategy based on the north declaring separation from New South Wales, now seen by him as an outlaw state. He consulted legal advisers and the state Country Party MPs Bruxner and Roy Vincent, then arranged for the journalists Thompson and Sommerlad to work on the northern press.[33] Page went public just eight days after Lang's announcement, in a speech he delivered at Glenreagh on the state's north coast. Default 'must automatically place New South Wales out of the Federal Union' and so 'the people of the North seem to have no other course but to cut adrift from New South Wales'.[34] Otherwise, he wrote privately, 'they become repudiators also and suffer the penalties of repudiation – no capital for development in the next generation; withdrawal of capital by all who can because once a government has repudiated in one direction it cannot be trusted not to in others'.[35]

Page's leadership of this campaign demonstrated his aggressive readiness to seize opportunities. It was he who summoned northern delegates to an Annual New States convention at Armidale on 28 February to endorse his proposals to form a provisional executive and submit a draft constitution to federal parliament.[36] He assured delegates that 'now is the psychological moment when the whole of Australia is stirred, and when our requests for admission are unanswerable', and called for petitions

---

32  Michael Cathcart, *Defending the National Tuckshop: Australia's Secret Intrigue of 1931*, McPhee Gribble/Penguin, Fitzroy, Vic., 1988, p. 22; Brett, *Australian Liberals and the Moral Middle Class*, pp. 108–9.
33  Page, *Truant Surgeon*, p. 204.
34  Quoted in Ellis, *New Australian States*, pp. 205–6.
35  Page to R. Jones of Canowindra, 7 March 1931, Ellis papers, NLA, MS 1006, box 14, folder 44.
36  Page, *Truant Surgeon*, p. 205.

to the Commonwealth and British governments seeking recognition.[37] Page blamed Scullin's fiscal policies and the Lang left of the ALP for threatening the Financial Agreement, New South Wales and indeed the entire nation. The new state's constitution would impose limits on taxes and borrowing to protect rural Australia from such urban profligacy. Page the fiscal conservative was always loath to concede that any of his own plans could impose on the public purse. A self-governing, frugal New England would attract investors and set an example to be copied across the nation. Privately, he told Ellis that northern MPs should leave state parliament at once and establish a government based at Armidale.[38]

This was all a typical Page strategy: seizing an opportunity to implement a long-held aim that would normally lack support; lining up important contacts; issuing strident public calls for immediate action; and then trying to push through the necessary arrangements, all with only as much regard for constitutional requirements and other inconveniences as was necessary. His approach was shadowy but teasingly semi-public. Page also rallied the New England New State Movement at a pivotal convention in Maitland in April 1931, which endorsed its constitution and working with other new state movements. Page exhorted his fellow new state militants to see themselves not as rebels but as loyalists intent on returning their territory to the national fold by rejecting Lang's effective withdrawal of New South Wales from the federation.[39]

Lang's threats were also important in the convening of the meetings that had brought Page and Hardy together in the UCM and where Page assumed ascendancy. At a rally at Wagga Wagga on 28 February 1931, Hardy issued an ultimatum to the state government to meet local demands by the end of the following month. Page recounted that, soon afterwards, Hardy privately confessed that he had no idea what to do if Lang stood firm – which the premier indeed did. Follow the lead of the New Englanders, advised Page, by now clearly the movement's leader.[40] Like Drummond, he was troubled by Hardy's countenancing weak local councils rather than the sovereign entities of the bona fide new stater. Page also hoped to keep open the option of a properly constitutional route

---

37 Speech by Page to New States Convention 28 February 1931, New England New State Movement, Armidale, UNE Archives, A1, box 14.
38 Ulrich Ellis, *A Pen in Politics*, Ginninderra Press, Charnwood, ACT, 2007, p. 174.
39 Speech of 7 April 1931, in Ellis papers, NLA, MS 1006, box 12, series 6A, folder 33. For details of the Maitland conference, see Ellis, *New Australian States*, pp. 210–13, 256–9.
40 Page, *Truant Surgeon*, pp. 205–6.

to new states. In parliament in April he called on Scullin to recognise New England and the Riverina, either by a referendum to adopt the Peden formula for new states or by persuading the British Parliament to intervene.[41]

Page was not merely 'flirting briefly and somewhat reluctantly with right-wing revolutionary politics', as has been claimed.[42] Documentation such as the diary and memoirs of his observant chronicler Ellis indicate that Page was absolutely determined in leading a properly bold response to what he saw as an unprecedented challenge to the very fundamentals of governance. Nor was he one to forgo a rare opportunity to implement an important element of his personal vision. Ellis recalled in his history of new statism, published soon after these events, that whenever the movement seemed divided over the wisdom of such militancy, it was Page who rallied them. He pointed to Page's strident speech at Glenreagh invoking the West Virginians' self-declared secession from their mother state of Virginia at the onset of the American Civil War in 1861, 'when the Constitution was infringed, so their honour might be unsmirched, their reputation untarnished, their obligations fulfilled and their progress and development as an integral part of the Federal Union assured'.[43] Dedicated new staters frequently drew a parallel with West Virginia, despite the vastly different historical circumstances. Ellis's detailed diary of the lead-up to the Maitland convention provides further evidence of Page's commitment. Page confided that achievement of a new state would rank alongside the Nymboida power scheme and the Financial Agreement as his lifetime achievements.[44]

Ellis also captured Page's confidence that he was far ahead of all others in thought and action. He wrote of Page convening an all-day and night meeting on 22 March 1931 at Parliament House, Sydney, with state and federal MPs in an attempt to secure their support for secession, only to be

---

41   Ellis, *New Australian States*, pp. 213–14; *Commonwealth Parliamentary Debates*, 16 April 1931, pp. 924–8.
42   Carl Bridge, 'Page, Sir Earle Christmas (1880–1961)', *Australian Dictionary of Biography*, National Centre of Biography, Australian National University, adb.anu.edu.au/biography/page-sir-earle-christmas-7941/text13821, published first in hardcopy volume 11, Melbourne University Press, Parkville, Vic., 1988.
43   Page quoted in Ellis, *New Australian States*, p. 206.
44   Typed text of diary in Ulrich Ellis papers, NLA, MS 1006, box 12, series 6A, folder 33, entry for 24 February 1931. This diary was quoted at length in Ellis's posthumously published memoirs. Parts of the original handwritten version survive in the Ellis papers and differ only in very minor details; see MS 1006, box 14, series 6, folder 44.

subsequently disappointed by their caution. Hardy is shown in the diary as soon after again looking to Page and the northerners for a lead, such as by proposing that Riverina adopt the New England constitution.[45] Bruxner makes a telling comment that Page had not only started the campaign in 1915 but ever since 'his continual activity had kept it alive'.[46] Page also wrote to Drummond on his consultations with MPs who could form the 'Governing Body' of the new state using terms that affirm the depth of his determination. He reiterated that 'this is the psychological moment and possibly our only ever chance of ever getting away with it'. If it failed, then 'so far as I am concerned I am finished with politics completely and will devote myself to my professional work and leave it to another generation to gather the results of the seed we have sown'.[47]

Nearly a year later, in April 1932 when Lang was threatening further repudiations in defiance of Commonwealth legislation, the UCM executive telegrammed the recently elected Prime Minister Lyons to demand a referendum on 'the immediate reconstruction of the state of New South Wales into smaller federal units'.[48] Lyons opposed separation. Ellis penned an extraordinary letter to a contact in Brisbane in which he used personal euphemisms to describe how Page – dubbed by Ellis the 'President' – had just approached federal Cabinet in a bid for support for his proposed breakaway state. Lyons was similarly labelled by Ellis the 'Chairman of Directors', Assistant Treasurer Bruce was the 'Cashier', and Attorney-General Latham was cast as the 'Lawyer'. Bruce was quoted as commenting that 'he thought the Chairman of Directors would have to fight our branch [i.e. the new state movement] if we adopted the attitude outlined by the President'. But he added that 'there are other people in the world he wants to fight more and with more reason'.[49] Ellis had a well-developed sense of the dramatic, but this subterfuge is not wholly outlandish. The political tensions of these months were sufficient to raise fear of conflict between the law enforcement forces of the Commonwealth and those of New South Wales.

---

45  Ellis, *A Pen in Politics*, p.179; also Ellis diary, 28 and 30 March 1931, ibid.
46  Ellis diary, 28 March 1931, ibid.
47  Page to Drummond, 18 March 1931, Ellis papers, NLA, MS 1006, box 14, folder 44.
48  Moore, *The Secret Army and the Premier*, p. 176.
49  Ellis to his school friend Jack Ridler, 7 March 1932, Ellis papers, NLA, MS 1006, box 14, folder 45. Page provides a brief account of this meeting in *Truant Surgeon*, pp. 210–11.

The UCM leadership met on 17 April 1932 at Page's Wollstonecraft residence in Sydney, followed the next day by a meeting of the UCM at which its executive revealed the intended plan for secession. This would begin with all 'loyal state members' being called together 'for the purpose of subdividing New South Wales into four units'.[50] Local conventions were to be held at Armidale, Wagga Wagga, Dubbo and Sydney to appoint provisional governments, which would then each proceed to seek Commonwealth recognition followed by a referendum to ratify a new state constitution. Finally, the constitution and boundaries would be submitted to the Commonwealth Parliament with an appeal to recognise the new states and to guarantee payments until elections were held for permanent governments.[51]

But UCM delegates raised doubts immediately, especially over timing. Although Page as leader had a strong personal network throughout the movement, he was not in complete control. The conspiracy had become increasingly diverse with the addition of Hardy and others. Page wanted to set a definite date for action, but Hardy – no longer an antipodean Cromwell – managed to persuade them all to wait for one more 'overt act' by Lang. Page described Hardy as having been 'theatrical' at this meeting: the leader of the Western Movement, E.J. Body, was 'timid'. The most Page could elicit was agreement on a coded telegram from the executive to the various movements as the signal to implement the plan when the time finally came.[52] In public, Page broadcast by radio that if the Commonwealth Government did not act to 'reconstruct New South Wales and remove its rebel government', then 'the country men will be forced to take the lead themselves by creating their own governments who will obey the Federal law and Constitution, protect the people, develop resources, and defy the rebel elements in the community'.[53] In parliament, a Labor MP asked the attorney-general whether action would be taken against Page for preaching sedition.[54]

---

50  Page, *Truant Surgeon*, pp. 209–10.
51  Ellis in his *A History of the Australian Country Party*, pp. 188–9, provides a similar description of the action proposed, but gives a different date for what appears to be the same executive meeting, 8 April 1932; and in his memoirs refers to the Emergency Committee of the UCM as meeting on 9 April 1932, *A Pen in Politics*, p. 184.
52  Page, *Truant Surgeon*, p. 210.
53  *Newcastle Morning Herald and Miners' Advocate*, 21 April 1932, p. 8.
54  Rowley James, *Commonwealth Parliamentary Debates*, 14 April 1931, p. 757.

On 12 May Lang refused to comply with federal legislation enabling the Commonwealth to reclaim from New South Wales monies it had spent to meet the state's debts, whereupon the state governor, Sir Philip Game, dismissed him from office. The speed with which this took the wind out of militant new statism implies much about its capacity to sustain Page's ultimate national goals. There is no indication anywhere that resentment of Lang, intense as it was in rural New South Wales, amounted to a popular groundswell favouring unilateral independence of the north, the Riverina or anywhere else. Over a year earlier Sommerlad had informed Page that he 'was rather surprised to find during my stay in the North that the secession idea is by no means as popular as we fondly imagined' and that 'if a referendum were taken on the question of the new state, it would have no chance of being carried so far as the Tableland is concerned'.[55] Nor did the movement's supporters have a strong enough presence within local governments, police, essential services and other vital points to have ever been able to assert control. Ellis had noted in his diary the paucity of support from state MPs. In his memoirs, he also observed a decline in Riverina interest in a new state, which he attributed to the expectation that all would be well once Lang was removed.[56] Page's advocacy of rebellion had been all the more daring for being led by a militant few rather than by public demand.

The Lang dismissal suddenly removed a shared focus from a narrow group of rebellious rural political, newspaper and business leaders. Page himself worked to a different dynamic than most new state sympathisers, who were at heart driven by short-term considerations of the state of the rural economy and dread of Langism. These years provided him with a seeming opportunity to redesign the federal system that he promptly seized with minimal concern for its unorthodoxy. Page was much more a man of ends rather than of means. He had greater ability than any other new state leader to provide continuity and attract wider attention, if not necessarily actual support. He also had superior capacity to cope with day-to-day events and to propose strategy in response than did passing rivals like Hardy. Hardy, incidentally, lost his Senate seat in 1937 before serving with the civilian defence effort in World War Two. He died in an air crash in Queensland in August 1941.

---

55   Sommerlad to Page, 17 March 1931, Ellis papers, NLA, MS 1006, box 14, folder 51.
56   Ellis diary, 27 February 1931, NLA, MS 1006, box 12, series 6A, folder 33; Ellis, *A Pen in Politics*, pp. 182–3.

For over six years following Lang's demise, Page again let new states and decentralisation drift as he, Bruxner and Drummond re-entered government and the Depression slowly receded. His political focus from 1934 shifted to nurturing a successful coalition with the UAP. Although Page found Lyons more pliable than Bruce had been, the prime minister's own engagement with new states remained inconsistent and driven by his efforts to manage his fluctuating relationship with the Country Party. Lyons in 1931–32 took some interest in a constitutional convention when it seemed likely that the Country Party would partner the UAP in a coalition. The shared policy program that he and Page produced in October 1931 included the elimination of overlapping federal–state powers, 'new self-governing Federal units' and referenda on the division of New South Wales.[57] Soon after, Lyons drew on Peden's findings of 1929 to propose clarification of the Constitution's provisions on new states and in June 1933, as prime minister, unsuccessfully proposed to the states a constitutional convention.[58]

New statism gained one other genuine new proponent in the political mainstream during this decade: Bertram Stevens, Lang's successor as premier. Like Page, Stevens has been underrated as a policy visionary. He was weighed down by his personal lack of political skills. Stevens showed distinct signs of taking cues from the Country Party, having a relationship with his coalition partner Bruxner that appeared closer than that with his own UAP colleagues. He came to office on a joint platform with the United Country Party that provided for a referendum on new states. In March 1932 Stevens used strikingly Page-like references when speaking on constitutional change, such as subdivision into 'new Federal units' and safeguards to prevent these putative entities from ever repudiating debt.[59] In February 1934 he succeeded in convening a conference in Melbourne of the state premiers to discuss constitutional reform, only to have proceedings overshadowed by Western Australia's announcement of intended secession.[60]

---

57  Page, *Truant Surgeon*, pp. 208, 214; the full text of the policy program is at pp. 391–2.
58  Speech by Lyons, 2 December 1931, New States, UNE Archives, A1, box 14. The proposed convention is mentioned in a history by Ellis of constitutional conventions; Ellis papers, NLA, MS 1006, box 22, series 7B, folder 97. For summaries of what was proposed and critical reactions by two states, see the *Advertiser*, 12 June 1933, p. 8, and the *Geraldton Guardian and Express*, 17 June 1933, p. 2.
59  Bertram Stevens's speech on constitutional reform, 25 March 1932, New States, UNE Archives, A1, box 14.
60  Mentioned in Ellis's history of constitutional conventions, NLA, MS 1006, box 22, series 7B, folder 97. See the *Sydney Morning Herald*, 26 February 1934, p. 8, for a summary of this conference.

Stevens's main contribution to the cause was the 1933–35 Nicholas Royal Commission. This was widely called the Boundaries Commission as it was restricted to delineating suitable boundaries for new states. It defined two suitable areas: a northern state that included Newcastle; and a large central, western and southern region encompassing the Riverina, Wollongong and the south coast. Page claimed to see this as a vindication, but the royal commission, for the time being, came to nothing. Most of the New South Wales UAP had no enthusiasm for new states and Bruxner rejected a referendum in the north as likely to be defeated by a strong 'no' vote from the Newcastle area.[61] Many new state activists did not want Newcastle and Wollongong included in new states. The main long-term legacy of the Nicholas Royal Commission was that a 1967 northern new state referendum failed when a strong 'yes' vote in the far north was indeed negated by opposition from around Newcastle.

In 1938–39 Stevens would be the only state premier to support Page's National Council planning initiative. Along with Richard Casey, he was the senior political figure most in tune with Page's developmentalist vision. Stevens later recalled that 'over the years, I have felt that the name and entity of the Country Party correspond to something deep down in the consciousness of many thoughtful people, by no means confined to the rural areas'.[62] Stevens and Casey encouraged Page but, over time, both became so marginal in their own parliamentary parties that they could not provide the decisive support he needed.

Yet Page in these inter-war years still managed to reignite and uphold the idea of a new state in northern New South Wales. Despite this, some new staters made known their disappointment with him. Looking back, Thompson implicitly criticised Page by opining that the movement's decisive need had long been a clear lead from the Commonwealth Government, such as by declaring a new state in Australia's far north.[63] Such assessments are harsh. Although he could not assert full control of the wider new state movement as it diversified, Page remained by far its most visible and respected figurehead. Few contemporary observers thought Page a poor political practitioner of day-to-day political arts. Hughes did briefly, but soon learnt better.

---

61    See Ellis, *A Pen in Politics*, pp. 197, 200; Page, *Truant Surgeon*, p. 382; also Aitkin, *The Colonel*, pp. 159, 163.
62    Stevens in the *Scrutineer and Berrima District Press*, 26 June 1948, p. 2. Stevens was writing rejecting post-war proposals to amalgamate the Liberal and Country Parties.
63    From Thompson's history of the new state movement, EPP, folder 2146, p. 6.

Page's intermittent withdrawals from the new state cause were not due to his using the issue primarily for local advantage but had more to do with his obligations to the Bruce–Page and Lyons governments. His very different political standing from other new state enthusiasts generated a special tension that he managed by assuming the role of national spokesman only when compatible with his status in parliament. Page's vision of an entire nation restructured along regional lines further distinguished him from the bulk of the movement and made him an important link to the wider regionalism that later evolved from new statism. Ellis and Thompson were among his few consistent allies as he outgrew northern New South Wales and put himself to the even harder task of reorganising all Australia into his federal units.

## Page's 'spirit of Oxford or Cambridge'

Involvement in the new state movement between the wars fortuitously drew Page to an important related issue. New state advocates had long contrasted educational facilities in rural areas, especially for higher education, with what was available to city dwellers. Most of the leading proponents of a new university to be located in Armidale, notably Drummond, were also ardent new staters. Their long campaign led to an appeal to Page to lend his support as the north's most prominent public figure. His subsequent involvement helped mark him as one of Australia's few political advocates of higher education as a valued end in itself.

When Page began his public career in the 1910s, mass primary education was well established. But public secondary education had barely begun, tertiary education on an appreciable scale was still decades away and the entire management of state education was centralised in capital cities. Campaigning by the Country Party and its antecedents for better educational opportunities in rural areas dated back to the 1890s and mainly concerned primary, technical and agricultural schooling. Between the wars, this was particularly strong in New South Wales and acquired an additional focus on tertiary education.[64] The Cohen Royal Commission recommended that all new teachers' colleges in the state be based in the countryside, that local governments play a role in education and that

---

64 James Belshaw, 'David Henry Drummond 1927–1941: A case study in the politics of education', *Armidale and District Historical Society Journal and Proceedings*, no. 26, March 1983, p. 47; Alan Barcan, *A History of Australian Education*, Oxford University Press, Melbourne, 1980, p. 244.

consideration be given to a university for rural-based students.[65] Such goals had Drummond's support as state education minister 1927–30 and 1932–41, leading to the establishment of the Armidale Teachers' College in 1928. Despite his long-standing commitment to education, Page was not especially prominent in early campaigning for rural tertiary institutions other than as an aspect of his engagement with new statism. He included the absence of a university in the north in his evidence to the Cohen Royal Commission, but other new state advocates such as the New England pastoralist Colin Sinclair (the sole dissenting member of the royal commission) and the indefatigable Thompson were more consistently focused on this.[66]

Page was asked to join the New England University cause just as it was becoming more organised, a decade after the royal commission. In July 1934 the secretary of the Provisional Council raising funds for a university college invited him both to join the council and to lead a delegation to Drummond.[67] In November 1938, Page became chairman of the Advisory Council for the newly established New England University College, responsible to the University of Sydney as the college's parent body. This was alongside a solidly rural elite membership of local graziers, town-based professionals and Country Party figures that included the fellow ardent new staters Phillip Wright and Bruxner. Once fully on board, his political rank and familiar energy soon made him prominent. Drummond later wrote of Page's 'great and widespread influence' as comparable to that of eminent chancellors of Sydney University, Percival Halse Rogers and Charles Blackburn.[68]

Campaigning for a fully fledged University of New England led Page towards a vision of tertiary education that drew on his broader philosophy of rural community and of the proper scale of social institutions. He came to see rural-based universities not only as important local amenities but also as means of community-building and shaping. Page told

---

65  Parker, 'Why New States?', p. 11.
66  Page, *The New State in Northern New South Wales*, pp. 17–18; also Matthew Jordan, *A Spirit of True Learning: The Jubilee History of the University of New England*, UNSW Press, Sydney, 2004, pp. 25–6.
67  R.L. Blake and J. Laurence to Page, letter, 17 July 1934, EPP, folder 1788.
68  David Drummond, *A University Is Born: The Story of the Founding of the University of New England*, Angus and Robertson, Sydney, 1959, pp. xviii–xix, 70.

Drummond in late 1938 of how he saw the new institution in Armidale as having 'an extraordinary influence ultimately on the development and concentration of rural thought in Australia'.[69] He foresaw that:

> It is by having in the centre of these northern districts an institution of this sort, with teachers able to make personal contact with the boys and girls that the full advantage of university life may be realised. Within universities such as this, there may be something of the spirit of Oxford or Cambridge, rather than London, for in big cities the commercial over-rides the cultural life.[70]

This is not just an early statement of his concept of an ideal university – small, rural and teaching-focused – but also of Page's fundamental distaste for cities and commercialism.

Although there was little reaction to these views in the 1930s, they were the starting point of Page's more fulsome contributions to the national debate on higher education that emerged in the 1940s and 1950s. His vision of rural education based on scale and community went well beyond anything proposed by Drummond, the most prominent Country Party advocate of education during the inter-war years. Although always personally close to Page, Drummond was more conventionally oriented towards vocational education that met the immediate needs of particular regions and industries. Drummond also helped to found Junior Farmers' Clubs to encourage young people to stay on the land and, under Bertram Stevens, tried unsuccessfully to regionalise technical education via district technical education councils.[71]

## Transport and agriculture: Page champions cooperative federalism

The 1930s proved more important for cooperative federalism than for new states or rural higher education. Yet this did not start well, as Page began by trying to re-establish institutionalised cooperation in the fraught field of national transport. This mainly served to illustrate the difficulties involved, but did affirm him as Australia's prime advocate of cooperative federalism.

---

69  Page to Drummond, 6 December 1938, EPP, folder 1090.
70  Page, November 1938, quoted in Drummond, *A University Is Born*, p. 70.
71  Belshaw, 'David Henry Drummond 1927–1941', pp. 51–2, 65; Bruxner's paper 'The Potentialities of Australian Agriculture', undated, EPP, folder 2308.

Page resumed his engagement with transport, even before the Country Party rejoined the coalition, by pushing the new Lyons Government to revive the Federal Transport Council. In his policy speech for the 1931 election he promised to re-establish the council so as to 'co-ordinate the activities of road, rail, sea, and air transport services to ensure that each branch of the service is fully utilised in those avenues of work for which they are best suited', a step towards the ultimate goal of 'the greatest degree of progress and development'.[72] The Governor-General's speech at the opening of the new parliament in February 1932 mentioned this council, and Page used his address-in-reply to again call for its revival.[73] Public service advice to the Minister for the Interior a few months later acknowledged Page's pressure by warning that 'apart altogether from the urgency of the problem, it is clear from recent press statements that the transport question will be made a live one by the Country Party immediately the House meets'.[74]

Page had a receptive audience. State governments in the early 1930s were increasingly concerned by financial losses inflicted on their rail systems by road transport, and raised this at a series of ministerial meetings. In September 1932, Lyons proposed the re-establishment of a ministerial council for transport. A June 1933 conference of transport ministers discussed amalgamating railways under a national railway corporation, itself responsible to a federal transport council with a brief to promote national uniformity and conduct investigations, but only served to illustrate the fragility of cooperative federalism by promptly falling foul of state opposition.[75] Page almost alone continued to promote the institutionalised coordination of transport. In his policy speech for the 1934 election he proposed that a central purchasing authority set railway fares and uniform rates for the entire nation.[76] Page later took time out from 1936 trade talks in London to cable Lyons about engaging Northcott, the chair of the 1929 Commonwealth Transport Committee, to conduct a study of overseas transport policy.[77]

---

72   Australian Country Party, *Honesty, Security: A Frank Statement of Country Party Policy by Dr Earle Page*, Bureau of Publicity, Information and Research, Sydney, 1931, p. 11.
73   *Commonwealth Parliamentary Debates*, 18 February 1932, pp. 95–6.
74   'Notes for Speech by the Minister for the Interior – the Federal Transport Council', August 1932, NAA, A431, 1946/888.
75   Lyons to Premiers, 30 September 1932, EPP, folder 489; NAA, A659, 1939/1/8829; memo of 8 June 1935 reporting on conference of transport ministers, EPP, folder 495; brief for Minister of the Interior, EPP, folder 492.
76   Ellis, *A History of the Australian Country Party*, p. 295.
77   Page to Lyons, cable, 10 July 1936, EPP, folder 496.

To work, federal-led coordination needed either the imposition of the Commonwealth's fiscal power or a common self-interest in responding to a clearly pressing national issue. Page harnessed the latter to successfully establish the Australian Agricultural Council (AAC), the most important and lasting of state–Commonwealth policy coordination bodies. As early as 1925 he had proposed a Commonwealth department of agriculture to coordinate the production and marketing of agricultural exports.[78] Creation of a Commonwealth–state entity took a decade longer and only after a clash with Britain over trade policy provided a casus belli. Like most of his initiatives in this decade, it had its origins in Page's talent for turning an unexpected problem into an opportunity.

Early in 1933 the Lyons Government received a proposal from the British Government to cut imports of Australian dairy produce. Cabinet – then still without Country Party members – reacted surprisingly favourably, reasoning that a smaller local industry would recover more quickly from the Depression.

Page was temporarily absent from parliament at the time following the sudden death of his eldest son on 14 January 1933, struck by lightning when driving cattle to Heifer Station. Earle junior had completed veterinary studies at Sydney University and was managing the station. His father's account in *Truant Surgeon* tells of his other son Iven riding through the storm to another nearby homestead for help, after which vague news reached Heifer Station. Earle senior rushed forth to nearby Copmanhurst where the body had been taken to a doctor's surgery and there confirmed the worst. So shaken was Page that he initially proposed resigning the Country Party leadership and even considered dropping out of parliament entirely. Drummond's regard for Page was so immense that he feared that without him the federal party 'would be very close to a leaderless rabble' that would not survive in federal politics. Ethel Page suffered a stroke but recovered sufficiently to continue her role in family and public life.[79] After some persuasion, it was agreed that Paterson would act as leader while Page took nine months leave from active politics, an unprecedented break for this otherwise tireless campaigner.

---

78   Undated minute 'Department of Agriculture', EPP, folder 2128. Ellis indicates it was prepared for Cabinet in 1925; see *A History of the Australian Country Party*, p. 102.
79   Drummond to Harold F. White, 31 January 1934, Drummond papers, UNE Archives, A248, V3010, folder B, part 4; see also Page, *Truant Surgeon*, pp. 225–6, 263.

This absence did not change Page's policy outlook nor, ultimately, his determination. He was aghast when he heard about Cabinet's intention to comply with 'this shattering proposal' from the British, not least as Grafton was a dairy producing area.[80] The major trade issue otherwise facing Australia at this time was trade diversification by Britain that restricted Australian exports, and so he riposted that the British should instead cut their dairy imports from non-Empire nations. This led to his proposing, in a series of speeches over the following year, the establishment of the AAC 'on the lines of the Australian Loan Council', to 'elevate agriculture to its proper place in our national life and make Australia realise its value and importance'.[81] Page was drawing on his established ideas about coordinated national action to fight for the sector of the economy that mattered most directly to him.

The AAC had a partial forerunner in the Standing Committee on Agriculture, created in 1927 under the aegis of the CSIR and originally focused on research cooperation between the Commonwealth and the states. It is widely accepted that Page was the main mover behind the establishment of the AAC as a much more influential ministerial body; the Rural Reconstruction Commission, for example, later matter-of-factly described him as such.[82] Page misleadingly assured the Graziers' Federal Council in December 1934 that the AAC was 'purely a consultative and advisory body'.[83] But his other statements were more expansive. In his 1934 election policy speech, Page called the AAC 'a board of directors for Australian agriculture' that would 'eliminate needless waste of public and private capital' and 'counteract restriction policies'.[84] In a November 1934 Cabinet submission he made clear that although the British trade proposal was the immediate motivation for creating the AAC, the split of agricultural policy responsibility between the Commonwealth (exports) and the states (domestic production) necessitated a mechanism for their working together. Page foresaw 'an intimate form of consultation between Commonwealth and states on the whole question of agricultural policy

---

80    Page, *Truant Surgeon*, pp. 391–2.
81    Speech by Page at Bellingen, 21 March 1933, quoted in *Truant Surgeon*, p. 232; also his 1934 election policy speech, referred to in Ellis, *A History of the Australian Country Party*, p. 213.
82    Rural Reconstruction Commission, *Tenth Report, Commercial Policy in Relation to Agriculture*, The Commission, Canberra, 1946, p. 197.
83    Page to Graziers' Federal Council, 5 December 1934, EPP, folder 183 (part 2).
84    Speech reproduced in *The Australian Country Party Monthly Journal*, vol. 1, no. 8, 1 September 1934, p. 7.

similar to the existing form of consultation in financial policy through the Loan Council'.[85] Privately, he wrote to his wife in March 1935 revealing how dearly he wanted a powerful planning body:

> I think I have a chance to do for agriculture in Australia what I have already done for finance – only agriculture must be organised as well in its different industries in addition to having a national policy laid down and that takes a tremendous amount of time and knowledge to find out just what are the right lines and what is the right method to follow. But I feel that with the extraordinary capable head of the Department I have picked up in Murphy – who has a forward constructive courageous mind something like my own backed by an immense amount of knowledge he has acquired since the B/P [Bruce–Page] Govt established the Development Commission, that I will be able not merely to create an organisation but to breathe the breath of life into it so that it will grow into one of the fundamental factors [of] our national scheme of government and of progress.[86]

'Murphy' is J.F. (Frank) Murphy, secretary of the Department of Commerce 1934–45 and one of the few public servants Page spoke of effusively.

The AAC was formally created at a December 1934 ministerial conference. It consisted primarily of agriculture ministers but with other ministers attending when necessary: the May 1935 inaugural meeting was considered important enough for representation from the states to also include no less than six premiers and acting premiers, with two state attorneys-general in tow. Supporting the ministers was the Standing Committee on Agriculture, comprised mainly of public service heads of agricultural agencies and CSIR's executive leadership. Page agreed that agendas were to be prepared from submissions put forward by the states, plus 'subjects which directly affect the Commonwealth'.[87] Unlike the Loan Council, the AAC remained a voluntary organisation rather than a statutory body with a constitutional basis. Despite its origins in a trade policy crisis it was, in practice, more heavily engaged with domestic policy. The inaugural meeting worked its way through a long agenda that

---

85 Cabinet paper, 'Australian Agricultural Council', signed by Page, 20 November 1934, EPP, folder 182.
86 Page to Ethel Page, 10 March 1935, copy provided by Helen Snyders.
87 'Proceedings and Decisions of Council, Australian Agricultural Council, First Meeting, 28, 29, 30 May 1935', p. 63, EPP, folder 2630.

reads like a stocktake of issues, from the organisation of the dairy industry to debt relief for farmers, the powers of marketing boards, soil erosion, wire netting, food preservation, the Wheat Royal Commission and the grasshopper problem. The expansiveness evident here is highly suggestive of Page's influence.

Although the AAC was never as powerful or planning-oriented as Page wanted, it quickly became central to agricultural policy and an important example of how coordinating machinery could smooth a complex, still unresolved federation. Its cast of ministers and their most senior officials debated issues vigorously and in full. Victoria's Agriculture Minister Edmond Hogan and his Queensland counterpart Frank Bulcock were especially vocal. (Hogan was a one-time Labor premier who defected to the Country Party, the two parties in Victoria then having a close relationship). From the start, the AAC promoted voluntary cooperative federalism by resolving that the states pass nationally consistent legislation, such as a proposal at its first meeting to set restrictive terms for the marketing of margarine.[88] (These terms concerned the colour of margarine so as to clearly differentiate it from butter.)

The AAC succeeded largely as it was based on cooperation amongst equals, rather than the Page-led arrangement he had fondly imagined. Page was often the initiator, but discovered that his state counterparts were very prepared to query his judgement. The biggest single issue facing the early AAC was the implications for orderly marketing legislation of section 92 of the Constitution prohibiting restriction on free trade between the states, specifically whether it invalidated Commonwealth orderly marketing legislation to the extent that this sought to regulate interstate trade. At the inaugural meeting there were very mixed responses to Page's dire warning that 'chaos will prevail' should the courts decide that section 92 did indeed apply to the Commonwealth, and his proposal for a referendum to alter this section. Victoria's premier and agriculture minister, Albert Dunstan and Hogan, bluntly warned of a failed referendum creating further problems; South Australia opposed compulsory schemes led by the Commonwealth; and Western Australia only reluctantly offered support. Proceedings ended in indecision by the issue merely being referred to a committee of all attorneys-general.[89]

---

88 Ibid., pp. 27–8; NAA, A11702, 3.
89 'Proceedings and Decisions of Council, Australian Agricultural Council, First Meeting, 28, 29, 30 May 1935', pp. 14, 23, EPP, folder 2630.

The centrality and versatility of the AAC is reflected in Page using it to develop a national response to the 1934–36 Royal Commission on the Wheat, Flour and Bread Industries. The agreed response to its findings involved a home consumption price, compulsory marketing and the licensing of flour millers and warehouses, all to be organised jointly by the Commonwealth and the states.[90] Criticisms of the AAC only emerged a decade later: in 1946 the Rural Reconstruction Commission (RRC) said it had 'not realized the high hopes of its founder' due to political considerations leading to the 'absence of a really national outlook'.[91] The RRC concluded that although such a ministerial body was essential, to work well it needed to be backed by an industry-led hierarchy of local, state and national bodies based on farming industry representation and focused on the responsibilities of farmers rather than their perceived rights. The prominent and intellectually uncompromising agricultural scientist Samuel Wadham disparaged the Standing Committee as having proposed schemes 'frequently difficult to administer or inequitable in their effects', as some of its member Commonwealth officials 'were not fully versed' in agricultural industries.[92] The AAC still had post-war defenders, such as public servant F.O. Grogan who said it was 'perhaps not an exaggeration to suggest it is the most successful example of such cooperation in Australian Commonwealth–State relationships'.[93]

The AAC was nonetheless much more successful than its ineffectual transport counterpart. The British trade issue gave the AAC a strong initial impetus: it was built on cooperation between governments in orderly marketing that dated back to the 1920s; government action was supported by producers; much agriculture competed internationally rather than nationally, easing interstate rivalry; and industries that produce homogenous products tend to experience common problems. The AAC was to be the main means by which Page consolidated co-operative

---

90  See text on wheat marketing policy, briefing note on orderly marketing schemes prepared for the Rural Reconstruction Commission, typed copy in EPP folder 2630, pp. 22–4; also Page, *Truant Surgeon*, pp. 236–8.
91  Rural Reconstruction Commission, *Tenth Report*, pp. 197, 201.
92  L.R. Humphries, *Wadham: Scientist for Land and People*, Melbourne University Press, Parkville, 2000, p. 138.
93  F.O. Grogan, 'The Australian Agricultural Council: A successful experiment in Commonwealth–state relations', *Public Administration*, vol. 17, no. 1, 1958, p. 12; J.G. Crawford, *Australian Agricultural Policy*, The Joseph Fisher Lecture in Commerce, University of Adelaide, Adelaide, 1952, pp. 47–8.

federalism in policy formulation. It operated by its original name up to 1992 and has a current equivalent in the form of the Agriculture Ministers' Forum.

Page was encouraged by the early success of the AAC. Typical of his optimism and ambition, he proceeded to call for a veritable constellation of voluntary coordinating councils. A 'parliament of governments' would serve as 'a kind of super-Senate' across agriculture, transport, health and social services without any need to amend the Constitution.[94] Praise for Page's efforts on cooperative federalism came from a familiar source, F.A. Bland. Speaking in 1935 on his efforts to revive the Federal Transport Council, Bland called for the 'elimination of political control' by using statutory policy commissions as advocated by Page.[95] He also praised Page in *Australian Quarterly*, then Australia's main current affairs journal, for his roles in creating the Loan Council and the AAC, and how he had been 'at considerable pains to popularize his ideas' by proposing similar new councils. Bland concluded that 'these proposals of Dr Earle Page not only prelude an eventful chapter in working the Federal system, but offer unlimited possibilities for inventiveness in the arts of public administration'.[96] In a draft letter a few years later to Casey, then treasurer, Page again mooted new bodies for coordination in transport and communications, so that the Commonwealth would 'be able to call a national tune with some real harmony in it'.[97]

Page used the AAC to respond nationally to the most serious interwar challenge to orderly marketing. The result showed the limitations of co-operative federalism and marked a shift in his approach to constitutional reform. A South Australian dried fruit grower, Frederick James, so strongly objected to state and Commonwealth authorities seizing his shipments to enforce orderly marketing legislation regulating interstate trade that he pursued a long series of legal challenges right up to the Privy Council. Essentially, the orderly marketing schemes he challenged elevated domestic prices to compensate for low export prices, and imposed production quotas set by the states and export quotas set by the Commonwealth. The Commonwealth legislation also

---

94 'Dr Page's New Plan – National Co-ordination councils – parliament of governments', *The Australian Country Party Monthly Journal*, vol. 2., no. 18, 1 July 1935, p. 3.
95 F.A. Bland, *An Administrative Approach to Australian Transport Problems*, lecture to the New South Wales Centre of the Institute of Transport, Sydney, 1935, copy in EPP, folder 489.
96 Bland, 'Inventing constitutional machinery', *Australian Quarterly*, pp. 19, 21.
97 Page to Casey, EPP, folder 407; undated draft, but evidently from 1938–39.

regulated interstate marketing of primary products, the focus of the Privy Council's ruling. In July 1936 the council declared that section 92 of the Constitution applied to the Commonwealth, thereby effectively striking down its legislation concerning such marketing for dried fruits, dairy products and wheat. This decision validated Page's earlier warnings but came at a difficult time for him. As commerce minister he was already struggling in trade talks with Britain on the beef trade. What followed gave him a focus for his determination to change the Constitution, and drew forth a string of Page pronouncements that made him its leading public critic.

The James case led the AAC to finally accept Page's calls for a constitutional amendment. The resultant March 1937 referendum proposed enabling the Commonwealth to make laws on marketing without being inhibited by section 92, with a concurrent referendum to give it powers over air navigation. Page in campaigning mode showed absolutely no reverence for the Constitution. He spoke of its 'faulty wording' thwarting Commonwealth action and of how 'no real democracy' would accept such restraints. The referendum was 'a straight-out fight for the maintenance of Australian living standards'.[98] Similarly, 'it is obvious' that aviation was a continental rather than a local matter, despite which the states had failed to collectively legislate and the High Court had invalidated Commonwealth regulations. Page cast these referenda as harbingers of a 'general Constitutional referendum' to fully revamp this troublesome document.[99]

Yet there turned out to be little public appetite for change. The question on marketing was rejected in all six states. The aviation referendum also failed, albeit less comprehensively. The strength of the 'no' votes was met with widespread bafflement. The *Sydney Morning Herald* postulated that it was simply a generalised protest against the Lyons Government. Page concluded that in future the only way to educate the public and win approval for change was through a constitutional convention.[100] He had been supported by other ministers only to the extent of protecting orderly marketing: few, if any, echoed his wider condemnation of the entire Constitution. Page had led a major revival of cooperative federalism but

---

98  'Statement by the Minister for Commerce (Dr Earle Page) 2nd March 1937', EPP, folder 934.
99  Document titled 'Referendum Campaign', no author or date but wording and internal references clearly suggest Page in 1937, EPP, folder 2140.
100  Both comments from the *Sydney Morning Herald*, 8 March 1937, p. 8.

needed a specific and material issue to do so and could not extend this to broader constitutional reform. Following the failure of this referendum, the AAC during 1938 successfully reformulated a coherent strategy for wheat based on complementary legislation by the Commonwealth and the states, along with a voluntary arrangement for dried fruits based on complementary state legislation.

Page's calls to protect orderly marketing again indicate that although such schemes were significant to him, he still treated them as being of secondary significance, components of his wider view of the nation's workings. During the referendum campaign, he linked orderly marketing to his long-standing goal of balancing the entire economy. The Commonwealth needed to regulate interstate trade so as to give primary producers protection comparable to that provided to manufacturers. Without farmers being able to afford to buy factory produce, manufacturing and ultimately the whole economy would falter; indeed, he considered this the cause of 'the late Depression'. Legislation had protected dried fruit and dairy producers since the 1920s by manipulating production and prices, but had only lately been extended to wheat – hence, concluded Page, the latter's persistent need to be subsidised.[101] Page maintained a wider policy vision than nearly all his Country Party colleagues, most of whom during the referendum campaign were otherwise preoccupied with a home consumption price for wheat, recommendations concerning rural loans by a Royal Commission on Banking and yet another Victoria-based party rift over coalitions.

In the March 1935 letter to his wife, Page had reflected on his work in creating the AAC as part of his higher calling. It was a fine example of a policy 'which has an infinitely greater and more far reaching effect on the happiness and welfare of the people of Australia than any work I could do in my profession or running my own place'. After dwelling briefly on the pressures he had faced in public life, he exulted in 'the pleasure and the joy in altruistic constructive work that will lift the standards of living and comfort of us all and specially of the country people for ever and make certain that my spirit lives after I am gone'. He concluded that 'my spirit would rest better if I felt that the torch I have lighted and borne would still flame through the world perhaps to illume it fully'.[102] Page fully retained the driving sense of special purpose that imbued his

---

101 Document titled 'Referendum Campaign', EPP, folder 2140.
102 Page to Ethel Page, 10 March 1935.

1917 speech, viewing even the AAC as an inspiring opportunity to leave a legacy. Three years later, he was to attempt a yet grander policy creation, the National Council.

## Electrification re-sparked

During the early to mid-1930s, Page's successive preoccupation with the northern new state, building a coalition with the UAP and establishing the AAC resulted in his standing back from the Clarence and electrification. He still considered electrification an essential part of his vision, but was inhibited by a low level of wider political engagement with developmentalism and an absence of professional interest in hydroelectricity. When the Depression receded in the latter 1930s, Page resumed his pursuit of electrification as a key to national development. As with new states, he seized unexpected opportunities, briefly restoring him as Australia's foremost champion of hydroelectricity.

The two initiatives he pursued involved very different approaches, typical of his stress on ends over means. One sought to exploit imperial ties to gain access to technology and investment. The other involved working with Bertram Stevens and his New South Wales government to use state-owned railways as a basis for electrification. Both showed how Page struggled to secure support from urban-based interests, always a severe constraint on his nationwide ambitions. They also suggest that despite the economic recovery of the late 1930s, there was less of a corresponding revival of the developmentalism that had characterised the 1920s. Ambitious development proposals wilted in the face of contrary vested interests: Australian optimism was to take several more years to recover.

During the 1930s, Australian policy on trade, migration and overseas investment remained solidly cast in an imperial context. In 1936 Australia adopted a trade diversion policy of discrimination against Japanese and US exporters in favour of British suppliers, the aim being to secure better access to the British market by offering tariff concessions on British manufactures. Page went along with this strategy, challenging it only at the margins such as by occasionally proposing migration and tourism from the United States and continental Europe.[103] Page rushed to London

---

103 See for example his 1929 exchange of letters with Leslie H. Perdrian (?) of Cambridge, Massachusetts, on promoting Australia as a tourist destination; Earle Page papers, UNE Archives, A180, box 10, folder 78.

in 1936 to appeal to the British Government not to shift meat imports to Argentina, considered by the Australians to be a direct threat to the principles of the Ottawa Agreement. Page on international missions had a habit of digressing into initiatives more directly geared to his own idea of Australian development. Having secured an acceptable agreement that protected Australian beef exports to Britain for the next three years, he set out to negotiate with the British Board of Trade what even he called an ambitious scheme for electrification based on British technology, finance and migration.

Page had long seen the imperial connection as a powerful platform for Australian development. As long before as September 1920, he and William Corin had corresponded on working with the Canadians to convene an imperial conference 'on the question of water power in the Empire'.[104] Page now sought to harness British interest in overseas investment in manufacturing and in coordinating industrial development within the Empire, both responses to the Depression-related breakdown of multilateral trade. Although based on the imperial connection, Page's strategy is broadly consistent with interpretations of Australian trade policy of the time as being driven more by national development policy than by any slavish attachment to imperial sentiment.[105]

Page and the Board of Trade tentatively agreed on the tariff-free entry of advanced heavy capital equipment into Australia for at least 10 years, the resumption of large-scale British migration, and either the British Electrical Association or the British Government itself arranging a long-term loan to extend 'electrical reticulation' throughout Australia.[106] 'The heads of electrical manufacturing concerns', Page later recalled, offered to 'bring out 58,000 migrants drawn from all classes and make available £30 million to enable governments to increase their electricity supplies and expand reticulation if they received certain concessions concerning the admission of major and very specialised electrical equipment.'[107] This proposal had a strong precedent dating from the 1920s when British legislation guaranteed finance for power

---

104 Corin to Page, 17 September 1920, EPP, folder 400.
105 Such as A.T. Ross, 'Australian overseas trade and national development policy 1932–1939: A story of colonial larrikins or Australian statesmen?', *Australian Journal of Politics and History*, vol. 36, no. 2, 1990, pp. 184–204.
106 Page, *Truant Surgeon*, p. 245.
107 Speech, 28 July 1958, Perth, National Party of Australia records, NLA, MS 7507, series 1, box 1.

development overseas that used British-produced plant.[108] Now Page was taking it upon himself to revive singlehandedly the Migration Agreement of that decade.

He claimed to have secured the support of British industry and of all but one of Australia's state manufacturing associations. Typical of his ready faith in the private sector, he fully expected them to proceed to resolve among themselves such details as the technical definitions of specific goods.[109] He was mortified to instead find his ambitious plan 'blocked by certain Australian manufacturing interests'.[110] He publicly blamed the engineer and UAP state parliamentarian F.P. Kneeshaw, long a critic of the Ottawa Agreement's concessions to Britain and president of the only state association opposed to Page's proposal, the New South Wales Chamber of Manufactures.[111] In a speech to the Country Party federal executive in July 1958 recounting his long engagement with electrification, Page attributed this failure more fundamentally to a lack of national ambition: 'Australia failed to take up the offer, which typifies what still could be done if the will exists'.[112]

Page's only significant domestic ally on electrification during the late 1930s was Stevens. In his policy speech for the 1935 state election, Stevens declared an intention to create a statewide grid based on coal and hydroelectricity, including the Nymboida facility and new hydroelectric plants on the Shoalhaven and other rivers.[113] The premier's convergent agenda encouraged Page to resume a long-standing interest in using New South Wales railways as a basis for rural electrification, something he first explored during the 1920s. The New South Wales Railways and Tramways Department had played a central role in electrification during the early twentieth century, partially acting as a statewide electricity authority by using its generators to supply power in bulk to local government distribution authorities.[114] In the late 1930s New South Wales had no

---

108 Cochrane, *Industrialisation and Dependence: Australia's Road to Economic Development*, University of Queensland Press, St Lucia, Qld, 1980, p. 38.
109 Page, *Truant Surgeon*, p. 245.
110 Memo by Page of 30 January 1950 on the new Department of National Development, EPP, folder 2072.
111 Page, *Truant Surgeon*, p. 245.
112 Speech, 28 July 1958, NLA, MS 7507, series 1, box 1.
113 Wigmore, *Struggle for the Snowy: The Background of the Snowy Mountains Scheme*, Oxford University Press, Melbourne, 1968, p. 93.
114 See Butlin, Barnard and Pincus, *Government and Capitalism*, pp. 254–5; also 'Memorandum on the Development and Organisation of the Electricity Supply Industry in New South Wales', by H.R. Harper, formerly chief engineer, State Electricity Commission of Victoria, 1938, p. 2, EPP, folder 1059.

less than six different electricity providers, including the Clarence River County Council focused on hydroelectricity. A central power authority appeared only gradually in New South Wales, between 1938 and 1950.[115]

In November 1936, Page sought an opinion on rural electrification from Australian General Electric's Tim Clapp, a favoured Page sounding-board in the business world. Clapp's advice was that the only practical strategy was through 'electrification of part of the main lines of the New South Wales Government Railways'. But he added that the load was too small to enable electricity to be supplied at low cost: as ever, sparse population and distance were fundamental constraints.[116] Yet just two months later, Stevens submitted an ambitious plan to his Cabinet that drew on discussions with Page and his own recent visits to Sweden and Britain. This proposed rural electrification using 'tapering subsidies' flagged a new central power authority empowered to raise its own funds and reported that the state's Electricity Advisory Committee was preparing a long-term strategy to link major power stations.[117] That Page's personal papers include a copy of a New South Wales Cabinet document is indicative of his ties to Stevens.

Most of Page's political colleagues showed little interest in such ambitions. An April 1939 conference in Sydney of Commonwealth and state ministers on water conservation and irrigation in calling for Commonwealth funding and a nationwide survey of water resources barely mentioned hydroelectricity.[118] Page, caretaker prime minister at the time, did not attend. Stevens was removed from the premiership by opponents within his own party in August 1939, partly in consequence of his being considered too close to the Country Party.

---

115 Allbut, *A Brief History of Some of the Features of Public Electricity Supply in Australia*, pp. 31–2.
116 Clapp to Page, 17 November 1936, EPP, folder 2086.
117 Cabinet minute by Stevens, 12 January 1937, EPP, folder 2612.
118 *Interstate Conference on Water Conservation and Irrigation: Held at Sydney, New South Wales 24th to 27th April, 1939*, Government Printer, Sydney, 1939, copy at EPP, folder 2111.

## The National Council planning initiative, 1938–39: Page sets out to shape the nation

Page's last major policy initiative of the 1930s also arose from an unexpected opportunity, this time mounting defence concerns. The National Council planning proposal of 1938–39 was a determined effort to recreate the DMC in a more powerful form. This effort to change the very fundamentals of national policy-making was by far Page's most ambitious attempt to realise his vision of Australia's development. He concentrated all of his formidable energy onto this, only to find its failure commensurately dismaying. It is well documented, including a full transcript of the October 1938 conference with the premiers at which Page first sought their commitment.

The National Council initiative briefly held the attention of the Commonwealth and all state governments. It helped to make economic planning an issue that lingered intermittently for the next two and a half decades. Yet it is mentioned only in a few histories of the period. Even the most detailed account, that by Paul Hasluck, does not fully recognise Page's dominant role and developmentalist aims, which were muddied by overlapping machinations concerning defence preparedness. Anne Henderson, in her biography of Lyons, provides an outline that does acknowledge Page's leading role and national development ambitions.[119] Most other histories of Australian foreign and defence policy of the late 1930s do not cover the National Council at all, mentioning Page only to note that post-1939 he was coy about his earlier support for appeasement.[120]

An understanding of Page's wider thinking and of the course of events makes it very clear that the foremost driver was his planning-based decentralist agenda. Asserting himself over his prime minister to call two conferences of state premiers on this issue was the high-water mark of Page's political influence in the 1930s, but also marks the start of his

---

119 Paul Hasluck, *The Government and the People 1939–41*, series 4 (Civil), volume 1, *Australia in the War of 1939–1945*, Australian War Memorial, Canberra, 1952, pp. 125–37; Henderson, *Joseph Lyons*, pp. 414–15.
120 See for example E.M. Andrews, *Isolationism and Appeasement in Australia: Reactions to the European Crises 1935–1939*, Australian National University Press, Canberra, 1970, p. 141.

decline. This singular episode is also an illuminating case study of Page's modus operandi, notably his blunt attempts to win over political colleagues and the states, and his misplaced optimism that business leaders would empathise with his developmentalist goals.

A new planning body had been proposed by then Opposition leader John Latham in late 1930. This was to be a non-party 'economic council' that could take charge during the crisis of the Depression, made up of federal and state political leaders – including Page – and of bankers. The then acting treasurer Joseph Lyons raised the idea with the Labor Caucus, which reportedly reacted with derision, possibly as members perceived collusion with the Opposition.[121] The Loan Council and premiers' conferences acted as an economic council during the Depression, but Page later publicly dismissed the deflationary Premiers' Plan of 1931 as 'an accountant's plan, not a statesman's plan' that misguidedly tried to 'tax people into prosperity'.[122] Revival of a DMC-like agency as a more powerful agent of developmentalism was one of his first proposals following the demise of the Scullin Government. In February 1932 he told the Constitutional Association of New South Wales that because of unplanned and unbalanced development 'we had peacocked industry as we had peacocked settlement'.[123]

Over the following two years, Page repeatedly called for a powerful federal export council of federal and state ministers as a statutory authority 'formed on the lines of the Loan Council, and given status and powers in the same way so far as the exporting industries are concerned'. This would 'rationalise' these industries and so 'direct our marginal producers into more profitable and stable lines of activity'. It would 'ensure for a definite term a payable Australian price' for exports that could later come down as lower tariffs reduced costs. This would be quite unlike 'the hopeless policy [of] giving bounties year after year to the wheat industry'. Like so many Page initiatives, he linked the federal export council to a currently topical issue – in this case, tariff reform. He tied the reduction of tariffs not just to 'harmony between the prices of the farm and the factory goods', but also to the restoration of world trade as 'lowered tariffs will enable investment

---

121 Cochrane, *Industrialisation and Dependence*, p. 126; see the Launceston *Examiner*, 11 December 1930, p. 7, for a detailed account of the Caucus reaction.
122 Quoted in a profile of Page in the Sydney *Daily Telegraph*, 14 August 1948, pp. 10–11.
123 Speech by Page of 15 February 1932 to the Constitutional Association, EPP, folder 384.

by creditor nations of their capital in equipment of debtor nations, and the debtor countries will be able to pay their interest again in the form of goods'.[124]

The federal export council idea and planning generally attracted little political reaction in the early 1930s. Governments were far more preoccupied with fiscal restraint. Later in the decade, rearmament and intellectual interest in planning gave Page a firmer basis for his National Council initiative. In brief, Page in 1938–39 sought to enlist ministers and experts from business and government with knowledge of manufacturing, agriculture, defence and engineering so as to direct national industry, trade, transport and energy policy across a timespan of several years. The resultant planning body would 'ignore state boundaries' in guiding the location of industries and the prioritisation of public works as it mounted an 'attack [on] the causes of excessive population in the vulnerable centres'.[125] Although bracketing development with defence was not a new idea in Australia, this was usually stated in simpler terms of the size and distribution of the nation's population, particularly in the sparsely populated north. Page's distinctive approach was to use growing security concerns and defence preparedness as a basis for seeking to plan the entire economy.

Tentative moves to ready the nation for war had begun in 1935 when the Australian Government consulted the states and industry on the content of the Commonwealth War Book, a detailed set of procedures to be followed upon the outbreak of war. By the time Page proposed the National Council in September 1938, preparations had already spawned an array of expert planning committees of officials, economists and business leaders. An Advisory Committee on Financial and Economic Policy included the leading economists L.F. Giblin, Roland Wilson and Leslie Melville, and mobilisation of secondary industry sat with an advisory panel chaired by BHP's formidable general manager Essington Lewis. Page would have been encouraged by increases in defence expenditure initiated by Lyons and Casey in 1937, a marked shift from the austerity of the previous few years as unemployment fell. This included a December

---

124 'Federal Export Council Proposed by Dr Earle Page for Continuous Australian Policy', speech by Page of 20 November 1933 to the Triennial Convention of the Australian Country Party Association, David Henry Drummond papers, UNE Archives, A248, V3010, folder 2(c). See also 'Speech by the Rt. Hon. Dr Earle Page MP, P.C., at the Western Divisional Conference of the United Country Party at Orange on Thursday February 22 1934', EPP, folder 1101.
125 'Memorandum to Cabinet', 18 October 1938, EPP, folder 1114.

1937 Cabinet direction to the Department of Works to give priority to defence projects.[126] Total defence expenditure climbed from 5.5 per cent of annual expenditure in 1933–34 to 9.4 per cent in 1936–37, and would reach 14.9 per cent by 1938–39.[127]

Page also gained some traction from growing intellectual interest in planning arising from the search for responses to the Depression. This, for the first and only time in his life, brought him into a willing alliance with professional economists. Planning was the subject of only the second summer school ever held by the Australian Institute of Political Science, in January 1934 in Canberra. Page did not attend, but the event still boasted an impressive cast of public policy intellectuals that included G.V. Portus, W. Macmahon Ball, Lloyd Ross, E.O.G. Shann, Leslie Melville, the Reverend E.H. Burgmann, Alan Watt, Bland, Wilson and Giblin. Discussion ranged from doubt about the very concept of economic planning to admiration for the USSR, but there was broad acceptance that some limited form of planning was needed to promote efficiency and equity. Bland was one of the few sceptics and condemned centralised planning as 'incompatible with the enjoyment of popular liberties'.[128]

Two participants, Wilson and Giblin, were later important players in Page's National Council proposal. In November 1938 Giblin prepared a short paper for Prime Minister Lyons supporting a 'general plan for national reorganisation' of the Commonwealth and the states as essential in this 'new era, in which concentrated and planned effort will have to be made by the people of all the democracies if they are to have a chance to survive'.[129] Page was also aware of ideas about planning circulating in British intellectual circles, having read G.D.H. Cole's 1935 *Principles of Economic Planning*. (Cole called for the full public ownership of industry, something Page found abhorrent.) In Britain the typical proposed goal

---

126 A.T. Ross, *Armed and Ready: The Industrial Development & Defence of Australia 1900–1945*, Turton & Armstrong, Sydney, 1995, pp. 113–15, 118.
127 Henderson, *Joseph Lyons*, p. 398.
128 F.A. Bland, *Planning the Modern State*, second edition, Angus and Robertson, Sydney, 1945 (first published 1934), pp. 67–8. Proceedings of the summer school were published in W.G.K. Duncan (ed.), *National Economic Planning*, Angus and Robertson in conjunction with the Australian Institute of Political Science, Sydney, 1934.
129 L.F. Giblin, 'The National Need', November 1938 (no specific date), EPP, folder 2082; see also Hasluck, *The Government and the People 1939–41*, p. 130.

of economic planning was to stave off crisis by rescuing capitalism from itself; in Australia, Page wanted to engineer the nation at last to fulfil its potential.[130]

A more immediately important factor in the National Council proposal was Page's political resurgence. The late 1930s was a Page purple patch. That he was knighted in the 1938 new year's honours list was the least of it. (Page had also been a Privy Councillor since 1929.) By 1938 he had built a strong personal relationship with Lyons. Enid Lyons recalled Page as being so close to her husband that it was rumoured to be the only known instance of Page being completely loyal to anyone else.[131] His determined efforts to promote the National Council proposal confirms the impression given in *Truant Surgeon* that he was only too willing to fill the vacuum created by Lyons's political and physical decline that would eventually led to his early death from coronary occlusion.

Page led an Australian trade delegation in Britain in 1938 to negotiate a revision of the Ottawa Agreement. These complex and inconclusive discussions dealt with access to each other's markets, the expansion of Australian secondary industry and also an understanding with Britain on trade agreements with third countries. The talks were also infused with growing fear of another major war: Australia's contribution to Empire defence and development was linked to increasing its population, seen by both countries as requiring the growth of secondary industry. Page in his memoirs recalled returning from these talks convinced war was inevitable. He at once 'began exploring means of co-ordinating Federal and State capital expenditure on defence and development and of allocating priorities to indispensable projects'.[132] Although this started with a proposal for agreement with the states to prioritise public works according to their defence value, the documentation that Page generated dwells far more on his own decentralist and developmentalist goals. There is no indication that he corresponded similarly with defence experts. Page's proposal also closely matched his DMC-inspired model for planning, including using business leaders as advisers and formal machinery for coordination

---

130 For accounts of British conceptions of planning, see Richard Overy, *The Morbid Age: Britain between the Wars*, Allen Lane, London, 2009, pp. 77–86; and Pemberton, 'The middle way', *Australian Journal of Politics and History*.
131 Enid Lyons, *Among the Carrion Crows*, Rigby, Adelaide, 1972, p. 75.
132 Page, *Truant Surgeon*, p. 262.

between levels of government. What followed is a fine example of Earle Page in full flight, utterly determined to seize an opportunity he had hoped for since the glory days of the Bruce–Page Government.

In October 1938 Page forcefully warned the Lyons Cabinet of the need to prepare for war, and so proposed that 'the Federal Government gives a lead and secures the complete cooperation of the other governments and the industrial leaders'. To this end he produced a confidential memo, evidently for Cabinet, entitled 'Financial Problems of Australian Defence and Development'. This earliest of the key documents generated by Page's National Council proposal stands as his magnum opus, a concentrated statement of self-belief devoid of any consideration of alternatives or foreseeable barriers.[133] It was clearly written by Page himself (or at least under his very close supervision), containing as it does such characteristic phrases as 'reproductive purposes' and 'it is obvious'.

The memo set out what was formally put to state premiers on 21 October 1938. An opening reference to 'the lessons of the last fortnight' reflects its preparation just after the Munich Agreement of September 1938. Australia's security necessitated not just the wise use of funds for defence procurement: Page also wanted 'industrial development in the widest national sense' to mobilise national resources and attract millions of new settlers. As funding through loans was limited, 'the height of wisdom is to plan the spending in the best possible way' by carefully identifying industries for expansion and locating them at the least vulnerable points, while 'promoting the best distribution of population'.[134]

All this would require state cooperation over the 'next seven or ten years' to jointly plan all sectors of the economy. Page also pondered here the possibilities of migration from continental Europe, especially settlers from the Netherlands and Denmark 'who would quickly assimilate the Australian character'.[135] New secondary industries would be sited at sources of raw materials, especially near seaports: Page thought it fortunate that many potential Australian ports were close to power sources, such as his adored Clarence River. A national electricity system would charge flat

---

133 See EPP, folder 2121; copies marked October 1938 and bearing Page's signature are at folder 1877 (part 1). Page's statement to the House outlining his plans drew heavily on this document; see *Commonwealth Parliamentary Debates*, 19 October 1938, pp. 903–5. Page also produced a memo to Cabinet dated 18 October 1938 providing furthers details of his intentions, EPP, folder 1114. The quote is from 'Financial Problems of Australian Defence and Development', p. 1.
134 'Financial Problems of Australian Defence and Development', EPP, folder 2121, pp. 1, 2.
135 Ibid., pp. 2, 10.

rates as a 'prime necessity for the decentralisation of industry'.[136] Planning would apply such tools as uniform railway gauges, tax privileges, new ports and manufacturing distribution centres, guided by 'experts who have the confidence of all Australia'.[137] As the international political environment darkened, 'now is the psychological moment for a definite call to national service, a national outlook, and a national programme'.[138] Reviewing the whole economy would also be consistent with agreement at the 1938 trade talks with Britain to assess Australia's lines of development of secondary industry so as to help frame trade policies.[139] As Page hoped to enshrine national development above party politics, he gave Opposition leader John Curtin an advance copy of his statement to parliament. Curtin noted the lack of detail but still approved sufficiently to claim credit for the ALP in first proposing machinery for collaboration with the states on public works.[140]

Page was indeed initially vague on how exactly this planning would be organised. It soon became evident he had in mind appointment by the Loan Council of a powerful joint advisory committee of Commonwealth and state officials and of business leaders.[141] This would undertake a 'survey of the lines which Australian industrial development should follow from now on'.[142] It would then submit recommendations to the Loan Council on the prioritisation of public works, including those not directly associated with defence. The most important would be 'reproductive' – electricity, road, railway, seaport and communications projects likely to stimulate production.[143] Page was effectively recasting the Loan Council, his great policy triumph of the previous decade, as a more powerful version of the DMC with a much more direct say in developmental expenditure.

Page broached his initiative with the convalescent prime minister by letter on 10 October 1938. In order to overcome 'the Loan Council deadlock', Page sought his agreement to a joint meeting of the Commonwealth, states, industry and Opposition to 'combine in one big progressive

---

136  Ibid., p. 6.
137  'Memorandum to Cabinet', 18 October 1938, EPP, folder 1114.
138  'Financial Problems of Australian Defence and Development', EPP, folder 2121, p. 2.
139  Ibid., p. 2. See Page, *Truant Surgeon*, pp. 394–5, for the relevant formal conclusions of these talks.
140  *Commonwealth Parliamentary Debates*, 19 October 1938, pp. 905–7.
141  Ibid., 19 October 1938, pp. 903–5.
142  Lyons speech to 21 October 1938 conference of premiers, in Australia, Parliament, *Conference of Commonwealth and State Ministers on National Co-operation for Defence and Development, Proceedings of Conference*, p. 3, copy in EPP, folder 581.
143  *Commonwealth Parliamentary Debates*, 19 October 1938, p. 904.

programme the Defence activities, the investigation of the plan of industrial development that the delegation arranged with the British Ministers [and] an enquiry into the location of the suggested new industries'.[144] Page also canvassed an old colleague. He wrote to Stanley Bruce, now Australian high commissioner in London, clearly indicating that defence preparedness provided an opportunity to pursue developmental planning: 'It has been quite obvious for some time that the Financial Agreement and the Loan Council would break down except something is done which would give real priority to worthwhile works', for which 'the Defence problem gives us an opportunity of putting this issue on to a plane that the general public can understand'.[145]

But attracting the interest of business leaders, always Page's preferred collaborators, proved difficult. He wrote to Essington Lewis, Tim Clapp and Sir Clive McPherson, the pastoralist. The letter to Lewis of 13 October 1938 is one of the most ambitious Page ever wrote. In order to achieve something 'of real and enduring value' for the nation, he sought 'the collaboration of the captains of industry in Australia, who have real vision' and asked for suggested names.[146] But Lewis's reply was characteristically formal, even cold. He had spoken with Robert Menzies (minister for industry and attorney-general) and T.W. White (minister for trade and customs), and thought the government already had access to the 'leading men'. Lewis did briefly list candidate industries for expansion, ranging from cotton and canned vegetables, to aluminium and shipbuilding. Extra protection would be required for them to be decentralised, he added.[147] Clapp and McPherson replied jointly that they would participate only if satisfied that the Commonwealth and states would endorse the recommendations of the 'Board of Control' – a near impossible precondition.[148]

The bureaucracy showed more enthusiasm. Page had a detailed memorandum prepared by three senior officials: Murphy of his Department of Commerce; Stuart McFarlane, secretary of the Treasury; and Roland Wilson, now Commonwealth statistician.[149] At the AIPS

---

144 Page to Lyons, 10 October 1938, EPP, folder 1621.
145 Page to Bruce, 12 October 1938, EPP, folder 407.
146 Page to Lewis, 13 October 1938; to McPherson, 14 October 1938; to Clapp, 12 October 1938; all EPP, folder 407.
147 Lewis to Page, 17 October 1938, EPP, folder 407.
148 Clapp to Page, 18 October 1938, EPP, folder 1621.
149 Page, *Truant Surgeon*, p. 263.

summer school four years earlier, Wilson had called for indicative planning that maintained private property and the profit motive, but with a 'central thinking agency' supervising the private sector.[150] The three public servants now outlined a 10-year plan of cooperative action by the Commonwealth and the states, starting by deciding on which industries to expand and their locations. The memorandum was sent to all state governments.

It says much about Page's influence in Cabinet that he secured support for his ill-defined and overstretched proposal. He was even confident that public opinion could force the states to cooperate.[151] Page dismissed likely criticism: the CSIR, the Loan Council and the NHMRC, he said, were all once 'ridiculed as impossible'.[152] He proceeded with two concerted attempts to secure the cooperation of the states. The first was the Conference of Commonwealth and State Ministers on National Co-operation for Defence and Development, convened in the House of Representatives chamber on 21 October 1938. All six state governments were represented, including by four premiers. Discussions were hampered by hurried preparation and a concurrent Loan Council meeting. Page's immediate aim was to have the states agree to participate in the advisory committee to the Loan Council. The results fell far short.

The conference presented a stark contrast between Page's high hopes and the exhaustion of a prime minister in terminal decline. Lyons, 'tired, dispirited and ill', was flown in from his sickbed in Devonport.[153] Even as he arrived in Canberra he knew the proposal in outline only: Page briefed him on the details during the drive from the airport. Lyons's opening speech was only half ready as he began to deliver it, obliging him to speak slowly while it was typed up and handed to him leaf by leaf.[154] The assembled state ministers would surely have been unimpressed. Even worse, a list of priority projects prepared by the Department of Defence was not ready for presentation.[155] Defence Minister Thorby (the Country Party's deputy leader) had just a week before asked his department to prepare a report

---

150  Duncan, *National Economic Planning*, p. 68.
151  'Memorandum to Cabinet', 18 October 1938, EPP, folder 1114; also Page to Bruce, 12 October 1938, EPP, folder 407.
152  'Necessity for Planning', undated, EPP, folder 2110.
153  Ellis, *A History of the Australian Country Party*, p. 235.
154  Page, *Truant Surgeon*, p. 263.
155  Hasluck, *The Government and the People 1939–41*, p. 127.

on public works of defence value. Cabinet only considered the resultant schedule on the day of the conference, and directed that it be revised to list projects in priority order.

Lyons instead broadly outlined to the states what Page had in mind, yet without mentioning him by name. He asked them to agree to the 'transfer of some part of your loan works programme from the works you already have in mind to works which have a defence significance', thereby encouraging projects that 'have a civil as well as a defence value'. The Commonwealth would deal with those works purely of defence significance. But as 'the whole of the defence plan must depend on the successful development of the country's resources and the increase of its wealth and population', there should also be a 'preparation of plans relating to the location of new industries and the public works necessary to ensure their success'. The advisory committee would 'have regard to both economic and strategic factors, including distribution of population and vulnerability of industry' in drafting a program 'of future industrial development' and 'an order of priority of public works'. Commonwealth and state experts could begin by meeting at defence headquarters in Melbourne.[156]

The reaction of the states demonstrated that their fear of loss of authority crossed party lines and far outweighed any faith in planning. Dunstan of Victoria was nominally Page's Country Party colleague but argued that the advisory committee should be denied substantive powers and exclude industrialists. Richard Butler of South Australia had similar concerns, despite being willing to countenance decentralisation 'if that can be done economically'.[157] Page himself was widely mistrusted. Initially he kept uncharacteristically quiet and later wrote that discussions were well advanced before the premiers 'recognised me as the author'. Two economic advisers, Douglas Copland from Victoria and Colin Clark of Queensland, wanted to know why his role had not been made clear at the outset.[158] William Forgan Smith, the Labor premier of Queensland, thought that the states risked coercion reminiscent of Page's abolition when treasurer of their per capita grants. This drew an indignant reply from Page that the states had been glad of the Loan Council ever since.[159]

---

156 *Conference of Commonwealth and State Ministers*, EPP, folder 581, pp. 3–4.
157 Ibid., pp. 6–7, 9–11.
158 Page, *Truant Surgeon*, p. 264.
159 *Conference of Commonwealth and State Ministers*, EPP, folder 581, p. 9.

Page's sole supporter was Bertram Stevens, who had already advocated Page's plan in a radio speech 10 days earlier. But even he was concerned by the proposed advisory committee and wanted an assurance of additional finance, including Commonwealth measures to secure the cooperation of the banks.[160]

The conference floundered its way to a noncommittal agreement by the states to 'examine the possibility of undertaking, within the limits of the local allocation of that state, any work of defence submitted by the Commonwealth'.[161] The whole meeting had lasted two hours, despite allowance for two days. 'Received cautiously by some Premiers' was the understated summary in the Commonwealth's press release of the next day. This reported that the advisory committee had been deferred rather than rejected and that the Commonwealth would seek 'a Committee with abridged powers' at the next meeting with the premiers.[162] Press coverage was much blunter. The *Sydney Morning Herald* editorialised on Page's 'disposition to obscure the substance of his proposals in a cloud of idealistic generalities'.[163] The Melbourne *Argus* reported a 'sometimes acrimonious discussion' that was a 'setback to Sir Earle Page'. It later added that one premier had been anxious to leave for Melbourne to attend a race meeting – Dunstan, no doubt.[164] Stevens alone wrote to Lyons promising manpower and appointing a committee to examine 'the organisation that would be set up to give effect to these proposals'.[165]

In parliament Page found himself awkwardly trying to defend the meeting with the premiers when speaking on a no-confidence motion moved by Curtin. He was reduced to attacking 'lying stories of intrigue and motives', which 'made worse an atmosphere which was already difficult'. He denied a report that the defence minister had left the conference just to attend a dance – it was actually the Journalists' Ball that he had gone to, as had most other conference participants, he explained to the House.[166] Page's assertions that the premiers had been keen on his proposals sounded hollow, and did not convince Curtin.

---

160 Ibid., pp. 4–8; Page, *Truant Surgeon*, p. 263.
161 *Conference of Commonwealth and State Ministers*, EPP, folder 581, p. 14.
162 'For Press', 22 October 1938, EPP, folder 583.
163 *Sydney Morning Herald*, 21 October 1938, p. 10.
164 *Argus*, 22 October 1938, p. 1; 24 October 1938, p. 3.
165 Stevens to Lyons, 3 November 1938, EPP, folder 395.
166 *Commonwealth Parliamentary Debates*, 3 November 1938, p. 1190.

But Page was not one to give up on something he had sought for so long. An unsigned and evidently draft Cabinet memo, probably prepared by Page or at least for his use, stated a determination to appoint an expert committee 'forthwith'. It warned that 'the Commonwealth Government has determined that with the cooperation of the states, if it can get it, or without that cooperation, if it cannot, it will endeavour to make a national effort commensurate with our needs and resources'.[167] The incorrigible Page wrote to Giblin insisting that the timing for planned development was still 'never better'. Although he feared that the government 'seemed to be falling apart', it was 'ready to make a fresh start'.[168] Page also assured his departmental secretary that 'I am quite sure that now we will really get a first class chance to secure co-ordination and planned development'.[169] He also kept pressing Lyons, who agreed to Cabinet reconsidering the whole idea. Page complained to the prime minister that a report by the Military Board on state cooperation was 'uninspiring', making it 'obvious that the whole question of future industrial development and location of industries and their strategic value does not enter into their thoughts' – reaffirmation that defence was not Page's first priority.[170]

Preparation for the second bout with the premiers was more thorough. On 25 October Cabinet finally approved a list of works for construction by the states.[171] Page directed Wilson to develop a new planning proposal. Wilson suggested a central coordinating committee of officials and industrialists to be called the Council of Industrial Development and Defence. This would be headed by a chief executive officer attached to the prime minister's office and supported by specialist advisory committees. The council would recommend projects to Commonwealth and state ministers, including when they met as the Loan Council. 'Planless development', warned Wilson, is 'possibly national suicide'. Perhaps dutifully, he described this proposal as so generous that 'the Commonwealth government does not entertain the least doubt that the Premiers will find it acceptable'.[172] Yet when the defence minister

---

167 EPP, folder 583, untitled and undated, but refers to the conference with the premiers as having been 'on Friday', p. 1.
168 Page to Giblin, 28 November 1938, EPP, folder 407.
169 Page to J.F. Murphy, 14 December 1938, Earle Page papers, UNE Archives, A180, box 3, folder 25.
170 Page to Lyons, 4 January 1939, EPP, folder 586.
171 Cabinet minute of 25 October 1938, NAA, A2694, VOLUME 19 PART 1, folio 71.
172 'Industrial Development and Defence', 1 November 1938, EPP, folder 1621; see also Hasluck, *The Government and the People 1939–41*, p. 130.

provided Page with a revised list of priority works, he imparted a sense of the difficulties faced by adding that Tasmania and Western Australia were reluctant to make supplies available to the Defence Department on Sundays.[173]

But then Page reconsidered the implications of the October conference for his need to allay state suspicions. A committee of officials and industrialists would overwhelm the Loan Council with requests for ministerial guidance. Page and his departmental secretary now proposed that 'the developmental and public works activity of Australia should be a ministerial body' – a National Council, supported by a full-time chief industrial adviser and an advisory committee of officials and experts.[174] Page was increasingly impatient. In a February 1939 memorandum to Cabinet he floated the idea of appointing an (unspecified) individual 'with status and authority to get right on with the consideration of the problems', thus 'leaving the lines of co-operation with the states to be traced as opportunity offers'.[175]

The conference with the premiers of 31 March 1939 was barely an advance on that of the previous October. It met in the shadow of Germany's invasion of Czechoslovakia on 15 March: Lyons opened proceedings with a grim warning to be ready for war. The National Council was still expected to extend well beyond defence needs to produce 'an ordered programme of national development, both primary and secondary'. Lyons tried pacifying the states by stressing the inclusion of their ministers in the council, but reiterated that because the Commonwealth faced too great a defence burden they would have to rearrange their own expenditures to cover the revised public works schedule.[176] Although a National Council of the prime minister and the premiers was at last endorsed, it was saddled with a debilitatingly obscure brief: 'to consider matters of concern as occasion arises and to bring about all the necessary co-ordination of

---

173 Geoffrey Street to Page, 3 February 1939, EPP, folder 588.
174 'Development and Defence', undated but clearly subsequent to Wilson's 'Industrial Development and Defence' proposal, EPP, folder 2121; see also Hasluck, *The Government and the People 1939–41*, pp. 131–2.
175 'Memorandum for Cabinet – Co-ordination of Development and Defence', 6 February 1939, EPP, folder 588. See also Page's memo of 28 March 1939, in which he proposed 'appointment of a special person as supremo on classification of public works', NAA, A2694, VOLUME 19 PART 2, folio 265.
176 'Speech for Prime Minister, Premiers' Conference, March 31st, 1939', EPP, folder 583; also 'Statement by the Minister for Defence', EPP, folder 592 (specific date not given).

the related activities of the Commonwealth and the states'.[177] A memo, evidently prepared for Cabinet so as to report in full on the meeting's outcomes, added agreement to such platitudes as 'close and continuous consultation concerning public works which are of value from the defence point of view' and to 'confer concerning ways and means of developing new industries needed for defence and supply'. The schedule of projects was consigned to discussion between Commonwealth and state officials.[178]

Even the Commonwealth doubted its own creation. The secretary of the Department of Defence thought the National Council 'should be confined to those problems which grow out of the Defence plans in relation to the national economic structure and primary and secondary industry', otherwise it would constitute 'an obvious duplication'. The chairman of the Defence Committee, Vice Admiral Colvin, warned that 'the National Council must be divorced from all strategical considerations'. Essington Lewis simply declared the Council best left to politicians, not business.[179] Nor did the proposed public works progress well. The only concrete Commonwealth offer was extended in December 1938 to 'co-operate with the states in works suitable for unemployment relief on the understanding that the state concerned would meet one fifth of costs and the works would have defence or civil aviation value'. Six months later the state cooperation liaison officer in the Department of Defence reported that the only works of defence value actually undertaken were a few road construction and repair works.[180]

In June 1939 the National Council met at the end of a premiers' conference, for the second and last time. (There had been a brief inaugural meeting just after the March premiers' conference.) Hasluck later concluded that since he could not find a record of discussions, and surviving participants were unable to recall any significant outcomes, it 'could not have had any marked consequences'.[181] Australia's best-placed and most ambitious attempt to plan the entire nation had already faded.

---

177  Hasluck, *The Government and the People 1939–41*, p. 133.
178  'National Security – Co-operation with the States and Co-ordination of Commonwealth Activities', 4 April 1938, EPP, folder 589.
179  Frederick Shedden, 'The National Council – its Functions in Their Relation to Defence', 5 April 1939; Vice Admiral Colvin to Shedden, 'Functions of National Council – Minute by Chairman, Defence Committee', 6 April 1939; Essington Lewis to Shedden, 12 April 1939; all EPP, folder 588 (part 2).
180  Hasluck, *The Government and the People 1939–41*, pp. 132, 135.
181  Ibid., p. 136. Press accounts of the council's inaugural meeting include the Melbourne *Argus*, 3 April 1939, p. 8, and *Age*, 3 April 1939, p. 12.

The National Council episode matches assessments by some historians that the later 1930s in Australia was a time of pessimism and a dearth of policy innovation.[182] Far from economic recovery opening the way for a resurgence of developmentalism, few policy-makers saw a need for radical change. Planning served no particular sectoral interest: apart from Page, support was limited to some economists and intellectuals. The Canberra-based *Australian National Review* was one of very few publications to endorse Page's ideas: 'the development of neglected power sources is essential not only for the decentralisation of manufacturing industries but the for realisation of the industrial expansion that Australian interest demands'.[183] Page stood out as a developmentalist visionary in an unambitious government focused on austerity-led recovery, but could not spark a renewed Bruce–Page-style commitment to development. The Depression era had so deadened the Australian sense of possibilities that its main additions to the nation's political imagination were some avowedly anti-political movements.

The National Council also recalls Bruce's weary comment that one of his tasks as prime minister was to restrain the many enthusiasms of Earle Page. Page unfettered was indeed prone to sudden bold moves when he spied an opportunity, instead of the slow process of building support by demonstrating how his ideas could actually work. Even as he rode high politically in the late 1930s, defence concerns and support from figures of the standing of Giblin and Wilson gave Page a starting point only. He had few close political confidants and did not habitually work with his political colleagues as policy equals. As the sense of economic urgency faded, Page's appeals to idealism attracted only already committed developmentalist thinkers like Stevens and Casey. It may be significant that Casey had originally trained as an engineer and had worked in mining and manufacturing, unusual for a politician then or now. Nor was the federal system as malleable as Page had hoped: state mistrust of the Commonwealth, and of Page himself, was strong.

The overall implication is that Page's power, although deep, was narrow. It encompassed only a federal Cabinet in which he headed the junior coalition party under a prime minister so weakened that he complied with a proposal he appears not to have fully understood. Page was much stronger in Lyons's Cabinet than in the business world. It also highlights

---

182 Such as Robertson, '1930–39', in Crowley, *A New History of Australia*, pp. 434–5, 448.
183 *Australian National Review*, April 1939, pp. 2–4.

how he had drifted from his own Country Party: few party colleagues supported his National Council and some, notably Dunstan, were openly hostile.

The end result was that Page overstretched himself badly. A telling indicator of his self-perception as a rationalist, not the emotive dreamer he really was, is that he rarely thought through the practical implementation of ideas such as planning. Planning was to Page self-evidently logical and thus assuredly workable. He was ultimately defeated by the difficulty of embedding comprehensive planning in a federal system, by sceptical political colleagues and by the indifference of private industry. Yet Page never forgot his 1938–39 planning proposal. As early as December 1940, in a speech on the war effort, he again called for 'a National Council of all the governments of Australia' that used 'the best brains of the community with all the necessary powers to deal with both defence and developmental problems'.[184] National economic planning is an important part of Page's vision, but did not give rise to a lasting personal legacy.

## Page's political crisis and fall

As a major failure in full view of his political peers, the rapid demise of the National Council almost certainly contributed to a decline in Page's political standing. He remained a formidable advocate, well capable in the years that followed of pushing his ideas into national political debate, including those on planning. But from 1939 onwards, Page was never again entrusted with a major leadership role in development policy. Political colleagues had lost faith in his grand visions.

Page's loss of the Country Party leadership in September 1939 is usually attributed to the events of his caretaker prime ministership five months earlier, primarily his infamous attempt to block the ascension of Robert Menzies. But Page's hold on the leadership had been slowly weakening for several years. Press reports appeared as early as 1932 of Country Party MPs being open to a change of leadership in favour of Thomas Paterson so as to clear the way for the formation of a coalition with the UAP. Reportedly, Page was saved by the unacceptability of the terms that Lyons offered.[185] John McEwen later said that when he entered federal parliament in 1934

---

184 Untitled speech, 16 December 1940, EPP, folder 591.
185 See George Paterson, *The Life and Times of Thomas Paterson (1882–1952): A Biography and History by His Elder Son George Paterson*, privately published, Caulfield East, Vic., 1987, p. 42.

'Page had already lost the support of a good section – not the majority, but a pretty important section – of his party'. For all Page's industry and imagination, he 'was determined to do what he wanted to do' and 'did not, except in a most passing way, consult his party members'.[186]

Others have attested to a personal antipathy between Page and McEwen. Page had in 1934 campaigned against McEwen in the federal seat of Echuca amid a bitter resurgence of the long-standing dispute between the Victorian Country Party and its federal counterpart over participation in coalition governments. The state party's central council had decreed that all candidates, whether state or federal, should sign a pledge that included refusal to support a coalition without the approval of the Victorian party organisation. Five sitting Victorian federal members including Paterson refused to sign, and W.C. Hill resigned from his seat of Echuca. At the ensuing 1934 national election the new candidate for Echuca endorsed by the Victorian organisation was none other than McEwen. Page directly entered the Echuca campaign in favour of two independent Country Party candidates backed by the federal parliamentary party.

McEwen won but, upon taking his seat, sided with the federal party and urged his Victorian colleagues to repair the breach. In 1937 McEwen blamed Page for blocking his elevation to the deputy leadership of the parliamentary party. Their mutual hostility also had much to do with very different respective backgrounds and policy priorities. Ian Robinson, much later Country Party MP for Cowper and the eponymous seat of Page, and who admired Page as 'an incredible man', said that this mutual disdain was 'so great that I don't think it could ever be properly or fully described'.[187] This is an overstatement – Robinson himself added that such antipathy did not harm the Country Party, so evidently they were still able to reluctantly work together.

In the wake of Lyons's death on 7 April 1939, the parliamentary Country Party passed a resolution that it was not prepared to remain in a coalition should Menzies accede to the prime ministership, largely due to Menzies's position that he would choose all ministers from both coalition parties himself. As Page himself told parliament, the decision by the governor-general, Lord Gowrie, to swear him in as caretaker prime minister pending the UAP's selection of a successor to Lyons was based on two special

---

186  John McEwen, *John McEwen: His Story*, edited by R.V. Jackson, privately published, place of publication n.a., 1983, p. 11.
187  See Davey, *Ninety Not Out*, pp. 19, 55, 61.

considerations. One was the lack of a direct line of succession within the UAP following Menzies's resignation as deputy leader the previous month. The other was that Lyons had died without having nominated a successor: the governor-general had even confirmed with two of the doctors attending the stricken prime minister that there was no possibility of his doing so.

Page had late the previous year persuaded Menzies not to leave the Cabinet; he condemned his resignation in March 1939 as especially 'unthinkable' by coming just as Hitler was about to invade Czechoslovakia and war seemed increasingly likely.[188] Menzies was provoked by the effective shelving of a national insurance scheme, supported by the Country Party on cost and other grounds but seen by him as exemplifying the government's wider decline. Page later wrote that the proposed scheme as originally recommended by British advisers brought out to Australia was simply too big and complex. It was 'a child of such size that only a Caesarean section would permit its parliamentary delivery, and both the offspring and mother might be killed in the process'. Page added that 'my predications proved exact' when the legislation was gradually emasculated by amendments.[189] Much of this arose from opposition within government ranks that included demands by dissident Country Party MPs for the inclusion of small farmers in the scheme. The scheme also ran increasingly foul of varying degrees of ambivalence and outright opposition from the medical profession, trade unions, state governments and employers, especially those in the pastoral industry concerned by the complexities and costs of including seasonal workers.[190] This resulted in the excision of much of the scheme's social welfare provisions and a narrowing of its focus down onto medical benefits, leading to Menzies's declaration that he could no longer meet promises that he had made in good faith to his electors.

Prime Minister Page took a predictably expansive approach to his caretaker status. He confirmed with his Cabinet senior appointments to the taxation office and the referral of cable manufacture to the Tariff Board. But Page does not appear to have made any concerted effort to extend his brief prime ministership. This was despite reported encouragement from Opposition leader Curtin, who Page claimed had, at Lyons's funeral at Devonport, offered to support his continuation in office until the next

---

188 Page, *Truant Surgeon*, p. 266.
189 Ibid., pp. 266–7.
190 Gillespie, *The Price of Health*, pp. 109–10.

federal election, due in 18 months. Page turned this unexpected offer down as he was not comfortable leading a government that lacked its own parliamentary majority.[191] Curtin was undoubtedly influenced by a similar arrangement between the ALP and the Country Party in Victoria that maintained Dunstan as premier.

Page was in fact determined to entice Stanley Bruce back from London to resume the prime ministership. He wrote in his memoirs that he returned from London in 1938 not only wanting a national planning agency, but also with a conviction that the likelihood of war raised the need for a national government formed from all the political parties represented in parliament. Bruce, unlike Menzies as Page saw him, had the necessary experience and stature to be 'the ideal figure to fulfil this exacting role', not least as he had been 'removed from the bickerings and disputes of the Australian parliamentary scene'.[192] Page even offered up to Bruce his own seat of Cowper as a base. *Truant Surgeon* provides the text of an exchange by cable with Bruce and transcripts of international phone calls that Page and Casey made to him soon after, Bruce then being in the United States on his way back to London. Bruce effectively refused by stipulating that he would only serve as prime minister without belonging to any political party and with the support of all the parties. Page took this to mean at the head of an all-party national government. Bruce's reluctance is another sign that he was not as close to Page as Page himself thought. He even added that he was prepared to come back not necessarily as prime minister but rather as 'a leader' who could 'give any help to Australia in the political arena': the qualification remained that this would not be as a member of any party.[193] Curtin and the Labor Party opposed a national government on the grounds that the only thing worse than a government of two parties was one of three.

The parliamentary Country Party on 18 April formally resolved not to serve under Menzies and to support the return of Bruce to lead a national government. Many UAP MPs also doubted Menzies's suitability to lead the party. His main rival for the prime ministership was the otherwise unlikely figure of the 76-year-old Hughes. There was also a suggestion from within the Country Party that the new prime minister be chosen

---

191 Ibid., p. 270.
192 Page, *Truant Surgeon*, pp. 270–1. The fullest description of the course of events following the death of Lyons is provided by Paul Davey in the chapter on Prime Minister Page in his *The Country Party Prime Ministers: Their Trials and Tribulations*, privately published, Chatswood, NSW, 2011.
193 Davey, *The Country Party Prime Ministers*, p. 273.

from the UAP's ranks by a joint meeting of the two governing parties, which would almost certainly not have anointed Menzies.[194] When the UAP party room met on 18 April, Menzies failed to secure a majority on the first vote running against Hughes, Casey and White. He defeated Hughes on the third ballot by just four votes. Bruce soon after told Menzies that Page had inadvertently been 'your fairy god-father' by elevating him to 'a sitting certainty' in the UAP ballot.[195] The Country Party's vow that it would not serve under Menzies was blunted by it also not threatening to bring a Menzies government down.

More personally, the seasoned journalist Roy Curthoys privately commented that he had heard Menzies speak of Page with such contempt that he 'gasped', and that these comments had gotten back to Page.[196] The two were very different in background and personality. Menzies is said to have acquired a distaste for the Country Party during his years in Victorian state politics. But Page particularly disdained Menzies for the pressure he placed on the ailing Lyons by his recent resignation from the ministry and deputy leadership. Enid Lyons reportedly attested to Page's anger being related to this perception.[197] Frank Green recalled Lyons immediately before his fatal heart attack ruefully reflecting that 'I should never have left Tasmania; I had good mates there, and was happy, but this situation is killing me'.[198] When Lyons lay dying in St Vincent's Hospital in Sydney the press gallery correspondent Harold Cox witnessed Page in the hospital reception room amid parliamentarians and journalists openly 'tracing the course of Lyons's heart condition as a doctor and linking its development to the attacks which he alleged Menzies had made on Lyons'.[199] Broadcasting news of Lyons's death to the nation, Page more obliquely implicated Menzies by attributing the premature demise of 'our beloved Prime Minister' to 'the intense strain and anxiety which accompanied his efforts to help Australia and the British Empire in their pressing hour of extremity'.[200]

---

194 *Argus*, 19 April 1939, p. 1.
195 Cameron Hazlehurst, *Menzies Observed*, George Allen & Unwin, Sydney, 1979, p. 166. Some sources say Menzies won by five or six votes.
196 Letter from Curthoys to James Darling, 24 April 1939, quoted in A.W. Martin, *Robert Menzies: A Life, Volume 2, 1944-1978*, Melbourne University Press, Carlton South, 1999, pp. 277–8.
197 Cameron Hazlehurst, 'Young Menzies', in Hazlehurst (ed.), *Australian Conservatism: Essays in Australian Conservatism*, Australian National University Press, Canberra, 1979, pp. 11, 25.
198 Green, *Servant of the House*, p. 116.
199 Harold Cox interview, quoted in Cameron Hazlehurst, *Ten Journeys to Cameron's Farm: An Australian Tragedy*, ANU Press, Canberra, 2013, pp. 8–9.
200 *Sydney Morning Herald*, 8 April 1939, p. 15.

## 6. PAGE AUDACIOUS

Privately, Page had written to his wife in November 1938 that 'Lyons has been very badly attacked by Menzies – but has survived with my aid' and of the 'bullets hitting the wrong victims and the P.M. emerging stronger than he was'.[201] Page pictured himself as holding the Cabinet together: the following month he reported that although Cabinet had been 'crumbling' he had inserted 'some cement joined in with the mortar … which I think will hold for some considerable time'.[202] Just eight days into his short prime ministership, Page wrote also to Drummond in wistful terms that hint at the stress he was feeling and of his most fundamental hopes. He wanted to write a book on 'the aspirations, ideals, philosophy and history of our work for those who come after us to have a touchstone for their job'. He would like to 'try and get a decent library together at Grafton and make it a Mecca for keen enthusiasts to come along and have a talk with me'.[203]

Was the failure of the National Council a further factor in Page's surge of hostility to Menzies? Almost certainly it was, adding policy substance to the personal gulf that lay between the two men. Page was conscious of the lack of support for this initiative from his federal colleagues. In *Truant Surgeon* he portrayed Menzies as petulantly throwing his pencil down and refusing to write another word of the prime minister's opening speech for the first conference with the premiers once he heard that Lyons was to be flown in to deliver it himself, the implication being that this was why the speech was not ready in time. Page added that during the subsequent proceedings Menzies 'adopted an aloof attitude'.[204]

Conversely, witnessing Page assume effective leadership of the government may well have been the last straw for Menzies's confidence in Lyons. Menzies's own notorious speech of the time was made to the Constitutional Club in Sydney on 24 October 1938, just three days after the premiers' conference. Page and Enid Lyons were among those who interpreted his comments on national leadership as a public attack on the prime minister.[205] Menzies consistently denied this, but Page responded

---

201 Earle Page to Ethel Page, 9 November and 10 November 1938, EPP, folder 2787 (part 3).
202 Earle Page to L.R. MacGregor, Australian Trade Commissioner New York, 14 December 1938, Earle Page papers, UNE Archives, A180, box 4, folder 25.
203 Page to Drummond, 15 April 1939, EPP, folder 2706.
204 Page, *Truant Surgeon*, pp. 263–4.
205 The fullest account of this speech is at Martin, *Robert Menzies: A Life, Volume 1*, pp. 241–4. This touches on the context of the speech being preceded by an unhappy meeting with the premiers, but does not draw out Page's role in this.

by delivering a radio broadcast a week later defending Lyons. 'Personality plus plan make up the essential qualities of leadership', he said. Having a plan was so essential that this explained the longevity of the Bruce–Page and Lyons governments.[206]

Public and parliamentary condemnation of Page's atypically personal attack was a critical step towards his eventual loss of the party leadership. Two Country Party MPs, including Arthur Fadden, at once sat as independent Country Party members; two others followed when parliament next met on 3 May. Fadden had endured his own personal attacks for not enlisting in the First AIF.[207] By contrast, the eight UAP ministers who had served under Lyons almost immediately produced for the incoming prime minister a jointly signed letter dissociating themselves from Page's comments.[208]

Most accounts of the fall of Earle Page imply that his attack on Menzies resulted in rapid banishment into the political outer. Page in fact survived as party leader for another five months. The Country Party stayed firm as a whole in its refusal to re-establish the coalition on Menzies's terms. Although Page's standing in the Country Party was seriously weakened, he was partially insulated by the absence of the four dissenters from the party room. There was also some muddying of waters from the intertwining of party refusal to serve under Menzies on political grounds with Page's more personal hostility.

Just four days after assailing Menzies, Page survived his first internal party test at a meeting of the central council of the New South Wales party. The state council supported rejection of a coalition under Menzies, but Page still faced internal criticism of his remarks; he dealt with them by issuing an unconvincing statement that they should not be interpreted as having 'cast a reflection on all non-returned soldier members of the various parties'.[209] But by July the state central council was warning Page to cease his continuing attacks on Menzies.

---

206 Adelaide *Advertiser*, 1 November 1938, p. 23.
207 Tracey Arklay, *Arthur Fadden: A Political Silhouette*, Australian Scholarly Publishing, North Melbourne, 2014, p. 43. Accounts of Page taking Thorby, Paterson and Cameron into his confidence about the nature of his forthcoming attack on Menzies are in Ellis, *A History of the Australian Country Party*, pp. 240–1 and Paterson, *The Life and Times of Thomas Paterson*, pp. 55–6.
208 Hazlehurst, *Ten Journeys to Cameron's Farm*, pp. 11–12.
209 *Sydney Morning Herald*, 25 April 1939, p. 7.

Page eventually resigned his compromised party leadership on 13 September 1939. This finally happened after a plan to vote out the Menzies Government over calls for a guaranteed price for wheat was suddenly overtaken by the outbreak of war. Page offered his support to what was now a wartime government, to which Menzies responded that he was open to having Country Party ministers in his Cabinet. Importantly, he added that while he still insisted on making the ultimate choice of all ministers, in doing so he would discuss names with the leader of the Country Party, and made clear that Page himself remained unacceptable in his Cabinet. Page publicly conceded that as party leader he was an impediment to a national government and that he should clear the way for at least a Country Party–UAP coalition.

At a long and difficult meeting on 13 September the parliamentary Country Party elected the South Australian Archie Cameron – 'a queer mixture of generosity, prejudice and irresponsibility' – as its new leader.[210] Cameron defeated McEwen with Page's support, and was decisively helped by the absence of the four dissidents. The coalition was finally re-established six months later after the UAP Government had been shaken by an unexpected by-election loss. In late October 1940, following the loss of three ministers in the Canberra air crash of 13 August and only narrowly surviving the September election, Menzies in an evident effort to strengthen his weakened Cabinet brought Page back as minister for commerce. Page now professed to have become a Menzies admirer after having witnessed his performance as a wartime leader. He even defended him from personal attacks following his return from a four-month overseas trip in May 1941 and 'as a doctor' advised the prime minister to rest – which, as he later pointedly noted, Menzies failed to do.[211] Menzies never fully forgave Page and singled him out in his memoirs for what he still well recalled as 'a bitter and entirely false attack upon me'.[212]

It is significant that Page failed to produce a fully like-minded successor as party leader to take up his policy vision. The temperamental Cameron sorely tested the patience of his party peers and resigned the leadership in October 1940. Page was far from being an outcast in the party, for the leadership ballot that followed resulted in a deadlock between himself and McEwen. This was only resolved by the leadership instead going to

---

210 Green, *Servant of the House*, p. 137.
211 Page, *Truant Surgeon*, p. 296.
212 R.G. Menzies, *Afternoon Light: Some Memories of Men and Events*, Cassell, Melbourne, 1967, p. 13.

Fadden as a compromise candidate, now back in the Country Party fold. This supposedly stopgap measure in fact frustrated McEwen's leadership ambitions until Fadden's retirement in 1958. Fadden was a less divisive party leader than Page. Paul Hasluck, in his capacity as both historian and colleague, recalled him as an 'affable, astute, story-telling man, untroubled by the deeper significance of problems'.[213] He was far more malleable on policy than Page. During the war years and in the post-war lead-up to the second Menzies Government, he was readily drawn to conventional policies on rural development. This helped consolidate the shift of the Country Party away from Page's vision of the nation.

Page could look back on the 1930s as his most mixed decade. His political fortunes fell, rose and then suddenly fell again at decade's end. Despite the closeness of their working relationship, Lyons had not provided the balance of opportunity and firm guidance that Bruce had. His priority of recovery from the Depression offered Page only limited basis for policy initiatives until he asserted himself on planning in 1938–39. Undeterred, Page adapted only his strategies to the greatly changed environment of the Depression, not his fundamental aims. Pragmatic opportunism became increasingly unavoidable as he had to be alert to limited opportunities. Page's own use of experts such as Wilson and Giblin late in the decade unwittingly marked a step towards the consolidation of the role of economists in government.

Yet Page still made major contributions to Australian political ideas in these years. He was the main bridge for developmentalist ideas into politics as he tried to harness such energetic business leaders as Gepp and Lewis, and established relationships with a select number of more abstract thinkers such as Bland. By seizing upon a succession of infrequent chances to implement dearly held ideas that now sat well outside the policy mainstream, he managed to promote most major elements of the vision he set out in 1917, albeit with very differing results. Although Page played leading roles in placing regionalism and planning on the political agenda, his most substantive achievement of the 1930s was the Australian Agricultural Council, a lasting landmark in cooperative federalism.

---

213 Hasluck, *The Government and the People 1939–41*, p. 266.

# 7
# POST-WAR PAGE
## Hopes amidst Frustrations

The domestic political outcomes of World War Two should have suited Page. The war fostered a planning-oriented culture that 'gave life to the argument promoted by inter-war new liberals that expert knowledge should determine resource allocation and social order'.[1] It also accelerated the centralisation of governmental power, foremost by the transfer of state income taxes to the Commonwealth. H.C. Coombs, director-general of post-war reconstruction, wrote in 1944 of the 'opportunity to move consciously and intelligently towards a new economic and social system', entirely unlike that of the Depression years.[2]

During the war, political attention began to return to developmentalism, making it central to post-war reconstruction. Many of the ideas for which Page had been the pre-eminent national advocate for over two decades finally entered the political mainstream, including regionalism, decentralisation and hydroelectricity. His wartime service in London and participation in the 1942 Constitutional Convention heightened his sense of entitlement to a major say in the policy priorities of the anticipated post-war era, reinforced by a conviction that wartime had made his policy prescriptions more acceptable to the general public.

---

1   Walter, *What Were They Thinking?*, p. 176.
2   Quoted in Stuart Macintyre, *Australia's Boldest Experiment: War and Reconstruction in the 1940s*, NewSouth Publishing, Sydney, 2015, p. 6.

But the changed political and policy-making precepts of this intellectually exciting period posed major new challenges for Page, and provide a sharp contrast to his political peak of the inter-war years. Much post-war policy thinking had troubling implications for such favoured fields of his as cooperative federalism. The economy was developing in directions that he found worrying: mechanisation reduced rural employment and the wartime boost to manufacturing combined with a housing backlog pushed public spending towards the cities. Above all, Page faced the paradox of his favoured policy themes being elevated to national policy amid a new technocratic and expert-oriented environment that he found unfamiliar and sometimes hostile. He responded to exclusion from official processes and dwindling personal power within his own party by personally lobbying governments and the media. His championing of the Clarence in preference to the Snowy Mountains Scheme provides a study of how he now found himself operating.

## Page's post-war expectations: The wartime setting

Page foresaw the looming post-war era as a rare opportunity. He attached great importance to taking full advantage of public tolerance of wartime measures as a basis for developmentalist initiatives. Despite being out of ministerial office from October 1941, the war years presented Page with two unexpected opportunities to pursue major elements of his policy agenda. These raised his hopes, but someone more self-aware might have seen them as signs of the difficulties he would face in trying to work with a post-war Labor Government.

The first opportunity arose courtesy of the short-lived government of Arthur Fadden. Following the resignation of the embattled Robert Menzies late in August 1941, Fadden was elevated to the prime ministership at a joint meeting of UAP and Country Party parliamentarians. This was evidently in the hope that he could repeat the relative harmony associated with his acting as prime minister during Menzies's recent absence overseas. In September, Page was appointed Australian minister resident in London, the outcome of four months of debate about Australian representation in the British War Cabinet. Menzies had earlier proposed representation at prime ministerial level, but his own and Fadden's Cabinet preferred a minister of less exalted rank.

Page received detailed written instructions from the new prime minister. These made it pointedly clear that he was expected to curb his anticipated enthusiasms and act primarily as an agent of his home government. His fundamental role in 'matters that require special consultation with the Government of the United Kingdom' were to be 'the strategical situation, with special reference to the Middle East' and 'Empire Defence and Foreign Policy, with special reference to the Far East'. En route to London he was to stop over in Singapore so as to familiarise himself with defence plans for 'Far Eastern Defence' and 'the Pacific situation', thereby acquiring 'the necessary background for your London discussions'. But with respect to 'operational plans' being developed, he should appreciate that 'there is no question of their review by you with the authorities at Singapore'. Upon reaching London, he was to be aware that 'Mr Menzies … during his visit covered all the major questions then outstanding which the Services desired to be discussed with the United Kingdom Government'. He would be advised at a pre-departure briefing with the three chiefs of staff 'whether any other matters have since arisen on which your assistance is required'. If any such questions of importance did arise in London, wrote Fadden, they 'should, of course, be submitted to me in order that the Ministers of the Departments concerned and, if necessary, the War Cabinet may be consulted, and the necessary directions prepared for your guidance'.[3]

Despite these instructions, Page at large in a world at war felt free to engage in his own very personal brand of diplomacy, as was typical of his vigorous pursuit of his own agenda in almost any circumstances. He was determined to uphold his own interpretation of the national interest, including a vision of international decision-making machinery reminiscent of his planning-based vision for the Australian economy. Page remained a steadfastly unconventional diplomat who produced long and didactic cables for Canberra's benefit as he pressed for an Australian say in British policy, the allocation of Allied resources to the Pacific region and the supply of Australian food and other commodities. His ebullience was to lead him into major difficulties, with implications both for his standing with his home government and his later historical reputation. Page kept a detailed diary of this wartime mission – a rich source not just on Page but also on wartime international relations more broadly. It provides a continuous narrative from Page's departure from Australia

---

3  Arthur Fadden to Page, 'Visit of Australian Minister to London', 16 September 1941, NAA, A5954, 475/1.

by seaplane in September 1941 to his August 1942 return, with addenda concerning a discussion with Douglas MacArthur in October 1942, the Constitutional Convention of November–December 1942 and a War Council meeting of 8 December 1942.[4]

Page was quick to signal his assumption that his on-the-spot status earned him a major say in Australian foreign and defence policy. Even when still in Singapore in early October he wrote to Prime Minister Fadden proposing a conference of the Australian Cabinet with regional Allied leaders including the British governor of the Straits Settlements, Shenton Thomas, the British minister resident there, Duff Cooper, and the governor-general of the Netherlands East Indies. Page was confident that 'the publicity given to such a conference and the statements made by the different visitors would be the best propaganda that we could have if we have to fight Japan, to enable the people to understand its inevitability'.[5] But the secretary of the Department of Defence, Frederick Shedden, curtly declared it 'dangerous to cut across the machinery or procedure that has up to the present been employed'.[6]

The Fadden Government was defeated on the floor of the House on 3 October 1941 while Page was still on his way to London. Its Labor successor led by John Curtin indicted that he should continue. This ultimately was to prove unfortunate for Page. It is evident from Page's diary that Prime Minister Churchill initially gave him a considerable amount of his time. By December Page had secured a position on British War Cabinet committees. In early 1942 he helped to establish the Pacific War Council, intended to advise on Allied operations in the Pacific theatre but which in practice did not become part of the chain of command as Page had hoped. Japan's sudden entry into the war dramatically increased tensions between London and Canberra over the defence of Singapore, and the simultaneous transformation of the United States into a full combatant greatly diminished Australia's relative importance as a British ally. Also woven into Page's day-by-day account is his continuing resentment of Robert Menzies, such as by recording gossip shared by Keith Murdoch that in losing the prime ministership Menzies had 'made some vicious speeches on his own people and seemed terribly sour'.[7]

---

4   Page's wartime diary is preserved in typed form at EPP, folder 2787 (part 2).
5   Page to Fadden, 2 October 1941, NAA, A5954, 475/1.
6   Shedden to Curtin, 'Sir Earle Page's Proposal for a Conference in Regard to Far Eastern Questions', 22 October 1941, NAA, A5954, 475/1.
7   Page's wartime diary, EPP, folder 2787 (part 3), entry for 21 November 1941.

Page, along with Stanley Bruce as high commissioner, bore the immediate brunt of Churchill's ire over the Australian criticism of strategy for the defence of Singapore, especially the notorious accusation that evacuation of the island would amount to an 'inexcusable betrayal'. As Page wrote in his memoirs, Churchill was 'human and there were times, with tempers frayed and nerves strained to breaking point, when electric passages-at-arms were staged around the War Cabinet table'.[8] Page's long diary entry on the War Cabinet meeting of 26 January 1942 records that 'Ch. [Churchill] then went off the deep end about the Austns. generally, and said if they were going to squeal he would send them all home again out of the various fighting zones'. This drew a long and firm riposte from Page that the Australian troops 'wanted to stay where the fighting was', and that far from looking out just for itself, Australia 'had been looking after the Empire all the time'.[9]

Page's personal standing with the Australian Government was seriously damaged by a major clash with both Curtin and his external affairs minister Herbert Evatt over the return of the Second AIF from the Middle East. This foremost instance of Page's readiness to conduct himself more as active player than loyal diplomat has been much publicised. He is usually strongly criticised; along with the April 1939 attack on Menzies, it has been recounted at length in histories and has distorted wider impressions of Page ever since.[10]

Essentially, in February 1942, Page deliberately hesitated in implementing through Churchill Australian Government instructions that elements of the 7th Division of the AIF, then at sea headed for the Netherlands East Indies (but eventually sent on to Australia) not be diverted to Rangoon at British behest in an attempt to save Burma from the Japanese. Although one of Curtin's instructing cables contained a short passage that could have been seen as signalling some openness to the diversion, in the whole Canberra's instructions were clear. Page's actions were not the result of his failing to master what the Australian authorities wanted, as John Dedman, Curtin's minister for war organisation of industry, later asserted.[11] Page in

---

8   Page, *Truant Surgeon*, p. 325.
9   Page's wartime diary, EPP, folder 2787 (part 3), entry for 26 January 1942.
10  Such as in Paul Hasluck, *The Government and the People 1942–1945*, series 4 (Civil), volume 2, *Australia in the War of 1939–1945*, Australian War Memorial, Canberra, 1970, pp. 73–87; and David Horner, 'Australia and Allied Strategy in the Pacific, 1941–1946', PhD thesis, The Australian National University, 1980, pp. 87–104.
11  John Dedman, 'The return of the AIF from the Middle East', *Australian Outlook*, vol. 21, no. 2, August 1967, p. 163.

fact agreed with the British assessment that it was important to try to save Burma so as to protect British India and maintain a land supply route that would help keep China in the war. He vigorously argued this case throughout this rare occasion when Australia found itself at the centre of Allied grand strategy by virtue of some of its troops happening to be in a strategic place at a critical time.

Page therefore mediated exchanges between Curtin and Churchill so as to leave open the possibility that the Australian Government would accede to British wishes. He did so until he was absolutely satisfied that the Australian Government was fully aware of the case for Burma, despite earlier indications that it was unlikely to shift its position. Page was overconfident that Curtin would reconsider and was 'staggered' when the Australian prime minister continued to insist that the troops should not go to Rangoon. At the same time, he discovered that a cable from the British commander in the Far East, Archibald Wavell, that presented the full case for Burma had not yet been sent to Canberra, with the result that he 'roared everybody up' to get the cable sent at once.[12] Page therefore delayed passing Curtin's reaffirmation on to Churchill as he thought that it had not been prepared in full knowledge of the considered British view. He told Curtin that he was thoughtfully 'holding your telegram secret till receipt further advice' and assured him that 'no instructions to divert its course from proceeding to Australia had been sent to the convoy'.[13] Far from not understanding the issues at stake, Page 'had [a] personal talk with Ch. [Churchill] and told him if he could give me certain assurances re [the] position in Burma I thought I could get their consent'. These were that in Burma the Australians 'would have a definite chance to retrieve the position completely'; second, 'that they could be got into Rangoon in reasonable safety'; and, finally, that if Rangoon fell 'they could be supplied if they fell back and operated in conjunction with [the] Chinese'.[14] This was all in Page's full knowledge that his youngest son, Douglas, was in the convoy being considered for Burma.

Page's understanding that the convoy had not yet been diverted proved empty when a few days later Churchill advised that he had discretely ordered it north towards Rangoon in anticipation of agreement from the Australians, probably influenced by Page's personal advice. Page was

---

12  Page's wartime diary, EPP, folder 2787 (part 3), entry for 18 February 1942.
13  Page to Curtin, 19 February 1942, *Historical Documents, Volume 5: 1941, July – 1942, June*, Department of Foreign Affairs and Trade (DFAT), 347 Cablegram P47 [NAA, A816, 52/302/142].
14  Page's wartime diary, EPP, folder 2787 (part 3), entry for 19 February 1942.

in good company in advocating the British position, including that of Stanley Bruce, President Roosevelt and the Opposition in the Australian parliament. But it remains that subsequent assessments of his actions are greatly coloured by a consensus that Australian troops landed in Rangoon would probably have shared the fate of their 8th Division comrades by becoming prisoners of the Japanese.[15]

Curtin concluded his debate over Burma with Page with an angry cable admonishing him that 'we were amazed to learn' that he had hesitated to send on advice that the troopships were not to be diverted. 'I cannot fail to point out to you that your cablegrams give no impression that the Australian point of view regarding the security of the Commonwealth as the ultimate base to be held in the south-west Pacific has been advocated by you' thundered the prime minister.[16] Page cabled back in typically verbose but hurt terms, declaring that 'my own personal and family record establishe[s] beyond question that the security of Australia has always been my first consideration' and reiterating the case for Burma. He added that he had devoted much thought 'to the establishment of cordial automatically working machinery of consultation on all planes between Australia and Britain', because 'in the scramble for priority' for receiving British armaments and technology 'maximum goodwill and [the] feeling that there will always be the utmost co-operation are tremendous assets'.[17] The tone is that he saw himself as an equal of Prime Minister Curtin.

Page in wartime retained a strong attachment to the possibilities of the imperial connection. This was despite steadily rising bilateral tension between Britain and Australia as their respective strategic and economic interests continued to diverge. Differences grew from the late 1930s over such issues as conservation of foreign exchange, expansion of Australian manufacturing at the expense of British exports and, prior to December 1941, whether to deter or seek compromise with Japan.[18] Page had long seen the Empire not just as a vehicle for Australian trade policy but also for the management of international trade, including 'Empire rationalisation'.

---

15   See for example Judith Marsh, 'Churchill versus Curtin, February 1942,' *Army Journal*, no. 260, January 1971, pp. 27–34.
16   Curtin to Page, cable, 25 February 1942, *Historical Documents, Volume 5*, DFAT, 374 Cablegram 33 [NAA, A3196, 1942, 0.5738].
17   Page to Curtin, 27 February 1942, *Historical Documents, Volume 5*, DFAT, 378 Cablegram P54 [NAA, A3195, 1942, 1.8581].
18   Kosmas Tsokhas, 'Dedominionization: The Anglo-Australian experience, 1939–1945', *The Historical Journal*, vol. 37, no. 4, December 1994, pp. 861–83.

In May 1936, for example, he had drafted an article for the *Farmers Weekly* proposing to organise Australia's trade in primary products via producer-controlled but government-backed national boards that would work with similar Empire boards for each product. Together, these would set production quotas, influence prices and manage imports from outside the Empire.[19] At the 1937 Imperial Conference he had mooted an empire agricultural council. Use of the Empire to manage international trade had numerous other eminent pre-war advocates such as Lionel Curtis, the Anglo-Canadian media baron Lord Beaverbrook and the then London-based Australian historian W.K. Hancock.

In London, Page's vision encompassed harnessing the Empire to manage the wartime and post-war production and pricing of major traded commodities and of manufactures such as steel. Early in 1942, Churchill and Roosevelt created joint Anglo-American boards to integrate Allied production and supply: Page wanted to balance these with machinery for the Empire management of supplies that also gave the Dominions a say. Reminiscent of his earlier ideas for planning the Australian economy, he set out in his memoirs a rationally organised pantheon of planning mechanisms ascending from the technical and departmental levels up to an empire supply or production board of British ministers and high commissioners with final authority to coordinate production across the Empire. Ideally, it would be headed by Beaverbrook.[20]

Page feared that growing ties with the United States posed a long-term threat to Empire integrity. He warned Curtin that although Australia had a strong relationship with Britain, 'it would be many years, if ever, before there was the same mutual sympathy, knowledge, understanding and common interest between the great masses of the people of Australia and America as between those of Britain and Australia'. Hence 'we should mobilise the support of the whole British Empire to bring maximum pressure on [the] United States to assure the fullest consideration and quickest attention to our military problems and needs'. A way to help achieve this, added Page, was 'the full functioning of the Empire clearing houses of the various supply organisations for munitions, raw materials and shipping brought into being by Roosevelt's and Churchill's agreement and the establishment of an Empire Production Council'.[21]

---

19  See EPP, folder 1802.
20  Page, *Truant Surgeon*, pp. 350–2, 356–7.
21  Page to Curtin, 13 March 1942, *Historical Documents, Volume 5*, DFAT, 410 Cablegram P66 [NAA, A3195, 1942, 1.10485].

Page's efforts to organise wartime production and supply had an additional agenda of extending these arrangements into peacetime to help stabilise world trade, as well as reinvigorate the Empire. He used his wartime travels to promote this extraordinarily ambitious yet ill-defined vision with an assortment of well-placed figures that included British civil servants, New York financiers and Oxford dons. In Washington en route to London he discussed with Vice-President Henry Wallace, even before the United States had entered the war, 'post-war reconstruction based on international collaboration with regard to surpluses of both primary and secondary industries'.[22] In London in November 1941 he raised with Bruce his ideas on how production surpluses could be used in an 'international way with a definite policy of restoring world trade and especially lifting the nutrition of the peoples of the world'. He was confident of securing Churchill's support and foresaw that his idea 'could be worked out by the industries themselves and not necessarily by the Governments'.[23] Publicly, he spoke of how 'the methods of co-ordination that are adopted for wartime action should be such as can be used for peacetime purposes and post-war planning', and 'not just vanish into thin air as they did after the last war'.[24] Soon after, as Singapore was about to fall to the Japanese, he spoke at All Souls College, Oxford, on the coordination of wartime supplies and the 'rationalisation of industry' between the Empire and other Allied countries through 'continuous and permanent machinery I have outlined for England & Australia'. Such machinery would at war's end 'overcome fierce competition that will bring trade dislocation and depressions'.[25]

Page echoed much of what he had said to the New South Wales Chamber of Manufactures in 1926 by now telling the British minister of labour, Ernest Bevin, of his hopes for a Commonwealth council of agriculture that would exceed the work of the Empire Marketing Board of 1926–33 by 'assuring production, distribution and marketing of our Empire goods in an orderly fashion'. The result would be that 'stabilisation of prices for agricultural products would tend to give such stability to industry and employment as to make industrial problems much smaller and easier to

---

22  Page's wartime diary, EPP, folder 2787 (part 3), entry for 19 October 1941.
23  Ibid., entry for 17 November 1941.
24  'Speech by Sir Earle Page at Second Wednesday Club, London, 7th January 1942', EPP, folder 1902 (part 2).
25  See EPP, folder 1819, for a summary outline of this 31 January 1942 speech; also Page's wartime diary, entry for 31 January 1942, including 'Note of Discussion at Balliol College, 31.1.42', EPP, folder 2787 (part 3).

handle'.²⁶ Speaking to the Empire Parliamentary Association in January 1942, he spoke of 'a review of the production capacity of each Dominion', an Empire-wide 'determination of sites and location of different industries' and even the planned industrialisation of India that would create post-war markets for Britain and Australia.²⁷ There are signs here, perhaps, of the reasons for the exasperated, and essentially unfair, comment from the chief of the Imperial General Staff, Field Marshal Alan Brooke, that Page had in the War Cabinet displayed 'the mentality of a greengrocer'.²⁸

The emphasis on global rationalisation, organisation and planning makes all this less a typical Australian conception of Empire than a distinctively Page view. He wrote in his diary of sending plans to Curtin, 'the symmetry of which was perfect and which would provide an insoluble bond of unity between Empire for good'. Page was then also preparing a statement on Empire production and supply, but feared 'that they may be so stupid as not to be able to understand without the actual practical operation of the system that I have had, how indispensable this system is and how permanent and indissoluble it will make the union'.²⁹ Page even mused about a federal union of the Empire and the United States.³⁰

Page's efforts far exceeded his personal influence and were contrary to the reality of a British Empire facing decline as the United States seemed increasingly likely to assume leadership of the post-war world. The policy and political opportunities of the 1940s were in many respects very different from those of the 1930s. The Australian Government's interest in international discussions concerning institutional arrangements for the post-war world economy shifted towards maintaining full employment. Although these various discussions did include trade in primary products, notably at the May 1943 Hot Springs Conference in the United States, their overall emphasis was on free trade and international financial stability rather than the production and price controls that attracted Page.³¹ There is no more striking instance of the extent of Page's policy ambitions and willingness to pursue these whenever an opportunity presented itself.

---

26  Page's wartime diary, ibid., entry for 25 June 1942.
27  Earle Page, *Improvement of Empire Communications and Methods of Consultation*, Empire Parliamentary Association, London, 1942, pp. 11–12, 13–14, copy at EPP, folder 642.
28  Field Marshal Lord Alanbrooke, *War Diaries 1939–1945*, edited by Alex Danchev and Daniel Todman, Weidenfeld & Nicolson, London, 2001, p. 212.
29  Page's wartime diary, EPP, folder 2787 (part 3), entry for 28 January 1942.
30  'Note of Discussion at Balliol College', EPP, folder 2787 (part 3).
31  See Macintyre, *Australia's Boldest Experiment*, pp. 241–53.

Page retained faith in the potential of the Empire, writing in his memoirs that had it 'developed the same common feeling as the United States' it would have remained a force for trade and international stability, a 'Commonwealth market' that the rest of world have wished to join.[32]

The events of the first few months of 1942 placed Page under great stress, resulting in a rare dampening of his otherwise incorrigible optimism. Late in March 1942 he came down with a near-fatal bout of 'double broncho-pneumonia'. Formally diagnosed on 28 March, his diary entry covering the next two days reads simply 'unconscious'. In a personal letter written as he recovered in hospital, Page told Curtin that 'I went through since January the worst period of acute mental distress of my whole life'. He looked forward to returning to Australia where 'I may be of real value to you in bringing to you a first-hand knowledge of their way of looking at things over here and the personal attitude of each man that counts'.[33] This is all a fine example not merely of Page's habitual conviction that he was the bearer of special knowledge but also his ultimate dedication to upholding what he perceived as the national interest.

Page departed Britain by air on 26 June 1942 to commence an extended return journey via the United States where he visited the Tennessee Valley Authority and met with President Roosevelt. As they flew into New York, he advised his fellow passenger the British Treasury adviser Frederick Leith-Ross 'not to form a general organisation to deal with the whole matter [of post-war reconstruction] but to take each major item by itself and have an executive organisation of the countries most interested in that subject to deal with it'.[34] In Washington, he prepared a press statement adding that 'pool controls' set up by Allied governments jointly to control production should be used after the war to 'automatically plan to meet the problems of peace', with 'international collaboration proceeding item by item'.[35] The President told Page that once Germany was defeated 'the surrender of Japan would follow almost immediately', which Page contested 'on the grounds of their fanaticism, the resources at their disposal, and of the difficulties of smashing them to bits'. He asked Page to take a message

---

32  Page, *Truant Surgeon*, p. 384.
33  Page to Curtin, 24 April 1942, NAA, A5954, 475/2.
34  Page's wartime diary, EPP, folder 2787 (part 3), entry for 28 June 1942.
35  'Statement by Sir Earle Page at Press Conference at Washington D.C. July 10th, 1942', EPP, folder 1902 (part 2).

to Curtin requesting that he visit.[36] In New York, the vice-president of General Electric, William Herod, recalled that Page had in 1936 'put up the proposal of a co-operative international electrical enterprise in Europe as the most certain way to prevent war'.[37]

Page was to remain defensive about his London experience, claiming to have helped contain the damage to bilateral relations. He never in hindsight conceded that he had been wrong about the Burma controversy. Later he wrote of his efforts to persuade Churchill and Curtin to moderate their dispute, with Churchill agreeing that Page could vet all his future cables to the Australians and the King personally honouring him for avoiding a split in the Empire by making him a Companion of Honour.[38] But the harm to his relations with the Labor Government almost certainly had implications for his hopes of a direct role in post-war reconstruction.

When Page returned to Australia in August 1942, he was greeted in Sydney by the prime minister who invited him to 'make up my mind what I would like to do'.[39] He resumed his place in a parliamentary Country Party still led by Arthur Fadden (also Opposition leader). Page remained undeterred by his decidedly mixed experiences overseas and at once sought a major say in guiding post-war reconstruction. He reported to parliament that in London he had been 'intimately associated' with 'the system of intergovernmental contacts' and was even 'largely instrumental in creating the Empire machinery associated with it'. On this basis, Page considered that he 'could be of use not only in the consideration of current problems, but also in planning for the post-war period, so that Australia shall be able to take its proper place in the affairs of the world'.[40] Although Page overstated his influence in London, he was nonetheless one of the few Australians to have operated at high levels in Allied capitals, and had a long-standing claim to expertise in prospective post-war issues of regionalism, planning and infrastructure.

---

36   Page's wartime diary, EPP, folder 2787 (part 3), entry for 21 July 1942.
37   Ibid., entry for 13 July 1942.
38   See note in EPP, folder 2577; also Page, *Truant Surgeon*, p. 365.
39   Page's wartime diary, EPP, folder 2787 (part 3), entry for 16 August 1942.
40   *Commonwealth Parliamentary Debates*, 9 September 1942, p. 109.

**Figure 9: Earle Page with Ethel Page on his return to Australia, August 1942.**
Source: Courtesy of Australian War Memorial, 150400, photograph by Harry Turner.

Page's second big wartime opportunity came when the Curtin Government appointed him as a delegate to the Constitutional Convention held in Canberra late in 1942. The government was already looking towards realising its anticipated post-war reconstruction program and gave Evatt (also attorney-general) the task of securing the greater constitutional powers this required. Page still had a largely workable personal relationship with Curtin, but the appointment had more to do with the need for a balanced party representation at the convention than any signal of a substantive post-war role.[41] Yet it both raised his hopes and came to demonstrate the extent to which his views had drifted from those of his immediate political peers.

The convention arose from a Bill introduced into parliament in October 1941 proposing an entirely new section of the Constitution expanding the Commonwealth's powers over industry, employment, health, transport and housing. It would also debar the High Court from interfering with legislation considered necessary for 'economic security and social justice'.[42]

---

41  Page's short (one and a half page) 'Diary of Constitutional Convention' notes simply 'I was chosen to represent the Country Party'; EPP, folder 2787 (part 3).
42  Macintyre, *Australia's Boldest Experiment*, pp. 137–8.

Faced with the unlikelihood of such radical alterations getting past the Senate let alone succeeding at a referendum, the Curtin Government resorted to convening a special convention of Commonwealth and state parliamentarians from all parties in the hope of securing broad-based political support. Membership was accordingly wide – eight members of the House of Representatives, four of the Senate, and the premier and the Opposition leader from each state, adding up to a total of 24 delegates evenly divided between the ALP and the non-Labor parties. The extended proceedings that followed were dubbed a Constitutional Convention, but Paul Hasluck, writing later as an official war historian, severely doubted that they deserved such an elevated title.[43]

Delegates convened in Parliament House, Canberra, from 24 November to 4 December 1942. It was soon clear that a referendum on greater Commonwealth powers lacked bipartisan support. Fadden rightly accused the Curtin Government of trying to insert the Labor Party's platform into the Constitution.[44] But Page treated the convention as an opportunity to present an ambitious and original policy plan. His main concerns were that the government had both misjudged its strategy and was missing an opportunity to achieve major reform. Unlike other non-Labor delegates, Page was not overly concerned by the dangers of a powerful central government. Instead, he proposed that for development projects 'the Commonwealth should plan and finance and … the states should administer and construct through their own agencies or through that of their local governments', making them 'the hands and fingers of the planning body'. He evoked past cooperative successes such as tied road grants, the Sydney–Brisbane railway and the Hume Dam on the Murray River. If 'the states could have some voice in the arrangement of the plan and of the general lines of policy, then there could be little objection to ample legal powers being in the hands of the Commonwealth'.[45] A National Council of the Commonwealth and the states should be appointed with a permanent secretariat 'to see what powers could be best handled co-operatively, which could be best handled by the Commonwealth or by states, and also should look at the changes necessary if any drastic reform of the Constitution in the direction of unification were found to be indispensable'.[46]

---

43  See Hasluck, *The Government and the People 1942–1945*, pp. 524–8.
44  Macintyre, *Australia's Boldest Experiment*, p. 139.
45  'Sir Earle Page – Constitutional Convention, Canberra, 1/12/42', EPP, folder 888.
46  'Diary of Constitutional Convention', EPP, folder 2787 (part 3).

Page was clearly seeking acceptance as a major contributor to post-war reconstruction. He was undeterred by the partisanship on display during and after the convention, instead indicating his own readiness to work across party lines. Although the convention concluded with delegates unanimously supporting the states using section 51(xxxvii) of the Constitution to voluntarily refer powers to the Commonwealth on a strictly temporary basis, in the event only two Labor states, New South Wales and Queensland, passed the requisite legislation. This resulted in a referendum in August 1944 for the direct acquisition of powers by the Commonwealth for a five-year period after the cessation of hostilities, including over the production and distribution of goods. In parliament, the Country Party initially voted with the government on the referendum legislation but later switched after failing to secure an amendment to strengthen powers over the marketing of commodities.[47]

Page's hopes and fears for post-war reconstruction were as much about means as ends, making him one of the first major public figures to articulate a comprehensive cooperative path to constitutional change. He had long experience of failed referendums thwarting constitutional reform, and saw the nation's wartime exigencies as presenting a chance to alter this pattern. In the parliamentary debate of March 1944 on the forthcoming referendum, he said that experience had convinced him that major reforms 'cannot be rammed down the throats of the states by a referendum', and wryly recalled that the only major referendum carried since Federation was the 1928 enshrinement of the Financial Agreement.[48] Although he thought that the states accepted much of what the Constitutional Convention and 1944 referendum proposed, Page saw the Commonwealth as courting failure by also proposing more controversial wider powers, such as over prices and company legislation. In other respects the proposed referendum was flawed by seeking merely 'partial and inadequate powers', particularly by omitting Commonwealth control of primary production and failing 'to acquire the whole of the railways of Australia'. If Australia were to compete successfully with countries like the Soviet Union, the United States and Canada, said Page, it must exercise proper national control of communications and energy.[49]

---

47   Hasluck, *The Government and the People 1942–1945*, pp. 534–5; Macintyre, *Australia's Boldest Experiment*, p. 257.
48   *Commonwealth Parliamentary Debates*, 8 March 1944, p. 1072.
49   Ibid., pp. 1071, 1077.

From the mid-1920s onwards, Page had increasingly found that in order to advance his developmentalist ideas, he needed to make accommodations with a constitution and a federal system that he otherwise disdained. As a patient and principled opportunist, Page was encouraged, even excited, by how wartime provided a unique chance to put this approach into practice. The most promising way forward in 1944, he said, was not a referendum but actually 'the co-operative method, exemplified by the Loan Council'.[50] The war had familiarised the states and the Australian public with the exercise of central power over railways, agriculture, marketing and energy. This created the conditions for reasoned, patriotic appeals for support of a voluntary temporary transfer of selected responsibilities to the Commonwealth. Page concluded that the Commonwealth should approach this carefully by first convening a special conference with the states to effect this transfer, and only much later following up with a referendum to make these changes permanent.[51] Page turned out to be essentially right in his fears about strategy: the referendum of August 1944 succeeded in only two states, an early signal that the public was tiring of wartime controls. This major failure forced the Curtin and Chifley governments to turn reluctantly to reliance on cooperation from the states, a major constraint on their post-war reconstruction program.[52]

## Page falters in the post-war environment

In wartime, there developed within the Commonwealth Government a confidence that post-war reconstruction would present a unique opportunity to build a fairer, more prosperous nation. Coombs later reflected that:

> we had faith in the intellectual model of the economic system and our capacity to manage it; we believed that it could in practice deliver benefits to both producer and consumer; we had the ear and the confidence of a Prime Minister and a Treasurer who combined vision with executive competence; we were conscious that there was in the community generally a conviction that a better world could be built.[53]

---

50   Ibid., p. 1072.
51   Speech to Convention by Page, 30 November 1942, EPP, folder 886.
52   Stuart Macintyre, 'The post-war reconstruction project.', in Samuel Furphy (ed.), *The Seven Dwarfs and the Age of the Mandarins: Australian Government Administration in the Post-War Reconstruction Era*, ANU Press, Canberra, 2015, p. 36.
53   H.C. Coombs, *Trial Balance: Issues of My Working Life*, Macmillan, South Melbourne, 1981, p. 27.

To this end, Curtin, Chifley and their intellectual supporters hoped that public acceptance of wartime planning and direction would carry over into a post-war tolerance of economic controls. This official optimism – perhaps more inspired hope – in practice ran up against the growing public weariness with government regulation that had helped defeat the 1944 referendum. Page should have prospered amid such optimism, but soon encountered the consequences of shifts in party politics and policy-making.

Page's vision of national development was outwardly compatible with the government's main strategies for post-war reconstruction: regionalism, infrastructure projects, communality and expert-led national policy planning. New planning-oriented agencies and inquiries had begun to appear early during the war. In June 1940, under the Menzies Government, the Loan Council appointed a coordinator-general of Public Works to assess the economic and military significance of works proposed by state governments.[54] The Curtin Government went further by proposing both a powerful national works commission to evaluate all new major construction projects and a reserve program of projects to be deployed if needed to cushion the employment consequences of demobilisation.[55] This idea fell foul of resistance from the states, but a National Works Council was established in 1943 as an adjunct to the Premiers' Conference to 'promote development of national resources according to a long-term programme' and make recommendations to the Loan Council on proposals submitted by the states.[56] The Commonwealth Housing Commission, also formed in 1943, described planning as 'a conscious effort to guide the development of the resources of the nation' and proposed a Commonwealth Planning Authority to bring together all agencies dealing with public works, industry and housing.[57]

Post-war reconstruction's similarity to Page's vision needs to be qualified in one important respect. Despite strong economic growth during the war years – real gross domestic product rose by 26 per cent between 1939 and 1946 – much of the Labor Government's planning for peacetime was motivated by an overarching fear of large-scale unemployment reminiscent

---

54   Heather Curtis, 'Planning for national development', *Australian Quarterly*, vol. 26, no. 3, September 1954, p. 55.
55   Macintyre, *Australia's Boldest Experiment*, p. 191.
56   Australia, Parliament, *Full Employment in Australia*, White Paper, Government Printer, Canberra, 1945.
57   Macintyre, *Australia's Boldest Experiment*, p. 182.

of the Great Depression.[58] David Rivett, chief executive officer of the CSIR, for example warned in 1941 that 'the only completely satisfactory method of dealing with unemployment devised by man seems to be war'.[59] Developmentalist policy of this time was frequently presented as a means of avoiding the economic disaster of the previous decade, hence an early post-war emphasis on direct public investment in growth. The Curtin Government's 1945 White Paper on Full Employment opened with the proclamation that 'full employment is a fundamental aim of the Commonwealth government'.[60] This crucially important goal rarely appeared in Page's own pronouncements on national development.

To his chagrin, Page was never given any formal role by the post-war Chifley Government. His invitation to the 1942 Constitutional Convention and service on the Advisory War Council in 1942–43 and 1944–45 remained temporary aberrations attributable to the necessities of war and politics, and to recognition of the expertise he had gained in London.[61] Page did not even earn a mention in *Regional Development Journal* produced by the Department of Post-War Reconstruction. He came to resent this exclusion from issues on which he felt past contributions gave him a rightful role transcending the party divide. There emerged a discernible bitterness in speeches in which he goaded government figures with whom he had formerly worked well, including Chifley himself. The government simply did not feel it needed Page's guidance.

Amid strident debates over whether post-war development should be led by government planning or private enterprise, Page, as so often, diverged from his party political peers. Harold Holt spoke in 1944 of the danger of 'a regimented Australia, a drab grey world in which every human being is pushed around'. Fellow Liberal Eric Spooner warned of 'some outdated theology which tried to make people come to heel by the threat of hell fire'.[62] Page did not place such stress on the rights of the individual and was far less suspicious of extending government-led planning into peacetime. Herbert Gepp, Charles Kemp of the Institute of Public Affairs and most other business leaders of the time tended to be more assertively individualist, perhaps in reaction to the socialist associations of a Labor Government. Despite newly acquired Keynesian sympathies, they tolerated

---

58 Yule in John Connor, Peter Stanley and Peter Yule, *The War at Home*, The Centenary History of Australia and the Great War, volume 4, Oxford University Press, South Melbourne, 2015, p. 77.
59 Quoted in Macintyre, *Australia's Boldest Experiment*, p. 66.
60 Australia, Parliament, *Full Employment in Australia*.
61 Page's own account stresses the latter motivation; see *Truant Surgeon*, p. 366.
62 Macintyre, *Australia's Boldest Experiment*, p. 261.

government-led planning only to the extent that it was a public–private collaboration that allowed private enterprise freedom of action, such as the very selective use of public works. Page agreed that private enterprise was critically important and fiercely opposed the Chifley Government's bank nationalisation, but remained more comfortable with government playing a central role in planning regionalisation and electrification that would harness the power of the private sector. At a 1945 celebration of his 25 years in parliament, he spoke of how 'the real challenge to Australian progress is fear and timidity in undertaking full tasks necessary to the fulfilment of our destiny': the nation's post-war future 'lies in a big, constructive plan of development'.[63]

Nor did Page have a particularly strong personal standing among the policy intellectuals who proliferated in the post-war environment. James Walter writes of diverse new groups of applied thinkers that included economists, bankers, academics, theologians, unionists, public servants and others, and divides them into 'bureaucratic reconstructionists' who favoured collective and state-directed action, and more technocratic 'business progressives'.[64] Although Page's ideas overlapped with those held by many of these thinkers, he did not fit neatly into either current of thought. He retained a strong rural bias, and the National Council episode of a few years earlier showed that his interaction with more thoughtful business leaders did not guarantee support for his brand of developmentalism.

Page's divergence from new post-war intellectual trends was a factor in his difficulty in coping with changes in the conduct of government, especially the role of the Commonwealth Public Service. The first post-1945 annual report of the Commonwealth Public Service Board recognised a wartime shift in the functions of government from 'regulation' to more 'positive and constructive responsibilities'.[65] Stuart Macintyre, the foremost historian of post-war reconstruction, sees the wartime increase in central direction as having demanded stronger economic and other policy skills in the federal bureaucracy, leading to 'an influx of younger, university-trained officers drawn from the networks in which the schemes of social meliorism and rational improvement were nurtured'.[66]

---

63   *Daily Examiner*, 1 November 1945, p. 3.
64   Walter in Brian Head and James Walter (eds), *Intellectual Movements and Australian Society*, Oxford University Press, Melbourne, 1988, especially pp. 244–63.
65   Quoted in Nicholas Brown, 'The Seven Dwarfs: A team of rivals', in Furphy, *The Seven Dwarfs*, p. 20.
66   Macintyre, *Australia's Boldest Experiment*, p. 471.

These changes resulted in a government with a very different way of analysing issues than Page's instinctive approach. Major departments now boasted an intelligentsia of economics-trained staff committed not only to Keynesian theory and a planning-oriented world view, but also the rigorous assessment of project proposals. Even before the war, outspoken young Australian academic economists were ahead of most of their international counterparts in taking a close interest in macroeconomic demand management.[67] The new post-war cohort of young economists had backgrounds quite unlike that of Page. Coombs himself had studied at the London School of Economics, and in post-war Canberra he built a powerful personal network of university-trained economists, bankers and public servants, including R.C. Mills, Douglas Copland, Leslie Melville, John Crawford, L.F. Giblin and Trevor Swan.[68]

Page had little empathy with this style of public service: he preferred advisers who validated his own predispositions. He supported a certain efficiency in resource allocation, as reflected in his cautious approach to tariffs, but repeatedly rejected discouraging findings about the likely returns on hydroelectric projects and doubts about the planned decentralisation of industry. Page favoured expenditure on public works mainly to provide rural infrastructure and to advance his vision of decentralisation. He was attracted only to those economists, such as Roland Wilson, with a strong interest in development and long-term growth. (Wilson was Commonwealth statistician for most of this immediate post-war period, during which time he continued to support planning but in a limited sense of coordinating the many forms of government policy intervention now in play.)[69] Page remained driven by his deep emotional commitment to regionalism and decentralisation, rather than openness to new intellectual trends that placed these goals within inclusive social policies and overarching economic management. His wartime diary details many meetings with important public figures in Britain but makes no mention of Keynes or his acolytes.

Changes in the conduct of government were also given an institutional basis by Australia being one of the few nations to draw together all the pressing policy challenges of these years – issues as diverse as demobilisation, conversion of munitions production, housing, immigration, social welfare

---

67  Alex Millmow, 'Australia and the Keynsian revolution', in Furphy, *The Seven Dwarfs*, p. 53.
68  Walter, *What Were They Thinking?*, pp. 181, 183–4.
69  Selwyn Cornish, 'Sir Roland Wilson – *Primus inter pares*', in Furphy, *The Seven Dwarfs*, pp. 135–6.

and education – under the one label of post-war reconstruction.[70] The Department of Post-War Reconstruction was established in December 1942 to provide policy oversight, with Chifley as minister. It initially oversaw the planning of a more productive and equitable economy through an array of expert commissions of inquiry, notably the Rural Reconstruction Commission, the Commonwealth Housing Commission and the Secondary Industries Commission. The department was to guide and coordinate these investigations and then draw on their findings in formulating policy for implementation by line agencies. As these various planning and policy commissions progressively completed their work, they were replaced by divisions of the department, including regional and rural divisions. This all made Post-War Reconstruction a small but powerfully placed agency, and the foremost target of Page's lobbying. Coombs failed to establish an outright department of economic planning.[71]

Page was frustrated but undeterred by his exclusion. As will be seen, he still pushed issues onto the Commonwealth Government's agenda through his persistent lobbying. He also appealed to public and elite opinion through non-governmental forums and the media, and maintained an occasional presence amongst the diverse milieu of post-war developmentalist thinkers. Page provided among the broadest of visions for the post-war nation by linking cooperative federalism, decentralisation, higher education, hydroelectricity, planning and regionalism, and by proposing emulation of the famed Tennessee Valley Authority (TVA), which had assumed 'totemic significance' in the post-war world.[72]

Page's attempt to engage with the Rural Reconstruction Commission proved an early instance of his difficulties with post-war expert studies. Wartime broadened direct Commonwealth regulation of primary industry, often by drawing on special powers that would have been politically unacceptable in peacetime. Persistently low prices for primary products throughout the preceding decade had encouraged an array of debt relief, financial assistance and dual pricing schemes that by propping up small, non-mechanised producers delayed adjustments and modernisation.[73] The Rural Reconstruction Commission was established in 1942 amid the wartime loss of markets and shortages of materials and

---

70  Macintyre, 'The post-war reconstruction project', in Furphy, *The Seven Dwarfs*, p. 32.
71  Ibid., pp. 36, 46–7; Macintyre, *Australia's Boldest Experiment*, p. 142.
72  Cullather, *The Hungry World*, p. 120.
73  Macintyre, *Australia's Boldest Experiment*, pp. 161–2.

labour that suggested a bleak outlook for rural industries. Page appears to have assumed that the commission would empathise with his views. In practice, it proved to be an independent-minded inquiry dominated by the banker C.R. Lambert and the agricultural scientist Samuel Wadham, with less input from fellow commissioners who included Page's former departmental head, J.F. Murphy.

The commission drew heavily on economic advice and made many compromises. The Bureau of Agricultural Research, under the direction of John Crawford, drafted its submissions to Cabinet and the Australian Agricultural Council vetted commission reports prior to publication.[74] The commission approached agriculture as essentially an industry like any other, and so should also be subject to considerations of scale and efficiency. Government support should not be based on subsidisation that made farmers mendicants, but rather should stress aiding skilled and enterprising producers such as by offering technical advice and social amenities.[75] Limiting its direct effectiveness was that most of the commission's recommendations required action by the states, not the Commonwealth.

Among the numerous underscored passages in Page's personal copy of the commission's third report, on land utilisation and farm settlement, is a glowing assessment of the DMC as 'a most beneficial influence by curbing the exuberance of many proposals'.[76] But he would have been gravely disappointed by the commission's failure to call unambiguously for revival of a similar such body. It instead vaguely recommended 'detailed machinery for co-ordination of public works' to 'ensure that productive capacity is correlated to prospective market demands'.[77] This evident compromise matches comments about differences between the commissioners and with the Department of Post-War Reconstruction on how to implement Commonwealth–state cooperation on long-term planning. Wadham, critic of the AAC's Standing Committee, thought that rural people would reject expert planners and so instead proposed leadership by selected progressive famers.[78]

---

74  Troy Whitford and Don Boadle, 'Australia's Rural Reconstruction Commission, 1943–46: A reassessment', *Australian Journal of History and Politics*, vol. 54, no. 4, December 2008, pp. 532–3.
75  Macintyre, *Australia's Boldest Experiment*, pp. 149–50, 168–73.
76  Rural Reconstruction Commission, *Third Report, Land Utilisation and Farm Settlement*, The Commission, Canberra, 1944, p. 93.
77  Ibid., pp. 93, 97.
78  Whitford and Boadle, 'Australia's Rural Reconstruction Commission', pp. 531–4.

# Page's bids to lead post-war cooperative federalism, regionalism and higher education

Page's efforts to influence post-war reconstruction strategies focused on federalism, regionalism, higher education and the Clarence River. His ideas had enough overlap with the Commonwealth Government's own vision for it at least to understand and formally respond to his many entreaties, but through a veil of refusal to share power with him.

Changes in modes of policy formulation and the rise of nationally led planning had significant implications for attitudes to federalism. A majority view emerged favouring centralism, which left Page playing an important contrary role as advocate of a cooperative federalism that institutionalised Commonwealth and state policy collaboration. The dominant intellectual attitude to federalism was that total Commonwealth ascendancy over the states was inevitable and desirable, as set out in the fullest contemporary study, the historian Gordon Greenwood's 1946 *The Future of Australian Federalism*. Greenwood considered federalism merely a stage on the way to a concentration of political power that matched the nation's growing economic unification, albeit with scope remaining to delegate policy implementation to the local level. Reminiscent as this was of Page's own national policy–regional implementation split, Greenwood otherwise assailed cooperative federalism as 'dilatory and ineffective', despite having been given a 'fair trial'.[79]

Active support for cooperative federalism did not extend much beyond Page and his confirmed admirers, notably Drummond. At the 1942 Constitutional Convention, Page had proposed Commonwealth–state coordinating councils that would elevate development to a national imperative, and 'the whole administration of this huge business organisation could be withdrawn from politics altogether'.[80] These would 'either induce the states to place definite agreed-on powers in the Constitution into the hands of the Commonwealth, or some agreement as to what parts of each of these subjects should be handled by the Commonwealth

---

79   Gordon Greenwood, *The Future of Australian Federalism: A Commentary on the Working of the Constitution*, Melbourne University Press, Carlton, Vic., 1946, pp. 298–9, 303–4.
80   'Sir Earle Page – Constitutional Convention, Canberra, 1/12/42', EPP, folder 888.

would be arrived at'. Page even suggested 'a permanent organisation' for determining state and Commonwealth powers, and harked back to his National Council idea of 1938–39.[81]

After the 1944 referendum, Page increasingly turned to public appeals via the popular press. He portrayed successful cooperative mechanisms ranging from the Loan Council down to the River Murray Commission as collectively establishing an unanswerable case for institutionalised cooperation across finance, industrial policy, transport and power generation: effectively 'a Cabinet of governments'.[82] Page in one post-war speech even made a Wellsian reference to federalism as a basis for eventual 'world government'.[83] Coombs noted a pattern of the Commonwealth using its financial powers to set post-war policy and then leaving implementation to state governments, but considered this a regrettable necessity following the Commonwealth's failure to secure the necessary constitutional authority for itself.[84]

Two other great Page passions proved more central than cooperative federalism to Commonwealth post-war reconstruction policy – regionalism and decentralisation. The mid-1940s marked the high point of official and intellectual interest in these related concepts. The policies of the Chifley Government bore distinct similarities to Page's views of a generation earlier, albeit amid differences on whether regional entities should have sovereign status. In the 1920s and 1930s such causes had mainly been driven by new statism, with Page the main figure to look further towards nationwide change. As the post-war period loomed, support for regionalism and decentralisation broadened beyond the Country Party–linked rural elite that Page knew so well. It attracted not just the policy-oriented intellectuals with which Australia abounded such as Bland (now a convert to new states) and MacDonald Holmes, but increasingly also more technocratic government-based figures including Coombs.

---

81   Speech by Page to Constitutional Convention, 26 November 1942, EPP, folder 888.
82   Page, 'Federal state conflict – co-operation needed for effective government,' *Sydney Morning Herald*, 20 February 1945, p. 2; also speech to Constitutional Association of New South Wales, Sydney, 13 September 1948, copy at EPP, folder 1033. Bland was the association's vice-president.
83   Page speech to Constitutional Association of New South Wales, Sydney, ibid. H.G. Wells had long been the foremost advocate of a united world government.
84   Coombs, *Trial Balance*, pp. 59–60, 62.

Page's sense of personally owning regionalism and decentralisation led him to expect a commensurately major role in their implementation. He used the press to help spread his perception that the TVA stood for regional planning at its best, drawing credibility from actually having visited it. Intermediate-level regional bodies should sit between the Commonwealth and the states, 'unifying the principles of local knowledge and initiative with those of central supervision and assistance'. The TVA was the model by which Australia could 'follow the American example of establishing regional organisations which control physical and geographical units which often may involve handling parts of different states', such as northern New South Wales and southern Queensland, and the Murray and Snowy region. Page also wanted greatly expanded tied Commonwealth grants to finance big projects that the states could not implement alone, such as airports and rural electrification, as 'federal aid unites skilfully the principles of local initiative and central supervision'.[85] Regional authorities would implement national policies determined by a federal power commission, a federal water commission and a ministry of food.[86] His enthusiasm evinced his not infrequent unawareness of how others might not be quite so moved by his visions: in December 1944 he made an international radio broadcast to the peoples of wartime Britain and the United States on the TVA model and the importance of the Clarence Valley.[87]

Page's expectation of receptiveness to these ideas ignored fundamental differences between his world view and that of the Commonwealth Government. He thought that decentralisation had been decisively encouraged by the wartime siting of munitions factories in country towns and the application of 'an Australian uniform rate book' to the transport of government goods by rail that overcame the centralised focus of rail systems. Page had long argued that differential rail freight rates channelled trade to capital cities rather than 'natural outlets'.[88] But contemporary official accounts instead attributed the elevation of decentralisation and regional planning into the policy mainstream to how the federal government organised the war effort. In its 1949 monograph *Regional*

---

85  Page in the *Sydney Morning Herald*, 20 February 1945, p. 2.
86  Page speech 'Australian Power and Water Development', 16 June 1945, EPP, folder 1205.
87  EPP, folder 1067.
88  'History of Decentralisation: Speech by Sir Earle Page', in Decentralisation and New State Movement Convention, *Decentralisation and New State Movement: Armidale Convention, June 1948*, The Convention, Armidale, NSW, 1948, pp. 27, 34.

*Planning in Australia*, the Department of Post-War Reconstruction pointed to the precedent of the wartime regional organisation of government administration. Regionally based structures were thought capable of continuing to function following the disruption of central command. The department also credited Curtin with being impressed by a 'marked tendency' for local councils to propose projects for their respective regions.[89]

The department's enthusiasm for community as a basis for a new social order took further inspiration from the cooperative efforts of the residents of the South Australian town of Nuriootpa to provide local facilities to help retain its young residents.[90] Coombs recalled other influences, including the TVA, writers such as Lewis Mumford and the Rural Reconstruction Commission's stress on the local provision of rural amenities. 'It is difficult in retrospect', he wrote, 'to recapture the intellectual excitement which these ideas generated'.[91] Coombs's department reissued an Army Education Service *Current Affairs Bulletin* that condemned centralism as contributing to every social ill from housing shortages to 'weakening of citizenship'.[92] As early as August 1944, Evatt publicly suggest a TVA-like body for the Murray Valley, an idea encouraged by the locally based Murray Valley Development League but disdained by state governments.[93]

---

89  Department of Post-War Reconstruction, *Regional Planning in Australia: A History of Progress and Review of Regional Planning Activities through the Commonwealth*, Department of Post-War Reconstruction, Canberra, 1949, pp. vii, 1.
90  Macintyre, *Australia's Boldest Experiment*, pp. 195–8; see also Coombs, *Trial Balance*, p. 61.
91  Coombs, *Trial Balance*, pp. 59–60.
92  'Regionalism', *Current Affairs Bulletin*, vol. 18, no. 5, 5 November 1945; copy in Ulrich Ellis papers, NLA, MS 1006, box 13, folder 35.
93  *Sydney Morning Herald*, 16 August 1944, p. 5.

7. POST-WAR PAGE

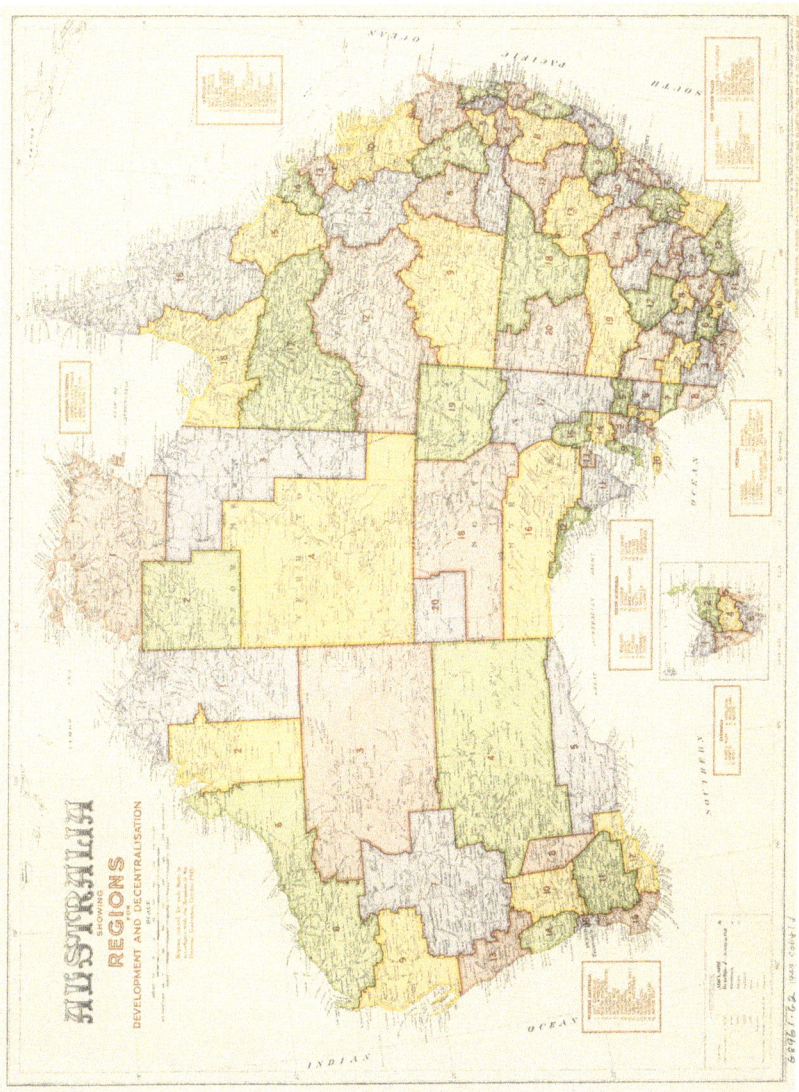

**Figure 10: Post-war Australia divided into 97 Regional Development Committees, as seen by the Chifley Government.**

Source: Courtesy of National Library of Australia, MAP G8961.G2 1949 (Copy 1), creator Department of Post-war Reconstruction. Regional Development Division, prepared by the National Mapping Section, Department of the Interior, 1949.

'NOW IS THE PSYCHOLOGICAL MOMENT'

In October 1944 Curtin proposed to all six premiers an ambitious program of cooperative regionalisation to promote decentralisation and national security. The states would define regional boundaries and survey local resources, then form 'representative regional advisory bodies'.[94] These were to collectively create a national network of 97 Regional Development Committees, through each of which state and local government representatives and other nominees would prepare local development plans. Curtin identified the Murray Valley, Newcastle and the Northern Territory as deserving particular attention – not the Clarence Valley.[95] His government was claiming the decentralisation–regionalisation concept as its own: its public pronouncements ignored Page, the Country Party and new state movements. (Nor was there reference, it appears, to antecedents in the ALP's pre-war platform.) Curtin's regionalism, however, gained only limited political traction. Committees were formed in just Victoria, New South Wales and Tasmania, and remained strictly advisory bodies that failed to gain the full commitment of state governments or local councils.[96]

Another problem here for Page was that the widening of interest in regionalism and decentralisation presented him with a far more diverse range of motivators and goals to navigate than had the Country Party–dominated agitation of the inter-war years. He would have applauded the call by F.K. Maher and J.I. Sullivan in a 1946 booklet for 'vigorous, self-governing regions', 'severe limitations' on construction in the big cities and the harnessing of river systems (which noted Page's efforts concerning the Clarence).[97] But the Methodist Page was not part of the lively strand of Catholic regionalist thought with which Maher was closely associated through the Australian National Secretariat of Catholic Action that he headed with B.A. Santamaria. Catholic social theorists were attracted by the religiosity of rural communities, hence the National Catholic Rural Movement advocating 'the spiritual restoration of the country' through rural settlement.[98] More secular intellectual support for decentralisation appeared in such journals as *Current Affairs Bulletin* and *Australian Quarterly*.[99]

---

94  Department of Post-War Reconstruction, *Regional Planning in Australia*, pp. viii, 13.
95  Ibid., p. 1.
96  Macintyre, *Australia's Boldest Experiment*, pp. 414–15.
97  F.K. Maher and J.I. Sullivan, *Regionalism in Australia*, Araluen Publishing Company, Melbourne, 1946, pp. 3, 45, 46.
98  Gerard Henderson, *Mr. Santamaria and the Bishops*, St Patrick's College, Manly, 1982, p. 57.
99  See for example 'Industries for the country', *Current Affairs Bulletin*, vol. 4, no. 2, 11 April 1949; and E.J. Tapp, 'Decentralisation and the individual', *Australian Quarterly*, vol. 20, no. 2, June 1948, pp. 82–90.

The diversity of interest was reflected in the range of speakers at a string of major conferences that addressed decentralisation. These included a January 1948 AIPS conference at Armidale, a New South Wales Local Government Association Local Government school of August 1948 and an All-Australian Federal Convention on constitutional change held in Sydney in July 1949. The latter event was convened by Bland's New South Wales Constitutional League, and amongst the other participants were Harold Nicholas (the same of the Boundaries Royal Commission), Alex Gibson, Richard Windeyer, MacDonald Holmes, H.L. Harris, Drummond and Bruxner. Most intellectual supporters of decentralisation linked regionalism to national and regional planning but some, including Bland and Gibson, saw it as a counter to centralised political control. Page's packaging of federal units with strong national government made it hard for him to use this Cold War–influenced argument. Bland, now well-established as Australia's leading scholar of public administration, became outspoken on inserting regional administrative entities between local and state governments so as to counter centralism. Gibson saw strong state and regional authorities as 'sure means by which the effect of centralised power and industrial concentration can be obviated'.[100] Interest in decentralisation also contributed to a modest revival in new statism. The New England movement reappeared in June 1948 when a new organisation was established at Armidale presided over by Phillip Wright. In March 1949 Premier Ned Hanlon of Queensland raised the subdivision of his home state, and a new local movement appeared at Townsville. Soon after, Premier Thomas Hollway of Victoria suggested a new state based on Gippsland and south-eastern New South Wales.[101]

Page contributed at least indirectly to this renewed interest in regionalism and decentralisation by having helped sustain such ideas in political discourse since the last revival in the early 1930s. Although most 1940s proponents worked to community-oriented agendas more focused on addressing rural poverty than Page's grander nationwide vision, some

---

100 See F.A. Bland, 'Post-war constitutional reconstruction', *Public Administration*, vol. 2, no. 3, September–December 1940, pp. 136–55; F.A. Bland, 'Towards regionalism', *Public Administration*, vol. 4, no. 8, December 1943, pp. 379–85; and F.A. Bland, 'Decentralization – the machinery of government', in H.L. Harris, H.S. Nicholas, F.A. Bland, A. Mainerd and T. Hytten, *Decentralization*, Angus and Robertson in conjunction with the Australian Institute of Political Science, Sydney, 1948, pp. 67–120. For Gibson, see 'The implications of decentralisation', in Decentralisation and New State Movement Convention, *Decentralisation and New State Movement*, pp. 7, 10.
101 See John Joseph Farrell, 'Opting out and opting in: Secession and the New State Movements', *Armidale and District Historical Society Journal*, no. 40, 1997, p. 148; and Ellis, *A History of the Australian Country Party*, p. 277.

nonetheless matched particular ideas he had long publicised nationally. At the AIPS conference, Harris was conceptually closest to Page's ideas about the potential of decentralisation to draw out the best social qualities. It would, he said, lead to 'a heightened social consciousness and a quickening of the community spirit with new standards and values and richer personalities'. Harris added that decentralisation was 'essentially a population policy directed to the preservation of the race and to the improvement of its quality', a racial cast that Page did not employ.[102] A 1944 booklet originally published as an article by the Institution of Engineers echoed Page's National Council by proposing the nation's division into six regions, all overseen by a national planning authority working with regional planning commissions.[103] Even Maher and Sullivan upheld the link between decentralisation and planning by recommending the use of freight schemes, tariffs and electrification as planning tools, much as Page had proposed.[104]

By the immediate post-war period, three decades of disappointment had made Page alert to opportunities to broaden his case for decentralisation and regionalisation. His major statements reflected the post-war interest in regional equity in social amenities. In his foremost speech of this period on new states, delivered in June 1948 to a convention in Armidale, Page declared that decentralisation would 'give equal opportunity to all Australian citizens in facilities of education, culture and health, in security of work for their families, in professional and business careers and in the provision of domestic amenities'. Page became increasingly prone to quoting selectively from major intellectual figures: his Armidale speech drew on Mumford's writings on self-governing political units large enough (as Page put it) to 'embrace a sufficient range of interests and small enough to keep these interests in focus and make them a subject of direct collective concern'.[105] With the advent of the Cold War, Page again employed defence-related arguments. 'Australia's great need', he told the All-Australian Federal Convention, 'is to get enough people

---

102 Harris et al., *Decentralization*, pp. 18, 20.
103 C.M. Longfield and T.A. Lang, *Regional Planning*, RAAF Educational Services, Melbourne, 1944 (first published in *The Journal of The Institution of Engineers, Australia*, August 1943), copy in Ellis papers, NLA, MS 1006, box 12, series 6A, folder 29.
104 Maher and Sullivan, *Regionalism in Australia*, p. 35.
105 'History of Decentralisation: Speech by Sir Earle Page', in Decentralisation and New State Movement Convention, *Decentralisation*, pp. 25, 29.

quickly to develop her latent resources and thus ensure the defence of our Continent', for which 'local self-government by the creation of new states with consequent acceleration of local development is the real answer'.[106]

The higher quality debate on regionalism helped develop Page's own ideas. He had long been neither clear nor consistent about how he defined a viable region for a new state or federal unit. But in speeches during 1945 he referred to their being delineated by common farming conditions and similar 'agricultural, scientific and research problems' of water, irrigation and fodder conservation.[107] His new federal units were also to include those parts of large states that were too distant to be governed effectively from an existing state capital. Page specified several regions as particularly suited for regional development, namely the Murray Valley, southern, central and northern Queensland, and northern and central New South Wales.[108] In 1949 he spoke of a prospective 18 new states as the beginning of a process of national subdivision into smaller units. He made clearer than ever his disdain for the 'boa-contractor' of the big city, beset by 'all sorts of social diseases', and proposed towns of from 30,000 up to 250,000 inhabitants.[109]

Decentralisation and regionalisation still struggled to be actually implemented even in this post-war period when the political portents had initially seemed good. Dwindling fears of a post-war slump removed the sense of urgency: gradually policy debate shifted away from regionalism and planning towards the politically popular dismantling of government controls. One casualty was enthusiasm for the TVA, an example of Page's tendency to leave drawbacks to be pointed out by others. William McKell, Labor premier of New South Wales since 1941 and a decentralisation enthusiast, visited the TVA in 1945 and publicly pronounced it 'not generally adaptable to Australian conditions'. Far from being the strong sovereign body of legend, the TVA received considerable federal funding and its regional powers were limited essentially to planning and research.[110] Significantly for Page's post-war role, McKell's findings were quoted at

---

106 Earle Page, 'Why New States?', speech to All-Australian Federal Convention 25–26 July 1949, in F.A. Bland (ed.), *Changing the Constitution: Proceedings of the All-Australian Federal Convention, 25th and 26th July 1949*, The New South Wales Constitutional League, Sydney, 1950, p. 95.
107 Speech entitled 'Australian Power and Water Development', 1945, EPP, folder 1994 (part 1).
108 *Commonwealth Parliamentary Debates*, 19 June 1945, p. 3270.
109 Page, 'Why New States?', in Bland, *Changing the Constitution*, pp. 99, 103–4.
110 W.J. McKell, *The Tennessee Valley Authority (USA): Report by the Hon. W.J. McKell KC, MLA, December 1945*, Government Printer, Sydney, 1945, pp. 13–14.

length in the Department of Post-War Reconstruction's *Regional Planning in Australia*.[111] Coombs himself later admitted that wartime interest in community-led regionalisation eventually dwindled to a more prosaic emphasis on local administrative efficiency and the delivery of specific projects. Regional planning, he said, 'flew in the face of the logic of the developing world economic system'.[112]

Another post-war policy field in which Page similarly attempted to engage with a surge in interest but then encountered a resistant political environment was higher education. Post-war reconstruction saw Australia's first extensive public debates on the role of universities. Attitudes to tertiary education changed greatly during the 1940s as the Commonwealth began funding universities as a national investment. Commonwealth grants for universities dated from 1936, but it was Curtin who in 1943 signalled a major commitment to widening access to tertiary education by establishing the Universities Commission to supervise the Commonwealth Reconstruction Training Scheme for returned servicemen and women.

The wider – and lively – post-war debate on universities is a further instance of Page's views being so strongly tied to decentralisation and regionalism that they veered far from the mainstream. Australian universities had for the first time played a major practical public role by providing technical support for the war effort, such as in manufacturing gun sights and controlling malaria. (Page assumed a significant role in malaria control, partly through his appointments to the Advisory War Council. In April 1943 he led an investigative party to New Guinea and pondered using malaria as a weapon by maximising Japanese exposure to mosquitos. Page remained proud of his work on malaria, to which he devoted a chapter of his memoirs.[113]) Tension developed between casting universities as bastions of civilising knowledge, or whether they should be reoriented towards a vocational role that addressed the goals of post-war reconstruction, as encouraged by Coombs.[114] Page sought to influence this emerging debate by proposing a unique alternative to the expansion of existing metropolitan universities. He does not appear to have been drawn to the view, common today, that the main merit of rural universities was

---

111 Department of Post-War Reconstruction, *Regional Planning in Australia*, p. 17.
112 Coombs, *Trial Balance*, p. 65.
113 See Page, *Truant Surgeon*, Chapter 41.
114 Hannah Forsyth, *A History of the Modern Australian University*, NewSouth Publishing, Sydney, 2014, pp. 25, 39, 49.

the direct boosting of economic prospects in their immediate regions. Instead, he drew on his ideals of decentralisation and institutional scale to propose that universities serve as tools of social construction. This was a fine example of how widely he could apply his basic views to produce a coherent alternative to the mainstream of opinion.

Page set out his vision of higher education in his May 1945 contribution to the parliamentary debate on the Re-establishment and Employment Bill to support the education of returned servicemen and women. They should not be relegated 'to large universities or big technical colleges, where they are regarded more or less as ciphers or numbers instead of personalities, [which] may wreck their whole future individual life and their value to the nation'. They should instead be directed to small institutions such as the New England and Canberra University colleges, 'where much more personal and intimate contact is made with the teachers'. (Page recalled how during his medical studies he was one of only 19 students.) He joined calls for the Commonwealth to take a firmer lead on funding universities and other levels of education via a central controlling body.[115] An adjunct here was Page's interest in a proposed national university in Canberra. This should also be cast as a small residential institution, which could train diplomats and 'make certain that boys and girls shall be able to obtain a first-class knowledge of international affairs'.[116]

Page's perception of education as a means of social engineering implies a not inconsiderable faith in human malleability. No more effusive statement of this exists than the prescription for secondary schooling he presented to the June 1947 Macleay River Teachers' Association Educational Conference. To Page, 'a district high school is a wonderful instrument' to 'mould the lives of students, influence the destiny of districts and, thereby, control the fate of the nation'. His ideal school would have 'noble buildings and grounds of ample proportion'. Curricula must create the 'groundwork of understanding' via rural, technical and cultural strands. The school library should impart 'a love of books that will carry on to adult life'. All country

---

115 *Commonwealth Parliamentary Debates*, 16 May 1945, p. 1793. There is contemporary evidence that university size indeed had a bearing on undergraduate performance. In 1944 the Commonwealth Universities Commission released data indicating that despite lower entrance standards, undergraduates at New England University College were ahead of their Sydney University counterparts after only one year of study; see statement by the Advisory Council, New England University College, 17 January 1945, 'The Great Success of New England University College; Statistical Report From the Commonwealth Universities Commission', EPP, folder 1088 (part 1).
116 *Commonwealth Parliamentary Debates*, 21 September 1944, pp. 1209–10.

high schools should offer free accommodation to help 'build a community spirit and interest in the school and the industries of the district'. Young men and women would 'get to know one another in a way that is not possible at present'. Children from local towns would experience 'a year or two of practical life on the land'.[117] As he recorded in notes for another speech on education, 'I have thought of everything and everything fits in its place'.[118]

Support for Page's vision came mainly from that hotbed of decentralism, New England. In 1948 the warden of New England University College, J.P. Belshaw, wrote in favour of residential institutions that used the tutorial system and reached out to local regions. A.J. Greenhalgh of Armidale Teachers' College called for state-run boarding schools where rural students could overcome the population dispersal that otherwise rendered rural area schools impractical.[119] But more prominent in national debate were a series of 11 widely read booklets issued by the influential Australian Council for Educational Research over 1943 to 1946. These were collectively entitled *The Future of Education* and reflect how singular were Page's views on decentralised education. Authors included such city-based academic figures as John Medley, vice-chancellor of Melbourne University, the historian John La Nauze and Eric Ashby of Sydney University Botany Department, who would become a prolific author on higher education.[120] Despite touching on many fundamental educational issues, they only fleetingly addressed Page's agenda. Ashby's *Universities in Australia* was an articulate defence of the traditional concept of a university that just passingly referred to founding junior colleges in country towns to teach matriculation. He was lukewarm about the practicality of rural universities, and rejected residential universities outright.[121]

---

117 Speech by Page, 'Educational Needs of a Rural Community', to the Macleay River Teachers' Association Educational Conference, Kempsey, 18 June 1947, EPP, folder 2504.
118 See speech notes, EPP, folder 2620; undated, but content suggests being from this same 1940s period.
119 J.P. Belshaw, 'Decentralisation of university education', *Australian Quarterly*, vol. 20, no. 4, December 1948, pp. 67–76; A.J. Greenhalgh, 'The plight of rural education', *Australian Quarterly*, vol. 21, no. 3, September 1949, p. 76.
120 W.F. Connell, *The Australian Council for Educational Research 1930–80*, Australian Council for Educational Research, Hawthorn, Vic., 1980, pp. 143–7.
121 Eric Ashby, *Universities in Australia*, The Future of Education series no. 5, Australian Council for Educational Research, Melbourne, 1944, pp. 26–8.

Page would also have hoped for something much more effusive in the Rural Reconstruction Commission's coverage of education. The sixth report, on farming efficiency and costs, covered technical training in some detail; the seventh, on rural amenities, offered broad support for rural high schools but added that this should recognise the reality that many rural schoolchildren would eventually find themselves in towns or cities.[122] It was cautious about tertiary education beyond concluding that more than one university in each state was 'unrealistic', while conceding some scope for rural university colleges or 'specially advanced schools'.[123]

## Page again champions hydroelectricity: The Snowy versus the Clarence

In the latter half of the 1940s, Page's interaction with the Chifley Government narrowed to focus on hydroelectricity and the damming of the Clarence River. This drew out his vision of post-war reconstruction to the fullest, but also his frustration that the Clarence did not feature centrally in Commonwealth policy. It nonetheless became the post-war reconstruction issue on which he had the most influence on government. Page's success in keeping this project under Commonwealth consideration and, to a lesser extent, that of two states is a case study of his undaunted persistence and tactical flexibility. Without Page, the Clarence would almost certainly have faded entirely in the face of criticisms by engineers and rivalry from the more glamorous and promising Snowy proposal. Post-war reconstruction presented Page with his best ever chance of getting this treasured project up and running, aided by the Commonwealth's fear that it needed major public works projects on hand should the post-war economic boom falter.

Page foresaw early that post-war reconstruction could create an opportunity for the Clarence region. In October 1943 he convened a meeting of state and federal parliamentarians, including Drummond and Bruxner, at Parliament House, Sydney, to discuss northern electrification.[124] They were especially interested in having a new transmission line link

---

122  Rural Reconstruction Commission, *Sixth Report, Farming Efficiency and Costs*, The Commission, Canberra, 1945, pp. 45–70; and *Seventh Report, Rural Amenities*, The Commission, Canberra, 1945, p. 23.
123  Rural Reconstruction Commission, *Seventh Report*, p. 24.
124  See open letter to the press concerning this meeting, 21 October 1943, EPP, folder 2083.

Newcastle, the Nymboida and Brisbane, and in August 1944 McKell agreed to have the Railways Department's power station at Newcastle connected to the Nymboida facility by a 66,000-volt transmission line.[125] This marks Page's only major practical success in rural electrification other than the establishment of the Nymboida station in 1923.

Page had many obstacles to overcome before the Clarence River could be harnessed. Proposals to exploit the Snowy had a longer provenance, dating back to an irrigation proposal of 1884, and a Snowy River Hydroelectric Development League appeared in 1936.[126] Debate during the 1930s indicates that although Page's ideas about hydroelectricity had gained some acceptance in the Country Party, much of this was channelled into support for the Snowy. His parliamentary deputy Thomas Paterson told the November 1936 Snowy River Hydroelectric Scheme Conference that electricity was 'perhaps the most important factor in your civilisation', and attributed the success of the Nymboida to a flat rate 'for farm and factory alike'. But he spoke primarily of the Snowy, stressing its potential to encourage industrial development east of the Great Dividing Range (encompassing his electorate of Gippsland).[127] The Snowy also had a clear edge among professional engineers. Gibson wrote in his 1929 report on power development that the Clarence had the disadvantage of requiring the construction of large storage reservoirs.[128] The president of the Institution of Engineers reported that the Clarence and the Nymboida were estimated to be capable of generating only a tenth of the hydroelectric power available in the Australian Alps.[129] Most media reports from the 1930s and early 1940s on Australia's water resources failed even to mention the Clarence.[130]

---

125 McKell to Page, 8 August 1944, EPP, folder 2086.
126 *The Australian Encyclopedia*, second edition, Angus and Robertson, Sydney, 1958, volume 8, pp. 171–2. D.J. Hardman, 'The Snowy Mountains Hydro-Electric Authority: Origins and antecedents', *Public Administration*, vol. 27, no. 3, September 1968, pp. 205–36, provides a full outline of early proposals to harness the Snowy.
127 Speech to the 'Snowy River Hydro-electric Scheme Conference', Cooma, 27 November 1936, EPP, folder 2704.
128 Gibson, *Report on Power Development in Australia*, p. 23.
129 H.R. Harper, 'Presidential Address', *The Journal of the Institution of Engineers*, Australia, vol. 6, no. 2, February 1934.
130 Such as Lewis R. East, 'Water conservation in Australia', *Walkabout*, vol. 2, no. 11, November 1936, pp. 33–8.

Today, the Snowy Mountains Scheme is commonly presented as the prime contrast between post-war nation-building and a latter-day absence of national foresight. Page became very aware of a growing possibility that this project would leave no room for the Clarence, and fought accordingly. Although he initially hesitated to directly criticise the Snowy – it was still a regional hydroelectric initiative, after all – what support he proffered was highly qualified, especially as he doubted its breadth of regional and national vision. He asserted that the Clarence could provide a starting point for a national grid by linking Sydney, Newcastle and Brisbane. It would be focused on power generation, whereas there was disagreement over the fundamental focus of the Snowy Mountains Scheme. This division was driven by state rivalries – New South Wales favoured irrigation, Victoria hydroelectricity – and delayed the Snowy's commencement.[131] Page's 1949 speech on the legislation to finally implement the Snowy is a statement of his hopes that it would be the starting point for a nationwide power scheme and that the Clarence would not be forgotten, using 'some standardised form of governmental machinery, of a type that could be used for general application throughout Australia'. This would be 'a separate authority for each scheme, but ... so closely interlocked that they will be able to pool men, machinery and equipment'.[132] In 1958, by which time the Snowy was well advanced, Page reminded the House that the project 'will lose its true significance if the water and power is not used to achieve that decentralised development in adjoining districts which is vital to the survival of the Australian nation'.[133]

Page's post-war vision of hydroelectricity came to incorporate three main strategies – local oversight by powerful regional authorities, national planning, and using The Gorge project on the Clarence as the starting point for a nationwide network of hydroelectric dams. This national synthesis readily distinguished him from innumerable other boosters of local projects. He spoke of how better land use via the utilisation of water and electricity could support a national population of 20 million, leading to the 'stabilisation of the land industries on a reproductive basis'. A unified national electricity grid would also have a fundamental social

---

131 Statement 'Australian Power Development – The Importance of the Clarence River Gorge Hydro-Electric Scheme', undated but clearly from this period, EPP, folder 2047. On state differences over the Snowy, see Hardman, 'The Snowy Mountains Hydro-Electric Authority', especially pp. 214–24.
132 *Commonwealth Parliamentary Debates*, 22 June 1949, p. 1353.
133 EPP, folder 2333. The Hansard record of this speech is somewhat different; see *Commonwealth Parliamentary Debates*, 13 May 1958, pp. 1742–5.

value, by 'giving the whole of the north of New South Wales and southern Queensland and, in time, the whole of Australia, a high common factor of mutual interest that must bind us together and help us all to appreciate, understand and sympathise with each other's local problems'.[134] Page again tied such ideas to the wider imperatives of the times by exploiting fears of war and famine, observing that development of the Clarence under a regional authority 'would aid that essential factor to permanent world peace – good food, and plenty of it'.[135] Since his time in London, Page had frequently dwelt on how food security could contribute to international stability, linking this to guaranteed prices for producers and surveys of nutritional needs. Such ideas had wide support, including from two figures well known to Page, Stanley Bruce and the Australian trade adviser in London, F.L. McDougall.

On local oversight, Page foresaw that development of the Clarence 'should be undertaken by a governmental partnership consisting of the Commonwealth, New South Wales and Queensland Governments, combined with a regional authority'.[136] As the Australian federal system had a 'blind spot' where no clear state or federal powers applied, a Clarence Valley Authority was needed, 'on all fours with the Tennessee authority'. Australia should emulate American initiative to 'annihilate the distances of space and time, and to bring the amenities of modern civilisation to the most remotely situated peoples in our land'.[137] Page complemented his appeals to governments with public proselytising, an increasingly common practice of his during this politically challenged phase of his career. He detailed this vision of a regionally managed Clarence in his short but lavish 1944 book *Clarence River Hydro-Electric Gorge Scheme*, replete with diagrams, photographs and maps. (A map from this booklet showing Page's proposed dam network is provided in Chapter 1, Figure 4.) Page personally arranged its production and the distribution of scores of copies to ministers, government agencies, private companies, Australian embassies, libraries and Curtin himself.[138]

---

134 'Dr. Earle Page's Prescription for National Health and Development', EPP, folder 2295.
135 Page, *Clarence River Hydro-Electric Gorge Scheme*, introduction and p. 1.
136 Ibid., quotes from introduction.
137 Broadcast by Page on 2NR (the ABC's Grafton station), 17 December 1944, text at EPP, folder 1077.
138 See for example Page to Curtin, 24 August 1944, NAA, A461, AK423/1/1.

**Figure 11: Cover of Page's 1944 booklet, *Clarence River Hydro-Electric Gorge Scheme*.**
Source: Courtesy of the Page family.

On national planning, Page in 1944 foresaw a future Australia with a more densely settled countryside that required 'a well-organised agricultural industry' supported by electricity, ample water and 'a guaranteed payable price for their products'. This necessitated guidance by planning authorities – his proposed federal power commission, federal water commission and ministry of food – but with electricity providing the catalyst. Implementation of this planning-based strategy was to be carried out through an array of TVA-style regional authorities with full executive powers.[139] The new national grid would encompass both hydro and thermal sources in exploiting 'hitherto neglected, isolated power possibilities'.[140]

Page's vision for an Australia-wide network of hydroelectric dams was set out in separate but essentially consistent statements over the next few years. The harnessing of the Nymboida back in 1923 had just been a stage one for the Clarence region, 'to make the surrounding district electricity conscious'. The second stage would be a 220-foot dam at The Gorge that could generate 'over 42,000 kilowatts continuously'. To enable this, 'an agreement for Clarence development with such wide regional and inter-state implications should be made between the Commonwealth, state and local governing authorities', using 'the pattern of the Migration Agreement between Australia and Britain'.[141] Damming the Clarence could be followed by a 'nationwide drive' to develop the continent, starting with the deployment of army surveyors to assess regional water resources before constructing new dams and hydroelectric stations tied to a national grid. All along the east coast, new railways would link inland power centres to deep water ports, including one at the mouth of the Clarence.[142] The spread of Page's Clarence model was to be funded by profits from the sale of electricity generated by each new dam, helped by a federal levy to fund grants that covered 50 per cent of the construction costs of expanding rural transmission.[143]

But persuading governments and experts posed a challenge for Page. In 1944–45 he had good grounds for hope, as the Commonwealth was beginning to cast around for public works projects to counteract the anticipated post-war slump. He had no hesitation in approaching the highest levels of government, including the prime minister. Curtin in March 1944 replied to Page noncommittally that the Clarence proposal was subject to prioritisation by the National Works Council and required state government support.[144] In December, Page switched his attention to

---

139 Page speech 'Australian Power and Water Development', 16 June 1945, EPP, folder 1205.
140 Page, *Clarence River Hydro-Electric Gorge Scheme*, p. 1.
141 Public address by Page at Lismore, 6 June 1947, EPP, folder 874.
142 'Dr. Earle Page's Prescription for National Health & Development', EPP, folder 2295.
143 Press release 'Full Development of the North Coast Rivers', August 1946, EPP, folder 1724.
144 Curtin to Page, 15 March 1944; also 'Collings' to Page on behalf of the Prime Minister, 11 July 1944, both EPP, folder 2086. (Probably Senator Joseph Collings, Minister for the Interior.)

Chifley as minister for post-war reconstruction, suggesting a joint expert study of the Clarence by the Commonwealth and state governments.[145] Harry Brown, Commonwealth coordinator-general of works, was so keen that his main concern was that a technical study led by the states could delay 'vitally urgent post-war public works programs': perhaps the Commonwealth could instil momentum by offering to act as an impartial chair for the study.[146] Following Page's approaches, Chifley wrote to the acting premiers of New South Wales and Queensland in May 1945 proposing a joint study by the three governments. He mentioned Page's support and described the project as possibly 'one of the most important in Australia', relevant to the regional planning then being discussed with premiers.[147] Page simultaneously pursued the engineering profession. In a rather technical speech to the Institution of Engineers, he predicted that the problem of limited local demand of only about 20–25,000 kWh would be overcome by linking the Clarence to a national grid, under which it would sell 50,000 kWh to Brisbane 'at less than half a penny a unit'.[148]

The federal system in practice proved a drag on Page's national developmentalism. Significantly for the Clarence's prospects, he attracted more interest from Queensland, which stood to benefit most from the electricity generated, than from the river's host state of New South Wales. The chairman of the Queensland State Electricity Commission, S.F. Cochran, told Coombs in early 1945 that his state was 'most interested'.[149] But the states responded to Chifley by rejecting Commonwealth involvement and making a half-hearted commitment to conduct a short joint study of their own.[150] This study in December 1945 merely concluded that a fuller technical assessment was needed. The New South Wales–led inquiry that followed – the Clarence River Water Resources Investigation Committee, commonly called the Technical Committee – dragged on into 1951 as one of no less than seven expert post-war studies

---

145 Page to Chifley, 2 December 1944, NAA, A9816, 1944/487 PART 1; see also Coombs to Harry Brown, Co-ordinator-General of Works, 19 January 1945, NAA, A9816, 1944/487 PART 1.
146 Harry Brown to Coombs, 9 April 1945, NAA, A9816, 1944/487 PART 1; see also Coombs to Chifley, 12 April 1945, NAA, A9816, 1944/487 PART 1.
147 The acting premiers were J.M. Baddeley of New South Wales and E.M. Hanlon of Queensland; Chifley letters of 18 May 1945, EPP, folder 1702.
148 Page speech to The Institution of Engineers, Australia, April 1944, EPP, folder 2090 (day not given).
149 Letter to Coombs, 8 January 1945, NAA, A9816, 1944/487 PART 1.
150 See for example letters to Chifley from acting Premier Baddeley of 12 June 1945 and from Premier McKell of 20 November 1946 to Chifley, NAA, A461, AK423/1/1.

of the Clarence Valley in general or The Gorge in particular. Each was properly cautious about consumer demand for a project of such scale: none provided the decisive endorsement Page sought.

Yet it is also clear that Page's efforts were keeping the Clarence at the forefront of high-level official attention, albeit amid persistent doubts. In May 1946 Chifley's successor as minister for post-war reconstruction, John Dedman, wrote to Page stating bluntly that a TVA-style authority was 'undesirable' but adding that the Commonwealth remained interested in the Clarence.[151] Dedman did not elaborate, but opposition from McKell would alone have rendered the TVA concept impractical. The paradox now facing Page was that the unexpected persistence of the post-war boom was working against big new projects. Far from unemployment being a problem, there were shortages of labour and materials. A year later the Commonwealth's Controller of Electricity Supply, H.P. Moss, advised the head of the Department of Munitions, John Jensen, that the Clarence proposal was still of interest but should be delayed until there was a need to alleviate unemployment or to cope with coal shortages.[152] When 'the feared unemployment following close on the transition did not eventuate', Commonwealth interest in public works–based developmentalism dwindled, especially that which involved large, longer range projects.[153]

Nor would Page have liked the Rural Reconstruction Commission's mixed findings on electrification. In its first report it had found that to help raise country living standards 'it should be a national objective to give every farm which is not too remote an opportunity to use electricity at a cost which is comparable with that which prevails in the cities'.[154] But in its seventh report, the commission directly challenged assumptions that hydroelectricity would be cheaper than thermal generation. It rejected uniform electricity tariffs as inequitable and likely to retard national electrification. The commission also now more clearly advised against the extension of electricity to all farms, some of which were simply too isolated.[155] In its eighth report, it found that in a continent as dry as Australia, human and animal consumption should have first claim on

---

151 Dedman to Page, 23 May 1946 (writing on behalf of the Prime Minister), EPP, folder 2090.
152 T. Murdoch on behalf of the Controller, Electricity Supply, to Secretary, Ministry of Munitions, 28 May 1947, NAA, MP61/1, 2/3/422.
153 Coombs, *Trial Balance*, pp. 66–7.
154 Rural Reconstruction Commission, *First Report, A General Rural Survey*, The Commission, Canberra, 1944, p. 46.
155 Rural Reconstruction Commission, *Seventh Report*, pp. 67, 73.

water use, followed by irrigation and only thirdly hydroelectricity. As for the Clarence, the commission paid far more attention to the Snowy and Ord rivers.[156]

So disappointed was Page with the Rural Reconstruction Commission's fleeting coverage of northern rivers that early in 1947 he invited the editors of 18 newspapers to join him on a grand tour of east coast rivers from the Brisbane to the Hunter.[157] As they set off, Page assured the seven who accepted that 'with your help, I am confident that wide public interest can be aroused in the vast scope of development which is possible in this richly endowed coastal area'.[158] Four hailed from local newspapers in Page's native northern New South Wales; only three joined from publications in other regions, the *Courier-Mail* and *Telegraph* from Brisbane, and the *Newcastle Herald*.

As enthusiastic as ever, Page led his little band up and down the coast. His Grafton *Daily Examiner* reported delegation members having 'rowed, rode, slithered and slashed their way up to the seat of the proposed dam and hydroelectric station'.[159] Social goals were still at the forefront: Page told the seven that 'it would be impossible to keep the people of the country in the country unless they had the amenities offering in the cities, and this has been shown by the Nymboida'.[160] One editor afterwards politely complained to Page about 'the sustained pressure of our tour'.[161] The Queensland press gave Page good publicity with such headlines as 'Surveys Prove Value of Scheme'. But even the sympathetic Brisbane *Telegraph* concluded that along the coastal belt from Newcastle to the Queensland border 'no market exists there for anywhere near 300,000 kilowatts of electricity, the planned output of the completed Gorge scheme', making Queensland's involvement crucial.[162]

Page remained so hopeful that he produced yet another booklet, *Clarence Water-Power Development*, its cover graced with a specially commissioned stylised map of proposed dam sites. This detailed his plan for a 220-foot dam at The Gorge, to be followed by the construction of supplementary

---

156  Rural Reconstruction Commission, *Eighth Report, Irrigation, Water Conservation and Land Drainage*, The Commission, Canberra, 1945, pp. 24, 58–70.
157  Page letters of 22 November 1946, EPP, folder 2105.
158  Page in the *Daily Examiner*, 31 January 1947, p. 3.
159  *Daily Examiner*, 4 February 1947, p. 2.
160  *Macleay Argus*, 14 February 1947, p. 3.
161  Lyne Young of the Lismore *Northern Star* to Page, 25 February 1947, EPP, folder 2106.
162  *Brisbane Telegraph*, 14 February 1947, p. 2 (headline and quote).

storages so that the whole Clarence system generated at least '125,000 kilowatts continuously' and irrigated 100,000 acres. As so often before, Page thought he had chosen his timing well: 'at this psychological moment, which might never recur, an early decision could launch this outstanding development on a most auspicious and sound basis'.[163]

As official interest shifted towards the Snowy, Page demonstrated his tactical flexibility by returning to the level of government and place where he had the most influence. Over 1948–49, he sought to reorganise local councils in the Clarence Valley into regional authorities based on the TVA model. He exhorted them to join forces so 'a united North could have a definite voice in the extent and manner of that [Gorge dam] development and the disposal and the distribution of the product'. Page proclaimed himself especially well qualified to lead this effort, as he had been personally responsible for both 'the inauguration of the Clarence County Council Scheme' and 'developing the Nymboida Power Station'. If the Commonwealth, New South Wales and Queensland governments were not interested, then they should leave the way open for private investors.[164] During 1949, Page succeeded in having councils form a 'Federation of all Electrical Supply and Distribution Bodies of the North Coast and Tablelands'.[165] 'A combined organisation, fully representative of the north', he said, could prevent the Commonwealth from using defence powers to bypass local government, as it had with the Snowy.[166] Yet lack of local government unity was impeding progress: councils failed to grasp that investment ought to be 'well ahead of immediate consumption demand' and that 'the economics of water power development schemes tend to improve with larger schemes'.[167]

Page continued his efforts at the national level. In 1949, he began openly criticising the Snowy, predicting that its steep slopes would cause such complications that the Clarence or even the Burdekin would be quicker to start generating power.[168] Page also continued to harry the

---

163 Earle Page, *Clarence Water-Power Development*, *The Bulletin Newspaper*, Sydney, 1947, pp. 3, 23.
164 Page to 'Council Clerk' (evidently an identical letter to all relevant councils), 14 July 1948, EPP, folder 2099.
165 'Northern Rivers Association of Municipalities & Shires Minutes of Conference Held at Lismore on Friday the 22nd April 1949, to Discuss and Consider Means of Expediting Completion of Survey, Investigation and Design of Proposed Clarence Gorge Hydro-Electric Scheme', EPP, folder 2099.
166 'Statement by Sir Earle Page at Conference of North Coast Local Governing Bodies Held at Lismore 22nd April 1949', EPP, folder 2102.
167 Statement by Page, 24 April 1949, EPP, folder 2083.
168 Statement by Page, 1 July 1949, reported in the Canberra Letter of The Associated Chambers of Manufacturers of Australia, EPP, folder 401.

Department of Post-War Reconstruction to the point that its director of regional development proposed formally asking him to desist from public statements suggesting the Commonwealth was an active participant in the Technical Committee.[169] The director-general of the department, now Allen Brown, commented that New South Wales 'has never appeared to be over-enthusiastic about pressing on with the investigations', especially as much of the project's benefit would go to Queensland. Another member of the department concluded that there was an assured market only for 50,000 kW for Queensland and about 5,000–10,000 kW for northern New South Wales, well short of Page's claimed 125,000 kW.[170] The president of the Institution of Engineers assailed misconceptions about the TVA and the availability of water in Australia as the ideas of 'ill-informed visionaries'.[171]

Amid this widespread scepticism and state government indifference, the fact that the Chifley Government never decisively rejected The Gorge proposal constitutes a success of sorts for Page. The prime minister continued to correspond with him well into 1949, reminding Page that state government support was essential and also asking New South Wales about the progress of the Technical Committee.[172] As late as July 1949 the director-general of Post-War Reconstruction wrote to his counterpart at Works and Housing recounting how earlier Commonwealth interest in the Clarence had been dampened by preference for the Snowy and 'the usual Treasury influence'. He suggested it be revived, partly as it might produce far more power than even Page thought and as water power was 'so limited in Australia we should be concerned to see that the maximum use is made of it'.[173] This led to a one-week field study in August 1949 by a Works and Housing engineer who, despite having been accompanied by Page throughout, produced another inconclusive report duly noting the Clarence's 'very large power potential' and calling for further investigation.[174]

---

169  C.R. Lambert, minute of 6 May 1949, NAA, A9816, 1944/487 PART 1. On Commonwealth inquiries with NSW, see for example Premier McGirr to Chifley, 24 November 1949, NAA, A9816, 1944/487 PART 2.
170  A.S. Brown, minute 'Clarence River Gorge Hydro-Electric Scheme', 3 June 1949, NAA, A461, AK423/1/1; T. Langford-Smith, 26 May 1949, NAA, A461, AK423/1/1.
171  William Nimmo in *The Journal of the Institution of Engineers, Australia*, no. 3, 1949, p. 29, copy in EPP, folder 1758.
172  Chifley to Page, 24 June 1949 and 18 July 1949, EPP, folder 2087.
173  A.S. Brown to L.F. Loder, 1 July 1949, NAA, A9816, 1944/487 PART 2.
174  Report by E.F. Rowntree, finalised October 1949, copy at EPP, folder 1077.

Page's doggedness in promoting the Clarence reflects the difficulties he faced in a policy climate that favoured so many precepts he had long nurtured but in political circumstances, which stood in the way of the major role he craved. He was pushed out to the margins by the irresistible pressures of party politics, a changed policy-making culture, and a growing isolation from colleagues in conservative politics that had been discernible in the 1930s and became more obvious post-war. Yet he remained the most outspoken non-Labor advocate of the possibilities of post-war reconstruction and of the spatial and rural-orientated perspectives he had long added to so many issues. His lobbying for causes by whatever means came to hand – via state governments, the press, intellectual policy groups and directly to federal ministers – gave him a continued major public and political profile. Although unable directly to determine policy, his tireless efforts to guide post-war reconstruction's engagement with federalism, regionalism, education and particularly hydroelectricity marked his distinctiveness and could at times still induce governments to respond to such sheer persistence. At the end of the 1940s, and of the life of the federal Labor Government, Page remained undeterred and looked forward to the advent of a new conservative regime as a chance to restore his own fortunes and advance those of his country.

# 8

# PAGE INDEFATIGABLE
## His Last Years in Public Life

When Page was appointed minister for health in the second Menzies Government, he saw himself as also becoming its leading advocate of developmentalism. In practice, he struggled to exert influence in a political environment that continued to evolve in ways he found uncongenial. Signs of the difficulties he would face were evident well before the government's election in December 1949. The alliance between the Country Party and the new Liberal Party was unlike coalitions Page had previously experienced, and a highly charged political contest between public sector–led development and private enterprise left less space for his brand of ambitious developmentalism.

Relations between the two conservative parties had reached a low point during the 1943 federal election campaign when Menzies, then a prominent backbencher, disowned part of the joint Opposition policy speech delivered by Fadden as Opposition leader. But the following year, after resuming the leadership of the UAP, Menzies invited the Country Party to attend the talks that led to the formation of the Liberal Party, raising the possibility of merger. Richard Casey as president of the Liberal Party over 1947–49 had doubts about amalgamation. The issue was further complicated by proposals of varying degrees of goodwill put forth at the state level, especially in New South Wales.[1] A merger did not eventuate, but collaboration between the two parties grew as each saw the other as an increasingly likely coalition partner.

---

1  Ellis, *A History of the Australian Country Party*, p. 275; Ian Hancock, *National and Permanent?: The Federal Organisation of the Liberal Party of Australia 1944–1965*, Melbourne University Press, Carlton South, Vic., 2000, pp. 76–80.

Page intervened early and strongly when the Country Party resumed its internal debate on coalition, a clear sign that he aspired to again play a major role in government. As Australian Country Party Association chair he assured his Liberal counterpart, T.M. Ritchie, in January 1946 that the Country Party would collaborate in 'securing the maximum goodwill between the parties', especially by managing how they contested seats.[2] The parties cooperated informally at the September 1946 federal election but their respective leaders still delivered separate policy speeches, with the result that Fadden was seen to be outbidding the Liberals on tax cuts. Resumption of a coalition became an even higher priority after the unexpectedly severe loss at this election, leading the two parties to form a joint Opposition executive to guide policy and tactics.

Page had temporary success during this immediate post-war period in injecting ideas into the federal Country Party's policy commitments. Fadden's 1946 policy speech included some ambitious developmentalist concepts that Page had long advocated – a national development and defence council, set prices for primary products, a flat national electricity rate and an invitation to the chair of the TVA to visit to advise on the Clarence, the Snowy, the Murray Valley and even the Bradfield Plan to irrigate the continent's interior.[3] These promises were made from the freedom of Opposition: their expansiveness is suggestive of a rhetorical riposte to the Chifley Government's avowed nation-building agenda.

Nor did they last. By 1948 Page felt compelled to produce his own press release on 'The Need of a Strong, Vigorous and Numerous Country Party' in an attempt to reaffirm the party's commitment to decentralisation.[4] Country Party–Liberal relations continued to improve over 1948–49, despite lingering discord at state level over competition for Lower House seats.[5] At a January 1949 meeting to plan for the forthcoming election, the federal Country Party proposed an electoral pact with the Liberals and offered to confer on policy.[6] Page was heartened by the likely revival of a coalition but also faced a continuing shift in public opinion against government-led planning, not a good sign for this inveterate planner.

---

2   Ellis, *A History of the Australian Country Party*, p. 266.
3   The text of this speech of 3 September 1946 is at EPP, folder 2618. The TVA chair, David Lilienthal, appears not to have visited Australia.
4   'The Need of a Strong, Vigorous and Numerous Country Party', EPP, folder 1994 (part 1). Undated, but data used suggests 1948 or 1949.
5   Hancock, *National and Permanent?*, pp. 101–5.
6   Ellis, *A History of the Australian Country Party*, p. 271.

The public increasingly wanted to be rid of irksome wartime controls and the Cold War context added unsavoury connotations to government intervention. 'The word "plan" was a dirty word then', recalled political journalist Frank Chamberlain.[7] The May 1948 referendum on Commonwealth control of rents and prices, conducted in the shadow of the Chifley Government's attempts to nationalise the private banks, was heavily defeated. Debate on the role of the state helped give the new Liberal Party a strong platform based on a commitment to individualism and private enterprise, but tempered by its qualified acceptance of a place for government in economic management and social welfare. The federal Country Party broadly agreed: at the January 1949 meeting with the Liberals it declared that 'to defeat communism, to preserve freedom in Australia and the driving force of individual initiative, it is most important to remove the Chifley socialistic government from power'.[8]

Improving relations between the Liberals and the Country Party imposed disciplines that left less space for Page's vision. For the December 1949 election, Menzies and Fadden affirmed a renewed coalition by delivering a combined Opposition policy speech. Their 'joint policy' proposed banning the Communist Party, combating industrial unrest, a national health scheme, stabilisation programs for the wheat and dairy industries, and the raising of loans to be managed by what became the Department of National Development.[9] In his own campaign speeches Fadden now gave priority to conventional causes of country roads, stabilisation of rural industries and an end to rationing – not planning or overtures to the TVA. He was especially vocal on petrol rationing, which the government had reintroduced to help conserve the sterling bloc's pool of US dollars – 'empty out the Chifley socialists and fill the bowsers'.[10]

Page did not play a major national role in the 1949 campaign. His main contributions were attacks on the Chifley Government's plans for comprehensive medical and pharmaceutical benefits schemes. A High Court decision striking down compulsory clauses in its legislation on pharmaceutical benefits opened the way, said Page, for a 'sane approach' based on the willing cooperation of health service providers.[11] Chifley

---

7   Frank Chamberlain, interview by Mel Pratt, 4 August 1972 and 19 January 1973, Mel Pratt Collection, NLA, TRC 121/39, FC:1:2/3.
8   Ellis, *A History of the Australian Country Party*, p. 271.
9   Ibid., pp. 271–2.
10  Macintyre, *Australia's Boldest Experiment*, p. 435; quote from Arklay, *Arthur Fadden*, p. 136.
11  *Sydney Morning Herald*, 8 October 1949, p. 1.

attributed his unexpectedly severe loss in the election – the ALP won just 47 seats in an enlarged 121-member House of Representatives – to public resentment of petrol rationing and bank nationalisation. Page's primary vote in Cowper reached its post-war peak of nearly 62 per cent.

The eternally optimistic Page welcomed the demise of the Chifley Government not merely as a party political triumph. After the baffling frustrations of post-war reconstruction under Chifley, Dedman and Coombs, he was again a Commonwealth minister in a government with a stated commitment to developmentalism. One of its first significant acts was to create a new portfolio of National Development, with Page's old friend Casey as minister. He even saw the election as offering hope at last for The Gorge project.[12] In practice, Page was only a nominal insider in the new government and over the next six years failed to spark a resurgence of his style of developmentalism. The government did engage with issues dear to Page, notably planning, power generation and higher education. But his nation-changing goals of decentralisation, regionalism and hydroelectricity diverged too far from the government's more immediate objectives for him to greatly influence its policy mainstream.

The 1949 election was also challenging for Page by marking a major generational change in parliamentary membership. It is widely appreciated that this was so for the Liberal Party, with the average age of its 38 first-timers in the House of Representatives (out of a total of 55 Liberal MPs) being a comparatively youthful 43. Most were imbued with a sense of having been elected at a pivotal time to oppose socialism. Less widely known is that there was also an influx of new Country Party MPs. Of the party's 19 members in the House, eight were entirely new to parliament.[13] Page, approaching 70 years of age when the election was held, was the only survivor from the Bruce–Page days; no doubt he took solace from David Drummond's transfer from the New South Wales Parliament to become the new federal member for New England. Page's views on Australian development were to diverge more than ever from all but a few of his party colleagues.

---

12   See for example his articles in the *Daily Examiner* of 29 October 1949, p. 9.
13   Ellis, *A History of the Australian Country Party*, pp. 281–2.

## Page returns to government: Triumph in the health portfolio but planning falters

Robert Menzies did not incur lasting damage from Page's 1939 attack. His return to government 10 years later was at the head of a revitalised new party with a clearer philosophy and stronger national organisation than its UAP predecessor. Menzies accepted an important role for government in both economy and society, provided this 'seemed to us to be the best answer to a practical problem'. The new prime minister upheld the Snowy Scheme, social welfare, increased public funding of universities and the policy-advising role of the public service. But this was within a wider context in which, as he reflected towards the end of his reign, his government's 'first impulse' was 'always to seek the private enterprise answer, to help the individual to help himself, to create a climate, economic, social, industrial, favourable to his activity and growth'.[14]

Helping consolidate this was a significant intellectual and governmental shift during the early 1950s from the social-democratic Keynesianism of the Chifley era to a more technocratic Keynesianism. Under the latter, 'maintaining continuous economic growth became the new goal of economic management, which was redefined as a matter for bureaucratic administration based on economic "science" rather than political contest'. Unexpectedly strong private sector demand had stabilised the economy at full employment, and so 'the idea of planning, of setting social goals and directing the economy accordingly, had given way to the lessor aims of management'.[15] John Crawford, now secretary of the Commonwealth Department of Commerce and Agriculture, encapsulated this major shift in a 1952 public lecture on agricultural policy. Crawford, who also chaired the Standing Committee of the Australian Agricultural Council and had the increasingly influential John McEwen as his minister, began by explaining that he would 'not be concerned to examine in any detail the relation between agricultural policy objectives and programmes and wider objectives of economic and social policy for the economy as a whole'. Instead, 'the 1952 policy is really one which makes enhanced agricultural production a matter of urgency because it is a principal means to the

---

14  Menzies speaking to the Liberal Party Federal Council, 6 April 1964, quoted in Walter, *What Were They Thinking?*, p. 207.
15  Paul Smyth, *Australian Social Policy: The Keynesian Chapter*, UNSW Press, Sydney, 1994, pp. 4, 127.

wider ends of national interest'.[16] Page found during this decade that such narrowing of perspective worked against preparedness to indulge his developmentalist vision of the nation.

The political dominance of Menzies from 1949 was alone sufficient to constrict Page's influence beyond his portfolio. Menzies's markedly improved relations with the Country Party did not fully encompass his new minister for health. Page was not, for example, part of a March 1952 meeting of senior ministers with the visiting president of the World Bank, Eugene Black, despite discussion of matters as vital to him as water and electrification.[17] His fraught relationships with Menzies and Fadden were not aided by a practice of peppering both with missives proposing new initiatives, only some of which concerned health policy. Menzies typically responded with icy formality.[18] Page had mentored the young Fadden in the 1930s, but did not remain close to him personally or politically.

Fadden, habitually a hearty friend to all, as Treasurer took little interest in Page's vision and schemes. He referred some of Page's correspondence to his departmental secretary Roland Wilson, who was dismissive of Page's hope of attracting private investment to infrastructure projects. Page's model for this involved granting a private corporation a franchise or charter to construct a dam at its own expense, after which it would reap revenues for a set period before the facility would 'become the property of the Authority giving the charter, debt free and fully functioning'.[19] Page's public pronouncements on this elicited a livid telegram from Fadden in August 1956 – it was strictly a matter for the states, said the treasurer.[20] Page was not deterred. Nor would relations have been improved by a *Daily Telegraph* editorial of the following year contrasting the 'elder statesman' Page with 'sit-on-your-hands' Fadden.[21] Page was trying to operate in political circumstances that relied more on cautious but assertive public

---

16   Crawford, *Australian Agricultural Policy*, p. 8.
17   See record of meeting of 12 March 1952, EPP, folder 2508.
18   Such as a 1951 letter from Menzies to Page rejecting a proposal to implement the new medical benefits scheme at once as 'half-cocked'; see EPP, folder 2366.
19   See for example Page to Fadden and Menzies, 3 November 1955, EPP, folder 1750 (part 1); on Page's private investment ideas, see 'Local Government Enquiry Commencing at Grafton on 10 September 1956, on Proposed Redivision of Local Government Boundaries – Evidence of Sir Earle Page, MP', EPP, folder 1798.
20   Fadden to Page, telegram, 1 August 1956, EPP, folder 2049.
21   *Daily Telegraph*, 31 July 1956.

service advisers than the rural activists and visionary industrialists with whom he empathised. Unintentionally, he became a contrarian in the government.

Economic policy in the 1950s had only a coincidental focus on elements of Page's agenda. Page nominally conformed to most precepts of the Menzies Government, and drew on these opportunistically to provide new arguments for old ideas. He used the language of the Cold War warrior in linking the 'the growing, sinister and secret influence of Communism' to the growth of cities.[22] Economic policy early in these Menzies years was dominated by short-term goals, first by carrying out the promise to scale back government regulation and then by managing the inflation associated with the Korean War wool boom via the 'Horror Budget' of 1951–52. A 1953 Cabinet submission on Queensland proposals to develop the Burdekin River and Tully Falls showed no trace of Page's electrophilia; it recommended Commonwealth support for their irrigation components but declared their hydroelectric elements uneconomic.[23]

Ellis's summary of what most exercised the wider Country Party in these years emphasises such issues as the appreciation of the pound, fiscal policy, responses to the wool boom, and tax averaging for primary producers prone to fluctuating incomes.[24] State governments gave priority to managing the pressures that urban growth imposed on education, transport and other services. Page's determination to improve rural living standards did not extend to applauding the consumerism that had burst forth from the pent-up demand of the war years, manifested in new household products and climbing rates of car and home ownership. Generally stable economic growth of over 4 per cent per annum during the 1950s made developmentalism, Page-style, seem less urgent. Menzies's chapter on development policy in his second volume of memoirs, prosaically entitled 'Stability, Capital and Development', limits itself to the wool boom, overseas investment and new mining ventures in the continent's far north-west.[25]

---

22 'The Need of a Strong, Vigorous and Numerous Country Party', EPP, folder 1994 (part 1).
23 See EPP, folder 2509.
24 Ellis, *A History of the Australian Country Party*, pp. 285–91.
25 Robert Menzies, *The Measure of the Years*, Cassell, London, 1970, pp. 98–108.

**Figure 12: The new Menzies Ministry 1949.**
Earle Page as minister for health is standing immediately behind Governor-General William McKell, former premier of New South Wales and TVA sceptic. Richard Casey is standing third from left, Enid Lyons sixth from left and John McEwen second from the right. Arthur Fadden is seated in the front row to the immediate right of McKell.
Source: Courtesy of National Archives of Australia (NAA, M4297, 10).

Page in this second Menzies Government is today best known for his role as health minister in creating Australia's first national public health benefits scheme. His return to this portfolio, which he previously held in 1937–38, elicited little public surprise: the *Sydney Morning Herald* editorialised that his 'personal claims to the portfolio can hardly be contested'.[26] The offer of Health to Page suggests that Menzies judged that his personal standing in the medical fraternity and tenacity in negotiation would be valuable in developing a scheme acceptable to the British Medical Association (Australia) (BMA), the profession's peak body. When Page assumed the Health portfolio, the public funding of medical services already had a long history as an unresolved issue. It had, for example, been unsuccessfully brought to the attention of two royal commissions during the Bruce–Page Government, that of 1925–27 on National Insurance and the 1925–26 Royal Commission on Health.

---

26   *Sydney Morning Herald*, 19 December 1949, p. 2.

Over 1944–49, the Curtin and Chifley governments pursued a comprehensive non-contributory scheme inspired by Britain's National Health Service that would have imposed a high degree of public control over health services. Efforts to negotiate an agreement with the BMA foundered over doctors' insistence on freedom to set their own fees. Menzies gave Page, himself a BMA member with a long personal history of resisting salaried medicine, a free hand in negotiations. Political contemporaries soon found that the new health minister was still a capable political operator. Paul Hasluck, a fellow minister, recalled him as a 'benign and shrewd old fox'.[27] Page seized the opportunity with typical alacrity in what Ellis, who Page engaged to publicise the proposed new scheme, later wrote of admiringly as 'a series of *coups d'état*'.[28]

According to Ellis, other ministers 'frankly confessed their inability to grasp the gist of Page's initial explanations', Treasury officials 'were puzzled and hostile by turn', and the Health Department 'saw obstacles as high as the Himalayas where Page saw only pimples'.[29] On his very first day as minister, Page sent telegrammed overtures to the BMA, the Pharmaceutical Guild and the friendly societies, calling them to a national conference the next month. He produced a Cabinet submission as early as 9 January 1950 proposing a program that would 'help those who helped themselves', 'strengthen the working of existing, voluntary insurance organisations' and 'provide a real nursery for democracy'.[30] The long gestation that followed was considerably more discordant and full of compromise than Page's account in his memoirs suggests.

The immediate political problem Page faced was that the government did not control the Senate, posing a potential barrier to new legislation. He at first tried to work around this by instead enacting much of his scheme through regulations that took their authority from the Chifley Government's own legislation. This changed only when the government won control of the Senate in the 1951 double dissolution, leading to the *National Health Act 1953*, the main item of legislation implementing the Page Scheme, as it became known. Page also had to reach a series of acceptable compromises with the BMA and the states. The BMA was sensitive to any perceived government control of its members. It strongly

---

27  Paul Hasluck, *The Chance of Politics*, Text Publishing, Melbourne, 1997, p. 41.
28  Ellis, *A History of the Australian Country Party*, p. 292.
29  Ibid., p. 292.
30  Page, *Truant Surgeon*, p. 375.

opposed suggestions of a contract-based capitation system under which fixed amounts of money per patient per unit of time would be paid by the Commonwealth in advance to practitioners, reflected in the long-standing tension between the BMA and friendly societies that used contracts.

The BMA was not pacified into ready compliance by Page's medical credentials and so the final form of his national health scheme diverged greatly from what he put to Cabinet early in 1950.[31] Page eventually settled on a BMA-supported model centred on the public subsidisation of fee-for-service-based private medical benefits. This was far less universalist than what Labor had sought, with access to benefits means tested and regulation largely left with the provider groups. Influential as the BMA was, the Page Scheme still owed much to his convictions about the proper role of government and the independence and privileges of the medical profession. He from the start envisaged a scheme 'based on a combination of government aid with nation-wide voluntary insurance against sickness and disease' that would not interfere in the 'personal relationship between doctor and patient', and give patients 'a definite sense of personal and social responsibility'. Page also sought to leave 'as much of the administration and control of the scheme as is possible' with doctors, chemists, hospitals and insurers. 'Subsidised voluntary health insurance' provided 'as far as possible through the machinery and administration of voluntary organisations which provide for prepaid health insurance' would avoid government nationalisation and (Page initially thought) enable quick implementation.[32]

The sequential introduction of the Page Scheme started in 1950 with the free provision of specified costly life-saving and disease-preventing drugs, policed by the medical and pharmaceutical professions themselves. Page had the necessary regulations issued when parliament was in recess, reasoning that when it resumed the public would have become so accustomed to these new arrangements that Labor would be reluctant to use its Senate majority to disallow them – reminiscent of previous instances when he argued that acclimatisation would ensure public acceptance of an important Page initiative. In his anxiety to get a scheme up and running,

---

31  Gillespie, *The Price of Health*, pp. 254–5.
32  Earle Page, 'A New Conception of a National Health Scheme for Australia', speech to the British Commonwealth Medical Congress, Brisbane, 23 May 1950, EPP, folder 1341.

he characteristically disregarded Treasury and Department of Health advice on cost controls. Page's pharmaceutical benefits quickly incurred major cost overruns from the overuse of expensive drugs.[33]

Other early measures also had strong public appeal: free milk for schoolchildren, a tuberculosis benefit scheme and the introduction in February 1951 of free medical treatment for pensioners, with free prescription medicines for pensioners commencing the following July. As the Commonwealth had powers only over quarantine and some social welfare benefits, the cooperation of the states was essential. Over 1950–51 Page negotiated with the states on complementary legislation for a Hospital Benefits Insurance Scheme based on means testing and voluntary insurance, largely successfully; only Queensland held out by insisting on free beds, until a change of state government occurred in 1957. In July–September 1951 he visited the United States and Canada to examine their voluntary systems of hospital and medical insurance, from which he concluded that 'the only practicable method that would relieve people from the fear of costly hospital and medical bills was through a system of voluntary insurance backed by governmental aid'.[34] The National Health Act passed in November 1953 marked the start of the Medical Benefits Scheme; its final item of legislation was passed in October 1955.

Page demonstrated skill and creativity as he put his scheme into place step by step over a five-year period, carefully designed around what the BMA would accept. The taxpayer-funded subsidisation of voluntary private insurance was provided on a claims basis as a refund for part of actual expenditure by patients for approved health care, not a more general subsidisation of private health insurance providers. The system was not universal – only means-tested pensioners received fully free medical services – and practitioners did not enter into direct contracts with the Commonwealth. Menzies later praised Page for his speech introducing the 1953 legislation as an exposition of the philosophy of maintaining the individual doctor–patient relationship and avoiding a fully nationalised, government-conducted scheme. He even declared health policy to be 'one of the high spots' of his prime ministership.[35]

---

33  Gillespie, *The Price of Health*, pp. 257–9.
34  Page, *Truant Surgeon*, p. 377.
35  Menzies, *The Measure of the Years*, p. 123.

Although the Page Scheme was the forerunner of subsequent public health benefits schemes, the foremost historian of Australian public health policy is critical of Page's efforts as 'a pragmatic, unplanned set of benefit programmes cobbled together in the face of intense suspicion from the BMA'.[36] Perhaps there was more consistency of purpose behind what Page designed than he is given credit for. In addition to wanting a system that supported self-help, he proposed the decentralisation and regionalisation of its administration. In a 1950 speech he told state health ministers he would leave management of national health policy to existing state machinery and that 'there should be an even further decentralisation of authority and administration'.[37] In a letter of 9 March that year to Bruce, he expressed a fear that a more generous scheme would degrade community independence, resulting in 'cynical indifference'.[38] The scheme stands as a major step in increased Commonwealth responsibility for health services.

Although Page remained proud of what is widely seen as one of his foremost achievements, in long, discursive speeches reviewing his career he portrayed this public health scheme as just one success alongside an array of developmentalist initiatives. Page still hankered for a major say in development policies. As he told the Cowper Federal Electorate Council in November 1956, 10 months after finally retiring from the front bench, 'my special position and knowledge made me of more value outside the Cabinet, although always ready and willing and available to give advice when needed'.[39] Even from the margins of political power, Page worked hard to draw the Menzies Government into accepting his developmentalist ideas.

One example is national economic planning. In the early 1950s, Page continued to bemoan the abolition of the DMC. He wrote to Bruce that, ever since, there had been 'no fact-finding nor comprehensive planning organisation in Australia adequate to deal with the problems facing us', and still decried 'the folly of Scullin's destruction of the organisation that was co-ordinating Federal and state policy as regards development

---

36  Gillespie, *The Price of Health*, p. 278. Other critics felt the Page Scheme was insufficiently targeted at low income groups; see for example Gwen Gray, 'Social policy', in Scott Prasser, J.R. Nethercote and John Warhurst (eds), *The Menzies Era: A Reappraisal of Government, Politics and Policy*, Hale & Iremonger, Sydney, 1995, p. 217.
37  Speech 15 August 1950, EPP, folder 2501.
38  EPP, folder 1821.
39  Speech by Page to Cowper Federal Electorate Council, 9 November 1956, EPP, folder 1805.

and collecting invaluable data'.[40] Despite the disdain of the public, planning remained a sufficiently persistent concept among policy-makers to nominally survive the advent of the second Menzies Government. Although Menzies abolished the Department of Post-War Reconstruction, many of its functions were shifted to other agencies, with the Industrial Development and Regional Resources divisions going to the newly created Department of National Development.[41] This new agency raised Page's hopes. His sense of personal ownership of planning remained so strong that he entered the new government telling Casey as the minister for national development how best to organise his department so as to hoist development and planning atop the government's agenda.

Page's relationship with Casey was important to him. They had worked together on the National Council in 1938–39 and shared an interest in the TVA. Days after the 1949 election, Ulrich Ellis produced a written proposal, almost certainly in consultation with Page, entitled 'A General Approach to the Organisation of a National Development Scheme'. This effectively sought to revive the National Council proposal. It called for a hierarchy of planning agencies headed by a national development council with members from industry, supported by state councils and regional or zone councils.[42] Both Page and Casey as new ministers were provided with a draft Cabinet paper on the Department of National Development prepared by the chair of the Public Service Commission, W.E. Dunk. This recommended very wide policy responsibilities for the department, including closer settlement, transport, water conservation, regional development, secondary industry and minerals. It would survey, plan and then enter into implementation agreements with state governments, again reminiscent of what Page had previously sought.[43]

Page himself wrote to Casey at length about the department in terms that recycled ideas from 1938–39. He wanted a powerful central agency that guided the rest of government and advanced his own agenda – 'the immediate objective of the Department of Development [sic] must be to provide a plan to halt the appalling drift from the countryside'.[44]

---

40  Page to Bruce, 9 March 1950 and 11 July 1951, EPP, folder 1821.
41  Macintyre, *Australia's Boldest Experiment*, p. 465.
42  Ellis, 'A General Approach to the Organisation of a National Development Scheme', 24 December 1949, EPP, folder 2076.
43  Draft Cabinet paper, with covering letter by W.E. Dunk, 12 January 1950 (earlier draft dated 27 December 1949), EPP, folder 2074.
44  Page to Casey, 9 January 1950, EPP, folder 2074.

It should be headed by someone the calibre of Essington Lewis, Tim Clapp or Charles Kemp. Like Dunk, he foresaw it coordinating policy with the states, including by surveying national resources and in promoting rural electrification. It would set long-term output targets for key industries including power, coal and steel. New sectoral planning authorities such as a joint coal board would bring governments together to 'carry out big schemes', and the Tariff Board would extend assistance to industries selected by the department.[45]

In practice, however, the Department of National Development was subject to complaints from state governments and soon lost staff and powers in a government elsewhere focused. It was further sidelined by not inheriting the Economic Policy Division of the old Department of Post-War Reconstruction, which instead went to the Prime Minister's Department.[46] Casey moved on to the External Affairs portfolio in 1951 but maintained an occasional personal interest in development. In June 1952 he suggested to Cabinet a near-revival of Page's 1938–39 proposal: 'consideration should be given as to what pressure can be brought to bear in the Loan Council on the state governments, to oblige them to agree to the setting up of a non-political body to screen and to create a list of priorities in respect of state, semi-governmental and local governing body works'.[47] The two corresponded throughout the 1950s, marking Casey as perhaps the only minister of the time to engage gladly with Page beyond his responsibilities as health minister. It was significant for Page that Casey was not a major influence in Menzies's Cabinet, and so was more friend and sounding-board than effective ally. Hasluck observed that 'Casey was ineffective in Cabinet. I doubt whether there was any other minister during the time he was in Cabinet with me who lost so many submissions'.[48]

Other recurrences of political interest in planning had an emphasis on defence strategy that overshadowed traces of Page's developmentalist vision. A National Security Resources Board modelled on an American

---

45   Undated document, 'Functions of the Department of Development', EPP, folder 2322.
46   A.J. Davies, 'National development', *Australian Quarterly*, vol. 37, no. 4, December 1965, p. 48; see also A.J. Davies, 'National Development Under Australian Federalism: Politics or Economics', a paper presented to the Australasian Political Science Association conference, August 1965; W.J. Hudson, *Casey*, Oxford University Press, Melbourne, 1986, pp. 208–11; David Lee, 'Cabinet', in Prasser, Nethercote and Warhurst, *The Menzies Era*, p. 127; and David Lowe, 'Menzies' national security state, 1950–53', in Frank Cain (ed.), *Menzies in War and Peace*, Allen & Unwin, St Leonards, 1997.
47   Submission by Casey to Cabinet, 24 June 1952, EPP, folder 2508.
48   Hasluck, *The Chance of Politics*, p. 86.

agency of the same name was established late in 1950 as a response to the Korean War. It was chaired by Menzies himself and had a mixed mandate to advise on the 'balanced allocation of the nation's resources as between defence, development, export production and the maintenance of the civilian economy'.[49] Despite Casey's urging, it never attained an executive role before ceasing to function three years later. The Country Party's November 1953 federal platform and policy called for 'Commonwealth-state machinery to determine the priority' of developmental projects.[50] In May 1954 Menzies proposed in his election policy speech a national development commission as 'a small advisory body of highly expert persons' that would report to the Commonwealth and the states, and depoliticise development policy – 'in the absence of such a body, Australian development may be actually hindered by election promises about specific local projects, made without regard to any Australian pattern'.[51] The commission was not formed as the states declined to be involved.[52]

Such attempts to institute planning in whatever muted form were echoes of a receding sense that the nation was underperforming. The planning concept that Page had long nurtured still lingered, but wider political opinion usually accepted that the economy was doing well enough without comprehensive guidance from government. Page was far from being Australia's only advocate of planning. S.J. Butlin wrote in 1955 that 'part of the general thinking of all Australians on economic affairs is a not very coherent prejudice in favour of an increase in total "production", specially the introduction of new industries, coupled with the assumption that the natural way to promote such new industries is government aid'.[53] John Crawford said at the end of the decade that 'we are all planners now' but in saying this employed a very expansive conception of planning, including by government establishing 'shared belief' in attainable objectives.[54] Page perhaps also owed something to the interest of economic and intellectual

---

49  Executive Member of the Board, economist E.R. Walker, quoted in Davies, 'National development', *Australian Quarterly*, p. 49. See also Davies, 'National Development Under Australian Federalism', pp. 19–26; Lee, 'Cabinet', in Prasser, Nethercote and Warhurst, *The Menzies Era*, pp. 128–30; and Curtis, 'Planning for national development', *Australian Quarterly*, pp. 52–3.
50  Earle Page papers, UNE Archives, A180, box 4, folder 41(a).
51  Menzies quoted in *Sydney Morning Herald*, 5 May 1954, p. 4.
52  Davies, 'National development', *Australian Quarterly*, p. 51.
53  S.J. Butlin, *War Economy 1939–1942*, series 4 (Civil), volume 3, *Australia in the War of 1939–1945*, Canberra, Australian War Memorial, 1955, p. 9.
54  Quoted in Smyth, *Australian Social Policy*, p. 194.

figures in the indicative planning then popular in western Europe.[55] The second Menzies Government only toyed with planning: the concept never attracted sufficient support beyond intellectual advocates and defence concerns to become established policy. But no other Australian federal politician of senior standing still pursued economy-wide planning with anything like Page's tenacity or scale of conception. As its foremost political advocate in the 1950s, he at least helped to keep the concept under government consideration, albeit intermittently.

Page's lack of traction on such issues as planning was also attributable to his increasing distance from the new generation of Country Party MPs. Aitkin later wrote of a fundamental change in the organisation of the Country Party from its founding as 'little more than an extra-parliamentary committee formed by two primary producer organisations' into a post-war 'mass political party of familiar type'.[56] The Country Party's policy ambitions changed, narrowing as the very worst privations of rural life were eased by such improved amenities as the road, phone and radio services that Page had championed. Mainstream rural politics gradually hardened into a focus on managing such priorities as price stabilisation schemes, tax concessions and subsidies on inputs.[57] This overtook the sense of exclusion that had helped motivate the pre-war Country Party to instead give it a strong stake in extracting benefits from embedded government practice. Countrymindedness lingered, but was expressed through more conventional and mainstream policies. Geoffrey Blainey adds that rural protest declined after 1945 due to generally good weather and high prices: 'in the Menzies years the big country towns oozed prosperity' and 'the Australian countryside lived on clover'.[58] This is an

---

55  On interest in planning in the latter 1950s, see Heinz Arndt, *A Course through Life: Memoirs of an Australian Economist*, Australian National University Press, Canberra, 1985, pp. 49–50; and Peter Coleman, Selwyn Cornish and Peter Drake, *Arndt's Story: The Life of an Australian Economist*, ANU E Press and Asia Pacific Press, Canberra, 2007, pp. 201–2.

56  Don Aitkin, *The Country Party in New South Wales: A Study of Organisation and Survival*, Australian National University Press, Canberra, 1972, p. 21. This reference was primarily to the New South Wales Country Party; the two organisations are the FSA of New South Wales and the Graziers' Association of New South Wales.

57  Lloyd provides a succinct summary of agricultural policy in the 1950s; Lloyd, 'Agricultural price policy', in Williams, *Agriculture in the Australian Economy*, pp. 362–3. He adds that in 1952 the Commonwealth Government with AAC endorsement announced production targets for 1957–58, 'Australian agriculture's nearest approach in peacetime to indicative planning'.

58  Geoffrey Blainey, *This Land Is All Horizons: Australian Fears and Visions*, Boyer Lectures 2001, Australian Broadcasting Commission, Sydney, 2001, pp. 37–8.

overstatement – the Korean War wool boom did not last and some rural industries sought protection from imports – but it remains that there was far less sense of rural crisis than in the inter-war years.

Page thus seemed a man out of time. Australia was now a more settled and prosperous nation, and his style of developmentalism became ill-fitted to a party increasingly sceptical of grand visions. A new consensus had emerged about Australian development being based on the steady management of national growth, and this was incorporated into structures of government that made only nominal provision for the visionary ventures of Earle Page.

There is no better illustration of Page's divergence from the rest of the Country Party than the contrasting world views presented in his speech of 28 July 1956 to its executive council in Perth and that on the same day in the same city by McEwen as minister for trade and industry to the annual general meeting of the Country Party of Western Australia. Page called for a national population of 30 million, new states and the emulation of the development of the United States, especially through decentralisation, mass migration, foreign capital and hydroelectricity. A national council of defence and development was needed to 'determine a pattern of development taking into account the economic and strategy factors associated with the size and locations of towns and cities'. McEwen's speech reported on recent economic growth, factory construction, exports and how stable commodity prices could encourage development in South-East Asia. His primary goal was stated simply and bluntly as 'fast and balanced growth'.[59] Page's post-war career draws out such changes in developmentalist thought. In the 1950s, developmentalism based on rural development was both challenged and supplemented by the nurturing of manufacturing, including outside the major cities, by protection from import competition, tax concessions and subsidised energy. Major enthusiasts for this approach included not only McEwen but also such prominent figures as Premier Thomas Playford of South Australia.[60] Development led by mining also began to gain prominence during the 1950s and 1960s, especially in Western Australia.[61]

---

59  Transcripts of both speeches are in the National Party of Australia records, NLA, MS 7507, series 1, box 1.
60  See David C. Rich, 'Tom's Vision?', in Bernard O'Neil, Judith Raftery and Kerrie Round (eds), *Playford's South Australia: Essays on the History of South Australia, 1933–1968*, Association of Professional Historians Inc., Adelaide, 1996, pp. 91–116.
61  Layman, 'Development Ideology in Western Australia'.

## Page's persistence: Higher education, new states and hydroelectricity

Higher education was another field where Page ventured beyond his own health portfolio in trying to influence the wider agenda of the second Menzies Government. Unlike planning, the development of universities had the government's committed attention, but Page's interventions served mainly to illustrate how different his views were. They also marked him as one of the few senior political figures – including Menzies himself – who looked beyond the vocational dimension of universities to their role in shaping society. Page's long-standing involvement with the New England University College gave him a platform for public pronouncements. This institution finally became the fully autonomous University of New England in 1954. Page was installed as its first chancellor, a personal career highlight. At his 1956 speech to the dinner marking his retirement from the ministry, he described providing 'equal opportunities to the country student' as one of his lifetime objectives.[62]

In retirement, Menzies recalled that during these years the numbers of young men and women seeking university entry 'had increased beyond all anticipation'.[63] Student enrolments almost doubled between 1945 and 1956 to reach 31,000.[64] Most political and educational commentators did not envisage a total re-engineering of universities but simply supported their expansion to cope with this burgeoning demand. Following prompting from the vice-chancellors of Australia's then nine universities, Menzies agreed to a more thorough inquiry into their needs than hitherto, and so in December 1956 appointed the Murray Committee on Australian Universities. Although Page's hope of reconfiguring higher education according to his ideas on decentralisation and the scale of institutions distanced him from the educational mainstream, his interest in education was sufficiently appreciated to earn him such invitations as to address the 1950 Canberra University College commencement ceremony on 'The Value of Decentralisation of University Education'. His public statements of this time are some of his most strident attacks on city life and are among the most passionate declarations of the importance of higher education by any Australian politician.

---

62 'Australian Country Party Complimentary Dinner to Sir Earle Page', EPP, folder 2358.
63 Menzies, *The Measure of the Years*, p. 82.
64 Martin, *Robert Menzies: A Life, Volume 2*, p. 397.

For Page, the central problem was not that existing universities were too small, but rather that they were too large to respond to rising demand. Their scale already imposed problems of the coordination of research and teaching that would only worsen should they continue to grow. Page concluded that 'very large universities in capital cities can now do little more than provide technical or professional vocational training'. To 'train good citizens in the true liberal tradition as well as good technicians' required small institutions of about 300 to 750 students that offered accommodation and tutorial-based learning. The result would make each student 'an active partner in a teacher–learner association rather than a passive recipient of pre-digested knowledge'.[65]

Such small universities were not feasible in big cities with their high costs and petty distractions 'so great that it would be very difficult to build up a corporate spirit upon which maximum success would depend'. So Page called for 'a number of small universities placed at strategic points throughout the country districts'. These would be critically important in reversing population drift by conducting regional research and nurturing community leaders – 'a united and properly balanced community must have available within itself all those factors which bind the region together and develop within it a community of interest'.[66] Ultimately, a national network of small universities would contribute to shaping the nation along Page's favoured regionalised lines. The University of New England would serve 'by example to inspire the launching of other similar enterprises in other parts of the Commonwealth to restore the balance in Australian development, to decentralise university education'.[67]

Page's speeches on education contain some of his most metaphysical and hyperbolic comments on decentralisation. His installation as chancellor provided a unique opportunity for him to proselytise before an audience that included vice-chancellors and government ministers. 'Nature had taught the country dweller the need for balance', he said, and 'if the machine is out of balance the harder it works, the sooner it

---

65   'Speech by Sir Earle Page at the Graduation Ceremony of the University of New England, Armidale, Saturday, 16th April, 1955, at 2.30 P.M.', EPP, folder 2636.
66   Earle Page, *The Value of Decentralisation of University Education in Australia: Being an Address Delivered at the Twenty-first Annual Commencement Ceremony of the Canberra University College on 28th March, 1950*, Canberra University College, Canberra, 1950, pp. 6, 8, 10.
67   'Speech by Sir Earle Page, Chancellor of the University of New England, Official Luncheon, Armidale, Thursday 4th August 1955', EPP, folder 2321.

destroys itself.' Restoring such balance was 'my own lifetime ambition'.[68] He told the University of Queensland in May 1960 that its university college at Townsville would help 'prevent the growth of the mind and culture of both teachers and students being overlaid by mercantile or industrial factors which may destroy them unwittingly like a child can be suffocated by its drunken parents in bed'.[69] Such proclamations reflect the depth of Page's habitual drawing together of disparate concepts into a reinforcing whole – in this case, decentralisation, balance on a national scale, institutions small enough to nurture individuality and an exemplar institution to guide the entire nation.

Page's views on education carried too much extraneous baggage to win wider acceptance during the post-war growth of universities. The Murray Report pondered how universities could provide 'a full and true education', but reached conclusions that diverged from Page's ideas in their orientation to meeting growing demand for workforce skills. It recommended concentrating future university expansion in population centres, with only passing reference to small rural universities. Its canvassing of university residences failed to incorporate Page's ideas about tutorial-based education.[70] There were more influential individual players in the 1950s on university issues such as A.P. Rowe, vice-chancellor of the University of Adelaide, whose memoirs mention neither rural universities nor Page.[71] Although Page's specific ideas were bypassed, A.W. Martin erred in stating that apart from Menzies it is 'hard to think of another federal politician at the time – with the very important exception of H.V. Evatt – who more revered, understood and often in an old-fashioned way romanticised, the ideal of a university'.[72]

---

[68] Page official dinner speech, 4 August 1955, on his installation as chancellor, transcript and as reported in the *Daily Examiner*, 5 August 1955; and speech at official luncheon on the same date; both at EPP, folder 2321.

[69] Speech to mark the jubilee of the University of Queensland, May 1960 (day not given), EPP, folder 2133.

[70] Committee on Australian Universities, *Report*, (the 'Murray Committee'), Commonwealth of Australia, Government Printer, Canberra, 1957, see pp. 8, 12, 39, 54–5, 89. The committee noted the relatively good performance of residential students.

[71] A.W. Martin, 'R.G. Menzies and the Murray Committee', in F.B. Smith and P. Crichton (eds), *Ideas for Histories of Universities in Australia*, Division of Historical Studies, Research School of Social Sciences, The Australian National University, Canberra, 1990, p. 104; A. P. Rowe, *If the Gown Fits*, Melbourne University Press, Parkville, Vic., 1960.

[72] Martin, 'R.G. Menzies and the Murray Committee', p. 99.

By contrast with his involvement in planning and higher education – two fields with some basis in the government's policies – Page as health minister largely suspended his public campaigning on new states. As in the Bruce–Page days, it would have been difficult to reconcile such activity with his status as a Commonwealth minister. His public comments on this topic became sporadic, such as his 1951 pondering of 'some biological reason' why cities over 50,000 cannot maintain themselves without absorbing rural migrants 'into their vortex'.[73] Page's absence from active campaigning is one reason why there was little effective political support for new states and decentralisation in the 1950s. Country Party and community interest dwindled: the party's 1953 platform made only vague references to new states, decentralisation and 'local control of local affairs'.[74] Governments were only politely sympathetic. In 1957 the Country Party premier of Queensland, Frank Nicklin, declared himself willing to test public opinion formally on dividing the state should he receive sufficiently large petitions: that this offer came to nothing was often remarked upon by remaining new staters.[75] There was more interest in intellectual quarters. *Current Affairs Bulletin* devoted an issue to new states in 1950 and four years later the Institute of Public Affairs produced a booklet advocating a petition-referendum formula for their creation.[76]

Ulrich Ellis temporarily assumed Page's role as the public face of new statism. From 1946 he effectively personally constituted the Canberra-based Office of Rural Research from which he issued a stream of publications before resigning in 1960 to concentrate on the New England separation campaign. Ellis was prominent at a major joint conference convened at Corowa in July–August 1951 of the New England New State Movement, the Murray Valley Development League and the Murrumbidgee Valley Water Users' Association. Visible as Ellis was, there are signs that Page was an influence behind the scenes. In October 1955 Ellis sought Page's comments concerning a draft bill on the division of assets and liabilities between parent states and their new state offspring.[77] A few stalwarts of the old Country Party–new state network remained active. Drummond now

---

73   Statement, 5 January 1951, EPP, folder 1627.
74   Country Party 1953 Platform, copy in EPP, folder 1685.
75   From the account of the new state movement written by Thompson for Page, EPP, folder 2146, p. 5.
76   'New states', *Current Affairs Bulletin*, vol. 6, no. 12, 28 August 1950; Institute of Public Affairs (New South Wales), *Safeguard Your Rights by Review of the Constitution*, IPA (New South Wales), Sydney, October 1954, p. 18.
77   Ellis to Page, 14 October 1955, EPP, folder 2020.

chaired the Australian Decentralisation and Development Committee (secretary, Ulrich Ellis) that lobbied premiers and federal ministers on the outcomes of the Corowa conference.[78]

Page was far less inhibited in publicly promoting the Clarence hydroelectricity project, evidently judging that his role as local member made this compatible with his ministerial status. In the early 1950s the Clarence issue was driven by a series of expert reports. Repeatedly disappointed but never deterred, Page kept seeking one that delivered the conclusively positive findings he needed. That these studies were undertaken at all owed much to his persistence. In 1951 the New South Wales Government's Technical Committee, appointed following Page's post-war lobbying, finally recommended a dual purpose flood mitigation and hydroelectricity dam, and the fuller investigation of the wider Clarence catchment.[79] The New South Wales director of public works, J.M. Main, later wrote to Page criticising these recommendations as having been 'of a preliminary nature particularly in regard to the economics of hydroelectric power generation'.[80] Main himself chaired the most substantive of all the Clarence reports, the 1951–55 'Clarence Advisory Committee on the Development of the Resources of the Clarence Valley'. This report dismissed the Technical Committee's findings and recommended that state electricity authorities be left to make their own decisions in the wider context of thermal and Snowy Scheme developments.[81] As the decade dragged on with little to show, Page was by 1954 floating a much smaller proposal to further develop the Nymboida.[82]

It is remarkable that Page managed to keep hydroelectricity on the agenda of governments at all given the results of these studies and further shifts in professional interest towards nuclear and thermal power. The Snowy Scheme did not spark wider support for hydroelectricity. Even William Hudson, manager of the Snowy, publicly conceded that hydroelectricity was limited by geography and high initial capital costs.[83] Local government also had doubts. Joe Cahill, as New South Wales minister for

---

78  Such as a deputation to the prime minister in April 1952; see Ulrich Ellis papers, NLA, MS 1006, box 22, series 7B, folder 99.
79  Extract from the Technical Committee report, EPP, folder 1798; this folder also has a copy of the 1951–5 report that summarises and critiques the Technical Committee.
80  Main to Page, 25 October 1957, EPP, folder 2595.
81  See copy of report in EPP, folder 2592.
82  'Abundant and Permanently Cheap Electricity for Progressive Northern Development' – a 'statement' by Page, no date but c. 1954, EPP, folder 2324.
83  N.R. Wills (ed.), *Australia's Power Resources: Papers Read at the 1954 Winter Forum of the Victorian Group of the Australian Institute of Political Science*, F.W. Cheshire, Melbourne, 1955, pp. 64–5.

local government, a long-standing Page target, claimed in January 1952 that the Clarence River County Council actually preferred a number of smaller schemes to The Gorge and pointed out that the state's Electricity Authority opposed reliance on hydroelectricity given 'the hydrological and field work which is required'.[84] Perhaps worst of all for Page, the Commonwealth minister for national development, Bill Spooner, estimated in 1955 that coal reserves in the three mainland eastern states would meet power requirements for the next 50 years.[85]

The British social historian Bill Luckin concluded that the British Electrical Development Association was most successful when it appealed to rural sentiment by drawing on 'existing cultural repertoires while simultaneously generating novel images of technological superiority, cultural modernity and near-universal access'.[86] There is some parallel here with how Page's hydroelectric activism was limited by failure to attract the interest of his various allies on other causes, even the new staters. That Page never entirely swallowed his disappointment at the choice of the Snowy over the Clarence further isolated him as the former became a national showcase. His efforts also affirmed that his political influence remained greatest in local government, not the state level that was responsible for most power projects. The locally run Nymboida power station of 1924 remained his foremost success in electrification.

## Page leaves the ministry to pursue his vision

Page announced his resignation from the Menzies ministry immediately after the government was re-elected in December 1955 and retired to the backbenches the following month. His last major official policy initiative had been legislation to amend his National Health Act of 1953. In announcing his retirement, Page listed the issues he would henceforth pursue: water conservation, hydroelectricity, new states and decentralisation.[87] He also lamented that although 'the only way Federation can continue to exist is through a series of co-operative partners', the 'city

---

84  Cahill to Page, 15 January 1956, EPP, folder 2056.
85  Quoted in Alice Cawte, *Atomic Australia 1944–1990*, UNSW Press, Kensington, 1992, p. 103.
86  Luckin, *Questions of Power*, p. 17.
87  *West Australian*, 13 December 1955, clipping at EPP, folder 1683.

people don't know about the country'. Page now thought that what the nation needed was 'cities of 200,000 people every 50 miles throughout this country, not just a few monster cities on the coast'.[88]

The second Menzies Government presided in the 1950s over a nation undergoing rapid change – high population growth, a younger population, rising material affluence and greater cultural diversity than ever before. But the decade was not to be an era of major innovation in development policy. In the latter 1950s there emerged a perception that Menzies himself was disengaged from many of the transformations over which his government presided. Articulate criticism of a seemingly unimaginative national leadership was led by such figures as John Douglas Pringle, the British expatriate editor of the *Sydney Morning Herald*.[89] (Menzies vigorously defended his domestic record, such as in his second volume of memoirs, *The Measure of the Years*.)

Page became the fortuitous beneficiary of this perception. Immediately he was free of the strictures of public office, Page campaigned as an effectively autonomous MP dedicated to realising what he saw as the missed opportunities of the post-war and Menzies eras. The reaction to his urging had two distinct dimensions. One suggests that political interest in interventionist-based national development was now at one of its lowest ebbs in twentieth-century Australian history. But against this, there remained a lively popular and cultural interest in grand developmentalist visions that was reflected in press coverage lauding Page for presenting an appealing contrast as the elder statesman of national development. Page tapped into this.

Page resumed trying to persuade the Country Party to make a practical rather than nominal commitment to new states and related causes, and did not hesitate to berate the government of which he was nominally still a member. He spoke only occasionally in the House but, when he did, it was often at length to reassert an entire vision of the nation's future. A typical effort was his response to the 1957–58 Budget. This speech ranged across northern development, regional self-government, public debt, the incidence of tuberculosis, mental health, decentralisation, foreign investment, new states, national productivity, the dairy industry, water use, marketing of Australian exports and hydroelectricity.[90]

---

88  Quoted in the *Daily Telegraph*, 17 December 1955, clipping at EPP, folder 1683.
89  John Douglas Pringle, *Australian Accent*, Rigby, Adelaide, 1978 (first published 1958).
90  *Commonwealth Parliamentary Debates*, 12 September 1957, pp. 600–5.

Page tied his late career ideas together more coherently when he spoke to the Australian Provincial Press Association conference in October 1956 – the very same forum he had addressed in 1917. Nearly four decades on, his goals for the nation's economy and society remained essentially unchanged but for a clearer stress on planning. Decentralisation would be 'greatly assisted by a system of priorities for government expenditure taking into account both defence and development projects along planned lines'. Councils should be empowered to enter into franchise agreements with the private sector on development projects. The local press had a positive duty to 'force the hands of government along the proper course of action that will give the best results'.[91]

One of the new backbencher's first initiatives was an attempt to revive national planning. Page had retained a curiosity about the wider world that dated back to his early travels in New Zealand and North America. In retirement, he scanned the constitutions and policy statements of recently independent former British colonies for ideas on planned development. After visiting the Indian subcontinent in March 1956, he told the House of the deep impression made on him by India's and Pakistan's planned use of rivers and by the Indian National Development Council. This council demonstrated that it was possible to resolve 'the eternal wrangling between the states and the Commonwealth over the disposal of revenue, and fix priorities for the undertakings necessary in Australia'.[92] It appears to have inspired Page's last concerted effort on planning. As in 1938, Page began by approaching a powerful business figure. In April 1956 he contacted the stockbroker and grazier Samuel Hordern, seeking to discuss:

> the leadership that might be given to the business and financial world in Australia by some one with your reputation, influence and contacts to make possible the earliest change in our long-range planning that would put in [sic] a position similar to that of the United States in its period of very active growth.[93]

But this 1956 effort seems have come to nothing.

---

91  Speech by Page to Australian Provincial Press Conference, Brisbane, no date but from 1956, EPP, folder 2607. The *Australian Newspaper History Group Newsletter* specifies 18 October 1956 and Sydney as the venue. The association changed its title from 'Australasian' to 'Australian' in 1925.
92  *Commonwealth Parliamentary Debates*, 22 May 1956, pp. 2319–23.
93  Page to Hordern, 23 April 1956, EPP, folder 2608. This appears to have been the Samuel Hordern who was born in 1909, not his father of the same name who in 1956 was a semi-invalid of 80 years of age and who died in June that year.

Page also resumed public campaigning for new states for the first time since 1949. His speech on the 1957–58 Budget praised Victoria as the most economically balanced of the six states: 'I believe that if we could have a number of states of the size of Victoria in this continent of ours we would see very rapid development'.[94] He corresponded with the Capricornia movement in central Queensland on their lack of success, attributed simply by Page to public apathy. Notwithstanding the disappointing Cohen experience of over 30 years earlier, he suggested they seek a royal commission.[95] In an October 1961 speech to the New England New State Annual Convention he proposed a fresh formula for his federal units: 'about 5 degrees of latitude of coastline and their capital cities no more than 200 miles from practically all parts of the state'. Page reminded the convention that he had been 'the leader of this movement in the Federal Parliament for over 40 years'.[96]

But the issue that attracted the greatest share of the elderly Page's still formidable energy was that which retained the greatest emotional resonance for him – the harnessing of the Clarence River. In a May 1956 speech to the House he complained of how the Department of National Development still lacked a strategy for the national integration of electricity systems. By contrast, the old DMC had worked well with the states so that 'magnificent projects were put into effect with complete amity and accord' – a considerable exaggeration, but with some basis.[97] Page even dealt with yet another report on the Clarence, commissioned by the Electricity Commission of New South Wales from the American consulting company Ebasco. Contrary to his idealisation of the private sector as more broad-minded than government, Ebasco cautiously concluded that The Gorge could best be developed after about 1980. For the present, local demand was just too small. This assessment attracted Page's bitter attacks for ignoring the potential stimulus to local development and how linking the Clarence and southern Queensland regions could make the project viable.[98] Page organised what must have

---

94   *Commonwealth Parliamentary Debates*, 12 September 1957, p. 603.
95   Page to A.E. Webb, Honorary Secretary, Capricornia New State Movement, 14 December 1959, EPP, folder 2310.
96   'Speech by the Rt. Hon. Sir Earle Page, MP at Annual Convention of New England New State Movement', Grafton, 13 October 1961, New England New State Movement, Armidale, UNE Archives, A547, box 33, pp. 1, 4.
97   *Commonwealth Parliamentary Debates*, 22 May 1956, p. 2320.
98   'Local Government Enquiry Commencing at Grafton on 10th September 1956', EPP, folder 1798, pp. 9–10.

been an awkward lunch with the chair of the Ebasco study. Page claimed the chair was puzzled as to why he had not been asked to investigate the project's wider benefits.[99]

Page responded to continued frustrations with his habitual fall-back strategy of trying to harness local councils. In 1956 he issued a new booklet reviving the Clarence Valley Authority idea, but now tied this to the restructure of local government. The authority would provide 'a ray of hope thrown out for our general future overseas financial relationships' and could even arrange international loans linked to migration (again reminiscent of the Migration Agreement of the 1920s).[100] The *Daily Examiner* dutifully supported a proposal to group shires into a new county council that could 'control the whole river'.[101] Despite such enthusiasm, Page took care to present his plans as measured and realistic. He scorned an intermittently appearing variant of developmentalism: proposals for gargantuan engineering projects to exploit water resources. The most famed of these are the Bradfield and Idriess plans to irrigate Australia's interior by such means as diverting water from Queensland rivers. Page responded by collecting material critical of them, including an assessment from the civil engineer John R. Burton that such proposals were 'physically impossible'. Page agreed that 'facts and not mere surmises' were what was needed.[102]

Page also engaged with two late and unexpected forums for his developmentalist agenda. These were novel in nature for him and each provided further confirmation of how the policy environment had changed. One was a major inquiry by a parliamentary committee into constitutional reform, the most comprehensive such review of the Constitution since the Peden Royal Commission. The other was an expert inquiry into the dairy industry which presaged the extension of market-oriented economic analysis to the rural sector. The results of both exercises underlined the decline in political appetite for major developmentalist-oriented change. But they also showed that Page remained well capable of presenting his ideas with force and clarity, and was adept at capturing attention.

---

99   *Commonwealth Parliamentary Debates*, 12 September 1957, p. 604.
100  Earle Page, *Unique Opportunity for Co-ordinated National Development Based on Proposals for the Clarence*, p. 6; no date or place of publication, but internal evidence suggests Grafton in 1956.
101  *Daily Examiner*, 16 June 1956, clipping in EPP, folder 1798.
102  Burton's 1959 assessment and other material on the Bradfield Plan and related issues by F.R.V. Timbury, Griffith Taylor et al. is in EPP, folder 1758.

The Joint Committee on Constitutional Review established in May 1956 attracted Page's last concerted attempts to amend section 124 on the creation of new states and to reform Australian federalism. New state activists had been lobbying for a constitutional review since the early 1950s. It was potentially a very influential inquiry, with membership that included Arthur Calwell, David Drummond, Alexander Downer and Gough Whitlam.[103] Page's fulsome evidence to the committee was perhaps the most comprehensive call for constitutional change by a senior political figure of this time. In his January 1957 submission, Page reflected that he had been pursuing constitutional reform for decades 'like Sisyphus', with the 1928 referendum his sole success. With characteristic optimism and overstatement, he asserted that there was now 'universal agreement that decentralisation of local administration and a balance in the Commonwealth Parliament are essential to efficient and satisfactory government'.[104] Page also identified himself as the creator of four major cooperative bodies – the Loan Council, the AAC, the National Health and Medical Research Council and the Federal Transport Council.[105]

Page detailed in his evidence several variations on the theme that authority to create a new state should be shifted from state parliaments to a formula based on local petitions, referenda within the state and the area concerned, and final approval by the Commonwealth Parliament.[106] His fundamental arguments for new states were increasingly ingenious but continued to reflect faith that a simple adjustment or two in governance would ensure the desired outcome. He told the committee that new states would hasten constitutional reform by making it easier to satisfy the requirement for a majority of states to support a 'yes' vote at referendums. With only six states, four needed to vote 'yes' to approve a constitutional amendment, a majority of two to one; with more states, the proportion required in favour would fall. New states, he seemed to assume, would surely be more open-minded on constitutional change. They would also, he said, improve consistency in national regulation of the economy by increasing the proportion of commerce crossing state borders and hence

---

103 The committee was said to have been important in forming Whitlam's ideas on constitutional reform and the aggressive use of section 96 tied grants to the states; see Jenny Hocking, *Gough Whitlam: A Moment in History*, The Miegunyah Press, Carlton, Vic., 2008, pp. 181–6.
104 'Statement by Sir Earle Page on Constitutional Amendments Made to a Meeting of the Federal Parliamentary Constitutional Committee Held in Sydney in January 1957', EPP, folder 1659, p. 1.
105 Transcript of Page's evidence to parliamentary constitutional review committee, 15 January 1957, Sydney, EPP, folder 1660, p. 52.
106 'Statement by Sir Earle Page on Constitutional Amendments …', EPP, folder 1659, pp. 5–13.

falling under nationally consistent federal law. Even more indirectly, Page thought that the existence of a greater number of states would encourage industry to work out formulae for preventing duplication in arbitration decisions.[107]

Page also proposed that national government now be radically reordered along cooperative lines using federal–state councils, akin to what he had called for in 1942 – 'Cabinets of the governments of Australia' that would take the Loan Council and the AAC as exemplars. They would operate initially on a voluntary basis 'that accustoms the public to their existence', prior to being put to referendum for elevation to constitutional status. He proposed a supplementary loan council to coordinate semi-governmental and local government finances; a new federal transport council that would also cover hydroelectricity and flood control; and a council of taxation to collect revenue for all governments. Education was also 'eminently suited to a combined Federal–state approach': perhaps the two levels of government could share tertiary or technical education, or the Commonwealth take responsibility for a particular subject.[108] Page additionally wanted a new interstate commission to deal with cross-border issues such as water use, and to investigate discrimination in interstate commerce and assistance to the states.[109]

He was also thinking about how to simplify amendment of the Constitution. Having long seen the Constitution as an obstacle to policy innovation, Page told the committee that parliament should be able to amend basic 'machinery of government' provisions itself. Only wider 'principles of government' changes should require a referendum, an idea borrowed from the Indian constitution. Eventually, he hoped, 'we can obtain amendment without referendum' by agreeing changes with the state parliaments alone.[110] Interestingly, Page commented here that the success of the 1928 referendum on the Financial Agreement owed something to the ballot paper presenting voters with a choice of '1' or '2' to tick rather than 'yes' or 'no', electors being reluctant to directly say

---

107  Ibid., pp. 3–5.
108  Ibid., pp. 14–17.
109  Ibid., p. 4; also transcript of Page's evidence to the committee, EPP, folder 1660, pp. 7, 45–6. An Interstate Commission was established in 1912 but achieved little before being effectively dissolved in 1920.
110  Transcript of Page's evidence, ibid., pp. 18–19, 48.

'yes' to more power for government. 'Fear', he reflected, 'is nearly always the dominating factor that determines the way people vote at an election or referendum.'[111]

Page was rarely one to advocate cautious incremental change, especially if he judged the time right for a realignment. His evidence to the Joint Committee on Constitutional Review is a good example. The committee's report handed down in 1958 included among its many recommendations the amendment of section 124 to enable creation of a new state if supported by referendum both in the area concerned and in the whole state affected.[112] Although Page in his memoirs contrived to hail this as finally signalling that 'the acceptance of the new states idea is no longer in doubt', this was almost the only Page proposal the committee adopted.[113] (It also called for new Commonwealth powers to overcome section 92's inhibiting of primary product marketing.)[114] As a multiparty entity, the committee was prone to compromise. Cooperative federalism was effectively ignored, and on constitutional amendment the committee merely recommended a limited watering down of the referendum formula by requiring approval by only three states. The committee, Page's last major engagement with issues of constitutional reform and cooperative federalism, effectively rejected his vision of radical change.

The other inquiry with which Page grappled in these last years of his career presented an even greater challenge, an encounter with rigorous economic analysis. The Commonwealth's 1960 Dairy Industry Committee of Enquiry was a pioneering study of the economic and social outcomes of rural industry assistance.[115] It arose from concerns that continuing subsidisation of the dairy industry was inefficient and had effectively institutionalised low-income small-scale farming. Page could not ignore this important review, especially given dairy's importance in the Grafton area. His evidence went far beyond the subsidisation that industry lobbyists so vigorously defended to instead propose nationwide action on such 'production side' issues as fodder conservation, water conservation, hydroelectricity, soft loans to fund irrigation, research and transport

---

111 Ibid., p. 3.
112 Australia, Parliament, Joint Committee on Constitutional Review, *Report from the Joint Committee on Constitutional Review*, Government Printer, Canberra, 1958, p. 21.
113 Page, *Truant Surgeon*, p. 382.
114 Joint Committee on Constitutional Review, *Report*, p. 19.
115 Australia, Parliament, Dairy Industry Committee of Enquiry, *Report of the Dairy Industry Committee of Enquiry on the Australian Dairy Industry*, Government Printer, Canberra, 1960.

coordination. He opposed any restriction of production, but his defence of subsidisation was lukewarm: this could 'scale down' in the long term once production issues had been dealt with.[116]

Significantly, the committee sought advice from two professors of economics, Richard Downing and Peter Karmel. They proved highly critical of the extent of assistance provided to the industry in reaching their conclusion that some of the capital and labour it employed 'could be more productively employed elsewhere'.[117] The committee's final report accorded Page's evidence a three-paragraph summary and analysis of its own, a somewhat flattering nod to his special prominence. It professed to recognise 'the value of national schemes of such importance' and went on to recommend that financial assistance to increase the productivity of eligible farmers covering, among much else, fodder conservation, irrigation and water conservation.

But the committee was otherwise deterred by the sheer scale of Page's proposals, concluding that 'they are of such magnitude and would be so costly as to require examination and evaluation by experts'. Its main findings were 'that the industry should be re-formed on a sounder economic basis', that 'direct financial assistance should be dispensed with as soon as possible' and 'the direction of assistance should be gradually changed from income-increasing to cost-reducing'. A small number of farms that could never be viable 'will need to be eased out of the industry'.[118] Although such conclusions were effectively dismissed by the government, this inquiry was a clear sign of a new preparedness to apply economic analysis to rural industries that continued to grow beyond Page's time. The federal government's response to the final report was classically dismissive. It committed itself only 'to discuss with the state governments and the industry the question of the reconstruction of the industry, taking into consideration the views of the industry'.[119]

---

116 Page's evidence of 1 March 1960, EPP, folders 1157, 2023.
117 A summary of Downing and Karmel's findings is provided in Dairy Industry Committee of Enquiry, *Report*, pp. 77–8.
118 Dairy Industry Committee of Enquiry, *Report*, pp. 101–2: the committee's findings are at pp. 115–17.
119 EPP, folder 2127.

## Page's final campaigns: 'I want to see the work completed before I die'

Page remained as active as ever to the very end, both on policy and personal fronts. Ethel Page died in May 1958. A year later Earle married his long-serving secretary, Jean Thomas, with Stanley Bruce best man at the ceremony at London's St Paul's Cathedral. The second Lady Page died in 2011. Ann Moyal, the young historian who worked with the elderly Page on his memoirs, recalled fondly his 'merriment and verve' even in this late stage of his life. Though Page was a 'fiery particle', she noted that he forgave political enemies.[120] Ellis agreed, himself recalling Page's long-standing tendency to separate policy disputes from personalities and his generally 'happy view of life'.[121]

But privately, Page in these final years remained baffled by his continuing failure to make substantive policy progress. With time and repeated disappointment, a sense of stridency entered his pronouncements as he sought to reverse declining interest in his brand of developmentalism. Ever one to seek out topical new arguments, he warned that by developing the coalfields stretching from the Hunter Valley to Port Kembla, the New South Wales Government was merely creating 'a neat target for atomic bombs'.[122] Page noted the ideas of physicist Marcus Oliphant on how decentralisation could limit the effects of nuclear attack.[123]

Continued lack of progress on the Clarence now loomed as his foremost anxiety. He professed himself 'amazed that no proper analysis has been made of what is called the ancillary benefits that would be gained from the harnessing of these waters'.[124] Page turned increasingly to appeals via the press. His now well-established persona as the elder statesman of national development provided a ready basis for articles ridiculing governments, most spectacularly a piece in *Australian Country Magazine* of September 1959 entitled 'Our Second Snowy – Wasted'. This presented a suite of photos of Page gazing out over the Clarence River and even drinking its waters. The accompanying text highlighted his 'all Australian, non-political

---

120 Ann Moyal, *Breakfast with Beaverbrook: Memoirs of an Independent Woman*, Hale & Iremonger, Sydney, 1995, p. 150.
121 Ellis, *A History of the Australian Country Party*, p. 240.
122 *Commonwealth Parliamentary Debates*, 12 September 1957, p. 604.
123 Undated notes titled 'Marcus Oliphant', possibly a record of discussion, EPP, folder 2035.
124 *Commonwealth Parliamentary Debates*, 12 September 1957, p. 604.

standpoint' and called Page 'energetic, nimble-minded'. Perhaps the end result of his campaigning would be dubbed the Earle Page Dam.[125] Even Gough Whitlam, Labor deputy leader and rising political star, applied the elder statesman tag to Page during the parliamentary debate on the report of the constitutional committee, without evident irony.[126]

Page had by the late 1950s also firmly grasped the mantle of party elder: no doubt this helped colleagues tolerate his hectoring on regionalism and planning. He was respected more for his longevity and role in the Country Party's early success than for his current policy views. At the party's April 1957 Annual Conference held at Rockhampton, he reminded colleagues what it had once stood for and listed its past 'many great reforms which stand out as bulwarks and milestones of national progress'. These included 'the co-operation of the sugar industry'; organised marketing of butter, wheat and canned fruit; the tariffs needed to 'sustain the system' of organised marketing; coordination of state and federal borrowing; a central bank; the rural credits system; the independence of the Commonwealth Savings Bank; tax concessions for rural development; the Federal Aid Roads system; the 'National Health Insurance Scheme'; tuberculosis eradication; the CSIR; free school milk; the Wool Research Organisation; and the Meat Board.[127] Page presented a slideshow to encourage delegates to take new states and the TVA seriously.[128] But while the party's 1958 federal platform provided for a Commonwealth–state commission to undertake the 'economic analysis of river basin projects', and for a Commonwealth–state planning authority 'accompanied by machinery to determine the priority of projects', neither was implemented.[129]

Not that Page admitted defeat – that would not have been the man. One of his last efforts on planning was a September 1960 speech to the House in which he again called for 'a permanent body' of experts to cover 'all the various forms of development and such matters as education', using 'the Loan Council machinery'.[130] Two months later, the now 80-year-old Page

---

125 *Australian Country Magazine*, September 1959, pp. 14–17, 91, copy at EPP, folder 2589. Another example of Page using the popular press is 'Wasted wealth of the Clarence', *Pix* magazine, 13 November 1948, Sydney, pp. 20–3, copy at EPP, folder 2553.
126 *Commonwealth Parliamentary Debates*, 13 April 1961, pp. 820, 822.
127 Page speech to Country Party Annual Conference, 12 April 1957, EPP, folder 2607.
128 A list of the slides is at EPP, folder 2622 but not the slides themselves.
129 Country Party Federal Platform and Policy, July 1958, Earle Page papers, UNE Archives, A180, box 3, folder 29, p. 7.
130 EPP, folder 2141; the wording recorded by Hansard is slightly different, see *Commonwealth Parliamentary Debates*, 7 September 1960, pp. 893–4.

returned to the fray at the Country Party Federal Council by pointing out that as the early party had faced an 'inelastic Australian Federal System, which limited combined national effort', it 'at once specialised on devising practical machinery for such fruitful governmental co-operation'. But he also regretted his own continued failure to harness the nation's water resources and so called on the council to endorse a permanent organisation of all tiers of government to develop a 'control programme of all the waters of Australia'.[131]

Right up to the very end of his life, Page remained the main parliamentary spokesman for new statism. Indeed, his last major parliamentary speech – effectively the end of his public career – was part of the 12 October 1961 debate on the Constitutional Committee's findings on new states. (His very last speech to the House was a shorter statement of 19 October on rail gauge standardisation; typically, he noted that the Bruce–Page Government had proposed this nearly 40 years earlier.) This debate was a last reminder of the difficulties he still faced. Page described the committee's report as the first ever unanimity in the federal parliament on constitutional reform. He recounted the Commonwealth's 1926 offer to take over Western Australia's north, wistfully inviting his audience to 'imagine the vast development that would have occurred under such a plan as this'.[132] Page's interest in Northern Australia was more often lukewarm: he had four months earlier pulled out of a parliamentarians' trip to the north so he could instead visit the United States at the behest of private insurance companies to help the 'fight against the nationalisation of medicine'.[133] His hopes of elevating development policy above party politics now received a last blow. In supporting the amendment of section 124, Whitlam added that although the ALP 'is not averse to new states' it was 'averse to sovereign states'.[134] Labor's Clyde Cameron added a well-researched yet still fundamentally unfair personal attack on Page for failing to push new states while a minister between the wars.[135] Support from his own Country Party, let alone the Liberals, was conspicuously thin. Only F.A. Bland, now a Liberal MP, chipped in supporting new states and local government as barriers to 'administrative centralisation which would destroy our democratic way of life'.[136]

---

131 Page speech to Country Party Federal Council, 25–26 November 1960, EPP, folder 2021.
132 *Commonwealth Parliamentary Debates*, 12 October 1961, p. 1985.
133 Page to C.S. Christian of CSIRO, 9 June 1961, EPP, folder 2031.
134 *Commonwealth Parliamentary Debates*, 12 October 1961, p. 1991.
135 Ibid., pp. 2013–16.
136 Ibid., p. 2001.

Page was ending his public life more politically isolated than ever. Although there was still support for elements of his ideas, few if any MPs other than Drummond shared his breadth of synthesis. The new state movement was by this time showing every sign of becoming one of Australia's greatest lost causes. This bewildered Ellis, Thompson and Page himself. Ellis wrote of the Country Party's 'inexplicable reluctance' to insist on decentralisation.[137] Page simply pointed to the self-interest of cities and local political ignorance. Yet creating new states out of old is difficult in any representative democracy. Political scientist R.S. Parker identified only three notable international instances: Kentucky, Maine and West Virginia in the United States.[138] Australia's own three breakaways came in the nineteenth century when boundaries were still formative; by the early 1960s Australians had long been accustomed to their existing states and were wary of constitutional change.[139] Although new state advocates complained vociferously about constitutional barriers, section 124 has the merit of clarity. Constitutions are meant to provide certainty, not the instability that would occur if a referendum were to be triggered whenever a local grievance arose. Nor could any constitutional formula avoid the immense practical difficulties of dividing old states into new.

Page in retirement from office remained unable to answer convincingly Cohen's devastating critique of three-and-a-half decades earlier. New state movements had only been effective when by combining widespread public support with political leadership from figures like Page they were able to secure additional government resources, notably in northern New South Wales. Popular support was far less stable than intellectual interest, hence historian R.G. Neal's observation that the new state movements were 'stronger as means to ends, than as ends in themselves'.[140] The importance of material concerns resulted in their fluctuating with local economic peaks and troughs. While such assessments underestimate the passions

---

137  Ellis, *A History of the Australian Country Party*, p. 8.
138  Parker, 'Why New States?', in Parker et al., p. 1. Harman also points to Canadian provinces created after confederation in 1867; see Harman, 'New State Agitation in Northern New South Wales', p. 26.
139  There are some more recent new state sympathisers. Geoffrey Blainey, for example, feels that although federalism is apt for so large a country, too few states were created for it to function well; see Wayne Hudson and A.J. Brown (eds), *Restructuring Australia: Regionalism, Republicanism and Reform of the Nation State*, The Federation Press, Sydney, 2004, p. 27; also 'Call for North Queensland to split', *Cairns Post*, 25 November 2009.
140  Neale, 'New States Movement', pp. 12–13, 23.

and ideals that the separatist cause was capable of raising at times, the rise of the Country Party probably helped head off new states by providing more conventional political means of dealing with regional grievances.

Page committed himself to leaving a written legacy by producing his memoirs. He had discussed this with Ellis prior to the war and in 1939 told Drummond that he hoped to write a book on 'the aspirations, ideals, philosophy and history of our work for those who come after us to have a touchstone for their job'.[141] In 1943 he tried to have Ellis released from the Department of Munitions to work on a book that would 'shed important light on post-war problems and the manner of their solution', eventually settling on an autobiography as the most effective approach. After various false starts, the writing process finally began in January 1956 with Page dictating much of the text and Ellis making refinements. By 1958 the draft 'was reaching alarming proportions', complicating Page's efforts to interest a London publisher. It was only rendered publishable posthumously in 1963 following extensive and skilful editing by Ann Moyal (then Mozley).[142] The result, *Truant Surgeon*, constitutes both an overt attempt to guide future policy and a tacit admission of unfinished business that he hoped others would conclude in his absence. Throughout he stoutly defended his record of policy achievement, attributing failures to others being unable to appreciate his vision of the nation. John Latham reviewed it favourably as 'a real contribution to Australian political history by a highly competent patriotic Australian', despite the drawback that Page 'does not say much about any contrary opinions'.[143]

Page also hoped to produce a separate book on electricity and water. This was to be called *Missed Opportunities: Turning Water into Gold* and may well have been more important to him.[144] Although this other volume was never completed, his published memoirs concluded with a succinct statement of his formula for Australian developmentalism that touched on his continuing commitment to regionalism, strong central government, hydroelectricity, cooperative federalism and planning:

---

141 Page to Drummond, 15 April 1939, EPP, folio 2706.
142 Notes by Ellis on the drafting of *Truant Surgeon*, 16 February 1963, Ulrich Ellis papers, NLA, MS 821.
143 John Latham, 'Sir Earle Page: *Truant Surgeon*', *Quadrant*, vol. 7, no. 4, Spring 1963, p. 85.
144 Advice from Page's granddaughter Helen Snyders indicates that the main text of this no longer exists; fragments survive in the EPP, folders 2776, 2777, 2778 and 2785.

with a background of over half a century's study, I am convinced that the simple remedy is at hand – one that has been applied in handling other major Australian problems, such as finance, marketing and roads – through a partnership of Federal, state and local authorities. In such a partnership, the Federal government, as the sole income-tax collector, should provide the capital for the headworks free of interest and redemption, the state government the water channels, and the local authorities, which in each case would be the local river basin authority, should advise and assist the water user on the spot.[145]

He quoted here his speech of 9 March 1961 to the House proclaiming the development of water resources to be 'the most important point of all', which should harness 'all the large rivers from the north to the south'. Finally, Page said of the Clarence 'I first became interested in this scheme forty years ago, and I want to see the work completed before I die'.[146]

He never did. In June 1961 Page hinted heavily to Ellis that he may well not return from the trip he was about to undertake to the United States. Four months later, feeling ill, he left early from a new state convention in Grafton.[147] Page succumbed to bowel cancer at the Royal Prince Alfred Hospital in Sydney – where he had been a young doctor at the start of the century – on 20 December 1961, at the age of 81 years and four months. Among the official mourners at St Andrew's Cathedral in Sydney two days later were Michael Bruxner, John McEwen and Gough Whitlam, and former prime ministers Arthur Fadden and Frank Forde. Robert Menzies was absent.

On the day of Page's death the result for Cowper in the federal election of 9 December was declared. The seat that he had held since 1919 returned a Labor member for the first time. Page had been an eminently successful local member who won 16 elections in succession. His achievements for his electors most visibly included the long-sought bridge over the Clarence. Most recently he had bombarded the postmaster-general with letters on extending television to northern New South Wales, entirely undeterred by increasingly terse replies.[148] (Page's *Daily Examiner* was keen on setting up a television company.) Only twice did his primary vote in Cowper

---

145 Page, *Truant Surgeon*, p. 384.
146 Ibid., p. 442.
147 Notes by Ellis on the drafting of *Truant Surgeon*, NLA, MS 821.
148 See correspondence in EPP, folders 2129 and 2132.

fall below 50 per cent, in 1943 when the ALP recorded its greatest ever national election victory, and now in 1961 when the government lost 15 seats in the wake of the credit squeeze. Page had earlier considered retirement from parliament should Ellis, one of the few people he trusted to uphold his national vision, succeed him in Cowper.[149] Once cancer had taken a grip Page could no longer campaign. His primary vote in 1961 fell by a massive 15 per cent from that recorded at the 1958 election, well above the overall swing against the government. Menzies privately blamed the loss of Cowper on Page's refusal to retire.[150]

Page's obituary in the *Medical Journal of Australia* praised his 'invincible optimism': 'Page never grew old', was a great reader and possessed an 'orderly mind' that made him precise in thought and action.[151] In the parliamentary tributes, McEwen recognised that Page 'was responsible for many monumental changes in the Australian political structure', while Arthur Calwell recalled his 'missionary's zeal'.[152] One newspaper obituary entitled 'Elder Statesman Colourful Figure', noted Page's consistent world view and 'leadership in the development of a new form of co-operative federation', with the Loan Council, the AAC and tied road grants his main achievements.[153]

It was his great confidant David Drummond who showed the most empathy with Page's life and vision. To Drummond, Page's 'outstanding characteristic was a wide and far-seeing vision', which put him 'far ahead of any other man in his own party or in most other political parties'. He recalled Page's commitment to constitutional reform and the harnessing of water power, and his role as 'the real driving force' in the early new states movement. All of this made him 'a realistic dreamer' with 'a vision and a practical idea of how to carry it into effect'. Drummond accurately told parliament that what Page had recently said before the Joint Committee on Constitutional Review was 'really expressive in very large measure, of the ideas that he had promulgated 30 or more years before'.[154]

---

149 Notes by Ellis on the drafting of *Truant Surgeon*, NLA, MS 821.
150 Heather Henderson (ed.), *Letters to My Daughter: Robert Menzies, Letters 1955–75*, Pier 9, Millers Point, 2011, letter Menzies to Henderson of 17 December 1961, p. 78.
151 Bell et al., obituary of Sir Earle Page.
152 *Commonwealth Parliamentary Debates*, 20 February 1962, pp. 15, 16.
153 *Canberra Times*, 21 December 1961, pp. 5, 10.
154 *Commonwealth Parliamentary Debates*, 20 February 1962, pp. 18, 19.

# CONCLUSIONS
## 'A Man's Reach Should Exceed His Grasp'

Earle Page's vision, longevity and political seniority make him twentieth-century Australia's most important developmentalist. He was the foremost representative of this strand in Australian politics when it peaked in influence, especially when treasurer in the 1920s. His story shows that Australian developmentalism has a far more varied and richer history than implied by observers such as Donald Horne and S.J. Butlin.

Page's determination and capacity for synthesis engaged him with, and so helps illuminate, such varied historical currents as regionalism, decentralisation, cooperative federalism and seemingly transformative technologies. That he was only partially successful in implementing his ambitious synthesis should not obscure his major and enduring influence on several of its specific components. Page's incessant proselytising was instrumental in giving these elements a bigger place in national political culture than they would otherwise have had. He made important contributions to cooperative federalism that are still influential today. He helped consolidate the Commonwealth's dominance through the 1927 Financial Agreement and the early systematisation of tied grants as means of extending its fiscal and policy influence. He gave regionalism lasting significance. And he helped uphold national economic planning over decades, including during periods when it was distinctly unfashionable.

Through the establishment of the Loan Council and the Australian Agricultural Council, and by promoting them as exemplars of federal cooperation, Page – as Ellis observed – 'gave this idea orderly and practical expression'.[1] His initiatives are antecedents of today's National Federation

---

1   Ellis, *A History of the Australian Country Party*, p. 327.

Reform Council and other cooperative bodies. The history of Australian federalism is broadly one of growth in central power and nationally imposed cooperation, set against a corresponding failure – despite repeated attempts – to strike an agreed and lasting balance between states and Commonwealth. Page probably increased this tension rather than resolved it, but he also contributed mightily (perhaps ironically) to shifting the balance of power towards the Commonwealth. State governments were to him obstacles around which he had to manoeuvre to implement his national vision. He was far from alone among Australian political leaders in confronting these issues, but set some basic strands of the debate via his own distinctive mix of centralism and regionalism.

By pioneering the use of tied grants to the states, Page helped usher in the Commonwealth's fiscal dominance and propensity to intervene in policy fields beyond its stated constitutional role. The importance of this only became fully apparent in the 1950s when the Commonwealth significantly broadened tied grants to fund university expansion. Under Gough Whitlam, tied grants reached about 40 per cent of total federal grants to the states, but it was Page who first gave them a firm place in Australian federalism.[2] Of all the policy issues Page pursued, his efforts to overcome federalism as a barrier to his nationwide agenda and the contribution this made to centralism had the most lasting national impact.

By contrast, new statism declined after Page's death, hastened by the narrow but decisive defeat of the 1967 referendum on the separation of northern New South Wales. But political interest in the allied concept of regionalism persists. Page did more than any other individual to embed this spatial and community-based dimension into modern Australian political thought. No one else of such political stature pursued regionalism and related decentralisation so intensively over such a period of time. Post-Page, a continuing sense that local government is too weak and state governments are too large has encouraged continued – and inconclusive – experiments in regional administrative structures, right up

---

2   For the proportion of tied grants out of total federal grants to the states, see Scott Bennett and Richard Webb, *Specific Purpose Payments and the Australian Federal System*, Parliamentary Library Research Paper no. 17, 2007–08, Parliament of Australia, Canberra, 2008, figure 1.

to the current Regional Development Australia committees.³ Page's most distinctive contribution here was his challenge to more conventional new staters that regionalism ought not just be an expression of local patriotism but should be used to spark economic and social vitalism across the nation.

Page left less of a policy legacy on hydroelectricity, rural residential universities and planning. The 1960–61 credit squeeze led to the 1965 Vernon Committee of Economic Enquiry that raised a flicker of renewed interest in planning by recommending 'more co-ordinated long-term planning of public investment between the states and the Commonwealth'.⁴ But by the time such findings were handed down, the economy had recovered and Vernon's proposed independent expert advisory bodies were summarily dismissed by Prime Minister Menzies.⁵

What Page did – and did not – achieve helps to provide a more nuanced understanding of Australian developmentalism by defining what the nation's political culture would tolerate. Over the course of his career, the Australian political imagination typically fell short of grand national visions and was increasingly limited to fostering steady improvement in material living standards. Reactions to his initiatives collectively challenge assumptions by some historians and other commentators that the Australian body politic of his time was firmly committed to ambitious nation-building. Government and public support for developmentalist proposals to shape Australia was usually very mixed indeed.

Support most consistently came from applied intellectuals such as Bland, Thompson, Holmes and Page himself. Page's grand ideas on national development were challenged from several quarters. His Country Party

---

3   Others include the Whitlam Government's Regional Organisations of Councils and the Keating Government's Regional Development Organisations. See Lyndon Megarrity, *Local Government and the Commonwealth: An Evolving Relationship*, Parliamentary Library Research Paper no. 10, 2010–11, Parliament of Australia, Canberra, 31 January 2011; and Andrew H. Kelly, Brian Dollery and Bligh Grant, 'Regional development and local government: Three generations of federal intervention', *Australasian Journal of Regional Studies*, vol. 15, no. 2, 2009, pp. 171–93. A.J. Brown refers to continuing 'conflict around a frozen territorial structure which is widely recognised as delivering *neither* the level of national unity *nor* the serious political decentralisation which many Australians have long desired'; Brown, 'Constitutional schizophrenia', p. 53.
4   Committee of Economic Enquiry, *Report*, Commonwealth of Australia, Canberra, 1965, p. 17.12. The committee was informally named for its chair James Vernon, managing director of Colonial Sugar Refining.
5   See Martin, *Robert Menzies: A Life, Volume 2*, p. 531, and *Commonwealth Parliamentary Debates*, 21 September 1965, pp. 1080–7. In recommending a Special Projects Commission, Vernon drew on British and Canadian exemplars, not Page's admired DMC; see Committee of Economic Enquiry, *Report*, pp. 3.16, 17.28.

colleagues preferred to see their party settle into protecting an established stake in the political mainstream. Vested interests, particularly among primary producers, gave little priority to the nationwide, production-side initiatives that Page advocated. Outright sceptics, such as press commentators who were dismissive of Page's ill-defined proposals for national planning, helped to ensure that these schemes were not taken seriously. Even more tellingly, Page was increasingly challenged by a growing body of professional expertise within and outside government. From often hard experience, such experts became increasingly aware of the constraints imposed by aridity, soil infertility, a small and dispersed population, isolation from international markets and the fundamental limits of government. Popular accounts of national development that dwell on such famed projects as the Snowy Mountains Scheme often fail to also consider the many development proposals that were rejected, of which Page was a fecund generator. Such rejection reflected the sound technical judgement of the times; it also suggests a more cautious past political culture than is realised today.

Page's developmentalism was thus restrained by cautious economists, engineers, officials, business leaders and state governments. The states in 1923 opposed national planning of electrical power. The Cohen Royal Commission clinically dissected the case for new states. The DMC and the New South Wales Government doubted Page's vision for the Clarence. Engineers scorned the practicality of hydroelectricity on most of mainland Australia. National planning proposals attracted the accusation that Page was a mere dreamer. Committees on constitutional review and the dairy industry declined to accept his call for nationwide action. Even an ostensible ally such as Herbert Gepp was wary of proposals for unlimited development as talk that 'damages our credit abroad and hampers the formation of rational plans for development'.[6]

Page's incessant campaigning and the responses he elicited unintendedly helped to draw out this growing realisation of national limitations. These were (and often still are) so fundamental that they could not be readily overcome by Page's public appeals. National optimism that Australia could be engineered to realise a near limitless development potential wilted in the face of experience and a growing emphasis on seeking benefits from within an increasingly hardened political culture. Development was

---

6    Gepp, *Democracy's Danger*, p. 27.

publicly supported throughout Australia during the twentieth century, but there was growing caution by decision-makers about how far such visions should extend. Over time, Page had fewer and fewer allies in government and business who shared his breadth of vision.

Nor was the Australian public's support practical and decisive. Local demands for amenities and a wider sense that Australia was falling short of its potential helped Page win attention, but were only occasionally sufficient for implementation of ambitious development projects. Popular enthusiasm, such as for new states, covered only selected elements of Page's vision and was readily assuaged, leaving him lamenting public indifference. Big projects like the Snowy Mountains Scheme were government initiatives that the public acquiesced in rather than demanded. Page's long career helps show that although developmentalism was a major theme in twentieth-century Australia, it has been strongest as an abstract national ideal that only occasionally bore fruit. It persisted at a shallow popular level but increasingly struggled as a vision that policy-makers were prepared to strive towards. By mid-century it often manifested as a form of nostalgia from which Page at the end of his career gained some belated public praise. This has not fundamentally changed in a nation in which policy debate commonly takes the form of an ongoing tension between populist and technocratic world views.

What Page was proudest of achieving was not he and his party's well-known work on orderly marketing or trade agreements, but rather such initiatives as the University of New England, the Financial Agreement and the AAC, each of which constituted a step towards his broader vision. Tireless though he was, Page's policy passions were not wholly his inventions – major policy initiatives are rarely solely the work of an individual. There are antecedents for the Loan Council and Financial Agreement, he pioneered but did not invent tied grants, and regionalism and decentralisation pre-date him. Aitkin's summation of Page as probably the most inventive federal politician of the twentieth century needs qualification, but he was entirely accurate in adding that Page is Australia's most under-regarded such figure.

Page's originality lies more in his capacity for synthesis, which made him a far wider visionary than other prominent developmentalists in government. Thomas Playford focused on outbidding rival states to secure manufacturing for South Australia. Queensland's William Forgan Smith favoured public works and primary industry. In Tasmania, Eric Reece as a minister and later premier considered hydroelectricity to be the key to decentralisation and industry. Page, by contrast, was a more truly national figure who assembled a far broader vision of a more developed Australia, one that incorporated a distinct social element. It was not his commitment to national development that drew criticism, but rather the seemingly limitless extent of his ambitions and the assumptions he made about how readily they could be realised. His vision was so broad as to draw concerns even in the optimistic 1920s – that it amounted to a full theoretical framework drew scepticism not praise.

Page offered an alternative role for government to W.K. Hancock's oft-repeated description of Australians seeing 'the State as a vast public utility'.[7] He instead saw it as applying triggers of regionalism, planning and electrification to catalyse communities and private enterprise into leading development. Page's devotion to this nationwide vision has been obscured by the wider Country Party's sectoralism, assumptions that Australian political thought is invariably derivative and a focus on the drama of his 1939 clash with Menzies. Also important was biographers' tendency until recently to conventionalise Australian political figures – overlooking Deakin's spiritualism and Curtin's depressiveness, for example. To these we can add Page's ambitious imagining of how the formative Australian nation of the first half of the twentieth century should be shaped.

Page's ideas are hard to classify collectively using traditional concepts of liberalism, conservatism and socialism. He fiercely opposed public ownership but wanted government and business to work together. Primarily, he saw himself as an innovator, who only selectively defended established paradigms such as the harnessing of imperial links. That he was so distinctive a visionary raises the question of why he held high office in a nation of supposed pragmatists. His personal resilience and stable support base around Grafton are just part of the explanation.

Page endured mainly as the Country Party did, despite the increasing divergence between them over time. It gave him public status, aided by allied civic movements. His foremost political achievement of a coalition at the national level with the urban-based conservatives struck a long-term balance between a separate persona for the Country Party and its scope to influence the political mainstream, in contrast to the mixed

---

7   Hancock, *Australia*, p. 55.

fortunes of rural protest parties in other nations.[8] The coalition also had indirect value to Page in that the senior partner tempered his impetuosity, especially under the watchful leadership of Stanley Bruce. The success of the coalition contributed to a personal prestige that for Page largely survived growing policy differences with his peers.[9]

Also integral to Page's endurance were his political skills. He drew on his national standing and sense of strategy to defend the coalition and outshine potential rivals such as Charles Hardy. He remained cannily alert to opportunities to promote his agenda. This made Page's insertion of ideas into the political process spasmodic. Yet such studied opportunism – his attempts to seize the psychological moment – is hardly uncommon in politics. The political journalist Henry Fairlie famously wrote of 'the patience of politics'.[10] Page could wait for decades, but once set on an outcome was relentless.

Page was active for so long that he was exposed to major changes in political culture. After the relatively ready optimism of his early career and first stint in government during the 1920s, the dwindling of policy-makers' faith in developmentalism was compounded by new economic theories and modes of governance. His career contributes to understanding how this rise of professional economic expertise redefined the reach of central government. The optimism of the 1920s faltered as that decade progressed and was then sidelined by the search for responses to the economic crisis of the Great Depression. This contributed to the rise of economic expertise that became central to the development of national policy and was harnessed to the resurgent optimism of the immediate post-war years. But as economic prosperity took hold, mainstream policy settings shifted by the early 1950s to more limited ambitions of managing steady growth, rather than trying to spark the comprehensive economic and social engineering Page continued to advocate.

---

8   Chapter 1 of Graham, *Formation of the Australian Country Parties*, provides a summary history of early twentieth-century agrarian political movements, especially in the United States and Canada.
9   Graham, ibid., also reflects on the importance of the coalition strategy to the Country Party and the role played in this by Page at the national level, and at the state level by figures such as Bruxner in New South Wales and Alex Monger in Western Australia, pp. 195, 295.
10  Henry Fairlie, *The Life of Politics*, Methuen, London, 1968, p. 84. Fairlie said that the phrase originated with R.A. Butler.

Nor did Page accept the de-radicalisation of his own Country Party, becoming the foremost critic of the narrowing of its focus onto defending rural incomes. He clung so tenaciously to his goals that he drifted towards marginalisation, something this ever-hopeful individual never accepted. Although Page held a high position in the party's organisation until his death, from the late 1930s he had only a handful of colleagues to whom he could relate on matters of policy. Generational change further eroded his personal political standing.

Page also had personal limitations. Ellis's descriptions of endearing strengths read also as shortcomings, such as his calling Page 'a crusader' without also noting the crusader's typical righteous inflexibility.[11] Outwardly, Page bears a distinct similarity to the 'active-positive' category in James David Barber's political typology of United States presidents. Characteristics include well-defined personal goals and a strong desire for results, but also a failure to take account of the irrational in politics, with a consequent difficulty in understanding why others can see things differently.[12] These similarities are reflected in Page's unwavering commitment to his vision of the nation and corresponding anger over the barriers he encountered.

Page saw his policy goals as so compellingly rational that he frequently failed to argue as persuasively as someone of his intelligence was capable. He never convincingly detailed how planning would work, why private investors would fund hydroelectric dams, or how regionalism could be reconciled with his instinctive centralism. As Bruce discovered, Page was not good at selling an idea, no small problem for someone with so big an agenda. Page was more likely to suddenly impose a goal when the time seemed right than slowly build support. He interacted with civic and political groups selectively and had too diverse a range of interests to secure broad backing. Australia in his time was open to incremental change, but less so to the sudden realignments he proposed. Tellingly, Page became sensitive to accusations of achieving less than he ought to have.[13]

---

11  Ellis, *A Pen in Politics*, p. 96.
12  James David Barber, *The Presidential Character: Predicting Performance in the White House*, third edition, Prentice Hall, Englewood Cliffs, 1985 (first published 1972), pp. 8–10.
13  For example, his angry exchange with the Labor Member for Adelaide, Cyril Chambers, *Commonwealth Parliamentary Debates*, 22 May 1956, p. 2324.

His successes and his failures suggest how difficult it has been in Australian public life to win support for a seemingly abstract vision of the entire nation, as against immediately pragmatic answers to specific issues. Progress is more likely to arise from incremental change based on a strong empirical case for clearly stated material goals, especially if this does not rely on collaboration between national and state governments. State–Commonwealth relations remain contested, with Page's contribution to the rise of Commonwealth power not being matched by an agreed commensurate shift in constitutional responsibilities away from the states. Tensions between countryside and city over the allocation of public resources have not been resolved by limited experiments in regionalism that fall far short of Page's nation-shaping federal units. His National Council and other planning proposals demonstrate the difficulty of implementing a coherent national economic policy in an unresolved federal system.

Yet as Australia's most significant developmentalist, Page still helps draw out currents of thought. His career supports revisionist arguments by James Walter and others that Australian political life was richer in ideas than often assumed, especially those promulgated by applied thinkers. He was a powerful exception to the 'Australian scepticism' identified by the sociologist John Carroll as a national trait, in which 'there are no grand visions of the past, the present, or the future' and no 'convinced belief that mundane institutions … can be radically transformed for the better, that idealistic passion can be translated into social progress'.[14]

Page's developmentalism helps enlarge understanding of what ideas define Australian civilisation. There is a widespread assumption that Australia reached a broad political consensus about 1910 based on the Deakinite vision, and that subsequent debate predominantly concerned its implementation.[15] In fact, Page offered a very different spatially oriented developmentalist vision of the nation. By doing so he also qualifies perceptions of the Country Party as predominantly a party of resistance. He affirms the endurance of the tradition created by European settlers that they could make much of a continent they saw as bearing no great burden of history and as having no previous owners of the land. Inspired

---

14  John Carroll, 'National identity', in Carroll (ed.), *Intruders in the Bush*, Oxford University Press, Melbourne, 1982, pp. 211, 214, 215.
15  See for example Geoff Stokes (ed.), *Australian Political Ideas*, UNSW Press, Kensington, NSW, 1994, p. 6; and Paul Kelly, *The End of Certainty: The Story of the 1980s*, Allen & Unwin, St Leonards, NSW, 1992, introduction.

by admiration of overseas development experience as he frequently was, Page's efforts to create an Australia according to his national vision amounted to a form of national pride.

Page thus shows how assessment of the career of an influential individual and the ideas they upheld can help illuminate the wider past and even cast light on the present. He is an example of the historical value of querying assumptions that prominent yet little studied national figures were merely reflective of the institutions in which they embedded themselves. An important minority of political figures such as Page ranged so widely in thought and vision that the study of their interactions with wider public culture can broaden interpretations of Australian history.

The strategic place of Page in Australian history is that he offered a full alternative to the Deakinite settlement. No one else of his political standing provided such a comprehensive challenge for so long to this mainstream national policy prescription. As ready faith in the nation's development narrowed to a predominantly popular ideal overshadowed by the management of steady growth, Page was increasingly lonely as one of the very few developmentalist optimists left in national politics.

In sum, Earle Page is historically important as Australian developmentalism's foremost standard bearer. He broadened developmentalist thought by providing a rare synthesis of ideas that were otherwise typically seen with little regard for how they could strengthen each other. This both delineated and stretched the breadth of visions and policies current in Australian politics. He was instrumental in giving elements of his vision, especially regionalism, cooperative federalism and a strong national government, greater and more lasting significance in Australian history than they would otherwise have had. Page's long career confirms that Australia has long inspired popular ideals of national development. Studying his life establishes his place in Australian history and, through this, contributes to establishing that of Australian developmentalism as a persistent ideal in public life but which as a practical concept was increasingly challenged during the twentieth century.

# BIBLIOGRAPHY

## Unpublished official sources

### National Archives of Australia (NAA)

A1, 1932/8838, Ministerial Transport Council – Minutes of First Meeting – 2nd August 1929, Department of Home Affairs.

A431, 1946/888, Co-ordination of Transport in Australian Government Policy and Federal Transport Council, Part 1 and 2, Department of the Interior.

A432, 1931/735, re Utterances of Dr Earle Page M.P., re New State Movement, Attorney-General's Department.

A461, AK423/1/1, Water and Electricity – General – Clarence River Hydro-Electric Development, Prime Minister's Department.

A461, AT326/1/3, Premiers' Conference – March 1939, Prime Minister's Department.

A571, 1924/5892, Australian Loan Council – First Informal Meeting – 1–2 February 1924, Department of the Treasury.

A659, 1939/1/8829, Co-ordination of Transport in Australia – Government Policy and Federal Transport Council, Part 3, Department of the Interior.

A786, I19/1, Conferences – Premiers' Conference 1929, Prime Minister's Department.

A786, R22/1, Development NSW Clarence Valley, Prime Minister's Department.

A2694, VOLUME 19 PART 1, Lyons and Page Ministries – Folders and Bundles of Minutes and Submissions, Part 1, Cabinet Office.

A2694, VOLUME 19 PART 2, Lyons and Page Ministries – Folders and Bundles of Minutes and Submissions, Part 2, Cabinet Office.

A2700, 1166, Seventh Report of Rural Reconstruction Commission – Rural Amenities, Cabinet Office.

A5954, 475/1, Far Eastern Defence, Sir Earle Page's Discussions in Singapore and London, 1941.

A5954, 475/2, Australian Representation in United Kingdom, Sir Earle Page's Mission Abroad September, 1941.

A9816, 1943/1298, Activities of the Development and Migration Commission, Department of Post-War Reconstruction.

A9816, 1944/487 PART 1, Clarence River Hydro-Electric Scheme by Sir Earle Page, Part 1, Department of Post-War Reconstruction.

A9816, 1944/487 PART 2, Clarence River Hydro-Electric Scheme by Sir Earle Page, Part 2, Department of Post-War Reconstruction.

A9816, 1944/487 PART 3, Report on Clarence River Gorge Hydro-Electric Scheme by Preliminary Committee of Technical Officers, Department of Post-War Reconstruction.

A11702, 3, Agenda Items of the First Meeting of the Australian Agricultural Council, 28 May 1935, Standing Committee on Agriculture.

B2455, PAGE EARLE CHRISTMAS GRAFTON, PAGE Earle Christmas Grafton: Service Number – Captain: Place of Birth – Grafton NSW: Place of Enlistment – N/A: Next of Kin – (Wife) PAGE Ethel.

CP103/11, 267, Information on Development and Migration Commission for Imperial Conference, 1930, Prime Minister's Department.

CP103/11, 818, Notes on Various Subjects to be Raised at Premiers' Conference, 1923, Prime Minister's Department.

CP211/2, 34/2, Investigations – New South Wales Clarence River Development, Development and Migration Commission.

CP211/2, 34/13, Investigations – New South Wales – Hydro Electric Scheme (Clarence River): 1928, Development and Migration Commission.

CP211/2, 57/4, Organisation – D. & M. [Development and Migration Commission] – Evidence for Royal Commission on Constitution – Commonwealth, Development and Migration Commission.

CP211/2, 57/7, Organisation - D. & M. [Development and Migration Commission] – Its Constitution and Functions – Memorandum by Mr Gepp, Development and Migration Commission.

CP211/2, 57/36, Organisation – D. & M. [Development and Migration] Commission – Minutes, Development and Migration Commission.

MP61/1, 2/3/422, Clarence River Water – Power Development, Department of Post-War Reconstruction.

# Manuscripts and recordings

## Australian Dictionary of Biography

Page, Earle, AU ANUA 312–7423, Noel Butlin Archives Centre, Australian National University Archives, Australian National University.

## Australian War Memorial

Earle Page papers, 1940–1942, 3DRL/3682.

## Museum of Australian Democracy

Uncatalogued acquisition of Page family papers.

## National Library of Australia (NLA)

Chamberlain, Frank, Interview by Mel Pratt, 4 August 1972 and 19 January 1973, sound recording, Mel Pratt Collection, National Library of Australia, TRC 121/39.

Papers of Douglas Berry Copland, 1907–1971, MS 3800.

Papers of Warren Denning, 1953–1965, MS 5129.

Papers of Ulrich Ellis, ca 1900 – ca 1968, MS 748; 6 February 1967, MS 821; 1900–1972, MS 1006.

Papers of Bruce Desmond Graham, 1921–1969, MS 8471.

Papers of Sir Robert Menzies, 1905–1978, MS 4936.

Records of the National Party of Australia, 1915–1983, MS 7507.

Papers of Sir Earle Page, 1908–1961, MS 1633 [EPP].

Speeches by Sir Earle Page, 1922–1960, MS Acc10.200.

Papers of Victor C. Thompson, 1931–1965, MS 2182.

Post-War Reconstruction Seminar Papers, 1941–1982, Australian National University, 31 August– 4 September 1981, MS 6799.

Post-War Reconstruction Seminar: Proceedings, 31 August–4 September 1981, sound recording, ORAL TRC 1096.

## University of Melbourne Archives

Papers of Sir Samuel McMahon Wadham, 1964.0014.

## University of New England and Regional Archives (UNE Archives)

David Henry Drummond papers, A248.

New England New State Movement records, A1.

New England New State Movement, Armidale; Anne Philp, including administrative records, A547a.

Page papers, A180.

New England New State Movement: Booklets by Ulrich Ellis, A811.

## Other

Page family papers provided by Helen Snyders – including summary biographies of Earle Page and his family members, press clippings and correspondence from Earle Page.

'The Trail of the Travelling Treasurer' by U.R. Ellis, unpublished account of travels in Australia with Page, 1936, copy provided by Max Ellis.

# Published official sources

Australia, Parliament, Dairy Industry Committee of Enquiry, *Report of the Dairy Industry Committee of Enquiry on the Australian Dairy Industry*, Government Printer, Canberra, 1960.

Australia, Parliament, *Full Employment in Australia*, White Paper, Government Printer, Canberra, 1945.

Australia, Parliament, Joint Committee on Constitutional Review, *Report from the Joint Committee on Constitutional Review*, Government Printer, Canberra, 1958 (full report published 1959).

Broderick, John Joyce, *Report on the Economic, Financial and Industrial Conditions of the United States of America in 1922*, Department of Overseas Trade, His Majesty's Stationery Office, London, 1923.

Bureau of Transport Economics, *Road Grants Legislation in Australia: Commonwealth Government Involvement, 1900–1981*, Bureau of Transport Economics Occasional Paper no. 48, Australian Government Publishing Service, Canberra, 1981.

Burke, R.H., *History of Commonwealth Government Legislation Relating to Roads and Road Transport, 1900–1972*, Bureau of Transport Economics Occasional Paper no. 8, Australian Government Publishing Service, Canberra, 1977.

Committee of Economic Enquiry, *Report* ('Vernon Report'), Commonwealth of Australia, Canberra, 1965.

Committee on Australian Universities, *Report of the Committee on Australian Universities* (the 'Murray Committee'), Commonwealth of Australia, Government Printer, Canberra, 1957.

*Commonwealth Parliamentary Debates*, House of Representatives, 1919–1962.

Commonwealth Transport Committee (Chairman, Major John Northcott), *Summary Report on the Co-ordination of Transport in Australia by the Commonwealth Transport Committee*, Canberra, 1929.

Department of Post-War Reconstruction, *Regional Planning in Australia: A History of Progress and Review of Regional Planning Activities through the Commonwealth*, Department of Post-War Reconstruction, Canberra, 1949.

Development and Migration Commission, *First Annual Report for Period Ending 30 June 1927*, Commonwealth of Australia, Melbourne, 1927.

Development and Migration Commission, *Second Annual Report for Period Ending 31st December 1928*, Commonwealth of Australia, Canberra, 1929.

Gibson, Alexander J., *Report on Power Development in Australia*, Government Printer, Canberra, September 1929.

Halsey, T.H., *Decentralisation: Its Scale and Economic Implications*, Commonwealth Division of Regional Development, Canberra, 1949.

*Interstate Conference on Water Conservation and Irrigation: Held at Sydney, New South Wales, 24th to 27th April, 1939*, Government Printer, Sydney, 1939.

McKell, W.J., *The Tennessee Valley Authority (USA): Report by the Hon. W.J. McKell KC, MLA, December 1945*, Government Printer, Sydney, 1945.

Royal Commission of Inquiry into Proposals for the Establishment of a New State or New States, *Evidence of the Royal Commission of Inquiry into Proposals for the Establishment of a New State or New States, formed wholly or in part out of the present territory of the State of New South Wales, together with the List of Exhibits and Printed Exhibits*, 6 volumes in 4, Government Printer, Sydney, 1925.

Royal Commission on the Constitution, *Report* ('Peden Report'), Parliamentary paper no. 16, Government Printer, Canberra, 1929.

Rural Reconstruction Commission, *Reports*, 10 volumes, The Commission, Canberra, 1944–46.

University of Sydney, *Calendar of the University of Sydney for the Year 1902*, Angus and Robertson, Sydney, 1902.

# Newspapers and periodicals

*Advertiser*, Adelaide
*Age*, Melbourne
*Argus*, Grafton
*Argus*, Melbourne
*Armidale Express*
*Australian*, Sydney
*Australian Country Magazine*, Melbourne
*Australian Country Party Monthly Journal*, Sydney
*Australian National Review*, Canberra
*Australian Newspaper History Group Newsletter*, Kingston, ACT
*Australian Quarterly*, Sydney
*Australian Town and Country Journal*, Sydney
*Brisbane Courier*
*Brisbane Telegraph*
*Cairns Post*
*Canberra Times*
*Cessnock Eagle and South Maitland Recorder*
*Clarence and Richmond Examiner*, Grafton
*Daily Examiner*, Grafton

*Daily News*, Perth
*Daily Telegraph*, Sydney
*Economic Record*, Melbourne
*Examiner*, Launceston
*Farmers' Advocate*, Melbourne
*Geraldton Guardian and Express*
*Glen Innes Examiner*
*Herald*, Melbourne
*Journal of the Institution of Engineers, Australia*, Sydney
*Kyogle Examiner*
*The Land*, Sydney
*Lithgow Mercury*
*Macleay Argus*
*The Methodist*, Sydney
*Murray Pioneer and Australian River Record*, Renmark
*New State Magazine*, Tamworth
*Newcastle Morning Herald and Miners' Advocate*
*News*, Adelaide
*Northern Star*, Lismore
*Pix*, Sydney
*The Primary Producer*, Perth
*Public Administration*, Sydney
*Quarterly Bulletin*, The Institution of Engineers Australia, Sydney
*Recorder*, Port Pirie
*Regional Development Journal*, Canberra
*Register*, Adelaide
*Riverine Herald*, Echuca
*Scrutineer and Berrima District Press*, Moss Vale
*Sun*, Sydney
*Sunday Times*, Sydney
*Sydney Morning Herald*
*Townsville Daily Bulletin*
*Walkabout*, Melbourne
*West Australian*, Perth
*Western Age*, Dubbo
*Wingham Chronicle and Manning River Observer*

# Secondary sources

Aitkin, Don, *The Colonel: A Political Biography of Sir Michael Bruxner*, Australian National University Press, Canberra, 1969.

Aitkin, Don, *The Country Party in New South Wales: A Study of Organisation and Survival*, Australian National University Press, Canberra, 1972.

Aitkin, Don, 'Countrymindedness: The spread of an idea', in Graeme Davison, John Hirst and Stuart Macintyre (eds), *The Oxford Companion to Australian History*, Oxford University Press, Melbourne, 1998, pp. 50–57.

Aitkin, Don, 'Page, Earle Christmas Grafton', in Graeme Davison, John Hirst and Stuart Macintyre (eds), *The Oxford Companion to Australian History*, Oxford University Press, Melbourne, 1998, pp. 488–89.

Alanbrooke, Field Marshal Lord, *War Diaries 1939–1945*, edited by Alex Danchev and Daniel Todman, Weidenfeld & Nicolson, London, 2001.

Alexander, Fred, *From Curtin to Menzies and After: Continuity or Confrontation?*, Thomas Nelson (Australia), Melbourne, 1973.

Alexander, Fred, *Australia since Federation: A Narrative and Critical Analysis*, third edition, Thomas Nelson, West Melbourne, 1976 (first published 1967).

Allbut, Guy, *A Brief History of Some of the Features of Public Electricity Supply in Australia: And the Formation and Development of the Electricity Supply Association of Australia, 1918–1957*, Electricity Supply Association of Australia, Melbourne, 1958.

Andrews, E.M., *Isolationism and Appeasement in Australia: Reactions to the European Crises, 1935–1939*, Australian National University Press, Canberra, 1970.

Arklay, Tracey, *Arthur Fadden: A Political Silhouette*, Australian Scholarly Publishing, North Melbourne, 2014.

Arklay, Tracey, John Nethercote and John Wanna (eds), *Australian Political Lives: Chronicling Political Careers and Administrative Histories*, ANU E Press, Canberra, 2006. doi.org/10.22459/APL.10.2006.

Arndt, Heinz, *A Course through Life: Memoirs of an Australian Economist*, Australian National University Press, Canberra, 1985.

Ashby, Eric, *Universities in Australia*, The Future of Education series no. 5, Australian Council for Educational Research, Melbourne, 1944.

Atkinson, Alan, J.S. Ryan, Iain Davidson and Andrew Piper (eds), *High, Lean Country: Land, People and Memory in New England*, Allen & Unwin, Crows Nest, NSW, 2006.

Australian Automobile Association, *A National Roads Policy for Australia*, Wynyard, NSW, c. 1950.

Australian Catholic Historical Society, australiancatholichistoricalsociety.com.au.

Australian Council for Educational Research staff, *A Plan for Australia*, The Future of Education series no. 2, Australian Council for Educational Research, Melbourne, 1943.

Australian Country Party, *Honesty, Security: A Frank Statement of Country Party Policy by Dr Earle Page*, Bureau of Publicity, Information and Research, Sydney, 1931.

*Australian Dictionary of Biography*, Melbourne University Press, Carlton, Vic., 1966–2012.

*The Australian Encyclopaedia*, Chisholm, Alec H. (editor-in-chief), second edition, Angus and Robertson, Sydney, 1958.

Australian General Electric Limited, *The Story of a Great Australian Industry*, Australian General Electric Limited, Sydney, 1937.

Barber, James David, *The Presidential Character: Predicting Performance in the White House*, third edition, Prentice Hall, Englewood Cliffs, 1985 (first published 1972).

Barcan, Alan, *A History of Australian Education*, Oxford University Press, Melbourne, 1980.

Barnard, Marjorie, *A History of Australia*, Angus and Robertson, North Ryde, NSW, 1976 (first published 1962).

Barr, Neil, *The House on the Hill: The Transformation of Australia's Farming Communities*, Land & Water Australia in association with Halstead Press, Canberra, 2009.

Bashford, Alison and Macintyre, Stuart (eds), *The Cambridge History of Australia*, 2 volumes, Cambridge University Press, Melbourne, 2013.

Beer, Andrew, Alaric Maude and Bill Pritchard, *Developing Australia's Regions: Theory and Practice*, UNSW Press, Sydney, 2003.

Bell, George, Henry Newland, W.F. Simmons and D.A. Cameron, obituary of Sir Earle Page, *Medical Journal of Australia*, 12 May 1962, pp. 731–4.

Belshaw, James, 'David Henry Drummond 1890–1930: The formative years', *Armidale and District Historical Society Journal and Proceedings*, no. 22, March 1979, pp. 19–42.

Belshaw, James, 'David Henry Drummond 1927–1941: A case study in the politics of education', *Armidale and District Historical Society Journal and Proceedings*, no. 26, March 1983, pp. 45–71.

Belshaw, Jim, 'Decentralisation, Development and Decent Government: The Life and Times of David Henry Drummond, 1890 – 1941', PhD thesis, Department of History, University of New England, submitted but subsequently put aside by its author, see newenglandhistory.blogspot.com.au/2010/06/decentralisation-development-and-decent.html, 3 June 2010.

Belshaw, J.P., 'Decentralisation of university education', *Australian Quarterly*, vol. 20, no. 4, December 1948, pp. 67–76. doi.org/10.2307/20633106.

Belshaw, Jim, *New England's History* [web blog], www.newenglandhistory.blogspot.com.au.

Bennett, Scott and Richard Webb, *Specific Purpose Payments and the Australian Federal System*, Parliamentary Library Research Paper no. 17, 2007–08, Parliamentary Library, Dept of Parliamentary Services, Canberra, 2008.

Bernie, K.N.J., 'The premiers' conferences: An historical sketch from the beginnings to 1930', *Public Administration*, vol. 6, no. 8, September 1947, pp. 410–17. doi.org/10.1111/j.1467-8500.1947.tb02096.x.

Bijker, Wiebe E., Thomas P. Hughes and Trevor Pinch (eds), *The Social Construction of Technological Systems: New Direction in the Sociology and History of Technology*, MIT Press, Cambridge, Massachusetts, 1987.

Bird, David S., *J.A. Lyons: The Tame Tasmanian: Appeasement and Rearmament in Australia, 1932–39*, Australian Scholarly Publishing, North Melbourne, 2008.

Blackbourn, David, *The Conquest of Nature: Water, Landscape and the Making of Modern Germany*, Jonathan Cape, London, 2006.

Blacklow, Nancy, '"Riverina roused": Representative support for the Riverina new state movements in the 1920s and 1930s', *Journal of the Royal Australian Historical Society*, vol. 80, no. 3–4, December 1994, pp. 176–94.

Blackwood, Robert, *Monash University: The First Ten Years*, Hampden Hall, Melbourne, 1968.

Blainey, Geoffrey, *Black Kettle and Full Moon: Daily Life in a Vanished Australia*, Penguin, Camberwell, Vic., 2003.

Blainey, Geoffrey, *The Great Seesaw: A New View of the Western World, 1750–2000*, Macmillan, South Melbourne, 1988. doi.org/10.1007/978-1-349-10086-6.

Blainey, Geoffrey, *A Land Half Won*, Sun Books, South Melbourne, 1983 (first published 1980).

Blainey, Geoffrey, *The Peaks of Lyell*, third edition, Melbourne University Press, Carlton, Vic., 1967 (first published 1954).

Blainey, Geoffrey, *This Land Is All Horizons: Australian Fears and Visions*, Boyer Lectures 2001, Australian Broadcasting Commission, Sydney, 2001.

Bland, F.A., 'The abolition of states and the increase of local government bodies', reprinted from *The Shire and Municipal Record*, November 1932.

Bland, F.A., *An Administrative Approach to Australian Transport Problems*, lecture to the New South Wales Centre of the Institute of Transport, The Institute, Sydney, 1935.

Bland, F.A. (ed.), *Changing the Constitution: Proceedings of the All-Australian Federal Convention, 25th and 26th July 1949*, The New South Wales Constitutional League, Sydney, 1950.

Bland, F.A., 'Decentralization – the machinery of government', in H.L. Harris, H.S. Nicholas, F.A. Bland, A. Mainerd and T. Hytten, *Decentralization*, Angus and Robertson in conjunction with the Australian Institute of Political Science, Sydney, 1948, pp. 67–120.

Bland, F.A., 'Inventing constitutional machinery: A study of Dr Earle Page's proposals for National Councils', *Australian Quarterly*, vol. 7, no. 28, December 1935, pp. 10–21. doi.org/10.2307/20629266.

Bland, F.A., *Planning the Modern State*, second edition, Angus and Robertson, Sydney, 1945 (first published 1934).

Bland, F.A., 'Post-war constitutional reconstruction', *Public Administration*, vol. 2, no. 3, September–December 1940, pp. 136–55.

Bland, F.A., *Shadows and Realities of Government: An Introduction to the Study of the Organisation of the Administrative Agencies of Government with Special Reference to New South Wales*, Workers' Educational Association of N.S.W., Sydney, 1923.

Bland, F.A., 'Towards regionalism', *Public Administration*, vol. 4, no. 8, December 1943, pp. 379–85. doi.org/10.1111/j.1467-8500.1943.tb02398.x.

Boadle, Donald, 'Regional water wars: River leagues and the origins of the Snowy Scheme', *Journal of the Royal Australian Historical Society*, vol. 80, pts 3 and 4, 1994, pp. 195–211.

Bolton, G.C., *A Thousand Miles Away: A History of North Queensland to 1920*, second impression, Australian National University Press, Canberra, 1970 (first published 1963).

Bongiorno, Frank, 'Search for a solution, 1923–39', in Alison Bashford and Stuart Macintyre (eds), *The Cambridge History of Australia*, volume 2, Cambridge University Press, Melbourne, 2013, pp. 64–87.

Booth, Edgar, *Decentralisation of University Education*, New England University College, Armidale, NSW, June 1943.

Booth, Robert R., *Warring Tribes: The Story of Power Development in Australia*, revised edition, Bardak Group, Doonan, Qld, 2003 (first published 2000).

Botterill, Linda Courtenay, 'Soap operas, cenotaphs and sacred cows: Countrymindedness and rural policy debate in Australia,' *Public Policy*, vol. 1, no. 1, 2006, pp. 23–36.

Bowen, Chris, *The Money Men: Australia's 12 Most Notable Treasurers*, Melbourne University Press, Carlton, Vic., 2015.

Bowers, William L., *The Country Life Movement in America, 1900–1920*, Kennikat Press, Port Washington, 1974.

Brady, Edwin J., *Australia Unlimited*, G. Robertson, Melbourne, c. 1918.

Brett, Judith, *Australian Liberals and the Moral Middle Class: From Alfred Deakin to John Howard*, Cambridge University Press, Cambridge, 2003. doi.org/10.1017/CBO9780511481642.

Brett, Judith, 'The country, the city and the state in the Australian Settlement', *Australian Journal of Political Science*, vol. 42, issue 1, March 2007, 1–17. doi.org/10.1080/10361140601158518.

Brett, Judith, *Fair Share: Country and City in Australia*, Quarterly Essay, issue 42, Black Inc., Collingwood, Vic., 2011.

Brett, Judith (ed.), *Political Lives*, Allen & Unwin, Sydney, 1997.

Bridge, Carl, *Earle Page: The Politician and the Man*, first lecture in the Earle Page College Thirtieth Anniversary Series, 9 March 1993, University of New England, Armidale, NSW, 1993.

Brown, A.J., 'The constitution we were meant to have: Re-examining the origins and strength of Australia's unitary political traditions', *Democratic Experiments: Lectures in the Senate Occasional Lecture Series 2004–2005*, Papers on Parliament No. 44, Department of the Senate, Parliament House, Canberra, 2006, pp. 41–65.

Brown, A.J., 'Constitutional schizophrenia then and now: Exploring federalist, regionalist and unitary strands in the Australian political tradition', in K. Walsh (ed.), *The Distinctive Foundations of Australian Democracy: Lectures in the Senate Occasional Lecture Series 2003–2004*, Papers on Parliament No. 42, Department of the Senate, Parliament House, Canberra, 2004, pp. 33–58.

Brown, A.J. and J.A. Bellamy (eds), *Federalism and Regionalism in Australia: New Approaches, New Institutions?*, ANU E Press, Canberra, 2006. doi.org/10.22459/FRA.08.2007.

Brown, A.J., 'Federalism, regionalism and the reshaping of Australian governance', in A.J. Brown and J.A. Bellamy (eds), *Federalism and Regionalism in Australia: New Approaches, New Institutions?*, ANU E Press, Canberra, 2006, pp. 11–32. doi.org/10.22459/FRA.08.2007.

Brown, A.J., 'Reform of Australia's Federal System: Identifying the Benefits', a discussion paper produced for the New South Wales Farmers' Association by The Federalism Project, Griffith University, May 2006.

Brown, A.J., 'Regional governance and regionalism in Australia', in Robyn Eversole and John Martin (eds), *Participation and Governance in Regional Development: Global Trends in an Australian Context*, Ashgate, Aldershot, 2005, pp. 17–41.

Brown, A.J., 'Subsidiarity or subterfuge?: Resolving the future of local government in the Australian federal system', *Australian Journal of Public Administration*, vol. 61, no. 4, December 2002, pp. 24–42. doi.org/10.1111/1467-8500.00297.

Brown, Archie, *The Myth of the Strong Leader: Political Leadership in the Modern Age*, Vintage Books, London, 2015 (first published 2014).

Brown, Nicholas, *Governing Prosperity: Social Change and Social Analysis in Australia in the 1950s*, Cambridge University Press, Cambridge, 1995.

Brown, Nicholas, *Richard Downing: Economics, Advocacy and Social Reform in Australia*, Melbourne University Press, Carlton South, Vic., 2001.

Brown, Nicholas, 'A sense of number and reality: Economics and government in Australia, 1920–1950', *Economy and Society*, vol. 26, no. 2, May 1997, pp. 233–56. doi.org/10.1080/03085149700000013.

Brown, Nicholas, 'The Seven Dwarfs: A team of rivals', in Samuel Furphy (ed.), *The Seven Dwarfs and the Age of the Mandarins: Australian Government Administration in the Post-War Reconstruction Era*, ANU Press, Canberra, 2015, pp. 3–30. doi.org/10.22459/SDAM.07.2015.

Burleigh, Michael, *Earthly Powers: Religion and Politics in Europe from the Enlightenment to the Great War*, Harper Perennial, London, 2006 (first published 2005).

Butcher, John (ed.), *Australia Under Construction: Nation-building Past, Present and Future*, ANU E Press, Canberra, 2008. doi.org/10.26530/OAPEN_458814.

Butler, A.G., *Official History of the Australian Army Medical Services, 1914–1918, Volume II – The Western Front*, first edition, Australian War Memorial, Canberra, 1940.

Butlin, N.G., A. Barnard and J.J. Pincus, *Government and Capitalism: Public and Private Choice in Twentieth Century Australia*, George Allen & Unwin, Sydney, 1982.

Butlin, S.J., 'The role of planning in Australian economic development', *Economic Papers*, no. 15 – *Planned and Unplanned Development*, The Economic Society of Australia and New Zealand, Sydney, 1962, pp. 5–26.

Butlin, S.J., *War Economy 1939–1942*, series 4 (Civil), volume 3, *Australia in the War of 1939–1945*, Australian War Memorial, Canberra, 1955.

Byrne, Graeme, 'Schemes of the Nation: A Design History of the Snowy Scheme', PhD thesis, Department of Art History and Theory, University of Sydney, October 1999.

Cain, Frank (ed.), *Menzies in War and Peace*, Allen & Unwin, St Leonards, NSW, 1997.

Calwell, A.A., *Labor's Role in Modern Society*, Lansdowne Press, Melbourne, 1963.

Campbell, Eric, *The Rallying Point: My Story of the New Guard*, Melbourne University Press, Carlton, Vic., 1965.

Canaway, A.P., *The Failure of Australian Federalism*, Oxford University Press, London, 1930.

Carboch, Dagmar, 'The fall of the Bruce-Page Government', in Aaron Wildavsky and Dagmar Carboch, *Studies in Australian Politics*, Cheshire, Melbourne, 1958, pp. 119–282.

Carey, John (ed.), *The Faber Book of Utopias*, Faber & Faber, London, 1999.

Carroll, John (ed.), *Intruders in the Bush: The Australian Quest for Identity*, Oxford University Press, Melbourne, 1982.

Carroll, John, 'National identity', in John Carroll (ed.), *Intruders in the Bush*, Oxford University Press, Melbourne, 1982, pp. 209–25.

Casey, R.G., *Double or Quit: Some Views on Australian Development and Relations*, Cheshire, Melbourne and London, 1949.

Cathcart, Michael, *Defending the National Tuckshop: Australia's Secret Intrigue of 1931*, McPhee Gribble/Penguin, Fitzroy, Vic., 1988.

Cathcart, Michael, *The Water Dreamers: The Remarkable History of Our Dry Continent*, Text Publishing, Melbourne, 2009.

Cawte, Alice, *Atomic Australia 1944–1990*, UNSW Press, Kensington, NSW, 1992.

Clarence River Historical Society Inc., *Clarence River Historical Society Inc. Diamond Jubilee 1931–1991*, Clarence River Historical Society Inc., Grafton, NSW, 1991.

Clarence River Historical Society Inc., *Grafton and the Early Days on the Clarence*, Clarence River Historical Society Inc., Grafton, NSW, 2009.

Clark, Colin, *Australian Hopes and Fears*, Hollis & Carter, London, 1958.

Clark, Colin, *The Organisation of a New State*, Australian Decentralisation and New States Movement, Sydney, 1952.

Clune, David and Ken Turner (eds), *The Premiers of New South Wales, Volume Two, 1901–2005*, The Federation Press, Sydney, 2006.

Cochrane, Peter, *Industrialisation and Dependence: Australia's Road to Economic Development*, University of Queensland Press, St Lucia, Qld, 1980.

Cockburn, Stewart (assisted by John Playford), *Playford: Benevolent Despot*, Axiom, Kent Town, SA, 1991.

Cockfield, Geoff and Linda Courtenay Botterill (eds), *The National Party: Prospects for the Great Survivors*, Allen & Unwin, Crows Nest, NSW, 2009.

Cole, G.D.H., *Principles of Economic Planning*, Macmillan, London, 1935.

Cole, Percival R. (ed.), *The Rural School in Australia*, Melbourne University Press, Melbourne, 1937.

Coleman, Peter, Selwyn Cornish and Peter Drake, *Arndt's Story: The Life of an Australian Economist*, ANU E Press and Asia Pacific Press, Canberra, 2007. doi.org/10.22459/AS.03.2007.

Coleman, William Oliver, Selwyn Cornish and Alfred Hagger, *Giblin's Platoon: The Trials and Triumph of the Economist in Australian Public Life*, ANU E Press, Canberra, 2006. doi.org/10.22459/GP.04.2006.

Collier, Sally, 'Earle Christmas Grafton Page: A doctor for the nation', *Armidale and District Historical Society Journal and Proceedings*, no. 39, 1996, pp. 1–11.

Collier, Sally, 'Sir Earle Christmas Grafton Page: A Doctor for the Nation', BA (Hons) thesis, Department of History, University of New England, June 1994.

Collis, Brad, *Snowy: The Making of Modern Australia*, Hodder & Stoughton, Sydney, 1990.

Collits, Paul, 'Australian Regional Policy and its Critics', paper presented at the 11th Biennial Conference of the Australian Population Association, Sydney, October 2002.

Connell, W.F., *The Australian Council for Educational Research 1930–80*, Australian Council for Educational Research, Hawthorn, Vic., 1980.

Connor, John, Peter Stanley and Peter Yule, *The War at Home*, Centenary History of Australia and the Great War, volume 4, Oxford University Press, South Melbourne, 2015.

Coombs, H.C., *Trial Balance: Issues of My Working Life*, Macmillan, South Melbourne, 1981.

Coopersmith, Jonathan, *The Electrification of Russia 1880–1926*, Cornell University Press, Ithaca and London, 1992.

Cornish, Selwyn, 'Sir Roland Wilson – Primus inter pares', in Samuel Furphy (ed.), *The Seven Dwarfs and the Age of the Mandarins: Australian Government Administration in the Post-War Reconstruction Era*, ANU Press, Canberra, 2015, pp. 125–41. doi.org/10.22459/SDAM.07.2015.06.

Costar, Brian and Peter Vlahos, 'Sir Earle Page', in Michellle Grattan (ed.), *Australian Prime Ministers*, New Holland, Frenchs Forest, NSW, 2000, pp. 168–73.

Costar, Brian and Dennis Woodward (eds), *Country to National: Australian Rural Politics and Beyond*, George Allen & Unwin, Sydney, 1985.

Crawford, Alan, *Electric Power*, Nelson Doubleday, Lane Cove, NSW, 1968.

Crawford, J.G., *Australian Agricultural Policy*, The Joseph Fisher Lecture in Commerce, University of Adelaide, Adelaide, 1952.

Crick, Bernard, *George Orwell: A Life*, Penguin, Harmondsworth, 1982 (first published 1980).

Crisp, L.F., *Australian National Government*, Longmans, Croydon, Vic., 1965.

Crotty, Martin and David Andrew Roberts (eds), *The Great Mistakes of Australian History*, UNSW Press, Sydney, 2006.

Crowley, Frank (ed.), *A New History of Australia*, William Heinemann Australia, Melbourne, 1974.

Crowley, V., 'A decentralisation policy: Plea for a big national scheme', *Australian National Review*, 1 August 1938, pp. 48–53.

Cullather, Nick, *The Hungry World: America's Cold War Battle Against Poverty in Asia*, Harvard University Press, Cambridge, Massachusetts, 2010.

Cumpston, I.M., *Lord Bruce of Melbourne*, Longman Cheshire, Melbourne, 1989.

*Current Affairs Bulletin*, 'Industries for the country', vol. 4, no. 2, 11 April 1949.

*Current Affairs Bulletin*, 'New states', vol. 6, no. 12, 28 August 1950.

*Current Affairs Bulletin*, 'Regionalism', vol. 18, no. 5, 5 November 1945.

*Current Affairs Bulletin*, 'The Snowy: An appraisal', vol. 31, no. 13, 13 May 1963.

Currie, George and John Graham, John, *The Origins of CSIRO: Science and the Commonwealth Government 1901–1926*, Commonwealth Scientific and Industrial Research Organisation, Melbourne, 1966.

Currie, George and John Graham, 'The origins of the Standing Committee on Agriculture', *Public Administration*, vol. 27, no. 1, March 1968, pp. 23–38.

Curtis, Heather, 'Planning for national development', *Australian Quarterly*, vol. 26, no. 3, September 1954, pp. 52–65. doi.org/10.2307/20633462.

*Daily Examiner, The Book of a Century: Grafton's 100 Years of Civic Life, 1859–1959*, Grafton, NSW, 1959.

Dales, John H., *Hydroelectricity and Industrial Development: Quebec 1898–1940*, Harvard University Press, Cambridge, Massachusetts, 1957. doi.org/10.4159/harvard.9780674491878.

Dallas, K.M., *Water Power: Past and Future*, privately published, Hobart, 1970.

Davey, Paul, *The Country Party Prime Ministers: Their Trials and Tribulations*, privately published, Chatswood, NSW, 2011.

Davey, Paul, *The Nationals: The Progressive Party, Country and National Party in New South Wales 1919 to 2006*, The Federation Press, Leichhardt, NSW, 2006.

Davey, Paul, *Ninety Not Out: The Nationals 1920–2010*, UNSW Press, Sydney, 2010.

Davidson, Jim, *A Three-Cornered Life: The Historian W.K. Hancock*, UNSW Press, Sydney, 2010.

Davies, A.J., 'Australian Federalism and national development', *Australian Journal of Politics and History*, vol. 14, no. 1, April 1968, pp. 37–51. doi.org/10.1111/j.1467-8497.1968.tb00611.x.

Davies, A.J., 'National development', *Australian Quarterly*, vol. 37, no. 4, December 1965, pp. 45–55. doi.org/10.2307/20634087.

Davies, A.J., 'National Development under Australian Federalism: Politics or Economics?', a paper presented to the Australasian Political Science Association conference, August 1965.

Davies, A.J., 'The New England New State Movement: A Political Analysis', paper to the Australasian Political Studies Association, Ninth Annual Conference, Melbourne, 21–24 August 1967.

Davies, Ronald E., *History of Clarence River and of Grafton 1830–1880*, reprints from the *Daily Examiner*, Grafton, NSW, 1957.

Davis, S.R., 'Co-operative federalism in retrospect', *Historical Studies*, vol. 5, no. 19, 1952, pp. 212–33.

Davis, S.R., *Theory and Reality: Federal Ideas in Australia, England and Europe*, University of Queensland Press, St Lucia, Qld, 1995.

Davis, S.R., 'A unique federal institution', *University of Western Australia Annual Law Review*, December 1952, pp. 350–404.

Davison, Graeme, *Lost Relations: Fortunes of My Family in Australia's Golden Age*, Allen & Unwin, Crows Nest, NSW, 2015.

Davison, Graeme, John Hirst and Stuart Macintyre (eds), *The Oxford Companion to Australian History*, Oxford University Press, Melbourne, 1998.

Davison, Graeme and Marc Brodie (eds), *Struggle Country: The Rural Ideal in Twentieth Century Australia*, Monash University ePress, Clayton, Vic., 2005.

Davison, Graeme and Kate Murphy, *University Unlimited: The Monash Story*, Allen & Unwin, Crows Nest, NSW, 2012.

Decentralisation and New State Movement Convention, *Decentralisation and New State Movement: Armidale Convention, June 1948*, Armidale, NSW, 1948.

Dedman, John, 'The Return of the AIF from the Middle East', *Australian Outlook*, vol. 21, issue 2, August 1967, pp. 151–64. doi.org/10.1080/ 10357716708444272.

Department of Foreign Affairs and Trade, *Historical Documents, Volume 5: 1941, July – 1942, June* [webpage], dfat.gov.au/about-us/publications/historical-documents/Pages/volume-05/1941-july-1942-june-volume-5.aspx.

Dickey, Brian, *No Charity There: A Short History of Social Welfare in Australia*, second edition, Allen & Unwin, North Sydney, 1987 (first published 1980).

Doherty, Muriel Knox, *The Life and Times of Royal Prince Alfred Hospital, Sydney, Australia*, New South Wales College of Nursing, Sydney, 1996.

Dollery, B. and A. Johnson, 'Enhancing efficiency in Australian local government: An evaluation of alternative models of municipal governance', *Urban Policy and Research*, vol. 23, no. 1, March 2005, pp. 73–85.

Dore, J. and J. Woodhill (eds), *Sustainable Regional Development: Final Report: An Australian-Wide Study of Regionalism Highlighting Efforts to Improve the Community, Economy and Environment*, Greening Australia, Canberra, 1999.

Drummond, David, *Australian Problems of Government: Federation vs. Unification*, Armidale, NSW, c. 1934.

Drummond, David, *The Future of Education in Australia*, Armidale, NSW, 1954.

Drummond, David, *A University Is Born: The Story of the Founding of the University of New England*, Angus and Robertson, Sydney, 1959.

Duncan, C.J. and W.R. Epps, 'The demise of "countrymindedness": New players or changing values in Australian rural politics?', *Political Geography*, vol. 11, no. 5, September 1992, pp. 430–48. doi.org/10.1016/0962-6298 (92)90035-R.

Duncan, W.G.K. (ed.), *National Economic Planning*, Angus and Robertson in conjunction with the Australian Institute of Political Science, Sydney, 1934.

Dyne, R.E., 'Local variations in cost of government', *Economic News*, vol. 25, no. 4, July 1956, pp. 1–9.

East, Lewis R., 'Water conservation in Australia', *Walkabout*, vol. 2, no. 11, November 1936, pp. 33–8.

Edwards, Cecil, *Bruce of Melbourne: Man of Two Worlds*, William Heinemann, London, 1965.

Edwards, Cecil, *The Editor Regrets*, Hill of Content, Melbourne, 1972.

Eggleston, Frederick, *Reflections of an Australian Liberal*, F.W. Cheshire, Melbourne, 1958.

Eggleston, Frederick, *State Socialism in Victoria*, P.S. King & Son, London, 1932.

Ellis, Ulrich, 'Australian Agricultural Council, its significance and value – new status for agriculture', *The Australian Country Party Monthly Journal*, 1 March 1935, p. 13.

Ellis, Ulrich, *The Case for Australia: An Interpretation of the Policy of the Australian Country Party*, Australian Country Party, Sydney, 1932.

Ellis, Ulrich, *The Country Party: A Political and Social History of the Party in New South Wales*, F.W. Cheshire, Melbourne, 1958.

Ellis, Ulrich, 'Federal reconstruction', *Australian National Review*, 1 April 1939, pp. 18–26.

Ellis, Ulrich, *A History of the Australian Country Party*, Melbourne University Press, Parkville, Vic., 1963.

Ellis, Ulrich, *New Australian States*, The Endeavour Press, Sydney, 1933.

Ellis, Ulrich, *A Pen in Politics*, Ginninderra Press, Charnwood, ACT, 2007.

Ellis, Ulrich, 'The sower of the seed', *The Australian Country Party Monthly Journal*, 1 March 1935, p. 6.

Emy, Hugh, *The Politics of Australian Democracy: Fundamentals in Dispute*, second edition, Macmillan, South Melbourne, 1978 (first published 1975).

Eversole, Robyn and John Martin (eds), *Participation and Governance in Regional Development: Global Trends in an Australian Context*, Ashgate, Aldershot, 2005.

Fadden, A.W., *Policy Speech of the Australian Country Party, Federal Elections 1949*, Australian Country Party, Sydney, 1949.

Fadden, A.W., *They Called Me Arty: The Memoirs of Sir Arthur Fadden*, The Jacaranda Press, Milton, NSW, 1969.

Fairlie, Henry, *The Life of Politics*, Methuen, London, 1968.

Farrell, John Joseph, 'Bones for the Growling Dog?: The New State Movements in Northern New South Wales 1915–1930', MA (Hons) thesis, Department of History, University of New England, 22 July 1997.

Farrell, John Joseph, 'Opting out and opting in: Secession and the new state movements', *Armidale and District Historical Society Journal*, no. 40, 1997, pp. 139–48.

Ferguson, Arch (ed.), *High: The Centenary History of Sydney High School*, Child & Henry, Brookvale, NSW, 1983.

Fitzgerald, Ross, *"Red Ted": The Life of E.G. Theodore*, University of Queensland Press, St Lucia, Qld, 1994.

Fitzgerald, Ross, with the assistance of Adam Carr and William J. Dealy, *The Pope's Battalions: Santamaria, Catholicism and the Labor Split*, University of Queensland Press, St Lucia, Qld, 2003.

Forster, Colin (ed.), *Australian Economic Development in the Twentieth Century*, George Allen & Unwin Ltd, London and Australasian Publishing Company, Sydney, 1970.

Forster, Colin, *Industrial Development in Australia 1920–30*, Australian National University Press, Canberra, 1964.

Forsyth, Hannah, *A History of the Modern Australian University*, NewSouth Publishing, Sydney, 2014.

Forsyth, W.D., *The Myth of Open Spaces: Australian, British and World Trends of Population and Migration*, Melbourne University Press, Melbourne, 1942.

Freeberg, Ernest, *The Age of Edison: Electric Light and the Invention of Modern America*, Penguin, New York, 2013.

Frost, A.C.H., *Hydro-Electricity in Australia: Water 2000: Consultant's Report No. 6*, Department of Resources and Energy, Canberra, 1983.

Frost, Warwick, 'Australia unlimited?: Environmental debate in the age of catastrophe, 1910–1939', *Environment and History*, vol. 10, no. 3, August 2004, pp. 285–303. doi.org/10.3197/0967340041794295.

Furphy, Samuel (ed.), *The Seven Dwarfs and the Age of the Mandarins: Australian Government Administration in the Post-War Reconstruction Era*, ANU Press, Canberra, 2015. doi.org/10.22459/SDAM.07.2015.

Galligan, Brian, *A Federal Republic: Australia's Constitutional System of Government*, Cambridge University Press, Melbourne, 1995. doi.org/10.1017/CBO978 1139084932.

Galligan, Brian and Winsome Roberts (eds), *The Oxford Companion to Australian Politics*, Oxford University Press, South Melbourne, 2007. doi.org/10.1093/acref/9780195555431.001.0001.

Gascoigne, John (with the assistance of Patricia Curthoys), *The Enlightenment and the Origins of European Australia*, Cambridge University Press, Cambridge, 2002.

Gates, R.C., 'The search for a state growth tax', in R.L. Matthews (ed.), *Intergovernmental Relations in Australia*, Angus and Robertson, Cremorne, NSW, 1974, pp. 159–77.

Gepp, Herbert, *Democracy's Danger: Addresses on Various Occasions*, Angus and Robertson, Sydney, 1939.

Giblin, L.F., *The Growth of a Central Bank: The Development of the Commonwealth Bank of Australia 1924–1945*, Melbourne University Press, Parkville, Vic., 1951.

Gilbert, R.S., *The Australian Loan Council in Federal Fiscal Adjustments, 1890–1965*, Australian National University Press, Canberra, 1973.

Gillespie, James A., *The Price of Health: Australian Governments and Medical Politics 1910–1960*, Cambridge University Press, Melbourne, 1991. doi.org/10.1017/CBO9780511470189.

Gojak, Denis, 'Gara River: An early hydro-electric scheme in northern New South Wales', *Australian Journal of Historical Archaeology*, vol. 6, 1988, pp. 3–11.

Goldberg, S.L. and F.B. Smith (eds), *Australian Cultural History*, Cambridge University Press, Cambridge, 1988.

Golding, Peter, *Black Jack McEwen: Political Gladiator*, Melbourne University Press, Parkville, Vic., 1996.

Gollan, Robin, *The Commonwealth Bank of Australia: Origins and Early History*, Australian National University Press, Canberra, 1968.

Graham, B.D., *The Formation of the Australian Country Parties*, Australian National University Press, Canberra, 1966.

Grattan, Michelle (ed.), *Australian Prime Ministers*, New Holland, Frenchs Forest, NSW, 2000.

Gray, Gwen, 'Social policy', in Scott Prasser, J.R. Nethercote and John Warhurst (eds), *The Menzies Era: A Reappraisal of Government, Politics and Policy*, Hale & Iremonger, Sydney, 1995, pp. 211–27.

Gray, John, *Black Mass: Apocalyptic Religion and the Death of Utopia*, Penguin, London, 2008 (first published 2007).

Green, Frank C., *Servant of the House*, Heinemann, Melbourne, 1969.

Greenhalgh, A.J., 'The plight of rural education', *Australian Quarterly*, vol. 21, no. 3, September 1949, pp. 72–80. doi.org/10.2307/20633181.

Greenwood, Gordon, *The Future of Australian Federalism: A Commentary on the Working of the Constitution*, Melbourne University Press, Carlton, Vic., 1946.

Grogan, F.O., 'The Australian Agricultural Council: A successful experiment in Commonwealth–state relations', *Public Administration*, vol. 17, no. 1, March 1958, pp. 1–21.

Hamilton, Alexander, James Madison and John Jay, *The Federalist Papers*, selected and edited by Roy P. Fairfield, Doubleday, New York, 1961.

Hancock, Ian, *National and Permanent?: The Federal Organisation of the Liberal Party of Australia 1944–1965*, Melbourne University Press, Carlton South, Vic., 2000.

Hancock, W.K., *Australia*, Jacaranda Press, Brisbane, 1961 (first published 1930).

Hancock, W.K., 'Then and now', *IPA Review*, vol. 22, no. 4, 1968, pp. 90–95.

Hannah, Leslie, *Electricity before Nationalisation: A Study of the Development of the Electricity Supply Industry in Britain to 1948*, Macmillan, London, 1979. doi.org/10.1007/978-1-349-03443-7.

Hardman, D.J., 'The Snowy Mountains Hydro-Electric Authority: Origins and antecedents', *Public Administration*, vol. 27, no. 3, September 1968, pp. 205–36.

Harman, Grant, 'New State agitation in northern New South Wales, 1920–1929', *Journal of the Royal Australian Historical Society*, vol. 63, part 1, June 1977, pp. 26–39.

Harper, H.R., 'Presidential Address', *The Journal of the Institution of Engineers, Australia*, vol. 6, no. 2, February 1934, pp. 79-95.

Harrigan, Nicholas, 'The "Australian Settlement" in the Countryside: Small Farmers and the Rise of Statutory Marketing in Australia', paper presented to the Australasian Political Studies Association Conference, 29 September–1 October 2004.

Harris, H.L., H.S. Nicholas, F.A. Bland, A. Mainerd and T. Hytten, *Decentralization*, Angus and Robertson in conjunction with the Australian Institute of Political Science, Sydney, 1948.

Hart, Philip R., 'J.A. Lyons: A Political Biography', PhD thesis, The Australian National University, 1967.

Hartnett, Con, *Curtin and McKell: Architects of Regionalism in Australia*, The Hunter Valley Research Foundation, Tighes Hill, NSW, 1984.

Hasluck, Paul, *The Chance of Politics*, Text Publishing, Melbourne, 1997.

Hasluck, Paul, *The Government and the People 1939–41*, series 4 (Civil), volume 1, *Australia in the War of 1939–1945*, Australian War Memorial, Canberra, 1952.

Hasluck, Paul, *The Government and the People 1942–1945*, series 4 (Civil), volume 2, *Australia in the War of 1939–1945*, Australian War Memorial, Canberra, 1970.

Hawker, Geoffrey, 'Hardy, Charles (1898–1941)', *The Biographical Dictionary of the Australian Senate, Online Edition*, undated, biography.senate.gov.au/index.php/hardy-charles/.

Hawkins, John, 'Sir Earle Page: An active treasurer', *Economic Round-up*, Commonwealth Department of the Treasury, no. 4, 2009, pp. 55–67.

Hazlehurst, Cameron (ed.), *Australian Conservatism: Essays in Twentieth Century Political History*, Australian National University Press, Canberra, 1979.

Hazlehurst, Cameron, *Menzies Observed*, George Allen & Unwin, Sydney, 1979.

Hazlehurst, Cameron, *Ten Journeys to Cameron's Farm: An Australian Tragedy*, ANU E Press, Canberra, 2013. doi.org/10.22459/TJCF.11.2013.

Hazlehurst, Cameron, 'Young Menzies', in Cameron Hazlehurst (ed.), *Australian Conservatism: Essays in Australian Conservatism*, Australian National University Press, Canberra, 1979, pp. 1–28.

Head, Brian (ed.), *The Politics of Development in Australia*, Allen & Unwin, Sydney, 1986.

Head, Brian and James Walter (eds), *Intellectual Movements and Australian Society*, Oxford University Press, Melbourne, 1988.

Headford, C.G., 'The Australian Loan Council – Its origin, operation and significance in the federal structure', in W. Prest and R.L. Mathews (eds), *The Development of Australian Fiscal Federalism: Selected Readings*, Australian National University Press, Canberra, 1980, pp. 164–77. doi.org/10.1111/j.1467-8500.1954.tb02532.x.

Henderson, Anne, *Joseph Lyons: The People's Prime Minister*, NewSouth Publishing, Sydney, 2011.

Henderson, Anne, *Menzies at War*, NewSouth Publishing, Sydney, 2014.

Henderson, Gerard, *Mr. Santamaria and the Bishops*, St Patrick's College, Manly, NSW, 1982.

Henderson, Heather (ed.), *Letters to My Daughter: Robert Menzies, Letters 1955–75*, Pier 9, Millers Point, NSW, 2011.

Henderson, Heather, *A Smile for My Parents*, Allen & Unwin, Crows Nest, NSW, 2013.

Heydon, Peter, *Quiet Decision: A Study of George Foster Pearce*, Melbourne University Press, Carlton, Vic., 1965.

Higgins, Benjamin and Krzysztof Zagorski (eds), *Australian Regional Developments: Readings in Regional Experiences, Policies and Prospects*, AGPS Press, Canberra, 1989.

Hirst, John, *Looking for Australia: Historical Essays*, Black Inc., Melbourne, 2010.

Hirst, John, 'The pioneer legend', in John Carroll (ed.), *Intruders in the Bush: The Australian Quest for Identity*, Oxford University Press, Melbourne, 1982, pp. 14–37.

Hocking, Jenny, *Gough Whitlam: A Moment in History*, The Miegunyah Press, Carlton, Vic., 2008.

Hodgins, Bruce W., James Struthers, John J. Eddy and Shelagh D. Grant (eds), *Federalism in Canada & Australia: Historical Perspectives 1920–1988*, Frost Centre for Canadian Heritage and Development Studies, Trent University, Peterborough, c. 1989.

Hodgins, Bruce W., Don Wright and W.H. Heick (eds), *Federalism in Canada and Australia: The Early Years*, Australian National University Press, Canberra, 1978.

Holmes, J. Macdonald, *The 'New States' Idea and Its Geographic Background*, New Century Press, Sydney, 1933.

Holmes, J. Macdonald, 'Regional planning in Australia', *The Geographical Journal*, vol. 112, nos 1/3, July to December 1948, pp. 78–92.

Hornadge, Bill, *The Search for an Australian Utopia*, Imprint, Bondi Junction, NSW, 1999.

Horne, Donald, *Money Made Us*, Penguin Books, Ringwood, Vic., 1976.

Horner, David, *Defence Supremo: Sir Frederick Shedden and the Making of Australian Defence Policy*, Allen & Unwin, St Leonards, NSW, 2000.

Horner, David, *Inside the War Cabinet: Directing Australia's War Effort 1939–45*, Allen & Unwin in association with the Australian Archives, St Leonards, NSW, 1996.

Horner, David Murray, 'Australia and Allied Strategy in the Pacific, 1941–1946', PhD thesis, The Australian National University, 1980.

Howard, Michael, *Advocacy and Resistance: The Question of a Post-war Commonwealth Government Role in Community Facilities, Town Planning and Regional Planning, 1939–52*, Urban Research Unit Working Paper No. 9, Australian National University, Canberra, 1988.

Hudson, W.J., *Casey*, Oxford University Press, Melbourne, 1986.

Hudson, W.J. and Wendy Way (eds), *Letters From A 'Secret Service Agent': F.L. McDougall to S.M. Bruce 1924–1929*, Australian Government Publishing Service, Canberra, 1986.

Hudson, Wayne and A.J. Brown (eds), *Restructuring Australia: Regionalism, Republicanism and Reform of the Nation State*, The Federation Press, Sydney, 2004.

Hughes, Colin A., *Mr Prime Minister: Australian Prime Ministers 1901–1972*, Oxford University Press, Melbourne, 1976.

Hughes, Thomas P., *Networks of Power: Electrification in Western Society 1880–1930*, The Johns Hopkins University Press, Baltimore, 1983.

Humphries, L.R., *Wadham: Scientist for Land and People*, Melbourne University Press, Parkville, Vic., 2000.

Institute of Public Affairs (New South Wales), *Safeguard Your Rights by Review of the Constitution*, Institute of Public Affairs (New South Wales), Sydney, October 1954.

Irving, Helen, *The Centenary Companion to Australian Federation*, Cambridge University Press, Melbourne, 1999.

Irving, Helen, *To Constitute a Nation: A Cultural History of Australia's Constitution*, Cambridge University Press, Cambridge, 1997.

Jones, Barry, 'Leadership: Ranking our prime ministers', *The Weekend Australian*, 12–13 June 1996, p. 25.

Jones, Evan, 'Nugget Coombs and his place in the postwar order', *The Drawing Board: An Australian Review of Public Affairs*, vol. 4, no. 1, July 2003, pp. 23–44.

Jordan, Matthew, *A Spirit of True Learning: The Jubilee History of the University of New England*, UNSW Press, Sydney, 2004.

Kass, Terry, *Grafton: Jacaranda City on the Clarence – A History*, Clarence Valley City Council, Grafton, NSW, 2009.

Kelly, Andrew H., Brian Dollery and Bligh Grant, 'Regional development and Local Government: Three generations of federal intervention', *Australasian Journal of Regional Studies*, vol. 15, no. 2, 2009, pp. 171–93.

Kelly, Paul, 'Building from the base', *The Australian*, 28 October 2009.

Kelly, Paul, *The End of Certainty: The Story of the 1980s*, Allen & Unwin, St Leonards, NSW, 1992.

Kelly, Vince, 'Doctor's remorse', *Nation*, 23 February 1963, p. 10.

Kemp, C.D., *Big Businessmen: Four Biographical Essays*, Institute of Public Affairs, Melbourne, 1964.

King, J.E. (ed.), *A Biographical Dictionary of Australian and New Zealand Economists*, Edward Elgar, Cheltenham, 2007.

Kingsbury, Stanley, *A Sydney Critic's Catechism of the State Reconstruction Movement*, Australian Country Party Bureau of Publicity, Information and Research, Sydney, 1932.

Kirkpatrick, Rod, 'Correcting years of confusion: The APPA presidents', *Australian Newspaper History Group Newsletter*, no. 48, July 2008, pp. 13–6.

Kirkpatrick, Rod, 'How newspaper editors helped the country become politically articulate', *Australian Journalism Review*, vol. 22, no. 1, 2000, pp. 117–36.

Knott, John William, 'The conquering car: Technology, symbolism and the motorisation of Australia before World War II', *Australian Historical Studies*, vol. 31, no. 114, April 2000, pp. 1–26. doi.org/10.1080/10314610008596113.

Koshin, Jillian, *Electric Eric: The Life and Times of Eric Reece*, Bokprint, Launceston, Tas., 2009.

La Nauze, J.A., *Education for Some*, The Future of Education series no. 3, Australian Council for Educational Research, Melbourne, 1943.

Lake, Marilyn, *The Limits of Hope: Soldier Settlement in Victoria, 1915–38*, Oxford University Press, Melbourne, 1987.

Landes, David S., *The Unbound Prometheus: Technological Change and Industrial Development in Western Europe from 1750 to the Present*, Cambridge University Press, Cambridge, 1969.

Lang, Jack, *The Great Bust: The Depression of the Thirties*, McNamara's Books, Katoomba, NSW, 1980 (first published 1962).

Lang, Jack, *I Remember: Autobiography*, McNamara's Books, Katoomba, NSW, 1980 (first published 1956).

Lang, John Dunmore, *The Coming Event or Freedom and Independence for the Seven United Provinces of Australia*, Sampson Low, Son and Marston, London, 1870.

Lang, John Dunmore, *Freedom and Independence for the Golden Lands of Australia: The Right of the Colonies, and the Interest of Britain and of the World*, Longman, Brown, Green and Longmans, London, 1852.

Lang, J.D., *Australian Water Resources: With Particular Reference to Water Supplies in Central Australia*, RAAF Educational Services, Melbourne, 1944.

Lang, T.A., *Regional Planning of Natural Resources*, State Rivers and Water Supply Commission, Melbourne, 1942.

Larcombe, Frederick A., *The Development of Local Government in New South Wales*, F.W. Cheshire, Melbourne, 1961.

Latham, John, 'Sir Earle Page: Truant Surgeon', *Quadrant*, vol. 7, no. 4, Spring 1963, pp. 82–3, 85.

Layman, Lenore, 'Development ideology in Western Australia 1933–1965', *Historical Studies*, vol. 20, no. 79, October 1982, pp. 234–60. doi.org/10.1080/10314618208595682.

Lee, David, 'Cabinet', in Scott Prasser, J.R. Nethercote and John Warhurst (eds), *The Menzies Era: A Reappraisal of Government, Politics and Policy*, Hale & Iremonger, Sydney, 1995, pp. 123–36.

Lee, David, *Stanley Melbourne Bruce: Australian Internationalist*, Continuum, London, 2010.

Leybourne, Marnie and Andrea Gaynor (eds), *Water: Histories, Cultures, Ecologies*, University of Western Australia Press, Crawley, WA, 2006.

Little, Graham, *Politics and Personal Style*, Nelson, Melbourne, 1973.

Lloyd, A.G., 'Agricultural price policy', in D.B. Williams (ed.), *Agriculture in the Australian Economy*, second edition, Sydney University Press, Sydney, 1982 (first published 1967), pp. 353–82.

Local Government School, *Decentralisation: Proceedings of the Fourth Local Government School*, Local Government Association of NSW and Shires Association of NSW, Sydney, 1948.

Logan, Greg, 'An urban revolution for rural Australia: The genesis of agricultural colleges in colonial Australia', in R.C. Petersen and G.W. Rodwell (eds), *Notes from Essays in the History of Rural Education in Australia and New Zealand*, William Michael Press, Casuarina, 1993, pp. 199–221.

Logan, James, 'Charles D. Hardy Jnr (1898–1941)', *Charles Sturt University Regional Archives & University Art Collection, Regional Records On-Line Guide*, undated, www.csu.edu.au/research/archives/collection/regional/agencies/cdhardy.

Longfield, C.M. and T.A. Lang, *Regional Planning*, RAAF Educational Services, Melbourne, 1944 (first published in *The Journal of The Institution of Engineers, Australia*, August 1943).

Louis, L.J. and Ian Turner (eds), *The Depression of the 1930s*, Cassell Australia, North Melbourne, 1968.

Loveday, Peter, 'Anti-political political thought', 'The Great Depression in Australia', special issue of *Labour History*, no. 17, 1970, pp. 121–35.

Loveday, Peter, 'Liberals and the idea of development', *Australian Journal of Politics and History*, vol. 23, no. 2, August 1977, pp. 219–26. doi.org/10.1111/j.1467-8497.1977.tb01240.x.

Lowe, David, 'Menzies' national security state, 1950–53', in Frank Cain (ed.), *Menzies in War and Peace*, Allen & Unwin, St Leonards, 1997, pp. 41–54.

Luckin, Bill, *Questions of Power: Electricity and Environment in Inter-War Britain*, Manchester University Press, Manchester, 1990. doi.org/10.1086/ahr/96.5.1549.

Lucy, Richard (ed.), *The Pieces of Politics*, second edition, Macmillan, South Melbourne, 1979 (first published 1975).

Lupton, Roger, *Lifeblood: Tasmania's Hydro-Power*, Focus Publishing, Edgecliff, NSW, c. 2000.

Lyons, Brendan, *They Loved Him to Death: Australian Prime Minister 'Honest Joe' Lyons*, privately published, King's Meadows, 2008.

Lyons, Enid, *Among the Carrion Crows*, Rigby, Adelaide, 1972.

McEwen, John, *John McEwen: His Story*, edited by R.V. Jackson, privately published, place of publication n.a., 1983.

McEwen, John and Don Veitch, *McEwen's Way*, edited by John Seale, David Syme College of National Economics, Public Administration & Business Ltd, Flemington, NSW, 1996.

Macintyre, Stuart, *Australia's Boldest Experiment: War and Reconstruction in the 1940s*, NewSouth Publishing, Sydney, 2015.

Macintyre, Stuart, *A Colonial Liberalism: The Lost World of Three Victorian Visionaries*, Oxford University Press, South Melbourne, 1991.

Macintyre, Stuart, *A Concise History of Australia*, Cambridge University Press, Cambridge, 1999.

Macintyre, Stuart, 'The post-war reconstruction project', in Samuel Furphy (ed.), *The Seven Dwarfs and the Age of the Mandarins: Australian Government Administration in the Post-War Reconstruction Era*, ANU Press, Canberra, 2015, pp. 31–51. doi.org/10.22459/SDAM.07.2015.02.

Mackerras, Malcolm, 'Menzies the Top Bob amid the greats', *The Australian*, 16 August 2008.

Mackerras, Malcolm, 'Ranking Australia's prime ministers', *Sydney Morning Herald*, 25 June 2010.

McLachlan, N.D., 'The future America: Some bicentennial reflections', *Historical Studies*, vol. 17, no. 68, April 1977, pp. 361–83. doi.org/10.1080/10314617708595557.

McLachlan, Noel, *Waiting for the Revolution: A History of Australian Nationalism*, Penguin Books, Ringwood, Vic., 1989.

Maclaurin, William Rupert, *Economic Planning in Australia 1929–1936*, P.S. King & Son Ltd, London, 1937.

McMinn, W.G., *A Constitutional History of Australia*, Oxford University Press, Melbourne, 1979.

McMinn, W.G., *Nationalism and Federalism in Australia*, Oxford University Press, Melbourne, 1994.

Maddison, Michelle, 'Senator Charles Hardy and the Riverina Movement', Collection Highlights, Museum of the Riverina, Wagga Wagga City Council, 2005, www.museumriverina.com.au/collections/highlights/senator-charles-hardy-and-the-riverina-movement#.WPX5naKLmUk.

Maher, F.K. and J.I. Sullivan, *Regionalism in Australia*, Araluen Publishing Company, Melbourne, 1946.

Maiden, H.B., *The History of Local Government in New South Wales*, Angus and Robertson, Sydney, 1966.

Main, J.M., 'The development of the Snowy River', *The Journal of the Institution of Engineers, Australia*, vol. 17, no. 10–12, October–December 1945, pp. 209–16.

Maley, William, 'The political philosophy of F.A. Bland', *Political Theory Newsletter*, vol. 5, 1993, pp. 25–38.

Marchant, Sylvia, 'Things Fall Apart: The End of the United Australia Party 1939 to 1943', Master of Letters thesis, The Australian National University, 1998.

Marr, David, *Political Animal: The Making of Tony Abbott*, Quarterly Essay, issue 47, Black Inc., Collingwood, Vic., 2012.

Marsh, Judith, 'Churchill versus Curtin, February 1942', *Army Journal*, no. 260, January 1971, pp. 27–34.

Martin, A.W., 'R.G. Menzies and the Murray Committee', in F.B. Smith and P. Crichton (eds), *Ideas for Histories of Universities in Australia*, Division of Historical Studies, Research School of Social Sciences, The Australian National University, Canberra, 1990, pp. 94–115.

Martin, A.W., *Robert Menzies: A Life, Volume 1, 1894–1943*, Melbourne University Press, Parkville, Vic., 1993.

Martin, A.W., *Robert Menzies: A Life, Volume 2, 1944–1978*, Melbourne University Press, Carlton South, Vic., 1999.

Martin, A.W. and Janet Penny, 'The Rural Reconstruction Commission, 1943–47', *Australian Journal of Politics and History*, vol. 29, no. 2, 1983, pp. 218–36. doi.org/10.1111/j.1467-8497.1983.tb00191.x.

Martin, A.W., *The 'Whig' View of Australian History and Other Essays*, Melbourne University Publishing, Carlton South, Vic., 2007.

Mathews, R.L. (ed.), *Intergovernmental Relations in Australia*, Angus and Robertson, Cremorne, NSW, 1974.

Mathews, R.L. (ed.), *Responsibility Sharing in a Federal System*, Research Monograph no. 8, Australian National University Centre for Research on Federal Financial Relations, Australian National University Press, Canberra, 1975.

Mathews, R.L., *Revenue Sharing in Federal Systems*, Centre for Research on Federal Financial Relations, Australian National University, Canberra, 1980.

Mathews, R.L. and W.R.C. Jay, *Federal Finance: Intergovernmental Financial Relations in Australia since Federation*, Thomas Nelson (Australia), Melbourne, 1972.

Matthews, Trevor, 'The All For Australia League', 'The Great Depression in Australia', special issue of *Labour History*, no. 17, 1970, pp. 136–47.

Maxwell, James A., *Commonwealth–State Financial Relations in Australia*, Melbourne University Press, Carlton, Vic., 1967.

Medley, J.D.G., *Education for Democracy*, The Future of Education series no. 1, Australian Council for Educational Research, Melbourne, 1943.

Megarrity, Lyndon, *Local Government and the Commonwealth: An Evolving Relationship*, Parliamentary Library Research Paper, no. 10, 2010–11, Parliamentary Library, Dept of Parliamentary Services, Canberra, 31 January 2011.

Melleuish, Gregory, *Cultural Liberalism in Australia: A Study in Intellectual and Cultural History*, Cambridge University Press, Oakleigh, Vic., 1995.

Mellor, Lise, *150 Years, 150 Firsts: The People of the Faculty of Medicine*, Sydney University Press, Sydney, 2006.

Mellor, Lise, *Page, Earle Christmas Grafton* [webpage], Faculty of Medicine Online Museum, University of Sydney, 2008, sydney.edu.au/medicine/museum/mwmuseum/index.php/Page,_Earle_Christmas_Grafton.

Menzies, Robert, *Afternoon Light: Some Memories of Men and Events*, Cassell, Melbourne, 1967.

Menzies, Robert, *Central Power in the Australian Commonwealth: An Examination of the Growth of Commonwealth Power in the Australian Federation*, University Press of Virginia, Charlottesville, 1967.

Menzies, Robert, *The Measure of the Years*, Cassell, London, 1970.

Meyers, Jeffrey (ed.), *The Biographer's Art: New Essays*, Macmillan, Basingstoke, 1989.

Miller, J.D.B., *Australian Government and Politics: An Introductory Survey*, Duckworth, London, 1954.

Miller, J.D.B., *The Nature of Politics*, Penguin, Harmondsworth, 1965 (first published 1962).

Millmow, Alex, 'Australia and the Keynesian revolution', in Samuel Furphy (ed.), *The Seven Dwarfs and the Age of the Mandarins: Australian Government Administration in the Post-War Reconstruction Era*, ANU Press, Canberra, 2015, pp. 53–79. doi.org/10.22459/SDAM.07.2015.03.

Millmow, Alex, *The Power of Economic Ideas: The Origins of Keynesian Macroeconomic Management in Interwar Australia 1929–39*, ANU E Press, Canberra, 2010. doi.org/10.22459/PEI.05.2010.

Mills, R.C., 'The financial relations of the Commonwealth and the states', *The Economic Record*, May 1928, pp. 1–14.

Mirams, Sarah, '"The attractions of Australia": E.J. Brady and the making of *Australia Unlimited*', *Australian Historical Studies*, vol. 43, no. 2, 2012, pp. 270–86. doi.org/10.1080/1031461X.2012.677457.

Mitchell, George H., *Growers in Action: Official History of the Victorian Wheat and Woolgrowers' Association, 1927–1968*, The Hawthorn Press, Melbourne, 1969.

Montmarquet, James A., *The Idea of Agrarianism: From Hunter-Gatherer to Agricultural Radical in Western Culture*, University of Idaho Press, Moscow, 1989.

Moore, Andrew, *The Secret Army and the Premier: Conservative Paramilitary Organisations in New South Wales 1930–32*, New South Wales University Press, Kensington, NSW, 1989.

Morse, A.L. and A.C. Marshall, *Review of the Electricity Section*, Local Government Association of New South Wales and Shires Association of New South Wales, Sydney, 1959.

Moyal, Ann, *Breakfast with Beaverbrook: Memoirs of an Independent Woman*, Hale & Iremonger, Sydney, 1995.

Munro, C.H., *Australian Water Resources and Their Development*, Angus and Robertson, Cremorne, NSW, 1974.

Murphy, John, *A Decent Provision: Australian Welfare Policy, 1870 to 1949*, Ashgate, Farnham, 2011.

Murray, Robert, *The Confident Years: Australia in the Twenties*, Allen Lane, Ringwood, Vic., 1978.

Museum of Freemasonry, *Prime Minister Earle Page* [webpage], undated, www.mof.org.au/articles/prime-ministers/86-prime-minister-earle-page.html.

Myers, Walter Harold, *The Supply of Electricity in Bulk*, Institution of Engineers, Australia, Sydney, 1929.

Neale, R.G., 'The New State Movement in Queensland: An interpretation', *Historical Studies*, vol. 4, no. 15, November 1950, pp. 198–213.

Neale, R.G., 'New States Movement', *Australian Quarterly*, vol. 22, no. 3, September 1950, pp. 9–23. doi.org/10.2307/20633275.

Nethercote, J.R. (ed.), *Liberalism and the Australian Federation*, The Federation Press, Leichhardt, NSW, 2001.

Nethercote, J.R., 'Liberalism, nationalism and coalition 1910–29', in J.R. Nethercote (ed.), *Liberalism and the Australian Federation*, The Federation Press, Leichhardt, 2001, pp. 113–33.

Noble, David F., *America by Design: Science, Technology, and the Rise of Corporate Capitalism*, Knopf, New York, 1977.

Nolan, Sybil, 'The snub: Robert Menzies and the Melbourne Club', *Australian Historical Studies*, vol. 48, no. 1, March 2017, pp. 3–18. doi.org/10.1080/1031461X.2016.1259337.

North Coast Development League for the Grafton Chamber of Commerce, *The Clarence Gorge Hydro-Electric Scheme: Harnessing 100,000 Horse-Power*, The League, Grafton, NSW, 1919.

Northcott, Clarence H., *Australian Social Development*, Columbia University, New York, 1918.

Northern New State League, *Australian Subdivision, Effect on Development, The Case for Northern New South Wales*, Examiner Printing Works, Glen Innes, NSW, 1920 (title page reads *Australia Subdivided: The First New State*).

Nye, David E., *America as a Second Creation: Technology and Narratives of New Beginnings*, MIT Press, Cambridge, Massachusetts, 2003.

Nye, David E., *American Technological Sublime*, MIT Press, Cambridge, Massachusetts, 1994.

Nye, David E., *Consuming Power: A Social History of American Energies*, MIT Press, Cambridge, Massachusetts, 1998.

Nye, David E., *Electrifying America: Social Meanings of New Technology 1880–1940*, MIT Press, Cambridge, Massachusetts, 1990.

Nye, David E., *Technology Matters: Questions to Live With*, MIT Press, Cambridge, Massachusetts, 2006.

O'Hara, J.B., 'A doctor in the House: Earle Page 1915–1920', *Armidale and District Historical Society Journal*, no. 14, April 1971, pp. 87–99.

O'Hara, J.B., 'The Entry into Public Life of Sir Earle Christmas Grafton Page (1915–1921)', BA (Hons) thesis, Department of History, University of New England, 1969.

O'Neil, Bernard, Judith Raftery and Kerrie Round (eds), *Playford's South Australia: Essays on the History of South Australia, 1933–1968*, Association of Professional Historians Inc., Adelaide, 1996.

Osmond, Warren G., *Frederick Eggleston: An Intellectual in Australian Politics*, Allen & Unwin, Sydney, 1985.

Overy, Richard, *The Morbid Age: Britain between the Wars*, Allen Lane, London, 2009.

Page, Earle, *Australian Industries: The Interdependence of 'Primary' and 'Secondary'*, Simmons Ltd, Sydney, 1926.

Page, Earle, *Clarence River Hydro-Electric Gorge Scheme*, The Bulletin Newspaper, Sydney, 1944.

Page, Earle, *Clarence Water-Power Development*, The Bulletin Newspaper, Sydney, 1947.

Page, Earle, 'Dr. Earle Page's new plan – National Co-ordination Councils – parliament of governments', *Australian Country Party Journal*, 1 July 1935, p. 3.

Page, Earle, *Improvement of Empire Communications and Methods of Consultation*, Empire Parliamentary Association, London, 1942.

Page Earle, *The New State in Northern New South Wales, Resources, Finance, Government: Statement of the Case*, Northern New State Movement, Tamworth, NSW, 1924.

[Page, Earle], *A New State: Proposed Separation of Northern New South Wales: A Statement Compiled and Published by the Committee appointed at a Public Meeting held in Grafton, in January 1915*, Grafton, NSW, 1915 (no author given but has Page's characteristic phraseology, e.g. 'the psychological moment', p. 22).

Page, Earle, *New States: Why They Are Necessary in Australia: Speech*, delivered at the New State Convention, Rockhampton, October 1923, Northern New South Wales New State Movement, Tamworth, NSW, 1923.

Page, Earle, 'New States', *Stead's Review*, 3 July 1925, pp. 27–30, 72.

Page, Earle, *A Plea for Unification: The Development of Australia*, Grafton, NSW, 1917.

Page, Earle, *A Policy for the People*, Australian Country Party, Sydney, 1928.

Page, Earle, *The Value of Decentralization of University Education in Australia: Being an Address Delivered at the Twenty-first Annual Commencement Ceremony of the Canberra University College on 28th March, 1950*, Canberra University College, Canberra, 1950.

Page, Earle, *Truant Surgeon: The Inside Story of Forty Years of Australian Political Life*, edited by Ann Mozley [Moyal], Angus and Robertson, Sydney, 1963.

Page, Earle, *Unique Opportunity for Co-ordinated National Development Based on Proposals for the Clarence*, [Grafton, NSW], c. 1956.

Page, Earle, *What Price Medical Care?: A Preventative Prescription for Private Medicine*, J.B. Lippincott, Philadelphia, 1960.

Page, Earle, 'Why New States?', speech to All-Australian Federal Convention 25–26 July 1949, in F.A. Bland (ed.), *Changing the Constitution: Proceedings of the All-Australian Federal Convention, 25th and 26th July 1949*, The New South Wales Constitutional League, Sydney, 1950, pp. 94–135.

Page, Geoff, *Collected Lives*, Angus and Robertson, North Ryde, NSW, 1986.

Page, Geoff, *Gravel Corners*, Angus and Robertson, Pymble, NSW, 1992.

Page, Geoff, *Selected Poems*, Angus and Robertson, North Ryde, NSW, 1991.

Page, Jim, *Great Uncle Harold: Harold Hillis Page 1888–1942*, privately published, no date.

Page, Jim, *The History of Heifer Station*, privately published, no date.

Paine, Kay, *History of Grafton Hospital*, revised edition, Clarence River Historical Society, Grafton, NSW, 2015 (first published 2005).

Parker, R.S., 'Why new states?', in R.S. Parker, J. Macdonald Holmes, J.P. Belshaw and H.V. Evatt, *New States for Australia*, Australian Institute of Political Science, Sydney, 1955, pp. 1–19.

Parker, R.S., Holmes, J. Macdonald, Belshaw, J.P. and Evatt, H.V., *New States for Australia*, Australian Institute of Political Science, Sydney, 1955.

Parry, E., 'The economics of electric-power distribution', *New Zealand Journal of Science and Technology*, vol. 1, January 1918, pp. 49–55.

Paterson, George, *The Life and Times of Thomas Paterson (1882–1952): A Biography and History by His Elder Son George Paterson*, privately published, Caulfield East, Vic., 1987.

Peck, Don (photographs by Marion Cooney), *From Rivertree to the Sea: Early Days along the Clarence River*, Clarence River Historical Society, Grafton, NSW, 2004.

Pemberton, Joanne, 'The middle way: The discourse of planning in Britain, Australia and at the League in the interwar years', *Australian Journal of Politics and History*, vol. 52, no. 1, 2006, pp. 48–63. doi.org/10.1111/j.1467-8497.2006.00407a.x.

Pemberton, Joanne, '"O brave new social order": The controversy over planning in Australia and Britain in the 1940s', *Journal of Australian Studies*, vol. 28, no. 83, 2004, pp. 35–47. doi.org/10.1080/14443050409387972.

Petersen, R.C. and G.W. Rodwell (eds), *Notes from Essays in the History of Rural Education in Australia and New Zealand*, William Michael Press, Casuarina, NT, 1993.

Pope, Barton, Macfarlane Burnet and Mark Oliphant, *Challenge to Australia*, Rigby, Adelaide, 1982.

Pope, Barton, 'Planning for the next one hundred years', in Barton Pope, Macfarlane Burnet and Mark Oliphant, *Challenge to Australia*, Rigby, Adelaide, 1982, pp. 6–21.

Portus, G.V. (ed.), *Studies in the Australian Constitution*, Angus and Robertson, Sydney, 1933.

Powell, J.M., *Griffith Taylor and 'Australia Unlimited'*, The John Murtagh Macrossan lecture 1992, University of Queensland Press, St Lucia, Qld, 1993.

Powell, J.M., *An Historical Geography of Modern Australia: The Restive Fringe*, Cambridge University Press, Cambridge, 1988.

Powell, J.M., *Plains of Promise, Rivers of Destiny: Water Management and the Development of Queensland 1824–1990*, Boolarong, Brisbane, 1991.

Prasser, Scott, J.R. Nethercote, J.R. and John Warhurst (eds), *The Menzies Era: A Reappraisal of Government, Politics and Policy*, Hale & Iremonger, Sydney, 1995.

Prest, W. and R.L. Mathews (eds), *The Development of Australian Fiscal Federalism: Selected Readings*, Australian National University Press, Canberra, 1980.

Pringle, John Douglas, *Australian Accent*, Rigby, Adelaide, 1978 (first published 1958).

Radford, Paul, *A Scholar in a New Land: Lewis Bostock Radford*, privately published, Lower Mitcham, SA, 1979.

Radford, William C., *The Educational Needs of a Rural Community*, Educational Research series no. 56, Melbourne University Press, Melbourne, 1939.

Radi, Heather, '1920–29', in Frank Crowley (ed.), *A New History of Australia*, William Heinemann Australia, Melbourne, 1974, pp. 357–414.

Rankin, D.H., *The Philosophy of Australian Education*, The Arrow Printery, Melbourne, 1941.

Reeves, William Pember, *State Experiments in Australia and New Zealand*, Macmillan, South Melbourne, 1969 (first published 1902).

Reynolds, Wayne, *Australia's Bid for the Atomic Bomb*, Melbourne University Press, Carlton, Vic., 2000.

Rich, David C., 'Tom's vision?', in Barnard O'Neil, Judith Raftery and Kerrie Round (eds), *Playford's South Australia: Essays on the History of South Australia, 1933–1968*, Association of Professional Historians Inc., Adelaide, 1996, pp. 91–116.

Richards, Eric, *Destination Australia: Migration to Australia since 1901*, UNSW Press, Sydney, 2008.

Richardson, Sarah, 'Higher education and community benefits: The role of regional provision', *Joining the Dots: Research Briefings*, Australian Council for Educational Research, vol. 1, no. 5, September 2011, pp. 1–11.

Richmond, W.H., 'S.M. Bruce and Australian economic policy 1923–9', *Australian Economic History Review*, vol. 23, no. 2, 1983, pp. 238–57. doi.org/10.1111/aehr.232004.

Robertson, John, *J.H. Scullin: A Political Biography*, University of Western Australia Press, Nedlands, WA, 1974.

Robertson, J.R., '1930–39', in Frank Crowley (ed.), *A New History of Australia*, William Heinemann Australia, Melbourne, 1974, pp. 415–57.

Robin, Libby, *How a Continent Created a Nation*, UNSW Press, Sydney, 2007.

Robson, L.L., *Australia in the Nineteen Twenties: Commentary and Documents*, Nelson, Melbourne, 1980.

Roe, Michael, *Australia, Britain, and Migration 1915–1940: A Study of Desperate Hopes*, Cambridge University Press, Cambridge, 1995.

Roe, Michael, *Nine Australian Progressives: Vitalism in Bourgeois Social Thought 1890–1960*, University of Queensland Press, St Lucia, Qld, 1984.

Ross, A.T., *Armed and Ready: The Industrial Development & Defence of Australia 1900–1945*, Turton & Armstrong, Sydney, 1995.

Ross, A.T., 'Australian overseas trade and national development policy 1932–1939: A story of colonial larrikins or Australian statesmen?', *Australian Journal of Politics and History*, vol. 36, no. 2, 1990, pp. 184–204. doi.org/10.1111/j.1467-8497.1990.tb00652.x.

Rowe, A.P., *If the Gown Fits*, Melbourne University Press, Parkville, Vic., 1960.

Rowse, Tim, *Australian Liberalism and National Character*, Kibble Books, Malmsbury, Vic., 1978.

Rowse, Tim, *Nugget Coombs: A Reforming Life*, Cambridge University Press, Melbourne, 2002.

Royal Prince Alfred Hospital, *Royal Prince Alfred Hospital: 125 Year Anniversary*, Royal Prince Alfred Hospital, Camperdown, NSW, 2007.

Russell, Charles W., *Country Crisis*, W.R. Smith & Paterson, Brisbane, 1976.

Ryan, J.S., 'Prelude – Uplands always attract', in Alan Atkinson, J.S. Ryan, Iain Davidson and Andrew Piper (eds), *High, Lean Country: Land, People and Memory in New England*, Allen & Unwin, Crows Nest, NSW, 2006, pp. 1–9.

Ryan, Peter, *It Strikes Me: Collected Essays 1994–2010*, Quadrant Books, Sydney, 2011.

Santamaria, B.A., *The Earth – Our Mother*, Araluen Publishing, Melbourne, 1945.

Santamaria, B.A., *The Fight for the Land: The Program and Objectives of the National Catholic Rural Movement*, National Catholic Rural Movement, Melbourne, 1942.

Santamaria, B.A., *Santamaria: A Memoir*, Oxford University Press, Melbourne, 1997.

Sawer, Geoffrey, *Australian Federal Politics and Law 1901–1929*, Melbourne University Press, Parkville, Vic., 1956.

Sawer, Geoffrey (ed.), *Federalism: An Australian Jubilee Study*, F.W. Cheshire, Melbourne, 1951.

Schama, Simon, *The American Future: A History*, Bodley Head, London, 2008.

Schedvin, Boris, *Australia and the Great Depression: A Study of Economic Development and Policy in the 1920s and 1930s*, Sydney University Press, Sydney, 1970.

Scott, Roger (ed.), *Development Administration and Regional Projects: Proceedings of a Seminar on Development Administration held at the Canberra College of Advanced Education, February 6–20, 1975*, Canberra College of Advanced Education, Canberra, 1975.

Scruton, Roger, *The Palgrave Macmillan Dictionary of Political Thought*, third edition, Palgrave Macmillam, Basingstoke, 2007 (first published 1982).

Scullin, J., 'Call for revision of Constitution', *Australian National Review*, February 1939.

Serle, Geoffrey, *From Deserts the Prophets Come: The Creative Spirit in Australia 1788–1972*, Heinemann, Melbourne, 1972.

Serle, Geoffrey, *John Monash: A Biography*, Melbourne University Press, Carlton, Vic., 1982.

Sesquicentenary Anniversary Committee, *Grafton's Sesquicentenary of Local Government 1859–2009: The First City on the North Coast*, Clarence Valley Council, Grafton, NSW, 2009.

Shedden, K.R., *Pioneering Hydro-Electric Development in Australia: Notes on the Life and Work of William Corin*, Taree, NSW, c. 1963.

Sinclair, W.A., 'Capital formation', in C. Forster (ed.), *Australian Economic Development in the Twentieth Century*, George Allen & Unwin Ltd, London, and Australasian Publishing Company, Sydney, 1970, pp. 11–65.

Sinclair, W.A., *The Process of Economic Development in Australia*, Cheshire, Melbourne, 1976.

Skene Smith, Neil, *Economic Control: Australian Experiments in 'Rationalisation' and 'Safeguarding'*, P.S. King & Son, London, 1929.

Smith, F.B. and P. Crichton (eds), *Ideas for Histories of Universities in Australia*, Division of Historical Studies, Research School of Social Sciences, The Australian National University, Canberra, 1990.

Smyth, Paul, *Australian Social Policy: The Keynesian Chapter*, UNSW Press, Sydney, 1994.

Souter, Gavin, *Acts of Parliament: A Narrative History of Australia's Federal Legislature*, Melbourne University Press, Parkville, Vic., 1988.

Soutphommasane, Tim, 'What happened to our nation-building optimism?', ABC Radio National *Mongrel Nation* program website, 5 August 2013, www.abc.net.au/radionational/programs/mongrelnation/mongrel-nation/4864688.

Spann R.N., and G.R. Curnow, *Public Policy and Administration in Australia: A Reader*, Wiley, Sydney, 1975.

Staley, A.A. and J.R. Nethercote, 'Liberalism and the Australian Federation', in J.R. Nethercote (ed.), *Liberalism and the Australian Federation*, The Federation Press, Leichhardt, NSW, 2001, pp. 1–10.

Stanley, Massey, 'Page on the attack', *Nation*, 23 February 1963, pp. 8–9.

Stirling, Alfred, *Lord Bruce: The London Years*, The Hawthorn Press, Melbourne, 1974.

Stokes, Geoffrey (ed.), *Australian Political Ideas*, UNSW Press, Kensington, NSW, 1994.

Stokes, Geoffrey, 'The "Australian Settlement" and Australian political thought', *Australian Journal of Political Science*, vol. 39, no. 1, March 2004, pp. 5–22. doi.org/10.1080/1036114042000205579.

Stokes, Geoffrey, 'A rejoinder', *Australian Journal of Political Science*, vol. 39, no. 1, March 2004, pp. 43–7. doi.org/10.1080/1036114042000205632.

Strange, Carolyn and Alison Bashford, *Griffith Taylor: Visionary, Environmentalist, Explorer*, National Library of Australia, Canberra, 2008.

Sugden, Edward H., *Wesley's Influence upon Australia*, The Methodist Book Depot, Melbourne, 1930.

Swain, E.H.F., *Forests and Regionalism in the Clarence River Region of N.S.W.: An Address Given by E.H.F. Swain in the Town Hall, Grafton, on 4th August 1944, Under the Auspices of the Grafton Chamber of Commerce (Mr. W.G. Johnson, Chairman)*, N.S.W. Forestry Commission, Sydney, 1944.

Swain, E.H.F., 'Forests and regionalism on the Clarence', *Public Administration*, vol. 5, no. 6, June 1945, pp. 264–80. doi.org/10.1111/j.1467-8500.1945.tb02597.x.

Sydney Boys' High School, 'Sydney Boys' High School Jubilee: 1883–1933', special issue of *The Magazine of the Sydney Boy's High School*, vol. XXV, no. 2, October 1933.

Tapp, E.J., 'The colonial origins of the New England New State Movement', *Journal of the Royal Australian Historical Society*, vol. 49, part 3, 1963, pp. 205–21.

Tapp, E.J., 'Decentralization and the individual', *Australian Quarterly*, vol. 20, no. 2, June 1948, pp. 82–90. doi.org/10.2307/20631557.

Thompson, Victor C., *Constitutional Position: Regarding Creation of New States as Provided in Present Federal Constitution: A Review*, Northern New South Wales New State Movement, Tamworth, NSW, c. 1922.

Thompson, Victor C., *The New State, Embracing Northern New South Wales: A Series of Articles Published in the Daily Observer, Tamworth, and Addenda*, Daily Observer, Tamworth, NSW, 1920.

Tink, Andrew, *Air Disaster Canberra: The Plane Crash That Destroyed a Government*, NewSouth Publishing, Sydney, 2013.

de Tocqueville, Alexis, *Democracy in America*, translated by Henry Reeve, Everyman's Library, Alfred A. Knopf, New York, 1994.

Todd, Jan, *Colonial Technology: Science and the Transfer of Innovation to Australia*, Cambridge University Press, Cambridge, 1995.

Tsokhas, Kosmas, 'The Australian role in Britain's return to the gold standard', *Economic History Review*, vol. 47, no. 1, February 1994, pp. 129–46. doi.org/10.2307/2598223.

Tsokhas, Kosmas, 'Dedominionization: The Anglo-Australian experience, 1939–1945', *The Historical Journal*, vol. 37, no. 4, December 1994, pp. 861–83. doi.org/10.1017/S0018246X00015120.

Tsokhas, Kosmas, *Markets, Money and Empire: The Political Economy of the Australian Wool Industry*, Melbourne University Press, Carlton, Vic., 1990.

Turner, Ian (ed.), *The Australian Dream: A Collection of Anticipations about Australia from Captain Cook to the Present Day*, Sun Books, Melbourne, 1968.

Turney, Clifford (ed.), *Sources in the History of Australian Education: A Book of Readings 1788–1970*, Angus and Robertson, Sydney, 1975.

Tyquin, Michael B., *Neville Howse: Australia's First Victoria Cross Winner*, Oxford University Press, South Melbourne, 1999.

Wadham, Samuel, *These Empty Spaces: The Problems of Decentralisation*, Platypus Pamphlet no. 6, Commonwealth Office of Education, Sydney, 1950.

Wadham, Samuel, R. Kent Wilson and Joyce Wood, *Land Utilization in Australia*, fourth edition, Melbourne University Press, Parkville, Vic., 1964 (first published 1939).

Walker, R.B., *Old New England: A History of the Northern Tablelands of New South Wales*, Sydney University Press, Sydney, 1966.

Walter, James with Tod Moore, *What Were They Thinking?: The Politics of Ideas in Australia*, UNSW Press, Sydney, 2010.

Ward, Russel, *A Nation for a Continent: The History of Australia 1901–1975*, Heinemann Educational Australia, Richmond, Vic., 1975.

Warhaft, Sally (ed.), *Well May We Say…: The Speeches That Made Australia*, Black Inc., Melbourne, 2004.

Waterhouse, Richard, *The Vision Splendid: A Social and Cultural History of Rural Australia*, Curtin University Books, Fremantle, WA, 2002.

Wettenhall, Roger, *Public Enterprise and National Development: Selected Essays*, Royal Australian Institute of Public Administration (A.C.T. Division) in association with the National Council, Royal Australian Institute of Public Administration, Canberra, 1987.

White, Colin, *Mastering Risk: Environment, Markets and Politics in Australian Economic History*, Oxford University Press, South Melbourne, 1992.

White, Richard, *Inventing Australia: Images and Identity 1688–1980*, Allen & Unwin, Sydney, 1981.

Whitford, Troy and Don Boadle, 'Australia's Rural Reconstruction Commission, 1943–46: A reassessment', *Australian Journal of History and Politics*, vol. 54, no. 4, December 2008, pp. 525–44.

Whitlam, Gough, *The Whitlam Government 1972–1975*, Viking, Ringwood, Vic., 1985.

Whitwell, Greg, *The Treasury Line*, Allen & Unwin, North Sydney, 1986.

Wigmore, Lionel, *Struggle for the Snowy: The Background of the Snowy Mountains Scheme*, Oxford University Press, Melbourne, 1968.

Wildavsky, Aaron, 'The 1926 referendum', in Aaron Wildavsky and Dagmar Carboch, *Studies in Australian Politics*, Cheshire, Melbourne, 1958, pp. 1–118.

Wildavsky, Aaron and Dagmar Carboch, *Studies in Australian Politics*, Cheshire, Melbourne, 1958.

Williams, D.B. (ed.), *Agriculture in the Australian Economy*, second edition, Sydney University Press, Sydney, 1982 (first published 1967).

Williams, George, 'Bryan Pape and his legacy to the law', *University of Queensland Law Journal*, vol. 34, no. 1, 2015, pp. 108–27.

Williams, Raymond, *The Country and the City*, Chatto & Windus, London, 1973.

Wills, N.R. (ed.), *Australia's Power Resources: Papers Read at the 1954 Winter Forum of the Victorian Group of the Australian Institute of Political Science*, F.W. Cheshire, Melbourne, 1955.

Wilson, Roland, *Economic Co-ordination*, The Joseph Fisher Lecture in Commerce, University of Adelaide, Adelaide, 1940.

Wiltshire, Kenneth, *Planning and Federalism: Australian and Canadian Experience*, University of Queensland Press, St Lucia, Qld, 1986.

Wood, F.L.W., *The Constitutional Development of Australia*, George G. Harrap, London, 1933.

Wright, Don and Eric G. Clancy, *The Methodists: A History of Methodism in New South Wales*, Allen & Unwin, St Leonards, NSW, 1993.

Young, John Atherton, Ann Jervie Sefton, and Nina Webb (eds), *Centenary Book of the University of Sydney Faculty of Medicine*, Sydney University Press for the University of Sydney Faculty of Medicine, Sydney, 1984.

# INDEX

Note: numbers in italics indicate figures or illustrations.

agricultural support schemes, 66
agricultural theory, 41–42
agriculture. *see* primary industry
America
    agricultural development, 41–42
    hydroelectricity, 52
anti-socialist fears, 79, 91, 100, 258, 289. *see also* communism
Australian Agricultural Council (AAC), 240
    creation, 207–208
    origins, 206
    response to orderly marketing, 210–212
    state dynamics, 208
    success of, 209–210
Australian Commonwealth Engineering Standards Association, 119
Australian Country Party Association (ACPA), 148–150
    Page as chair, 150
Australian Farmers' Federal Organisation (AFFO), 74
    formation, 63
    relationship with Country Party, 148–149
    resistance to electoral pact, 145
Australian geography, 69
    constraints on production, 39, 164

impacts on development, 7, 12, 123, 216, 308
Australian Institute of Political Science (AIPS), 182–183, 220
Australian Labor Party (ALP), 72–73, 85, 141, 179, 235
Australian Provincial Press Association, 18, 311
Australian Wheat Board, 74

banking sector, 97–99
    central bank, 98–99
Bland, F.A., 72, 186, 210, 320
    regionalism, 269
Brigden Enquiry, 159
Brigden, James, 159
Britain
    direction of Australian troops to Burma, 245–247
    economic planning, 220–221
    embargo on gold exports, 98
    *Empire Settlement Act 1922,* 153
    funding from, 214–215
    migration from, 11, 115, 153, 214
    as Mother Country, 11
    Page visits to, 221–222, 243–247
    post-war recovery, 153
    relationship with Australia, 243
    relationship with United States, 248
    return to gold standard, 165

379

tensions with Australia, 247
trade relations with, 139, 182, 205, 206, 209, 213–214, 247–248
British Empire
admiration of, 57
Australian duty towards, 139–140
decline, 250
loyalty to, 11
brown coal. *see* coal
Bruce–Page Government. *see also* Development and Migration Commission (DMC)
Commonwealth–state cooperation, 100–108
developmentalism, 138–142
dynamics, 143–144
electoral pact, 145
fall of, 175–178
Financial Agreement, 165–170
fiscal policy, 128–133
Maritime Industries Bill, 176
portfolio allocation, 94
roads, 128–133
Bruce, Stanley
economic approach, 140
offer of prime ministership, 235
opinion of Page, 1
relationship with Page, 94, 133, 139–141, 142–143, 235, 318
Treasurer, 182

Cameron, Archie, 239
Canada, 21
hydroelectricity, 60, 113
Canberra, 81, 273
Casey, Richard
minister for national development, 299
president of Liberal Party, 287
relationship with Page, 299–300
Catholic regionalism, 268
centralisation. *see also* decentralisation; regionalism

acceleration of, 241
barrier to electrification, 112
criticisms of, 266
disadvantages of, 18, 82–83
population, 39
as wastefulness, 65–66
Chifley Government, 290–291
national health insurance scheme, 295
Chifley, Ben, 281
Churchill, Winston, 244, 245, 252
cities
criticism of, 82
population concentration, 39, 86–87, 125, 305
public works, 82
Clarence River, 31. *see also* Nymboida River; Snowy River Hydroelectric Scheme
alternative to Snowy River Hydroelectric Scheme, 277
assessments for hydroelectricity, 281–282, 285, 308
*Clarence River Hydro-Electric Gorge Scheme,* 278, *279*
Clarence Valley Authority, 276, 313
*Clarence Water-Power Development,* 283–284
criticisms of proposal, 285, 312
hydroelectricity scheme, 20, 46, 47–49, 111, 162–163
nationwide hydroelectric scheme, 280
post-war reconstruction project, 275–276
publicity, 283, 318–319
Clarence Valley, 19–20, *29*
medical services, 42–43
transfer to Queensland, 32
coal
development, 318
versus hydroelectricity, 113–114, 164

INDEX

Cohen Royal Commission
  brief, 122
  findings, 125–126
  Page as witness to, 122–125
Cold War, 270, 289
Commonwealth Bank, 98–99, 169
Commonwealth Government
  Commonwealth Public Service, 259
  Department of Post-War Reconstruction, 261, 266, 285
  financial powers, 70, 167–168
  funding for universities, 272, 273
  health, 297–298
  as leader in intergovernmental cooperation, 105–106
  migration, 153
  national development, 138–139
  as national planner, 105–106, 153
  reach of powers, 70–71, 73
  wartime taxation, 104–105
Commonwealth Housing Commission, 257
Commonwealth Planning Authority, 257
Commonwealth–state policy cooperation
  agriculture, 205, 206–213
  coordinated borrowing, 105
  coordinating bodies, 171–172, 210, 219
  efficiency, 107
  electrification, 117–120
  fears of centralism, 170
  Financial Agreement, 165–170
  financial relations, 104–105, 107–108
  health, 297–298
  hydroelectricity, 281
  Loan Council, 107–108, 167–168, 218, 223–224
  national planning, 102–103, 221–223, 262
  necessity of, 70–71

  Page's contributions to, 325–326
  post-war reconstruction, 253–256
  proposals for, 263–264, 314–315
  resistance to, 225–227, 333
  roads, 130–132
  through voluntary collaboration, 102–103
  tied Commonwealth grants, 128–133
communism, 289, 293. *see also* anti-socialist fears
community engagement, 23, 27, 30–31, 67
  and regionalism, 270
Constitution
  Constitutional Convention, 253–255
  criticisms, 21, 103, 211
  Joint Committee on Constitutional Review, 314
  new state section (section 124), 34, 90, 314, 316, 320
  Peden Royal Commission into the Constitution, 171, 172–173
  reform, 69, 71, 100–101, 211, 313–316
Coombs, H.C.
  director-general of post-war reconstruction, 241
  economics background, 260
Corin, William, 47–48, 49, 164
  Nymboida River, 115
Council for Scientific and Industrial Research (CSIR), 97, 141
Country Party
  agricultural support schemes, 66
  Australian Farmers' Federal Organisation (AFFO), 148–149
  change in focus, 302–303, 332
  coalition with Liberal Party, 288
  coalition with Nationalists Party, 91–100, 144–147

381

coalition with United Australia
    Party (UAP), 180–181, 199,
    233–234, 239
electoral pact, 145
founding of, 4, 74–75
Hardy, Charles, 188
leadership, 73, 76, 95, 145–146,
    148–149, 232, 238–240
National Council support, 232
national planning, 152
new statism, 87–88
perceptions of, 110, 330–331
policies, 75, 77–78, 148–149, 288
resistance to tariffs, 184
support for free trade, 74
support for Snowy River
    Hydroelectric Scheme, 276
support for state intervention, 74
voting, 79
countrymindedness, 40–42, 302.
    *see also* regionalism
Curtin Government
    national health insurance scheme,
        295
    post-war reconstruction, 257,
        258, 280
    regionalisation, 268
    tertiary education support, 272
    World War II Burma controversy,
        245–247
Curtin, John, 244
    Commonwealth–state
        cooperation, 223
    relationship with Page, 234–235,
        245–247

dairy farming, 66
    British imports, 205
    Dairy Industry Committee
        of Enquiry, 316–317
    regulation, 62
    subsidies, 316–317
Deakin, Alfred, 22

Deakinite Australian Settlement, 10,
    333–334
decentralisation, 18–20, 80–86,
    264–272. *see also* centralisation;
    regionalism
    during wartime, 265–266
    and higher education, 304–306
Dedman, John, 282
Department of Post-War
    Reconstruction, 261, 266, 285
Development and Migration
    Commission (DMC), 141. *see also*
    Migration Agreement
    abolition by Scullin Government,
        177–178, 298–299
    Clarence Valley hydroelectricity
        plan, 162–163
    creation, 154
    scope, 151–152, 154–155, 161
developmentalism, 8–13
    assumptions about, 333–334
    *Australia Unlimited*, 12, 69
    in Australian history, 333–334
    Bruce–Page Government,
        138–144
    debates, 12
    ideology, 10
    lack of interest, 231
    and national identity, 9–10, 70
    optimism, 38
    Page's approach to, 329–330
    political culture, 327–328
    post-war reconstruction, 241,
        256–259
    post-war revival, 69–70
    public interest in, 310, 329
    scepticism, 178
Drummond, David, 44–45, 324
    education ministry, 127

economic planning, 71–72, 139–140,
    218–219, 223. *see also* finance
    averting depressions, 183
    Britain, 220–221

compared with management, 291
and manufacturing, 156–160
and national planning, 221
post-war reconstruction, 249–250, 255–258
and primary industry, 157
economists
  Brigden, James, 159
  impact on policy, 159
  role in policy-making, 178, 183, 219–220, 240, 260, 317
education
  higher education, 272–275, 304–306
  regional areas, 20, 24, 201–203, 273–274, 306
  secondary schooling, 273–274
  universities, 201–203
electrification
  central to Page's career, 110
  connection of Nymboida to Newcastle, 276
  as development, 112, 213, 276, 282
  funding of, 214–215
  impact on medical services, 44
  increase in power use, 113
  *Missed Opportunities: Turning Water into Gold*, 322
  nationwide, 117–120, 277–278, 279–280
  opportunities for regional Australia, 41
  price-setting, 116, 222
  standardisation, 117–118, 119
Ellis, Ulrich, 55, xvi
  Constitution League, 186
  national development, 299
  new statism, 307–308, 321
  and Page's memoirs, 322
  writing on Page, 14, 54–57, 121, 195–196
  writing on water resources, 46

Fadden, Arthur, 238, 240, 292
  prime ministership, 242–243, 244
Farmers and Settlers' Association (FSA), 63
farming. *see* primary industry
Federal Reconstruction Movement (FRM), 187
  alliance with United Australia Party (UAP), 191
federalism
  cooperative federalism, 102
  criticisms of, 85
  debate, 70, 71
  the federal bargain, 103–104
  and manufacturing, 156–157
  post-war revival, 263–264
  reforms, 170–175
  strengths of, 102
Federation, 33–34
Federation Drought, 39
finance. *see also* Great Depression
  banking crash (1893), 35
  banking reform, 97–99
  budgets, 96–97, 177, 293
  coordinated borrowing, 105
  customs and excise duties, 70
  debt, 165, 167
  deficit, 171
  free trade, 158, 159
  gold standard, 165
  infrastructure funding, 131
  Loan Council, 107–108, 167–168, 218, 223–224
  private investment, 160
  protectionism, 158
  tied Commonwealth grants, 128–133, 325
  vertical fiscal imbalance, 65, 103, 105, 152
Financial Agreement
  background, 165–166
  referendum, 166–167
food security, 278
free trade, 158, 159

government. *see also* Commonwealth Government; state governments
  balance of power, 79, 92
  censure motion, 79
  central government, 85–86, 104
  coalitions, 91–100, 144–147, 180–181, 199, 233–234, 287–288
  conduct of, 260–261
  debate on role of state, 289
  efficiency, 71–72, 107, 137, 141, 155, 260, 272
  electorate competition, 145
  generational change, 290
  levels of, 105–106
  local government, 125, 126
  policy environment, 181–183, 231, 250, 259, 263, 310
  political culture, 331
  portfolio allocation, 94, 233, 239
  preferential voting, 73
  process, 7, 68–69
  public attitudes, 257, 289
  referenda, 165, 211, 255, 316
  Senate control, 295
Grafton, NSW, 22, 30
  as basis for Page's ideals, 81
  civic improvements, 48–49
Graziers' Association of New South Wales, 74
Great Depression, 179
  causes, 212
  impact, 231
  recovery, 181–183, 240
Great War. *see* World War I

Hardy, Charles
  *Cromwell of the Riverina*, 187
  death, 198
  paramilitary force, 188
  Riverina secession, 187–190
  senator, 190–191
  ultimatum to Lang, 194

health
  British Medical Association (Australia) (BMA), 294, 295–296
  infrastructure, 28
  medical technology, 36, 43–44
  National Health and Medical Research Council, 174
  pharmaceutical benefits programs, 296–297
  policy coordination, 173–174
  public health benefits scheme, 294–298
  social medicine initiatives, 297
Hughes, Billy
  horseriding injury, 88
  Nationalist Party formation, 73
  new statism, 88–89
  prime ministership, 73
  relationship with Page, 37–38, 78–79, 94
  resignation, 93, 94
hydroelectricity, 110–117
  versus brown coal, 113–114, 164
  Clarence River, 20, 46, 47–49, 111, 162–163
  global adoption of, 46–48
  Jackadgery, 116–117, 163
  limited by geography, 308
  national network of, 280
  Nymboida River, 112–117, 276
  private investment in, 292
  problems with, 164–165, 282–283, 308–309
  as regionalisation, 277

industrial action, 142, 175
industrial arbitration
  Commonwealth role, 176
  nationalisation, 157
industrial organisation, 21
industry. *see* manufacturing
infrastructure. *see also* railways
  funding, 131

health, 28
policies, 130, 131, 132
regional areas lack, 33
rural development, 81
rural roads, 128–133

Keynesian theory, 10, 260, 291

Labor Party. *see* Australian Labor Party (ALP)
Lang, Jack
  dismissal, 198
  legitimacy of government, 192, 193, 197
  and Page, 136, 169–170
  repudiating interest payments, 179–180, 185, 193, 196
  resistance to Migration Agreement, 162
Lang, John Dunmore, 32, 33
Latham, John, 93
Liberal Party, 72
  age of Members of Parliament, 290
  policies, 289
Loan Council, 107–108, 167–168, 218, 223–224
local–state government tensions, 82
Lyons Government, 199
  new state separations, 196
  policy priorities, 181–183
  portfolio allocation, 181
  public spending, 181
  role of Page, 240
Lyons, Joseph
  death, xv, 233
  leader of United Australia Party (UAP), 180
  leadership style, 180
  relationship with Page, 221
  sickness, 225, 236

malaria, 272
manufacturing
  development, 119
  economic planning, 156–158

recovery from Great Depression, 182
relationship with primary industry, 155–156
role in war preparations, 219
McEwen, John, 232–233
  economic growth, 303
  relationship with Page, 233
media, 264, 318
  mass communication, 56
  political role, 67–68
  radio broadcasts, 265
  rural newspapers, 67–68, 283
Menzies Government
  criticism of, 310
  Department of National Development, 299–300, 312
  economic policy, 293
  national planning, 291, 298–300, 302
Menzies, Robert
  attack on, xv–xviii
  Cabinet career, 234
  leadership of United Australia Party (UAP), 233, 235–236, 287
  legal challenges to Commonwealth legislation, 130
  praise of Page's health scheme, 297
  relationship with Lyons, 237–238
  relationship with Page, 142, 236, 237–238, 244, 292, 323
  war service, xix, xvi
Methodism, 23, 27
migration. *see also* Development and Migration Commission (DMC)
  cost-sharing, 153
  and hydroelectricity, 313
  linked to development, 214–215
  and national planning, 153
  resistance to, 161
  rural development, 11

Migration Agreement, 162. *see also*
    Development and Migration
    Commission (DMC)
  funding from, 153
  hydroelectricity funding, 115,
    116–117
military service
  Menzies, xvii–xix
  Page, 51–53, 243–247
Murray Valley, 266

nation-building. *see* developmentalism
National Council
  decline, 230
  endorsement, 229
  presentation to states, 222–224,
    228–229
  proposal for, 222–225
  states' responses, 225–227
national development. *see*
  developmentalism
National Health and Medical
  Research Council, 174
national insurance, 66, 97, 175–176
  Menzies proposal, 234
national planning, 20, 71–72.
  *see also* Development and
  Migration Commission (DMC);
  developmentalism
  attitudes towards, 301–302
  Commonwealth Housing
    Commission, 257
  Commonwealth Planning
    Authority, 257
  defence planning, 226
  electrification, 117–120
  lack of interest in, 327
  National Works Council, 257, 280
  Page's interest in, 151–152,
    301–302, 311
  planning bodies, 217–218
  proposal to states, 222–224,
    228–229
  proposed bodies, 300–301

roads, 130
war, 221–223
National Works Council, 257, 280
Nationalists Party
  coalition with Country Party,
    91–100, 144–147
  coalition with United Australia
    Party (UAP), 180–181
natural resources, 2
  and development, 140
  manufacturing, 156
  northern NSW, 19–20
New England, 32
  attempted secession, 192–201
  New State Movement, 194, 269
  potential for development, 124
  University of New England,
    201–203, 273, 274, 304
New Guard (paramilitary
  organisation), 188
new statism, 31–34
  Cohen Royal Commission,
    120–126
  confidence, 195–196
  Constitutional requirements, 34,
    315
  costs, 125
  decline, 321, 326–327
  federal proposals, 127–128
  Federal Reconstruction
    Movement (FRM), 187, 191
  and Federation, 33–34
  Hardy, Charles, 185, 187–191
  ideals of, 123
  Lang, John Dunmore, 32, 33
  leadership role, 50–51, 86–91,
    187, 195–196, 307–308, 320
  link with Country Party, 87
  movements, 82–84, 185
  national plan, 81, 89–90,
    186–187
  Nicholas Royal Commission, 200
  northern NSW, 32, 50, 87,
    90–91, 124, 192–201

Pearce, George, 127–128
Peden Royal Commission into the Constitution, 172–173
popular support, 90–91, 127, 193–194, 198, 307, 321–322
referenda, 200
and regionalism, 269
revival, 184–192
Royal Commission on Western Australian Disabilities Under Federation, 127–128
state separations, 31
Thompson, V.C., 82, 87, 200
unilateral secession, 188
United Country Movement (UCM), 187, 197
Northern Territory, 128
Nymboida River. *see also* Clarence River
connection of Nymboida to Newcastle, 276
hydroelectricity, 112–117, 276
water supply, 47–48

oil industry, 130–131
opportunism, 57, 84, 120, 194, 231, 256
orderly marketing, 66, 146–147, 157
impact on interstate trade, 208, 210–211
organised labour, 161

Page, Charles (father), 25
Page, Earle
career-opening speech, 18–22
chancellor of University of New England, 304
community engagement, 30–31
Constitutional reform, 101
Country Party leadership, 69, 73, 95, 145–146, 148–149, 232, 238–240
Country Party–Nationalists coalition, 91–100
death, 323–324
delegate to Constitutional Convention, 253–255
dislike of cities, 37, 40 (*see also* countrymindedness)
education, 26–27, 34–37
as elder statesman, 318–319
emphasis on central government, 85
evidence to Cohen Royal Commission, 122–125
evidence to Dairy Industry Committee of Enquiry, 316–317
expert witness to Joint Committee on Constitutional Review, 314–316
family background, 23–28, 67
in federal parliament, 79–80
Grafton improvements, 48–49
idealism, 22, 54, 57
ideology, 22
knighthood, 221
legacy, 4–8, 13–16, 129, 169, 212, 325, 329
marriage, 44–45, 318
mayoralty, 64
medicine, 36–37, 42–44, 52, 109, 294
Memorial Window, 23, *24*
military service, 51–53, 243–247
minister for health, 287, 294–298
minister resident in London, 242–252
opportunism, 57, 84, 120, 194, 231, 256
parliamentary service, 4, 6
persistence, 228, 275, 286, 304
personality, 54–58, 135–138, 318, 332
policy ideals, 4–5, 18–22, 80–86
political approach, 57
political campaigning, 64–66

prime ministership, 4, 234–235, 237
resignation from ministry, 309
responses to changing policy context, 183, 256–262, 286
responses to technical advice, 111, 163–164, 260, 308
seat of Cowper, 67, 323–324
sickness, 251
son's death, 205
suspicion of, 226
tied Commonwealth grants, 129
treasurer, 95–97, 135–138, 171
*Truant Surgeon*, 15, 143, 322
wife's death, 318
World War II Burma controversy, 245–247, 252
Page, Ethel (née Blunt) (wife), 44–45
death, 318
political activism, 45, 109
stroke, 205
Page, Geoff (grandson), 110
Page, James (grandfather), 23–25
pastoralism, 73
Pearce, George, 127–128
Peden Royal Commission into the Constitution, 171, 172–173
political campaigning, 64–66, 289
political parties, 72–73, 74–75, 78, 302. *see also under* individual parties
coalitions, 91–100, 144–147, 180–181, 199, 233–234, 287–288
rural parties, 62–63
tenuousness of, 148–149
population
concentration in cities, 39, 86–87, 125, 305
growth as defensive strategy, 11, 140, 270–271
growth of manufacturing, 221
impacts on development projects, 163
settlement patterns, 164

preferential voting, 73
primary industry, 41. *see also* orderly marketing
agricultural support schemes, 66
Australian Agricultural Council (AAC), 205, 206–213
competitiveness, 100
and development, 40
policy, 182, 291–292
price fixing, 63, 66, 73
protectionism, 73, 100, 146–147, 212
recovery from Great Depression, 182
relationship with manufacturing, 155–156
subsidies, 66, 99, 146–147, 316–317
tariffs, 159
wartime regulations, 62
working population, 39
private industry
growth, 291
investment in hydroelectricity, 284
and national planning, 224, 232
role in post-war reconstruction, 258–259

Queensland
interest in Clarence River, 281, 283
separation movements, 34, 49–50
state formation, 31–32
Queensland Farmers' Union, 63

railways
electrification, 215
federal control, 20
gauge standardisation, 174, 320
as means of regional development, 81
national railway corporation, 204
and new statism, 51

regional control, 123
unification, 132–133
regional interests, 65–66
regional resources, 31
regionalism, 18–20, 80–86,
  264–272. see also centralisation;
  countrymindedness;
  decentralisation
  local development, 80
  local government, 125
  major approaches, 84
  McKell, William, 271–272, 282
  motivators, 268–269
  national planning, 268–270
  and new statism, 264
  obstacles to, 271–272
  proposed regional development
    committees, 267, 268
  Tennessee Valley Authority
    (TVA), 265, 271
River Murray Commission, 71
Royal Commission on Taxation, 105
Royal Commission on Wheat, Flour
  and Bread Industries, 209
rural Australia
  activism, 61–63, 68, 77 (see also
    Country Party)
  concerns, 39–40, 192
  cultural norms, 193
  development projects, 11, 39, 81,
    115, 121, 127
  education opportunities, 24,
    201–203, 273–274, 306
  electrification, 216, 282
  Great Depression, 185
  medical services, 42–43
  perception of government neglect,
    64
  policy impacts on, 77
  poverty, 269
  quality of life, 282, 293, 302
  religiosity, 268
  roads, 128–133

Rural Reconstruction
  Commission, 261–262, 275,
    282–283
  sense of equality, 85
  universities, 201–203, 273, 274,
    305–306
rural–urban resentment, 73

Scullin Government, 177–178
secondary industry. see manufacturing
Snowy River Hydroelectric Scheme,
  308–309. see also Clarence River
  early proposals, 276
  Page's criticisms of, 284–285
  popularity of, 276
  post-war reconstruction project,
    277
socialism. see anti-socialist fears
state boundaries, 31
  new states, 197, 200, 271, 321
  Nicholas Royal Commission, 200
state governments. see also
  Commonwealth–state policy
    cooperation
  Constitutional Convention
    attendance, 254
  debts, 21
  distrust of Commonwealth, 170,
    231
  financial powers, 107–108
  hostility to Commonwealth
    interference, 119
  impact of, 117
  implementation of national
    planning, 106, 129, 254
  migration, 153
  national planning proposal,
    222–224, 228–229
  new states, 120–121
  participation in Australian
    Agricultural Council (AAC),
    208
  Premiers' Conferences, 106–107,
    118–119, 166, 171–172, 176

responses to National Council proposal, 225–227
revenue share, 104–105
tied Commonwealth grants, 128–133
state–federal governments. *see also* Commonwealth–state policy cooperation
cooperation, 21
overlapping powers, 199
tension, 19, 196
Stevens, Bertram
national planning, 227
Nicholas Royal Commission, 200
supporter of electrification, 215–216
supporter of new statism, 199
strikes. *see* industrial action
subsidies. *see* primary industry

tariffs, 73, 171, 181
impact on primary industries, 99
Massey-Greene tariff, 77–78, 99
role in economic planning, 158–160
wartime application, 62
Tasmania, 9, 47, 164
taxation
Commonwealth, 166, 241
double taxation, 107
government jurisdiction, 107
Royal Commission on Taxation, 105
wartime taxation, 104–105
technology. *see also* hydroelectricity
electrical triumphalism, 110
as means of regional equality, 44, 46
medical, 36, 43–44
The Gorge. *see* Clarence River
trains. *see* railways
transport. *see also* railways
Federal Transport Council, 204, 210

policy coordination, 174–175, 203–204
rural roads, 128–133
*Truant Surgeon,* 15, 143, 322

unemployment, 171, 182, 257–258
government impact on, 96
United Australia Party (UAP)
creation of, 190
leadership, xv–xvi, xvii
merger with Country Party, 190–191
origins, 180
United Country Movement (UCM), 187
new statism, 197
United States
post-war ascendancy, 250
relationship with Australia, 248
universities
debate over role, 272–273, 304–305
economic impact of, 273
role in war effort, 272
University of New England, 201–203, 273, 274, 304
urbanisation, 86–87

Victorian Farmers' Union (VFU), 63, 73
resistance to electoral pact, 145

war service
Menzies, xvii–xix
Page, 51–53, 243–247
water resources, 11–12, 111, 282–283, 285, 313
River Murray Commission, 71
underutilisation, 164
welfare. *see* national insurance
Western Australia
Royal Commission on Western Australian Disabilities Under Federation, 127–128
separation movements, 32

wheat farming, 182
    Australian Wheat Board, 74
    political activism, 63
    Royal Commission on Wheat, Flour and Bread Industries, 209
    wheat pool, 62, 74, 77–78
Whitlam Government, 326
    new statism, 320
Wilson, Roland, 260
women in politics, 109
wool industry
    prices, 73, 147
    wool boom, 293
Workers' Educational Association (WEA), 71, 72
World War I, 51–53, xvi
World War II
    7th Division direction to Burma, 245–247
    beginning, 229
    impact on Australia, 241
    post-war reconstruction, 249–250
    preparations for, 219–220, 222
    War Cabinet, 4, 244, 245
    wartime production, 249

www.ingramcontent.com/pod-product-compliance
Lightning Source LLC
Chambersburg PA
CBHW040337300426
44112CB00027B/2857